CU00766479

Masters of Warfare

Masters of Warfare

Fifty Underrated Military Commanders
from Classical Antiquity to the Cold War

Eric. G. L. Pinzelli

Pen & Sword
MILITARY

AN IMPRINT OF PEN & SWORD BOOKS LTD.
YORKSHIRE - PHILADELPHIA

First published in Great Britain in 2022 by
Pen & Sword Military
An imprint of
Pen & Sword Books Ltd
Yorkshire – Philadelphia

Copyright © Eric. G. L. Pinzelli, 2022

ISBN 978 1 39907 012 6

The right of Eric. G. L. Pinzelli to be identified as Author of this work has been
asserted by him in accordance with the Copyright, Designs and Patents Act 1988.

A CIP catalogue record for this book is available from the British Library.

All rights reserved. No part of this book may be reproduced or transmitted in any
form or by any means, electronic or mechanical including photocopying, recording
or by any information storage and retrieval system, without permission from the
Publisher in writing.

Typeset in Adobe Caslon Pro 10.5/13.5 by SJmagic DESIGN SERVICES, India.
Printed and bound in the UK by CPI Group (UK) Ltd, Croydon, CR0 4YY.

Pen & Sword Books Limited incorporates the imprints of Atlas, Archaeology,
Aviation, Discovery, Family History, Fiction, History, Maritime, Military, Military
Classics, Politics, Select, Transport, True Crime, Air World, Frontline Publishing,
Leo Cooper, Remember When, Seaforth Publishing, The Praetorian Press,
Wharncliffe Local History, Wharncliffe Transport, Wharncliffe True Crime and
White Owl.

For a complete list of Pen & Sword titles please contact

PEN & SWORD BOOKS LIMITED
47 Church Street, Barnsley, South Yorkshire, S70 2AS, England
E-mail: enquiries@pen-and-sword.co.uk
Website: www.pen-and-sword.co.uk

or

PEN AND SWORD BOOKS
1950 Lawrence Rd, Havertown, PA 19083, USA
E-mail: Uspen-and-sword@casematepublishers.com
Website: www.penandswordbooks.com

Contents

Introduction: Military Leadership through the Ages   viii

Part I: THE CLASSICAL ERA (600 BC – AD 500)

Chapter 1   Cyrus II 'The Great', founder of the Achaemenid Empire   2

Chapter 2   Themistokles, architect of the Greek victory against Persia   7

Chapter 3   Epaminondas, Ancient Greece's greatest tactician   12

Chapter 4   Demetrios Poliorketes, 'The Besieger'   18

Chapter 5   Bai Qi of Qin, 'The Butcher' of the Warring States   24

Chapter 6   Marcus Agrippa, Augustus' Lieutenant   28

Chapter 7   Germanicus, Rome's beloved general   33

Chapter 8   Attila the Hun, 'The Scourge of God'   38

Part II: THE MIDDLE AGES (AD 500 – 1490)

Chapter 9   Flavius Belisarius, architect of the Byzantine reconquest   44

Chapter 10   Khālid ibn al-Walīd, the 'Sword of Islam'   49

Chapter 11   Charles Martel, Commander of the Frankish kingdom   54

Chapter 12   Robert Guiscard, the Norman 'Terror of the World'   59

Chapter 13   Subotai 'The Valiant', Genghis Khan's strategist   64

Chapter 14   Aleksandr 'Nevsky', hero of Russia   70

Chapter 15   Bertrand Du Guesclin, hero of the Hundred Years' War   75

Chapter 16   John Hawkwood, mercenary and condottiero   80

Chapter 17   Jan Žižka, leader of the 'Warriors of God'   86

Chapter 18   Sultan Mehmet II, 'the Grand Turk', conqueror of Constantinople   91

Chapter 19   Matthias Corvinus, the 'Raven King'   99

Part III: THE EARLY MODERN ERA (1490 – 1790)

Chapter 20 Francisco De Almeida, Viceroy of the Portuguese Indies   106

Chapter 21 Gonzalo Fernández de Córdoba, 'The Great Captain'   110

Chapter 22 Hernán Cortés, conqueror of the Aztec Empire   114

Chapter 23 Khayr al-Dīn Barbarossa, Admiral of the Ottoman Navy   119

Chapter 24 Francis Drake, Elizabeth I's most famous privateer   125

Chapter 25 Yi Sun-sin, the legendary saviour of Chosŏn Korea   131

Chapter 26 Akbar, the greatest Mughal Emperor   138

Chapter 27 Tokugawa Ieyasu, unifier of Japan   144

Chapter 28 Michiel De Ruyter, 'The Lion of the Seas'   149

Chapter 29 Shivaji Bhonsle, founder of the Maratha Empire   155

Chapter 30 Grand Condé, Louis XIV's master tactician   160

Chapter 31 Francesco Morosini, Venetian God of War   167

Chapter 32 Jan III Sobieski, the liberator of Vienna   174

Chapter 33 Marquis de Vauban, Europe's foremost military engineer   181

Chapter 34 Karl XII, 'The Swedish Meteor'   187

Chapter 35 Duke of Marlborough, Britain's greatest commander   194

Chapter 36 Prince Eugene of Savoy, Austria's 'Noble Knight'   201

Chapter 37 Blas de Lezo, defender of Cartagena   208

Chapter 38 Robert Clive, founder of Britain's Indian Empire   214

Chapter 39 Nathanael Greene, Washington's most trusted commander 220

Chapter 40 La Fayette, hero of the American War of Independence   225

Part IV: THE MODERN ERA UP TO THE COLD WAR (1790–1991)

Chapter 41 Joachim Murat, Napoleon's dashing cavalry commander   232

Chapter 42 Simón Bolivar, the 'Liberator' of Latin America   239

Chapter 43 Colonel T. E. Lawrence, leader of the Great Arab Revolt   245

Chapter 44 Paul von Hindenburg, Germany's hero of the Great War   252

Chapter 45 Mustafa Kemal Atatürk, founder of modern Turkey   259

Chapter 46 Paul Emil von Lettow-Vorbeck, the 'Lion of Africa'   266

Chapter 47 Erich Von Manstein, Hitler's ablest battlefield commander 272

Chapter 48 Georgy Zhukov, Stalin's champion against the Third Reich 280

Chapter 49 Matthew Ridgway, the Airborne General   289

Chapter 50 Võ Nguyên Giáp, master of revolutionary warfare   296

Final Considerations   304

Select Bibliography   306

Introduction

Military Leadership Through the Ages

A prince ought to have no other aim or thought, nor select anything else
for his study, than war and its rules and discipline; the prince should read
histories, and study the actions of illustrious men, to see how they have borne
themselves in war, to examine the causes of their victories and defeat, so as
to avoid the latter and imitate the former; and above all do as an illustrious
man did, who took as an exemplar one who had been praised and famous
before him, and whose achievements and deeds he always kept in his mind,
as it is said Alexander the Great modelled himself on Achilles, Caesar on
Alexander, Scipio on Cyrus the Great.

Niccolo Machiavelli, *The Prince*

A handful of first-class commanders such as Hannibal, Alexander the Great,
Caesar, Genghis Khan, Timur, Pizarro, Friedrich II, Souvorov, Nelson, Napoléon
and Patton, are the objects of countless biographies. Their universal fame and
the sheer volume of comprehensive studies pertaining to these 'Gods of War'
overshadow untold numbers of other talented generals and admirals who have
also had a profound impact on history and by their actions shaped mankind's
destiny.

When it comes to the knowledge of history, mass culture, instrumental in
shaping public perception, has accentuated this tendency: people want to learn
more about what they have already become aware of through the internet, the film
industry or video games. This leads to an obvious causal nexus: industries, obeying
the cardinal axiom of supply and demand, in turn produce more of the same
material. These last decades, the focus has been overwhelmingly on the Second
World War alone, this phenomenon increasingly narrowing public acquaintance
with world history, instead of expanding it. Moreover, current creations highlight
and glorify national accomplishments to the detriment of factual history that is
often far from Manichean, but complex and nuanced.

The present study follows a diametrically divergent path, introducing warfare
through a selection of distinguished leaders from Classical Antiquity to the Cold
War. This represents an attempt at a balanced, continuous, global understanding
of war through time. The emphasis given to any given military leader is suggestive
and highly dependent on each person's perspective according to their individual
background. In the sample of 'underrated' commanders introduced in this book,

some may be more or less familiar to the reader. Fundamentally, this selection follows the criterion of legacy: their geopolitical impact on local or continental affairs, their distinctive contribution(s), their long-term influence on warfare and human history as a whole.

War, fundamentally destructive, immoral and unethical, has been mankind's most tragic, resource-consuming activity since the dawn of time. War is certainly not a mere 'symptom', but rather a fundamental force driving human history. It is an intimate part of the never-ending cycle of life and death: through war, civilizations arose, empires were dismembered, populations migrated, new states emerged. As 'three things are necessary in war, money, money and more money' (Raimondo Montecuccoli), war was always intimately linked to the inevitable development of more efficient economies, ideas, industries and government. As a consequence, it has influenced the whole direction of academic science, technological progress, production and governance. We may lament it, but the fact remains undeniable. Learning from past experience should be the pragmatic response.

Combat being an individual's ultimate test of valour, until recently the definition of heroism itself was pretty much universal. In most cultures it required rising to a challenge, sometimes making the ultimate sacrifice, regardless of the then applicable moral standards. Clearly, moral values are subject to change over time. Invading a foreign land, capturing its cities and enslaving its people are, for the most part, no longer acceptable, even less 'glorious'. Some of these fifty leaders undoubtedly qualify as legitimate 'heroes', others as full-blown mass murderers, regardless of whether or not they were forced to take up arms to defend their people, or chose to fight motivated by greed or personal advancement. In any case, some of these 'villains' may be regarded as proper 'heroes' in a different culture, since moral standards are not universal.

In examining their achievements, each of them qualifies as a highly effective commander, displaying superior leadership skills, performing superb personal feats and, when required, raising the spirits of their men in order to perform seemingly impossible tasks. Lao Tzu's *Tao Te Ching* (sixth century BC) lays down that an effective leader's behaviour requires both strength and flexibility; leading by personal example is advocated. US Admiral William 'Bull' Halsey once said, 'There are no great men, there are only great challenges.' According to Gary Yukl (*Leadership in Organizations*, 1981), leadership is a 'process of influencing others to understand and agree about what needs to be done and how to do it'. The leaders in our selection range from excellent tacticians to supreme strategists, in some instances happily combining both traits.

In contrast to John Keegan's standpoint as spelled out in *The Face of Battle*, it is argued here that the role of the individual commander is the key factor determining the eventual outcome of any military operation, more important than numerical superiority, logistics, morale, discipline, and of course weaponry.

As General Matthew Ridgway put it, the success of a unit is merely 'a reflection of the qualities of leadership possessed by its commander'. The large number of real-life examples that follow consistently demonstrate this point.

> There is a 'felt' element in troops, not expressible in figures, and the greatest commander is he whose intuitions most nearly happen. Nine-tenths of tactics are certain, and taught in books: but the irrational tenth is like the kingfisher flashing across the pool and that is the test of generals. It can only be ensued by instinct, sharpened by thought practising the stroke so often that at the crisis it is as natural as a reflex.'
>
> T. E. Lawrence, 'Guerrilla Warfare',
> *Encyclopedia Britannica*, 1929

Leadership always strives to achieve excellence, even in the face of insuperable odds, showing the rare ability to select the best course of action. Thus, the sample of outstanding leaders in this collection reflects a certain continuity of military talent and genius. Some of these men were exceptionally brave, others displayed uncommonly good judgment, a lesser number seemed to be naturally born to the business of war.

This diversity of origins, careers and fortunes enables the reader to follow the somewhat linear evolution of warfare, grand strategy and tactics through time, as adversaries adapt and learn from each other, or face annihilation. The short biographies are treated not in isolation, but firmly within the context of this historical evolution. Throughout time, the grim reality becomes apparent that there have never been generally acknowledged rules of war. When all is said and done, there was little honour also. Clever strategies and deception, the 'thieves of war' as the Ancient Greeks used to call them, were employed by all sides. The most professional warrior was ultimately 'only doing his job'. Civilians were caught in the crossfire, populations decimated, infrastructure and resources ruined, the landscape permanently scarred. The ultimate goal of a military leader was, and remains, to fulfil his objective, to execute the mission, if possible to achieve victory, all the while doing his best to preserve the men under his command.

The lion's share of the book is assigned to the Age of Exploration and Discovery (1450s–1700s) which witnessed a profound 'military revolution'. Pioneered by the Italian states, the Ottoman Empire and the Iberian kingdoms, this pivotal period in history saw the world coming together through intertwined trade and conquest. The prime goal of seizing control of the spices and riches of faraway oriental lands, together with the diffusion of Christianity, were the cornerstones of Western European expansion. The inevitable advent of gunpowder precipitated key developments. Guns triggered the emergence of bastionned fortifications at the end of the fifteenth century. A century later, new ship designs, functional cartography and an ensemble of navigation tools crowned sea power as the ultimate instrument of empire-building.

During the golden era of Early Modern siege warfare (1500–1750), the deployment of firearms, their concentration and their increasing range ushered in advanced battlefield tactics. The rediscovery of classical treatises induced a rebirth of the pike square, the combined-arms approach, the concept of the Spanish *tercio*; while seventeenth century Dutch and Swedish improvements led to the linear formation and better drilled infantry with enhanced discipline, 'the fundamental postulates of tactics' (Maurits van Oranje). Military campaigns focused on the methodical capture of enemy cities, the ultimate practitioner being Vauban, while set-piece battles became less decisive and less frequent, until the advent of the French Revolutionary and Napoleonic wars (1792–1815). With the mobilization of millions during the industrial revolution, warfare evolved at an increasingly fast and deadly pace, heralding the advent of total war.

Eurasia features prominently for four main reasons: the amount of sources and records available to reconstruct the past; the prevailing importance of the largest landmass of the planet; its population centres, breadbaskets of the ancient world; and its role in distant civilizations, when contact was made with them in the sixteenth century. Eurasia was the cradle of influential civilizations: the Celts, the Bronze Age Minoans, the Fertile Crescent, the Indus valley, China, Japan, all the way to the south-eastern Hindu kingdoms of the Iron Age.

Eurasia has been home to the greater part of the world population since the Neolithic age. According to Angus Maddison's estimates, 2,000 years ago, Asia already accounted for 74 per cent of the world population, Europe, 15 per cent, the rest of the world combined, only 11 per cent. Eurasia saw the giant nomadic empires of the steppes that extended for 8,000km, acting as a contact zone between Europe and the fabulously wealthy Far East, along the silk roads active since the heyday of Persia. As a result, kingdoms and empires have fought over it relentlessly.

Consequently, the super-continent has been the most contested part of the world. Xi'an (present-day Shaanxi Province) in central China has been captured fifty-one times in the last twenty-eight centuries. Adrianople (Edirne), at the crossroads of Europe and Asia, has been the focal point for migrations, invasions, battles or sieges seventeen times since its foundation by Emperor Hadrian in the second century AD. Byzantium/Constantinople was besieged or attacked thirty-six times until its final conquest by the Turks in 1453, Jerusalem at least twenty-two times in 3,000 years. The overwhelming number of military leaders in the book (48 out of 50) from Eurasia reflects this inescapable reality.

The research for this book was not intended to be exhaustive. An average of just five pages is dedicated to each military leader, and a more thorough analysis would have easily expanded the content tenfold. For further study, a short reference list at the conclusion of the book provides essential published primary and secondary sources, indicating their first publication date, together with up to date select biographies.

Note

For consistency, in the spirit of a multi-national essay, personal names retain their original spelling (e.g. Karl XII of Sweden instead of the anglicized 'Charles' XII) when dealing with individuals originating from the Latin and multilingual neo-Latin world.

Romanized transcriptions are used when dealing with different writing systems from the Ancient Middle East, Asia, the Turkic world or pre-Columbian America.

Pontifical names are given in Latin, not in their baptismal or anglicized forms.

Dates are all converted when needed and given as Day/Month/Year, in New Style.

Italic type is used for words in their original language (though sometimes converted).

Part I

THE CLASSICAL ERA
(600 BC – AD 500)

Pasargad: The tomb of Cyrus the Great. (*Wikimedia Commons*)

Chapter 1

CYRUS II THE GREAT
Founder of the Achaemenid Empire,
'King of the Four Corners of the World'

That Cyrus's empire was the greatest and most glorious of all the kingdoms in Asia – of that it may be its own witness. For it was bounded on the east by the Indian Ocean, on the north by the Black Sea, on the west by Cyprus and Egypt, and on the south by Ethiopia. And although it was of such magnitude, it was governed by the single will of Cyrus; and he honoured his subjects and cared for them as if they were his own children; and they, on their part, reverenced Cyrus as a father.

Xenophon, *Cyropaedia*, Book VIII

Our very first entry is also one of the most remarkable. Cyrus II, originally an obscure local ruler, led numerous military campaigns against powerful neighbouring kingdoms, uniting most of the Middle East through conquest, culminating in the creation of the Achaemenid Persian Empire, the largest and most efficient the world had ever seen. Cyrus's multinational empire stretched 3,600km from the Indus to the Aegean Sea. Covering an area of 7.5m square kilometres, Persian territories were even larger than the Roman Empire at its peak. Eduard Meyer estimated its inhabitants at c.50 million, accounting for a significant proportion of the entire world population at that time. Cyrus's empire would be the first to establish regular routes of communication between Asia, Europe and Africa.

According to the 'Cyrus Cylinder', an ancient clay cylinder written in Akkadian cuneiform and discovered in the ruins of Babylon, Cyrus's forefathers were the rulers of the city-state of Anshan in Elam. Early on, Cyrus (in Old Persian 'Kurush', c.600–529 BC) was referred to as the 'King of the City of Anshan' and his ancestors as 'the Great Kings of the City of Anshan'. It was from Anshan that Cyrus embarked on a series of conquests, making the city the nucleus of the formidable Persian Empire.

In Herodotus's *Histories* (Book I), Cyrus was recorded as the son of Cambyses I of Anshan and Mandane of Media, the daughter of Astyages, the King of the Medes. In his youth, the young prince received a formal military education. The conquest of the Middle East may have been achieved with the help of Kuru and Kamboja Indo-Aryan mercenaries from eastern Afghanistan and northern India. In their honour, the elder branch of the Achaemenids would name their princes from Cyrus I onward alternately as Cyrus (*Kurush*) and Cambyses (*Kamboja*).

> What conceivable use tactics could be to an army, without provisions and health, and what use it could be without the knowledge of the arts invented for warfare and without obedience? You made it clear to me that tactics was only a small part of generalship, I asked you if you could teach me any of those things, and you bade me go and talk with the men who were reputed to be masters of military science and find out how each one of those problems was to be met.
>
> Xenophon, *Cyropaedia*, Book I, dialogue
> between young Cyrus and his father

In 553 BC Cyrus revolted against the Median Empire, and in 550 BC succeeded in defeating the Medes. Harpagus, who was Astyages' general, switched sides and went on to become Cyrus's most successful general. Cyrus captured his grandfather Astyages and took the Median capital city of Ecbatana. He then proclaimed himself the successor to Astyages but treated the deposed king with honour, even allowing him to keep a position within his court.

After Astyages' overthrow, Croesus of Lydia marched against Cyrus, attempting to opportunistically use the war in Media to expand Lydia's eastern frontier. Before the start of his offensive, Croesus made an alliance with Sparta and King Nabonidus of Babylonia. At the end of an inconclusive campaign, Cyrus, with Harpagus at his side, defeated Croesus at the Battle of Thymbria in December 547 BC. Two weeks later, Sardis, the capital of Lydia, fell, and Cyrus captured Croesus. Harpagus was then tasked to push westward, and the Median general conquered Ionia, Caria, Lycia, Phoenicia and other regions of Asia Minor. To take fortified cities, Harpagus had earthwork ramps and mounds built, a method unknown to the Greeks. These fresh conquests, including the Greek cities of Ionia and Aeolis, were incorporated into Cyrus's already huge empire, and Harpagus was appointed Satrap (Governor) of Asia Minor.

According to Xenophon (*Cyropaedia*), Cyrus fielded almost 200,000 men during his campaign against Lydia. The Medo-Persian army was composed of Persians, Medes, Arabians and Armenians. The infantry consisted of Persian 'Immortals' equipped with bronze breastplates and helmets, but also pikemen, archers, slingers and light infantry/skirmishers. The standard tactic employed by frontline infantry was to form a shield wall, which rows of archers massed behind could fire over. The shield-bearers (*sparabara*) were equipped with a large rectangular wicker shield called a *spara* and armed with a short spear.

Apart from his infantry, Cyrus deployed elite horsemen, camel cavalry, 300 war chariots and siege towers, the latter used even during the set piece battles to provide longer range to his archers. At the Battle of Thymbria, the horses of the Lydian cavalry panicked at the smell of the dromedaries, a tactic apparently invented by Harpagus. The Persian light cavalry would usually initiate battle by throwing javelins and shooting arrows at the enemy.

From 546 to 539 BC Cyrus campaigned in Central Asia, subduing the ancient tribal kingdoms of Sogdiana, Drangiana, Arachosia, Margiana and Bactria. He converted them into satrapies and put natives in command, incorporating their troops into his own ever-expanding imperial army.

In 539 BC Cyrus was ready to invade the largest remaining power of the Middle East, the Neo-Babylonian Empire. King Nabonidus of Babylon was said to be unpopular among his subjects because of his suppression of the cult of Marduk, the city's traditional patron deity, and his elevation of the cult of the moon god Sin. Nabonidus sent his son Belshazzar to face the powerful invading force, but the Babylonian army was routed at the Battle of Opis. On 12 October, after Cyrus's engineers had diverted the waters of the Euphrates, a division of the Medo-Persian army led by Ugbaru entered Babylon. Nabonidus was captured and his life was apparently spared. Cyrus himself entered the city seventeen days later. The *Cyrus Cylinder* records that he entered the prestigious capital to be welcomed by its population. Cyrus' reputation had preceded him – he was known to spare those who yielded to him.

Cyrus at once took possession of the citadels and sent up to them guards and officers of the guards. As for the dead, he gave their relatives permission to bury them. He furthermore ordered the heralds to make proclamation that all Babylonians deliver up their arms; and he ordered that wherever arms should be found in any house, all the occupants should be put to the sword. So they delivered up their arms and Cyrus stored them in the citadels, so that they might be ready if he ever needed them for use.

Xenophon, *Cyropaedia*, Book VII

One of Cyrus's first acts was to allow foreign exiles to return to their homelands. He had the statues of the gods that had been seized in battle, and hoarded in Babylon, returned to their peoples. Babylon would never again rise to become the single capital of an independent kingdom, and Babylonia was absorbed into the Achaemenid Empire, becoming the satrapy of Babirush. The conqueror then entitled himself 'King of the Four Corners of the World'. The golden eagle became the emblem of his dynasty.

In all, Cyrus appointed twenty-six satraps ('protectors of the province'), who acted as viceroys, ruling in the king's name. The Empire was held together from Pasargadae (Iran), the capital, by a centralized, bureaucratic administration making use of Old Persian as its official language. In every corner of his domains Cyrus allowed his conquered subjects to retain their traditions, promoting a multicultural policy unheard of until his reign.

He used ancient Hittite and Assyrians roads during his campaigns. They would later be restored, and the network known as the Royal Road was extended, linking the Mediterranean to the Persian Gulf. Making use of this communication system, the 'Eye of the King', one of Cyrus's closest advisors, supervised intelligence gathering throughout the Empire:

By rewarding liberally those who reported to him whatever it was to his interest to hear, he prompted many men to make it their business to use their eyes and ears to spy out what they could report to the King to his advantage.

Xenophon, *Cyropaedia*

Cyrus died around 529 BC. Descriptions of the circumstances of his death differ radically. In Herodotus' *Histories* he is said to have died while campaigning against the Massagetes of the Caspian Sea; according to Ctesias of Cnidus' *Persica*, he was killed in northern India; while Xenophon believed that he died from natural causes in his capital. In any case, Cyrus was buried 1km away from Pasargadae, in a modest tomb containing his golden sarcophagus, his arms, some ornaments with precious stones and a cloak. In 331 BC Cyrus's final resting place was looted by the Macedonian army, but Alexandros III (Alexander the Great), who admired

Cyrus, had it restored, and it stands to this day. According to Strabo, an inscription on the mausoleum read:

> Passer-by, I am Cyrus, who founded the Persian Empire, and was king of Asia. Grudge me not therefore this monument.

Achievements

Cyrus, who founded the largest empire up to that time in a matter of decades, was acclaimed as one of the most benevolent conquerors of all time. The first universal ruler, he distinguished himself equally as a general and a statesman. Cyrus's conquest of the Greek cities of Ionia and Aeolis would bring the Greek world and Persia into conflict, culminating in the fifth century Persian wars. Rightfully earning his epithet of 'The Great', he skilfully assimilated and administered an astonishing diversity of lands, peoples, languages and cultures, allowing his subjects to live and worship as they pleased. Cyrus founded a viable politico-economical superstructure layered on top of deep-rooted local traditions that lived on for two centuries, until the Macedonian conquest. The Persians in the time of Herodotus already considered Cyrus as 'a father'. Today, he is more than ever celebrated as a national hero in Iran. Cyrus 'The Great' remains an essential figure in the nation's rich history and a powerful symbol of its immortality.

Themistokles. Roman copy 117–138 AD from a Greek original of c.400 BC, Vatican Museums. (*James Anderson*)

Chapter 2

THEMISTOKLES
Architect of the Greek victory against Persia

It was at the end of this period that the war with Aegina and the prospect of the barbarian invasion enabled Themistokles to persuade the Athenians to build the fleet with which they fought at Salamis . . . Our contingent of ships was little less than two-thirds of the whole 400; the commander was Themistokles, through whom chiefly it was that the battle took place in the straits, the acknowledged salvation of our cause.

Thucydides, *The Peloponnesian War*

Themistokles was a prominent Athenian soldier-statesman of the fifth century BC whose deployment of naval power was instrumental in winning the Persian wars. During the second Persian invasion in 480 BC he held supreme command of the Greek city-states' fleets at the Battle of Artemisium and at Salamis, one of the most decisive battles in history. Themistokles was one of the most important historical figures of Classical Greece whose vision set Athens on the road to empire and greatness.

According to Plutarch, Themistokles (c.524–460 BC) came from a modest middle-class family. His elevation was due solely to his own skills, and from an early age he was a popular, influential, public figure. According to Herodotus, the young man turned lawyer could greet every citizen by name. In 508–507 BC Athens had adopted Kleisthenes' direct democratic system of government, by which all eligible citizens were allowed to speak and vote in the Assembly.

In 493 BC the 30-year-old Themistokles was elected Eponymous Archon (chief executive officer in Athens). On the other side of the Aegean Sea, the formidable Achaemenid Empire had just succeeded in crushing the Ionian revolt. Since Athens and Eretria (in the island of Euboea) had supported this rebellion of Greek colonies against the Persians, Darius I vowed to take revenge on the two cities.

Themistokles foresaw the need to prepare for the Persian invasion and believed the key to saving Athens would be sea power. His main political rival during that period was Aristides, who favoured more traditional land-based tactics over naval expansion. Themistokles launched the construction works on the fortified naval base of Piraeus, which would become the largest naval base in the Greek world.

Among the refugees arriving from Ionia was Miltiades, a veteran of the Persian War against the Scythians (513 BC). During the Ionian Revolt, Miltiades had captured Imbros and Lemnos and ceded those islands to Athens. Themistokles supported Miltiades' election as general (*strategos*) of the Athenian army. In 490 the Athenians, led by Miltiades, halted the first invasion of the Persians at the Battle of Marathon. Themistokles himself commanded the centre of the Athenian formation. But following the failure of the expedition against Paros in 479 BC, Miltiades was incarcerated in Athens and died in prison.

At this point Themistokles may have been one of the few Athenians to realize that the Persians would come back. In those years intensified exploitation of a particularly rich vein in the mining district of Laurion worked by 20,000 slaves yielded 2.5 tons of pure silver. In 483 BC, rather than distributing this unexpected new bounty among the Athenian citizenry, Themistokles proposed to use it to construct 200 triremes, under the pretext of the ongoing conflict with the nearby island of Aegina. These 35-metre-long undecked warships using three banks of oars were armed with bronze rams. The Athenians would use this superior naval technology to compensate for their numerical inferiority against the Persians.

The measure was initially opposed by Aristides. Themistokles nevertheless managed to convince the Athenian Assembly to finance the building of 100 triremes, and soon more were under way . . . The Athenian navy expanded from 70 to 200 warships in a matter of months. With a total complement of 200 men per ship – 170 oarsmen and 30 marines (hoplites and archers) – this meant that every able-bodied Athenian male citizen would be required to man the navy.

During the Persian invasion of 480 BC Themistokles came up with a strategy to block the enemy's advance: while King Leonidas of Sparta would hold the pass of Thermopylae, the Greek allied navy would guard his flank at sea, near Cape Artemisium in Northern Euboea. Herodotus explains that the Euboeans bribed Themistokles with 30 silver talents (the equivalent of $655,000) to keep the combined Greek fleet of 271 triremes near Artemisium in order to protect their island. The entire southern Greek mainland was placed on high alert.

Resolved by the Council and the People on the motion of Themistokles, son of Neokles: to entrust the city to Athena the Mistress of Athens and to all the other gods to guard and defend from the Barbarian for the sake of the land. The Athenians themselves and the foreigners who live in Athens are to remove their women and children to Troizen. The old men and the movable possessions are to be removed to Salamis. The treasurers and the priestesses are to remain on the acropolis protecting the possessions of the gods. All the other Athenians and foreigners of military age are to embark on the 200 ships that lie ready and defend against the Barbarian for the sake of their own freedom and that of the rest of the Greeks, along with the Lakedaimonians, the Corinthians, the Aiginetans, and all others who wish to share the danger.

Themistokles' Decree, Troezen Inscription, 480 BC

While the 1,000 Spartans and Thespians were fighting for their lives at Thermopylae, the Athenians fought an indecisive naval battle off Artemisium before retreating. These delaying actions failed to halt the Persian advance, and Xerxes' gigantic army marched south through Boeotia. The Athenians were forced to evacuate their entire population; women, children and the elderly were transported in haste to the Peloponnese and to islands in the Gulf of Athens. The remaining free Greek city-states were staking their hopes of ultimate survival on the 'wooden walls' of their fleet.

Themistokles is thought to have divined the best time for fighting with no less success than the best place, inasmuch as he took care not to send his triremes bow on against the Barbarian vessels until the hour of day had come which always brought the breeze fresh from the sea and a swell rolling through the strait.

Plutarch, *Parallel Lives*, Book IV

By subterfuge on the part of Themistokles, in September the Allies lured the Persian fleet into the narrow strait of Salamis, thus negating the enemy's numerical advantage. Relying on speed and manoeuvrability to ram and disengage the more cumbersome enemy vessels one by one, the Greek fleet routed the Persians, sinking or capturing 200–300 ships, about half of the enemy's force, while losing only 40 of their own. The decisive Greek triumph at Salamis was the turning point of the invasion.

> No more brilliant exploit was ever performed upon the sea, either by Hellenes or Barbarians, through the manly valour and common ardour of all who fought their ships, but through the clever judgment of Themistokles.
>
> Plutarch, *Parallel Lives*, Book IV

In the aftermath of Salamis, the twin Greek victories at the land Battle of Plataea and over the Persian fleet at Mycale in Asia Minor (479 BC) decisively ended the second Persian invasion. The Ionian cities were freed from Achaemenid rule, and the Delian League was formed under the aegis of Athens (478 BC). The predominance and prestige of Athens would gradually turn the League into an Athenian maritime empire.

> It is said that when the next Olympic festival was celebrated [in 476 BC], and Themistokles entered the stadium, the audience neglected the contestants all day long to gaze on him, and pointed him out with admiring applause to visiting strangers.
>
> Plutarch, *Parallel Lives*, Book IV

Unfortunately for Themistokles, his glory was somewhat short-lived. His power provoked envy among rivals, and Sparta caused him to be accused of bribery, sacrilege and association with the Spartan traitor Pausanias, the victor of Plataea. As consequence, in 472 BC he was ostracized by his fellow citizens and exiled from Athenian territory. He moved from place to place, an outlaw, until he eventually fled Greece on board a merchant vessel under an alias, asked for and was granted asylum by King of Kings Artaxerxes I. Themistokles was made governor of Magnesia in Ionia, where coins were minted bearing his portrait. Ironically, the hero of Greece ended his days in the comfort of a Persian palace, far from home.

Achievements

At a time when Greece and the new-born Athenian democracy faced their most dangerous existential threat, Themistokles rose to become the inspired leader desperately needed by the Greek city-states who refused to bow down to the

Achaemenid Empire. Had Persia won the war, the history of western civilization would have been dramatically different. The Battle of Salamis, which itself altered the course of history, is regarded as one of the most tactically brilliant ever fought. The ambitious Themistokles was a great statesman, soldier, diplomat and admiral, and a strategist endowed with admirable foresight and ingenuity. He was capable of long-term planning, but could also adapt to changing situations to counter the tactics of his adversaries. Notwithstanding his eventual fall from grace, Themistokles' name remains forever attached to the fight for liberty and the foundation of the mighty Athenian thalassocracy (rule by sea power).

Ancient Messene, northern circuit wall and watchtowers. (*Author*)

Chapter 3

EPAMINONDAS THE LIBERATOR
Ancient Greece's greatest tactician

> Before the birth of Epaminondas, and after his death, Thebes was subject constantly to the hegemony of others; but, on the contrary, so long as he was at the head of the state, she was the leading city of all Greece. This fact shows that one man was worth more than the entire body of citizens.
> Cornelius Nepos, *Life of Epaminondas*

A resolute statesman and outstanding battlefield commander, Epaminondas of Thebes led expeditions in the Peloponnese, achieving long-lasting results. After defeating the superior forces of the Spartans by using revolutionary tactics, he liberated the Arcadians and Messenians from their Spartan overlords and freed the helots (slaves), permanently crippling Sparta. He founded the fortified cities of Messene and Megalopolis and set up a pro-Theban Arcadian League under Theban control. Governed by Epaminondas and his close friend Pelopidas, Thebes was elevated to the rank of a first-rate power, its hegemony lasting until the rise of Macedon, to which Epaminondas indirectly contributed.

Born in the 'seven-gated' *polis* (city) of Thebes into an impoverished aristocratic family, Epaminondas (c.418–362 BC) received a sound education. From his youth he was endowed with natural authority and displayed uncommon physical and intellectual abilities. The austere and upright Theban would never marry. According to Aelian, for the sake of virtue his sole possession seems to have been a single rough cloak. According to Plutarch, Epaminondas excelled in 'restraint and justice', his 'magnanimity' attested to by the fact that he never executed or enslaved his defeated enemies.

The long and bitter Peloponnesian War (431–404 BC), followed by the Corinthian War (395–386 BC), and a series of epidemics, had resulted in the collapse of Athenian power and the demographic decline of the Spartan population, weakening its ability to field armies. During the siege of the Arcadian *polis* of Mantinea in 385 BC, Thebes sent a contingent to fight on the side of the Spartans, their allies at the time. On this occasion, Epaminondas saved the wounded patrician Pelopidas, son of Hippoklas. This act of bravery cemented their lifelong partnership (Plutarch, *Parallel Lives*, *Life of Pelopidas*, Book XIV).

In 382 BC, in violation of the Peace of Antalcidas imposed by Artaxerxes II, Spartan general Phoebidas seized the ancient Kadmeia, Thebes' citadel since Mycenaean times, thereby giving Sparta control over the city. Although Phoebidas was relieved of command, the Spartans left behind a Laconophile (Spartan-favouring) oligarchy supported by a garrison.

Six years later, with support from Athens, the democratic party led by the returned exiles Pelopidas and Epaminondas triumphed. They expelled the Spartan garrison stationed at the Kadmeia, ousted the members of the oligarchy and established a new constitution. Pelopidas was elected to the office of *Beotarch* (chief executive) and Epaminondas became *Polemarch* (commander of the army). The two friends would be repeatedly re-elected in subsequent years. As leaders of the Theban democrats, they shared the vision of an aggressive expansionist policy with the ultimate goal of Greek unity under Theban hegemony.

As expansion is ultimately determined by military might, they needed to introduce radical changes, starting with the creation of an adequate military force to challenge the Spartans. They immediately set about implementing reforms in weaponry, training and tactics. The Theban phalanx received two-handed pikes with a longer reach, together with the lighter *dipylon* (the so-called 'Beotian shield'). The Theban cavalry was already considered the best in Greece, and some light infantry such as slingers and skirmishers (*hamippoi*), armed with javelins and a dagger, were tasked to support the horsemen.

According to Plutarch, the Sacred Band was formed by the Hipparch Gorgidas shortly after Thebes had regained its sovereignty. Comprising 150 pairs of male lovers consisting of an older erastês (ἐραστής – 'lover') and a younger erômenos (ἐρώμενος – 'beloved'), placed beside each other in battle, this unit would remain undefeated until it was wiped out by Philip II of Macedon at Cheronea in 338 BC.

In 374 BC, while Athens and Sparta were busy fighting each other again, Thebes subjugated the autonomous pro-Spartan Boeotian *polis*. Thespiae and Tanagra formally became part of the re-established democratic Boeotian confederacy. The following year, Theban *Beotarch* Neokles razed the Boeotian city of Platea, its traditional rival. In 371 BC a peace congress was summoned at Sparta to ratify the Peace of Callias. The Thebans refused to renounce their Boeotian hegemony. In response, the Spartans sent an army under King Kleombrotos to compel Theban acceptance. The two opposing forces met at Leuctra in Beotia on 6 July 371 BC.

Epaminondas and Pelopidas held supreme command of the Theban forces. Faced with the grim prospect of a decisive defeat that would lead to the utter destruction of his homeland, Epaminondas did the unexpected: he conceived and used the oblique order tactic (or refused flank) for the first time in history.

The Thebans were outnumbered by 10,000 to 6,000. To compensate, Epaminondas massed his cavalry and elite infantry, including the 300-man Sacred Band, on his left flank, facing the Spartan right flank under King Kleombrotos. In doing so, he defied centuries of convention by placing his best troops on his left flank instead of the right, the traditional position of honour. Rather than spreading his hoplites evenly in a standard formation, Pelopidas and the Sacred Band would spearhead a 50-rank-deep phalanx directly across the Spartan king's 12-rank-deep line, giving them enough mass to overwhelm the Spartans facing them. Epaminondas gambled that, with their best troops defeated, the rest of the Spartan army and their allies would lose heart and flee.

The weaker Theban centre and right flank were ordered to march at a very slow pace, while the heavily reinforced left flank would charge ahead, targeting the Spartan king and his bodyguards, the *Hippeis*. If the tactic worked, the only fighting would be done by the superior left flank, and the battle would end before the much weaker centre and right flank had to engage. A deep phalanx had been used fifty-three years earlier by Theban general Pagondas at the Battle of Delium (424 BC), although only twenty-five ranks deep, but the refused flank and interchanging the position of the reinforced phalanx to face the Spartans' elite warriors were Epaminondas' own innovations. His pep talk to encourage his troops was another mark of his leadership from the front:

Epaminondas convened an assembly and exhorted the soldiers by the appropriate pleas to meet the issue, they all shifted their resolutions, rid themselves of their superstition, and with courage in their hearts stood ready for the battle.

Diodoros Siculus, *Bibliotheca Historica*, Book XV

Not only did Epaminondas' battle plan work flawlessly, he remained in full control once it was set in motion. He was able to achieve total tactical surprise by clever screening and employment of his cavalry in front of his formation. Pelopidas, at the head of the Sacred Band, steamrollered the Spartans' right flank, penetrating all the way to Spartan King Kleombrotos, who was killed in the melee, the first time a Spartan King had been killed in action since Thermopylae. At the sight of their best troops defeated and their king slain, the Spartans lost heart and fled, followed by their allies.

The Thebans, once a minor power, had faced the famed Spartan hoplites on the field while outnumbered and had prevailed in spectacular fashion. Epaminondas had been able to defeat a numerically far superior enemy, displaying a remarkable economy of force. Out of 700 Spartan citizen-soldiers present, 400 were killed. The blow to the prestige of the Spartan military was resounding, its reputation shattered beyond repair.

> The highest praises were accorded to the general Epaminondas, who chiefly by his own courage and by his shrewdness as a commander had defeated in battle the invincible leaders of Greece.
>
> Diodoros Siculus, *Bibliotheca Historica*

In the aftermath, Epaminondas freed the *helots*, the slave class of Spartan society and one of the pillars of its economy. With Pelopidas, he founded the city of Megalopolis in Arcadia, uniting neighbouring communities, and Messene in the lower Pamisos Valley for the descendants of exiled Messenians as a fortified city-state independent of Sparta. The powerful walls and towers were erected in just eighty-five days. Together with the foundation of Megalopolis, and also Mantineia and Argos, it formed a strategic barrier conceived by Epaminondas to contain Spartan ambitions in the Peloponnese. Messene became the capital of the free Messenian state, following four centuries of occupation of its territory by the Spartans. General Pammenes, a friend of Epaminondas, was dispatched with 1,000 soldiers to defend Megalopolis.

On their return to Thebes, Epaminondas and Pelopidas were accused by their political rivals of having retained their command beyond the legal term. They were acquitted after Epaminondas brilliantly defended his actions:

> He denied none of the charges of his opponents, admitted everything that his colleagues had said, and did not refuse to submit to the penalty named in the law. He made only ONE request of the judges, namely, that they should enter the following record of his sentence: 'Epaminondas was condemned to death by the Thebans because at Leuctra he compelled them to vanquish the Lacedaemonians [Spartans], whom before he took command no Boeotian

had dared to face in battle, and because in a single contest he not only saved Thebes from destruction, but also secured freedom for all Greece and so changed the situation of the contending parties that the Thebans attacked the Lacedaemonians, while the Lacedaemonians were satisfied with being able to save themselves; and he did not bring the war to an end until by the restoration of Messene he placed Sparta in a state of siege.' When he had said this, there was laughter and merriment throughout the assembly and no juror ventured to vote for his condemnation. Thus from a capital charge he gained the greatest glory.

Cornelius Nepos, Life of Epaminondas

In 366 BC Epaminondas led another Theban expedition to Achaea, aiming at securing the allegiance of the Achaeans and reinforcing Theban control over the Arcadians and other allies. After the Thebans had forced their way through the fortified Isthmus of Corinth, the Achaeans submitted. In the north, Thebes was by then the arbitrator of Macedonian affairs. The young Filippos (Philip) of Macedon, son of Amyntas III and Eurydice I, was held hostage in Thebes, where he remained for three years. Treated as an honoured guest, Filippos received his military and diplomatic education from Epaminondas himself, living under the care of Epaminondas' friend Pammenes.

With the backing of Persia, Epaminondas also sought to challenge Athens by building a navy from scratch, and by 364 BC 100 warships had been launched. Epaminondas led the Beotian naval force to Rhodes, Chios and Byzantium, establishing alliances with the Athenian League's wealthiest members. That same year, Pelopidas was killed fighting the Thessalians at Cynoscephalae. Although the battle was won by the Thebans, his death was a serious blow to the *polis* and to Epaminondas himself.

Spartan King Agesilaos II assembled an army from numerous Peloponnesian *poleis* dissatisfied with Theban hegemony, including Athenians, Achaeans, Eleans and some of the Arcadians. In the vicinity of Mantinea, on 4 July 462 BC, some 50,000 to 60,000 men faced each other from the four corners of Greece, in what became the largest hoplite showdown in history. Employing once again a battle formation with a reinforced left flank 'like a trireme' that he led from the front, Epaminondas prevailed once more, but was mortally wounded.

Epaminondas having received a mortal wound at Mantinea, and being brought (yet alive) to the tents, called for Daiphantus, that he might declare him General. When they told him that he was slain, he called to Iolaidas. When they said that he also was dead, he counselled them to make peace and friendship with their Enemies, because the Thebans had no longer any General.

Aelian, Varia Historia

The liberator was buried on the battlefield itself, with his fellow countrymen. Although Epaminondas was no more, the old King Agesilaos was not able to re-establish Spartan ascendancy. In the Third Sacred War with its neighbour Phocis (356–346 BC), Thebes lost its predominance in central Greece and gradually sank back to the position of a secondary power. In the final confrontation at Chaeronea in 338 BC Thebes and Athens, utterly crushed, would be forced to yield to Filippos II. The Macedonian *hegemon* would assume the leadership of Greece on the ruins of Epaminondas' city. Taking advantage of these unified warring forces at his disposal, Filippos would turn them against the mighty Persian Empire.

> Epaminondas, perhaps the most original genius in military history … He not only broke away from tactical methods established by the experience of centuries, but in tactics, strategy, and grand strategy alike laid the foundations on which subsequent masters have built. Even his structural designs have survived or been revived. For in tactics the 'oblique order' which Frederick made famous was but a slight elaboration of the method of Epaminondas.
>
> Basil H. Liddell Hart, *The Strategy of Indirect Approach*, 1941

Achievements

Hailed throughout the Greek world as champion of the oppressed, Epaminondas was a virtuoso tactician and military genius who shattered Spartan hegemony and established Theban supremacy. He and his colleague Pelopidas were assuredly the most gifted commanders and military innovators of their generation, the founders of cities and the creators of a new navy. Filippos of Macedon would learn the art of war from the two statesmen during his years of captivity in Thebes. Largely influenced by Epaminondas' reforms, Filippos would later introduce military innovations and tactics of his own that heralded Hellenistic warfare, ultimately realizing Epaminondas's vision of a united Greece.

Demetrios Poliorketes, Museo Archeologico Nazionale di Napoli. (*Marie-Lan Nguyen/ Wikimedia Commons*)

Chapter 4

DEMETRIOS POLIORKETES
'The Besieger'

Since Demetrios saw that the city of the Salaminians was not to be despised and that a large force was in the city defending it, he determined to prepare siege engines of very great size, catapults for shooting bolts and ballistae of all kinds, and the other equipment that would strike terror. He sent for skilled workmen from Asia. He constructed a device called the 'Helepolis'. It was divided into nine storeys, and the whole was mounted on four solid wheels each eight cubits high. He also constructed very large battering rams and two penthouses to carry them. On the lower levels of the Helepolis he mounted all sorts of ballistae, the largest of them capable of hurling missiles weighing three talents; on the middle levels he placed the largest catapults, and on the highest his lightest catapults and a large number of ballistae; and he also stationed on the Helepolis more than two hundred men to operate these engines in the proper manner.

Diodoros Siculus, *Historical Library*, Book XX, Chapter 48

Demetrios (337–283 BC), One-Eyed Antigonos' loyal son, was one of the most fascinating individuals of the Early Hellenistic era. Born in 336 BC, he belonged to the second generation of Alexander the Great's successors, and experienced great swings of fortune. He fought in the Third and Fourth Wars of the Diadochi (the rival generals of Alexander), survived his father's disastrous defeat at Ipsos, and even managed to hold the Macedonian crown for a few years. He was notorious for the incredible size of the siege engines he developed for his military campaigns.

Demetrios' first attempt at leading an army on his own turned out to be a disaster, however. At the Battle of Gaza (312 BC), 24-year-old Demetrios was no match for Ptolemaîos and Seleukos. They routed his troops, captured his camp and killed or captured all his forty-three elephants. Such a humiliation could have broken his determination to pursue a military career. After the battle, Ptolemaîos had the courtesy to send him back his personal effects 'with a humane and courteous message, that they were not fighting for anything else but honour and dominion' (Plutarch).

Filippos II of Macedon and his son Alexandros III (Alexander the Great) had improved on the techniques of classical Greek warfare epitomized by Miltiades, Leonidas and Epaminondas. Drawing on the legacy of those illustrious precursors, Hellenistic generals introduced combined-arms tactics. Elite *hypaspist* (shield-carrying) hoplites and heavy phalanx infantry units were supported by light-armed infantry (*peltasts*, or skirmishers, slingers and archers). Elephants, stationed in front of the ranks, would charge to disrupt enemy lines; cavalry would outflank the adversary's formations and cut down fleeing enemies. The bulk of the Macedonian and later Hellenistic war machine, however, was the phalanx armed with long pikes. The drilled pike *syntagma* (battalion) placed at the centre of the battle line was eight, ten, twelve, or sixteen men deep and the same number of men across.

Time and time again, this slow but formidable formation stood its ground on the battlefield against numerically superior foes. Up to five rows of overlapping 7-metre-long *sarissas* (long spears) projected towards the enemy. Nothing could stop a phalanx slowly moving forward as they outreached the enemy's spears. Archers taking cover behind were tasked to discharge a barrage of missiles over the formation and clear a path. Phalangites, wearing a helmet and a bronze breastplate or lighter linothorax (linen-based) armour, used sidearms such as swords and daggers for close combat. Mobile light infantry and cavalry units supported the phalanx according to the shifting battlefield environment:

The cavalry, like the light infantry, take their positions according to the demands of battle, and especially is this true of the skirmishers; for these are the most useful to draw first blood, to provoke the enemy to battle, to break their ranks, to repulse their horse . . . by their swift manoeuvring they render many valuable services in battle. The cavalry force is stationed, like the light infantry, sometimes before the phalanx, sometimes behind it, and at other times on the flanks, for which reason this arm of the service is called a supporting force (*epitagma*), as in the case of the light infantry.

Asclepiodotos, *Tactics*

In the highly professional Hellenistic armies, drill and accumulated experience were paramount. The seasoned Silver Shields, 'masters of war without a defeat or a reverse' (Plutarch), served no less than 35–45 years. They fought in countless encounters up to the Battle of Gabiene in 316 BC, crushing all their adversaries, even when pitted against much younger soldiers. At the Battle of Paraitakene, 3,000 of these experienced veterans routed 11,000 enemies without losing a man. These heroes attained almost immortal status.

During the Babylonian War (311–309 BC), shortly after the disbandment of the Silver Shields by Antigonos, Demetrios and his father attempted to wrest the eastern satrapies from Seleukos. Although they managed briefly to occupy (and loot) Babylon twice, they met severe local resistance and eventually had to retreat to Asia Minor, leaving Seleukos firmly in command of the entire Eastern provinces as far as the Indus Valley.

In the meantime, Ptolemaîos had occupied the island of Cyprus, taken the island of Kos, and captured the island of Delos, centre of the League of the Islanders. Antigonos decided to send Demetrios to retake control of the Aegean. During the Fourth War of the Diadochi (308–301), with a fleet of 250 huge polyreme ('with many banks of oars') warships, Demetrios swept through the islands, retook control of the Nesiotic League, landed unexpectedly at Athens (307 BC), where he expelled the garrison of Kassandros, who thus lost control of Southern Greece, before destroying Ptolemaîos' fleet at the Battle of Salamis off Cyprus (306 BC), where he used large 'supergalleys' and captured the island itself. Quinqueremes (galleys with five banks of oars), first built at the instigation of Dionysios I of Syracuse in 398 BC, were the mainstay of the Diadochis' Mediterranean fleets.

Ptolemy himself sailed to the attack with a hundred and fifty ships, and ordered Menelaus to put out from Salamis with sixty ships, and when the struggle was fiercest, to assail the ships of Demetrius in the rear, and throw them into confusion. But to these sixty ships Demetrius opposed only ten ships (for that small number sufficed to block the narrow exit from the harbour), while he himself, after first drawing out his land forces and encompassing the headlands that extended into the sea, put out to battle with a hundred and eighty ships. He made his onset with great impetus and force, and utterly routed Ptolemy. Ptolemy himself, after his defeat, fled swiftly with eight ships only (for only that small number were left from his whole fleet).

Plutarch, *Parallel Lives, Life of Demetrios*

This string of victories served as justification for Antigonos to claim the title of King, and he had another diadem sent to his devoted son. Demetrios then sailed to Rhodes, which he attempted to conquer in order to force the islanders to side with the Antigonids and distance themselves from the Ptolemaic alliance. The siege lasted a year. Apart from the scientific approach of the siege operations, Demetrios stunned his contemporaries with the size and quantity of siege machinery he deployed, including a giant 56m-long ram-tortoise built by Hegetor of Byzantium and propelled by 1,000 men. Demetrios also used a 25m-long moveable *korax* (drill) to bore holes through walls.

His most fearsome device was an enormous wheeled armoured tower called *Helepolis* ('Taker of Cities') built by Epimachos of Athens: it was nine storeys high, reinforced with iron plates on the front and sides, stood more than 40m tall and weighed a staggering 180 tons. Its armament made it particularly fearsome: carrying sixteen catapults and four dart throwers, the two top floors would shower down darts from above. *Helepolis* did not have a drawbridge; rather it was used as an early land 'gunship' or tank: its concentrated firepower would clear the enemy's walls of defenders, while its large catapults could even destroy ramparts and curtain-walls. Attackers could then bring up battering rams, undermine the walls or mount a traditional assault with ladders.

The *Helepolis* was mounted on eight oak wheels (5m in diameter) and propelled by a capstan and belt drive manned by 200 men. Additional thrust could be provided from the rear. During the siege, the Rhodians managed to knock out some of the iron plates, exposing the timber beneath to fire-arrows. To avoid it being destroyed, the huge tower was pulled out for repair.

A compromise with the Rhodians was eventually reached: they offered their loyalty to Antigonos and Demetrios and pledged to support them against all their enemies, except Ptolemaîos. This is when Demetrios' nickname, 'the Besieger', was earned (304 BC). The *Helepolis*, along with the other siege machinery left behind, was dismantled and sold by the Rhodians for 300 talents of silver. The money and the timber were used to build the colossal statue of the sun god Helios, one of the Seven Wonders of the Ancient World. When the Colossus was finished, it was dedicated with the following poem:

To you, O Sun, the people of Dorian Rhodes set up this bronze statue reaching to Olympus, when they had pacified the waves of war and crowned their city with the spoils taken from the enemy. Not only over the seas but also on land did they kindle the lovely torch of freedom and independence. For to the descendants of Herakles belongs dominion over sea and land.

From Rhodes, Demetrios sailed back to Greece, freed the entire Peloponnese and created a new Greek League of free and independent cities against Kassandros' Macedonian rule. His long series of victories came to a brutal end when Lysimachos and Seleukos clashed with Demetrios and his father at Ipsos (301 BC). With Antigonos' death on the battlefield and the loss of the Antigonid army, Demetrios had to escape with 9,000 men back to Greece, where he was no longer welcome.

In the following years Demetrios, who still had control of the sea, proved again to be amazingly resilient. Seleukos allied himself with him against Ptolemaîos, and the Besieger forced Athens to come to terms once again. By 294 BC Demetrios had reconquered the entire Peloponnese. He then intervened in Macedonia, which was torn by a dynastic struggle among Kassandros' heirs, and eliminated both young kings. The Macedonian army then proclaimed Demetrios king. When Demetrios returned to Athens from Kerkyra in 291 BC, the Athenians welcomed the King with a solemn procession, bestowing the title of 'saviour-god' on him:

How the greatest and dearest of the gods have come to the city! Hail son of the most powerful gods Poseidon and Aphrodite! For other gods are either far away, or they do not have ears, or they do not exist, or do not take any notice of us, but you we can see present here, not made of wood or stone, but real. So we pray to you: first make peace, dearest; for you have the power.
                    Ithyphallic hymn sung by the Athenians in 291 BC

These achievements came at a heavy price: Demetrios' possessions in Asia Minor were all seized by Ptolemaîos, Lysimachos and Seleukos. He was forced to abandon his kingdom, which was divided between Lysimachos and Pyrrhos of Epirus, and to intervene in the East, leaving behind his 31-year-old son Antigonos II Gonatas as governor of Greece.

Demetrios assembled his navy and embarked with 11,000 infantry and all his cavalry to attack Caria and Lydia, two provinces held by Lysimachos (287 BC). He was chased across Asia Minor by the armies of Seleukos and Lysimachos. By late 286 the remnant of his army had deserted him, and he was forced to surrender to Seleukos, who permitted him to live and installed him in a luxurious prison at Apamea on the Orontes, where he proceeded to drink himself to death (283 BC). However, by 276 BC, his son Antigonos II Gonatas was able to re-establish the family's control over Macedon, as well as over most of the Greek city-states.

Achievements

In Demetrios' time, naval warfare and siegecraft reached a new level of size and complexity, shaping the course of western history. Hailed as a living God, Demetrios, the most spirited military leader of his generation, became famous as the builder of the most gigantic warships and siege engines created up to that time. To take cities, his engineers devised a plethora of new machines that astonished his contemporaries, including giant catapults, armoured battering rams and armoured wheeled towers equipped with heavy ballistic devices. After Demetrios, Macedonia would be ruled by Antigonids for the next century and a half, until Perseus' defeat at Pydna by Rome in 168 BC.

Terracotta Army Qin Dynasty general. (*David Castor/Wikimedia Commons*)

Chapter 5

GENERAL BAI QI OF QIN
The 'butcher' of the Warring States

Thus Zhao Kuo was defeated, and 400,000 of his soldiers surrendered to Lord Wuan [Bai Qi], who devised some deception and had them all massacred, sending only 240 of the youngest ones back to Zhao. Counting earlier and later actions, he took prisoner or cut off the heads of 450,000 men, leaving the people of Zhao trembling with fear.

Sima Qian, *Records of the Grand Historian*

During the two centuries and a half of the Warring States period (475–221 BC), the *Records of the Grand Historian* mention no fewer than 186 large-scale conflicts. Toward the end of that chaotic era, the brutal Bai Qi led his armies in some seventy engagements and captured eighty-six walled cities. Never defeated, he allegedly killed nearly one million enemies in his military career. As General in Chief of the Kingdom of Qin, Bai Qi, one of the most infamous generals in the entire history of China, practised total war, leaving behind him a trail of death and destruction for which he is remembered to this day. His murderous campaigns, eliminating most foreign opposition, paved the way for Qin's strategic dominance and the later unification of what would be known as China under Qin Shi Huang in 221 BC.

Owing to the paucity of reliable historical sources surviving from that period, not a great deal is known about his life, but we know that Bai Qi (c.332–257 BC) was born in Mei (in Qin) into a noble family. However, since the legalist reforms of Chancellor of Shang Yang, in the state of Qin even young nobles had to prove their worth to be promoted. Bai Qi also owed his rise to the lasting support of Queen Dowager Xuan, the de facto ruler until the 270s BC, and Prime Minister Wei Ran, the young king's uncle.

In 294 BC Lord Mengchang of Qi's alliance system collapsed. The states of Han, Wei and East Zhou allied together to attack Qin. After Qi and Qin signed a truce, both kingdoms pursued their own interests: Qi moved south against the State of Song, whilst Prime Minister Wei Ran of Qin sent Bai Qi eastward against a superior Han/Wei allied force that he faced on the battlefield of Yique.

Capitalizing on the hostility between the Han and the Wei generals, Bai Qi was able to fight them separately, as each refused to come to the help of the other. He captured the Wei positions one by one, then turned against the Han forces. When the Han troops, trapped by Qin forces, tried to break out, the Qin cavalry ensured that none would escape. Bai Qi's troops proceeded to hunt down their defeated enemies, eventually decapitating 240,000 of them. The armies of Han and Wei had been wiped out. Both states were forced to cede lands to the Kingdom of Qin in return for temporary peace, but their eventual destruction was only a matter of time.

> The General is the bulwark of the State; if the bulwark is complete at all points; the State will be strong; if the bulwark is defective, the State will be weak.
>
> Sun Tzu, *The Art of War*

In 292 BC Bai Qi led the main Qin army against Wei, capturing Weicheng and sacking Yuanqu. Further campaigns against Wei took place the following years under Bai Qi. Fan Ju of Wei, fleeing his home state, arrived at the court of King Zhaoxiang. The future Chancellor was the one who devised the grand strategy of 'alliance with distant states while attacking the nearby ones'.

In 278 BC Bai Qi and Zhang Ruo attacked Chu on two different fronts. Bai Qi flooded the city of Yan by redirecting the Han river, drowning 100,000 people. Ying, the capital on the Yangtze river, was captured, and Chu's western lands on the Han River were annexed. Bai Qi now set up a new commandery, and the state of Chu was forced to relocate its capital to Chen. King Zhaoxiang then promoted Bai Qi to the position of 'Lord Wuan'.

In 262–260 BC, in the fight over the Shandang Commandery, Zhao's armies were led by the young Zhao Kuo, while King Zhaoxiang of Qin secretly appointed the veteran General Bai Qi as his overall commander. At the Battle of Changping in southern Shanxi, when Zhao Kuo left the protection of his fortifications, deceived by a feigned retreat of the Qin troops, Bai Qi used a pincer movement: his centre fell back, while his wings surrounded the Zhao army, cutting off their retreat and supply lines.

The showdown still lasted a month and a half, the starving Zhao troops even resorting to cannibalism before surrendering en masse. Bai Qi had the prisoners executed to avoid having to fight them again later, and a macabre mound was built with their skulls. The state of Zhao, having lost 450,000 men in this dramatic campaign, would never recover or pose a threat to Qin again. After Zhao's defeat, no single state was strong enough to face Qin on its own. The Battle of Changping is regarded as one of the decisive battles of Chinese history.

Naturally, we have to take with a pinch of salt the huge numbers of deaths reported in the chronicles; they are probably inflated for rhetorical effect. In 1995, the skeletal remains of 130 males dating from that period, bearing signs of battle trauma, were excavated from the battlefield site in modern Shanxi province (Yonglu No. 1 human remains pit). Though it was a significant discovery, it's still a far cry from the hundreds of thousands allegedly slaughtered (and buried) on the site. In 2020 more human remains from that era were discovered, and future findings could shed more light on what really happened.

Following this massacre, Bai Qi planned to finish off Zhao once and for all, as the remainder of the Zhao troops were in no condition to fight after suffering such huge losses. However, the Prime Minister of Qin, Fan Sui, who was made Marquis of Ying, probably fearing Bai Qi's power and influence, recommended halting the offensive, on the pretext that the Qin troops ought to be rested and that Qin needed to negotiate a favourable peace to gain territorial concessions.

> In the first month of the lunar year, both sides sheathed the sword. At this news, Lord Wuan held a grudge against Marquis Ying. In September, the State of Qin sent troops again and Viscount Wang Ling was ordered to invade Handan, the capital of Zhao.
>
> Sima Qian, *Records of the Grand Historian*

When King Zhaoxiang finally ordered Bai Qi to reinforce General Wang Ling at the siege of the well-defended Handan, capital of the Zhao, Bai Qi refused repeatedly, claiming he was too indisposed to lead any ongoing military operation. The battered forces of Wei and Chu eventually arrived on time to relieve (even if temporarily) Handan from the besieging Qin armies. These setbacks prompted the infuriated king to force Bai Qi to commit suicide in November 257 AD. Even the mightiest general was not immune from a dramatic reversal of fortune:

> The state of Chu measured several thousand li [Chinese miles] squared, and supported a million lance-bearers. Bai Qi led an army of several tens of thousands, engaging Chu in battle. In one battle he captured Yan and Ying, in another he put Yiling to the torch. He also crossed through Han and Wei to attack the powerful Zhao. In the north, he buried Lord Mafu and massacred his host of more than 400,000 soldiers. The blood flowed in rivers and cries rose up like thunder. Therewith he caused Qin to perform the task of the thearchs. Thenceforth, Zhao and Chu bowed down in terror and dared not attack Qin: this was the power of Bai Qi. He personally subjugated more than seventy cities. Yet when his merits had been accomplished, he was granted death at Duyou.
>
> Dialogue between Fan Sui and Cai Ze in *Annals of the Warring States*

Handan would eventually be taken by Wang Ling. Ying Zheng (Qin Shi Huang), the future first Emperor of China, was born in Handan during the siege. Fan Sui, who had a hand in Bai Qi's downfall, would himself be executed for treason a few years later. The Zhou royal principality was annexed by Qin in 256 BC, and Nan, the last king, died in captivity soon after, putting an end to the Zhou dynasty 790 years after its foundation.

Bai Qi is said to have been responsible for some 900,000 enemy deaths over his entire military career. Although this figure was probably exaggerated, as soldiers were paid by the number of enemies killed, it still confirms that warfare in China had reached an appallingly lethal level. Allegedly, Bai Qi was able to predict the outcome of any given battle. Instead of aiming at territorial conquests, he sought the complete destruction of the enemy's military capacity by annihilating his troops, even after they surrendered. The widespread misery and massacres of the period are one of the reasons for China's subsequent predilection for a strong, unified state.

Achievements

Bai Qi is among the 'Ten Wise Men' of the martial temples that list ancient China's best strategists. A ruthless general but an outstanding military tactician, Bai Qi severely weakened the different enemy states of Qin. Once Qin had emerged as one of the most powerful of the seven Warring States, Ying Zheng, the new king of Qin, advised by Chancellor Li Si, then unleashed the final campaigns to conquer the remaining six major states one by one, finally unifying China for the first time in history.

Agrippa, Musée du Louvre. (*Marie-Lan Nguyen/Wikimedia Commons*)

Chapter 6

MARCUS AGRIPPA
Augustus's lieutenant

Enjoying the favour of the winds and the gods, his head held high, Agrippa leads the army; on his forehead shines the naval crown, adorned with rams, a superb war distinction.

Virgil, *Aeneid*, Book VIII

Octavian, the skilled politician who became the first Emperor of Rome as Augustus, was anything but a soldier. It was Agrippa, his close childhood friend, who officiated as his personal advisor, general, admiral and chief state administrator. Agrippa's ascendancy is inseparably linked with that of Octavian. Together, they defeated Octavian's rivals one by one, until the two associates were the sole masters of the Roman world. Without the able Agrippa as his right-hand man, Octavian would have never seized ultimate power or established the foundations of the Roman Principate.

Although Marcus Vipsanius Agrippa's family were not patricians (members of the ruling, senatorial families), they seemed to have been wealthy enough to be raised to equestrian (knightly) rank. The young Agrippa (c.62–12 BC) was sent to Rome for his education, where he met Gaius Octavius, the great-nephew of the *Triumvir* (one of three rulers) Gaius Julius Caesar, leader of the *Populares* (popular faction), who at the time was involved in the conquest of Gaul. In 46 BC, when Octavian sailed to Hispania to join Caesar, Agrippa and Maecenas were at his side. Caesar defeated Pompey's sons Gnaeus Pompeius and Sextus Pompeius at the Battle of Munda in March 45 BC. Shipwrecked, the two young men travelled through hostile territory to reach Caesar's camp, arriving after the conclusion of the campaign.

The young Octavian and his companions must have made quite an impression on the seasoned general, for he appointed the 19-year-old Octavian as his *Magister Equitum* (cavalry commander), then sent his young great-nephew, Agrippa, Maecenas and the young soldier Quintus Salvidienus Rufus to Apollonia in Illryia to continue their studies and receive further military training. They studied under Athenodorus of Tarsus, a distinguished scientist.

By that time Roman legions had been the undisputed tool of conquest across the Mediterranean world for a century. During the Macedonian Wars (214–148 BC) the Romans had observed some of the few faults of the Hellenistic phalanx: it was vulnerable to both flank and rear attacks, it was slow and it could only be successfully deployed on flat terrain. These weaknesses had brought about the defeat of King Perseus at Pydna (168 BC) and Rome's subsequent supremacy over Greece following Corinth's utter destruction in 146 BC. More flexible maniples (small tactical units) had replaced the once-invincible phalanx.

It was at Apollonia that Octavian and his classmates received news of Caesar's murder (March 44 BC). When they returned to Rome, Octavian found to his surprise that Caesar had adopted him and had made him heir to his political position and personal fortune.

During the confused Civil War that followed, Octavian at times joined forces with Mark Antony against Caesar's assassins. At the Battle of Philippi, where the Caesarian army emerged victorious, Octavian handed over military command of his legions to Agrippa (42 BC). Brutus and Cassius died during the campaign; Julius Caesar's murder had been avenged.

Sextus Pompey still held out, however. Having been given command of the Italian fleet by the Senate in 43 BC, Pompey took control of Sicily, Corsica and Sardinia and blockaded Italy, shutting off the crucial supply of grain from Africa. Agrippa fought off Mark Antony and Pompey one after the other, defeating Antony at Perusia and Sipontum (40 BC). The following year, he put down a rebellion in Gaul and even crossed the Rhine to fight the Germanic tribes.

Appointed *Praetor* of Rome, Agrippa then turned admiral and architect. Despite having no prior naval experience whatsoever, he founded Portus Julius at Misenium, built a powerful fleet, then trained the crews in the Gulf of Baiae. Agrippa also came up with a new device, the *harpax*, a ballista-fired grappling-hook with a mechanical traction mechanism to draw ships together.

In 37 BC Agrippa, now in his mid-twenties, was awarded the rank of Consul for the first time, despite the fact that the minimum age was normally forty-three. The following year, with his naval force of 300 quinqueremes (the largest fleet built by Rome since the Second Punic War in the second century BC) armed with the *harpax* and *corvus* boarding ramps, Agrippa won the naval Battles of Mylae and Naulochus.

Three hundred ships were put in readiness on either side, provided with missiles of all kinds, with towers and whatever machines they could think of. Agrippa devised one called the 'grip', a piece of wood five cubits long bound with iron and having rings at the extremities. To one of these rings was attached the grip itself, an iron claw, to the other numerous ropes, which drew it by machine power after it had been thrown by a catapult and had seized the enemy's ships. When the appointed day came the rival shouts of the oarsmen were first heard, accompanied by missiles thrown by machines and by hand, such as stones, firebrands, and arrows. The 'grip' achieved the greatest success. Thrown from a long distance upon the ships, as it could be by reason of its lightness, it clutched them, as soon as the ropes pulled on it from behind. On account of the iron bands it could not be easily cut by the men whom it attacked, and those who tried to cut the ropes were prevented from reaching them by its length. As this apparatus had never been known before, the enemy had not provided themselves with scythe-mounted poles.

Appian of Alexandria, *The Civil Wars*

Pompey's threat was over, and Octavian was the undisputed master of the western Mediterranean. In recognition of his decisive victories, Agrippa was awarded the naval crown decoration (*corona rostrata*).

Meanwhile, relations had been deteriorating between Octavian and Mark Antony, dictator of the Orient. After Mark Antony's divorce from Octavia, Octavian's sister, renewed war was inevitable. The time had come for an epic showdown. Mark Antony and Kleopatra VII of Egypt took their fleet of about 200 large warships to Actium on the western coast of Greece, where they established their main base of operations.

Agrippa now took the offensive: he captured Methone and Corcyra, defeated an enemy squadron led by Quintus Nasidius, captured Corinth, then successfully ferried Octavian's legions across the Adriatic. Octavian's legions occupied Patrae and Corinth, cutting Antony's communications with Egypt and forcing him to take action. To make matters worse, his fleet was caught in a gale lasting four days. On the fifth day Antony embarked 20,000 infantry for the decisive naval showdown.

> Agrippa. . . was confident himself that he would conquer without difficulty, because in the meantime a violent rainstorm, accompanied by a mighty wind, had struck Antony's fleet, though not his own, and had thrown it utterly into confusion.
>
> Cassius Dio, *Roman History*, Book L

Agrippa led Octavian's 250 quinqueremes in the heat of battle, ordering his smaller, faster and more agile warships to ram and disengage before attacking other enemy vessels, avoiding boarding whenever possible:

> Caesar's followers, having smaller and swifter ships, would dash forward and ram the enemy, being armoured on all sides to avoid receiving damage. If they sank a vessel, well and good; if not, they would back water before coming to grips, and would either ram the same vessels suddenly again, or would let those go and turn their attention to others; and having done some damage to these also, so far as they could in a brief time, they would proceed against others and then against still others, in order that their assault upon any vessel might be so far as possible unexpected. For since they dreaded the long-range missiles of the enemy no less than their fighting at close quarters, they wasted no time either in the approach or in the encounter.
>
> Cassius Dio, *Roman History*, Book L

The fighting remained indecisive, until Kleopatra ordered the sails of her sixty warships hoisted in order to escape toward Egypt. This caused Antony to break off in turn and pursue her, abandoning his fleet and his legions. During the battle and in its immediate aftermath the Antonian fleet lost 300 ships. In the days that followed, the surrender of Antony's legions left behind in northern Greece transformed Octavian's advantage into total victory.

This last naval battle of the Civil Wars definitively established Octavian as the sole ruler of Rome and the entire vast territory of the Roman Republic. Agrippa then landed in Egypt, both Antony and Kleopatra committed suicide in Alexandria, and Octavian took personal control of the land of the Pharaohs. It was at the end of this extraordinary campaign that the Senate granted Octavian the additional name of 'Augustus'.

In 23 BC, when Augustus fell dangerously ill, he nominated Agrippa as his successor. After Augustus' recovery, Agrippa served as his *Imperator* (commander) and friend in the East. Agrippa married the 18-year-old Julia, Augustus' only biological child, after Maecenas advised Augustus: 'You have made him so great that he must either become your son-in-law or be slain.' Thus their children would be Augustus' heirs.

Agrippa also left a vast legacy of public works in Rome and throughout the Empire, such as his improvement of the public road network for the movement of troops (*Via Agrippa*). In the capital, he built the Pantheon on his own property in the Campus Martius. This engineering marvel was rebuilt by Hadrian after the fire of 110 AD, and today it stands majestically as one of the wonders of the Ancient World.

Governor of Gaul in 18 BC, Agrippa quelled uprisings and built new forts. After a last campaign on the Upper Danube, he retired to Campania, where he died in March 12 BC. His death was a terrible blow to Augustus, who mourned his companion for a month and had Agrippa's ashes placed in his own mausoleum on the Campus Martius.

Such was the end of Agrippa, who had in every way clearly shown himself the noblest of the men of his day and had used the friendship of Augustus with a view to the greatest advantage both of the emperor himself and of the commonwealth.

Cassius Dio, *Roman History*, Book LIV

Achievements

Agrippa rose to become Octavian's most trusted friend and military commander. A man of action, he displayed leadership, ingenuity and outstanding strategic abilities throughout his campaigns. Octavian's lieutenant also proved to be an exceptional administrator. The string of victories the young Agrippa won over his father-in-law's adversaries on land and at sea was essential to Augustus' ascendancy. He proved himself in all environments and all settings against a variety of enemies, in sieges, pitched battles, naval battles and counter-insurgency campaigns, fighting against Illyrians, Gauls, Germanic tribes and fellow Romans. The final decisive victory over Mark Antony established Augustus as the undisputed master of the Roman world and the entire Mediterranean. The Battle of Actium is considered a major turning point in the history of Rome: it marked the end of the Civil Wars and the Republic, heralding the dawn of the Empire. Secure from internal threats, Rome would expand further in both the West and the East. Caligula, Agrippina the Younger and Nero were all descended from Agrippa and Julia.

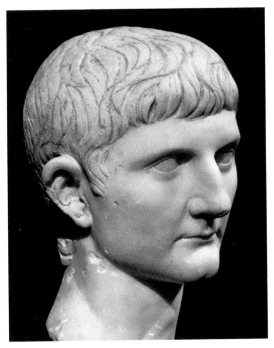

Germanicus, Musée de Saint-Raymond, Toulouse. (*Pierre Selim/Wikimedia Commons*)

Chapter 7

GERMANICUS
Rome's beloved general, heir to the Empire

Germanicus was gracious to his friends, temperate in his pleasures. He was too no less a warrior, though rashness he had none, and, though after having cowed Germany by his many victories, he was hindered from crushing it into subjection. Had he had the sole control of affairs, had he possessed the power and title of a king, he would have attained military glory as much more easily as he had excelled Alexander in clemency, in self-restraint, and in all other virtues.

Tacitus, *Annals*, Book II

Germanicus was the great-nephew of Augustus, grandson of Mark Antony, nephew, adopted son and heir of Emperor Tiberius, father of Caligula and grandfather of Nero. According to the biased Latin sources known to us, this member of the *Domus Augusta* (House of Augustus) who had a successful military career against the Germanic tribes was a natural-born leader. An immensely popular general and gifted diplomat, he was destined to become emperor, and his untimely and mysterious death in Syria shook the Empire to its core.

Nero Claudius Drusus 'Germanicus' (24 BC–19 AD) was the son of Drusus Claudius Nero, who was loved by the people and the Senate and was Augustus' choice as successor, before he died in a military campaign in 9 BC. The *agnomen* (name of honour) 'Germanicus' (Conqueror of Germany) had been given to Drusus and his heirs in the last weeks of his life. The 6-year-old Decimus Claudius Nero was renamed 'Germanicus' Claudius Nero. His younger brother, the future Emperor Claudius, also became Tiberius Claudius Drusus Nero 'Germanicus'.

As part of Augustus' succession scheme, the Emperor had the young Germanicus adopted by Tiberius in 4 AD, even though Tiberius had a son of his own called Drusus, while Augustus chose Tiberius as his heir and future *princeps* (first citizen). Germanicus was married to the last remaining member of the Julian family, his cousin Agrippina the Elder, the granddaughter of Augustus.

Quaestor (Senatorial rank, administrator of public funds) at the age of twenty-one, Germanicus served under Tiberius in Illyricum and on the Rhine (7–9 AD). In 9 AD the disaster at the Battle of the Teutoburg Forest, one of Rome's most humiliating defeats, made it clear that the Germanic tribes were a dangerous foe that had to be dealt with. Only a victory in Germania would restore the prestige of the Empire after Varus' resounding failure. In the year 12 AD, as Consul, Germanicus was given command of the eight legions stationed along the Rhine, a third of Rome's entire military strength.

In 14 AD, after Augustus's death, a mutiny broke out among the 1st, 5th, 20th and 21st legions, as the soldiers had not received the bonuses promised to them. Germanicus' personal popularity and charisma enabled him to quell the rebellion. He secured the loyalty of his legions by negotiation, successfully addressing their grievances and replacing the unsound officers. Although pressed to claim the throne for himself, Germanicus remained firmly loyal to Tiberius. Allegedly, he even threatened to commit suicide rather than accept his mutinous soldiers' offer to make him Emperor.

Immediately after the suppression of the mutiny, Germanicus had his 30,000 legionaries and auxiliary troops prepare for war. He knew that while the soldiers were undergoing harsh conditions on campaign, discipline could be maintained by the prospect of wealth and rewards from raiding Germanic territory. At first he moved against the Marsi tribe, members of the tribal federation led by Arminius. It was a punitive raid: his soldiers laid waste to the Germanic lands, destroying their sacred places and killing everyone in their path:

Neither sex nor age moved his compassion. Everything, sacred or profane, the temple too of Tamfana, as they called it, the special resort of all those tribes, was levelled to the ground.

Tacitus, *Annals*, Book I

The Bructeri, Tubanti and Usipeti were roused by the attack and ambushed Germanicus on the way to his winter quarters, but they were defeated with heavy losses. During the subsequent campaigns (14–16 AD), Germanicus crossed the Rhine with a larger army of 50,000 men to engage the tribes. Unlike Varus, Germanicus marched with his army fully anticipating an attack at any moment: 'The men were alert and ready, so arranged that the order of march could come to a halt in line of battle.'

Although the Germanic tribes avoided open battle, by repeated incursions Germanicus was able to force Arminius to respond. At the Battle of the Weser River, eight Roman legions, together with the Chauci and other auxiliaries, fought for an entire day against 50,000 warriors of the Germanic coalition. The clash was beyond brutal, with no quarter given. While Arminius sought to trample the Roman foot-archers in the centre, Germanicus attempted to trap his adversaries in a pincer movement using his cavalry positioned on both wings. Some of the Germanic warriors attempted to cross the river to safety, others sought refuge in the forest.

It was a brilliant victory. The enemy were slaughtered from the fifth hour of daylight to nightfall, and for ten miles the ground was littered with corpses and weapons. Among the spoils were found the chains which, without a doubt of the result, they had brought in readiness for the Romans.

Tacitus, *Annals* Book II

After this grisly fight, the Romans erected a trophy on the site of the battle, although a wounded Arminus had been able to escape once more. The vanquished Germanic warriors, instead of submitting, rallied against the invaders from all over Germania and attacked them in force at the so-called 'Angrivarian Wall'. Germanicus, who was expecting the assault, routed them again:

The Germans held their own; but they were handicapped by the nature of the struggle and the weapons. Their extraordinary numbers – unable in the restricted space to extend or recover their tremendous lances, or to make use of their rushing tactics and nimbleness of body – were compelled to a standing fight; while our own men, shields tight to the breast and hand on hilt, kept thrusting at the barbarians' great limbs and bare heads and opening a bloody passage through their antagonists.

Tacitus, *Annals* Book II

This was literally a war of annihilation. As Germanicus declared to his troops, 'Prisoners were needless: nothing but the extermination of the race would end the war!' Therefore, he subjugated and devastated entire regions in his path, recovering in the process two of the three legionary standards (eagles) lost by Varus at the Battle of the Teutoburg Forest. The recovered eagle of the 19th Legion was being carried around by the Bructeri tribe, and the other was held by the Marsi, who had buried it in a woodland area, keeping it under guard.

In 15 AD Segestes of the Cherusci defected to the Romans, handing over his own daughter Thusnelda, wife of Arminius. The Germanic tribes suffered heavy losses, while Roman military hegemony was partly reasserted from the Rhine to the Elbe, but the war was far from over. Arminius would be killed in 21 AD by Segestes and his clan. Varus' lost third eagle found its way into the hands of the Cauci tribe and would only be recovered in 41 AD by Publius Gabinius. Varus and his legions were finally avenged.

Germanicus' popularity and victories had aroused the jealousy and fears of Tiberius, who had him recalled to Rome while military operations were still in progress, before he could complete the conquest of *Magna Germania* (regions of Germania under Roman control). For Tiberius, there was little profit in dominating these northern regions. Thusnelda and her infant Thumelicus, Arminius' son, were presented at Rome in the lavish triumph Germanicus was allowed to celebrate on 26 May 17 AD, when he paraded the two eagles retrieved from the forests of Germania. The Roman populace replied to this glorious show from their dashing prince with absolute adulation.

A year after his triumph, Germanicus became Consul for the second time. This time, he was given command of the eastern portion of the empire to deal with the Parthians. Senator Gnaeus Calpurnius Piso was appointed as his legate and made governor of Syria. Tacitus suggests that Tiberius appointed Piso to act as a check, with full knowledge of his antipathy towards Germanicus.

Germanicus organized the previously independent client kingdoms of Cappadocia and Commagene into provinces, appointing governors. When he met King of Kings Artabanos (Ardawān) II of Parthia on an island in the Euphrates, the two men engaged in negotiations that ended with a peaceful compromise settlement to the Armenian succession, together with a friendship treaty between Rome and Ctesiphon that secured over a decade of peace between the two empires. War would not be necessary; it was a rare diplomatic achievement.

In January 19 AD Germanicus visited Alexandria, in defiance of the rules laid down by Augustus that prohibited members of the Senate from going to Egypt without the Emperor's consent. Travelling along the Nile as his grandfather Mark Antony had done, Germanicus put in place a series of measures which made him even more popular: he lowered prices and opened wheat silos to put an end to the hunger caused by a low flood in the Nile. All these actions enraged Tiberius, who criticized him publicly in the Senate, and Germanicus was forced to leave Egypt.

On Germanicus's return to Syria, the differences with Piso turned to open hostility, and Piso, who rejected Germanicus' higher authority, had to leave the province. Shortly afterward, Germanicus fell ill, convinced that Piso, through the latter's wife Plancina, had poisoned him. Germanicus died on 10 October, 19 AD at the age of thirty-four, just outside Antioch on the Orontes. His body was cremated in the forum. The news of his demise brought widespread outpourings of public 'grief and indignation' in Rome and throughout the Empire.

> There was some suspicion that he was poisoned; for besides the dark spots which appeared all over his body and the froth which flowed from his mouth, after he had been reduced to ashes his heart was found entire among his bones; and it is supposed to be a characteristic of that organ that when steeped in poison it cannot be destroyed by fire.
>
> Suetonius, *The Twelve Caesars, Caligula*

Tiberius was forced to order an official investigation, which pointed to Piso. Before he could be sentenced, however, Piso committed suicide, although Tacitus presumed that Tiberius had in fact had him murdered to clear himself from any implication in the plot to eliminate Germanicus. Among the six children of Agrippina the Elder and Germanicus who survived were the insane Emperor Gaius Caligula (37–41 AD) and Julia Agrippina, mother of the Emperor Nero. Many were born in army camps while Germanicus was on active service. Claudius, Germanicus' younger brother, would succeed Caligula (41–54 AD).

Achievements

A capable soldier and general and a skilled diplomat, Germanicus' highly praised charisma and *pietas* (patriotic devotion) made him genuinely popular among the army and beloved of the masses, even though Tiberius regarded his nephew's growing power as a threat to his own rule. Beyond the Rhine, Germanicus resumed the Roman policy of expansion through conquest and restored the legions' honour, which made him a genuine hero of the Empire. The war was left unfinished, however, and the Rhine eventually became the border between the Roman Empire and *Magna Germania*. In the eastern provinces, Germanicus' skills and reputation allowed him to negotiate a peaceful agreement with the Parthians, Rome's most dangerous adversaries. When Germanicus died, the rumours that Tiberius had arranged for his nephew's murder irremediably undermined the Emperor's reputation. The death of Germanicus changed history and set the Empire on a different path.

Huns, Askerî Müze, Istanbul. (*Author*)

Chapter 8

ATTILA THE HUN
'The Scourge of God'

He was a man born into the world to shake the nations, the Scourge of all lands, who in some way terrified all mankind by the dreadful rumours noised abroad concerning him. He was indeed a lover of war, yet restrained in action, mighty in counsel, gracious to suppliants and lenient to those who were once received into his protection.

Jordanes, *Getica*

The fifth century AD was a dark age of utter chaos and devastation that marked the final years of the Roman Empire in the West and the definitive shift of imperial authority to Constantinople. At that time, the pagan and nomadic Huns joined their former enemies the Visigoths in plundering Roman territory.

Attila, the mighty leader of the European Huns, would come to rule over a vast Hunnic Empire stretching from the Caucasus to the Rhine. In the course of two decades his armies sacked Roman cities and towns throughout Gaul, Illyricum, Moesia, Thrace and Italy, threatening Rome and Constantinople and literally holding the fate of Europe in his hands. Although his sudden death led to the rapid collapse of the meteoric Hunnic empire, the memory of Attila lived on throughout the medieval period and beyond.

Our knowledge of Attila (c.405–53 AD) comes from contemporary and prejudiced Greek and Latin chronicles written by his adversaries, who designated him *Flagellum Dei* (the Scourge of God). The Huns themselves left no written records. Succeeding his uncle Rugila, in 445 AD Attila began his personal rule by murdering his older brother Bleda to secure sole leadership of the Huns. The two brothers had made incursions as far as the Persian Empire, before returning and raiding settlements along the Danube.

> All livestock, any sort of fruit and wine which the enemy invader can seize for his own sustenance should be collected into strong forts secured by armed garrisons, or into very safe cities . . . Repairs to all walls and torsion-engines should be taken in hand in advance too, for if the enemy once find you unready, everything becomes confused in panic . . . Cities and forts should be defended by those soldiers who prove less useful in the field, equipped with arms, arrows, sling-staves, slings and stones, mangonels and catapults.
>
> Vegetius, *De Re Militari*

Attila's incursion into Germania drove large populations to flee across the borders of the Western Roman Empire and contributed to its later breakdown. Rome's weakness encouraged Attila to make and break treaties without fear of consequences. His wide-scale pillage, murder and rape in Roman territory met with little resistance, making it clear that the under-resourced Roman armies were no longer capable of defending the Empire. Attila's name became synonymous with the terror it instilled among the populations of the regions that his armies swept through.

Attila skilfully used the superstitions of his own people and his adversaries to forge his power and cause panic among his enemies. He hammered other tribes into submission, forging alliances with the Alans, Gepids and Ostrogoths. His ability to command a confederation of warrior tribes from various ethnic backgrounds was in contrast to Roman generals of his time, who had difficulty keeping the *foederati* (allied tribes) levies under control. Attila's commanding presence held his empire together through personal authority. He set up his capital in the heart of Pannonia, in the great Hungarian plain, and named it 'Sicambria', or Etzelburg

(Attila's town) in later German sources. Priscus of Panium, who visited it, has left us a vivid description:

> Attila was lord over all the Huns and almost the sole earthly ruler of all the tribes of Scythia; a man marvellous for his glorious fame among all nations. The historian Priscus, who was sent to him on an embassy by the younger Theodosius, says this among other things: Crossing mighty rivers – namely the Tisia and Tibisia and Dricca . . . we arrived at the village where King Attila was dwelling – a village, I say, like a great city, in which we found wooden walls made of smooth-shining boards, whose joints so counterfeited solidity that the union of the boards could scarcely be distinguished by close scrutiny. There you might see dining halls of large extent and porticoes planned with great beauty, while the courtyard was bounded by so vast a circuit that its very size showed it was the royal palace. This was the abode of Attila, the king of all the barbarian world; and he preferred this as a dwelling to the cities he captured.
>
> Jordanes, quoting Priscus of Panium, *Getica*

Attila's gigantic empire was built in a decade. He made the Huns the most effective fighting force of the time. His mobile cavalry probably used saddle stirrups, a key development in the art of war and riding technology. Hunnic horsemen were armed with lances and powerful composite recurved bows made with alternating layers of horn, wood and sinew. Learning from the Romans themselves, Attila's armies also used siege engines to assault and conquer walled cities.

In 447 he took advantage of an epidemic devastating Thrace to sack the province, then raided the dioceses of Dacia and Macedonia. The walled city of Serdika (Sofia), birthplace of the Emperor Galerius, was captured and destroyed by his troops. *Magister Militum per Orientem* (Commander of the East) Zeno rushed to Constantinople in order to reinforce the defences of the imperial capital, but the Eastern Roman Empire was relatively less vulnerable than the West due to its more capable leadership.

> The barbarian nation of the Huns, which was in Thrace, became so great that more than a hundred cities were captured and Constantinople almost came into danger and most men fled from it. And there were so many murders and blood-lettings that the dead could not be numbered. They captured the churches and monasteries and slew the monks and maidens in great numbers.
>
> Callinicus of Rufinianae, *Life of Saint Hypatius*

An assassination attempt on Attila's life fomented by Emperor Theodosius II failed. In August 450, after Theodosius' accidental death, the Emperor Marcian abrogated the past treaties with the Huns along with all the tribute due. This gesture of defiance would have to be answered, but for now Attila had other plans.

In 449 Attila had received a message with a signet ring from 31-year-old Justa Grata Honoria, sister of Western Emperor Valentinian III, offering him half of the West if he would rescue her from a forced marriage with a senator. Attila demanded that Honoria be given to him, along with half of the Western Roman Empire, but Valentinian rejected the ultimatum and braced himself for war. This fateful decision provided the pretext Attila had been looking for to march against the West.

In the spring of 451 AD Attila crossed the Rhine and launched his large-scale invasion of Gaul with a force estimated by Jordanes at half a million, as the King of the Huns was joined by his vassals the Vandals, Gepids and Ostrogoths. The huge army took Gallia Belgica with little resistance, sacking every city in its path until it encountered the stout Aurelianum (Orléans).

Attila was finally checked in June at the Battle of the Catalaunian Plains (or Châlons) by a coalition of *foederati*: Visigoths, Franks, Burgundians and Alans mustered by *Comes et Magister Utriusque Militiae* (official holding supreme military rank) Flavius Aetius. The Visigoths under Theodoric I only joined Aetius because they considered the Huns a greater threat than the Romans.

Here you stand, after conquering mighty nations and subduing the world. Despise their battle line. Attack the Alani, smite the Visigoths! Seek swift victory in that spot where the battle rages. For when the sinews are cut the limbs soon relax, nor can a body stand when you have taken away the bones. Let your courage rise and your own fury burst forth! Now show your cunning, Huns, now your deeds of arms! Even a mass of federated nations could not endure the sight of the Huns. I shall hurl the first spear at the foe.
Attila's address to his troops before the Battle of the Catalaunian Plains in Jordanes, *Getica*

Once the Ostrogoths were defeated by the Visigoths on the left flank, Theodoric attacked the Huns in the centre. Unable to make use of his mounted archers, with his left flank routed and his right struggling against Aetius, Attila ordered a retreat to his camp. The Battle of the Catalaunian Fields would be Attila's first and only defeat. In the aftermath of the engagement, Aetius moved his army away, while Attila crossed the Rhine with the spoils of his campaign.

The following year, Attila ravaged northern Italy, shadowed by Aetius. After sacking Verona, Aquileia and Mediolanum (Milan), he intended to march on Rome. According to Prosper of Aquitaine, Attila was so impressed by Pope Leo the Great that he eventually withdrew from the peninsula. In reality, his troops, struck by an epidemic, were simply too weakened, while an army from the Eastern

Empire was raiding deep into the great Hungarian plain, wreaking havoc on Attila's food supplies.

Returning to Pannonia, Attila threatened to avenge this stab in the back by invading Marcian's Eastern Empire the following year and conquering it entirely. These plans fell apart soon after, however, for in March 453 Attila, who had just taken a new wife called Hildico, died on his wedding night in obscure circumstances. In later High Germanic legends, Hildico would be renamed Kriemhild, the widow of Siegfried the dragonslayer, killing Attila to avenge the death of her people.

Two years after Attila's unexpected death, in June 455, King Genseric of the Vandals sacked Rome without encountering opposition. This time, Pope Leo the Great was not able to save the Eternal City. Aetius was no more, as he had been assassinated by Valentinian in September 454. Aetius was avenged in March 455, when two of his followers in turn murdered the Western Emperor on the Campus Martius.

Attila's three sons tried to hold his empire together but failed in the ensuing civil war, as one Germanic vassal after the other revolted. By 469 AD, when Dengizich, his last son, was no more, Attila's vast domains had broken apart, and the Huns were absorbed by other nomadic peoples. The location of Attila's tomb and his capital remains a mystery. The conqueror who had shaken the Roman world to its core managed to vanish entirely, leaving the grim memory of his deeds as only trace of his passage.

Achievements

Attila is remembered as a ruthless tactician who was perfectly aware of the weaknesses of the fading Roman world. He used his adversaries' tactics to his advantage, as he alternately allied with the Romans, extorted resources from them, then raided their territories. An exceptionally intelligent and sophisticated ruler, he held the Huns and their vassal tribes together against Rome and its allies through his sheer prestige and authority. Despite Aetius' victory at the Catalaunian Fields, the depleted Western Roman Empire would not survive for more than twenty-five years following this climactic battle. In order to deal with the challenge of nomadic warfare, the Eastern Romans would soon adopt the Hunnic model to reform their own armies, as attested in Maurice's and Syrianus Magister's *Strategikon*. The thirteenth-century *Nibelungenlied*, in which Attila plays a central part, would mirror the chaotic events of the Western Roman Empire's collapse and the dawn of a new era we now call the Middle Ages.

Part II

THE MIDDLE AGES
AD 500 – 1490

Belisarius, San Vitale, Ravenna. (*The Yorck Project/Wikimedia Commons*)

Chapter 9

FLAVIUS BELISARIUS
Architect of the Byzantine reconquest

The name of Belisarius was on the lips of all: to him were ascribed two victories, such as had never before fallen to the lot of any one man to achieve; he had brought two kings captive to Byzantium, he had brought back their wealth and restored it once more to the state, and recovered for the empire in a short space of time almost one half of its territory.

Procopius of Caesarea, *History of the Wars*, Book VII

In the sixth century the precarious Byzantine Empire was under siege, beset by enemies at its borders: the Persians in the east, Germanic tribes in the west and south, and Göktürks and pagan Slavs in the north. While Emperor Justin I had avoided any significant conflicts, his nephew Justinian I (482–565) was determined to turn things around. He launched aggressive wars to reconquer lost territory, reasserting Byzantine control in an ultimate attempt to restore the Roman Empire. Of all his generals, none was more capable than the legendary Belisarius, who in the course of just a decade succeeded in more than doubling the size of the Byzantine realm. The dream of a reunited Mediterranean seemed within reach.

Born in Thrace, and originally a palace guard (*doryphoros*) in Justin's retinue, Flavius Belisarius (c.500–565) was appointed commander of the *Bucellarii* (heavy cavalry bodyguards). Following Justin's death, Justinian was declared Emperor in August 527. That Belisarius' wife Antonina was a close friend of the Empress Theodora's was also a crucial factor in his rise and key to his lasting favour in the midst of shifting, murderous court intrigues.

As *Magister Militum* (generalissimo), Belisarius' first campaign in the East could well have been his last: after defeating a superior Sassanid force at Dara, Belisarius' army was eventually bested at the Battle of Callinicum (April 531), but an invasion of Byzantine Syria had been prevented. In September 532 the two sides agreed on the 'Eternal Peace' (which lasted less than eight years), both pledging to return all occupied territories. Furthermore, the Byzantines paid a heavy tribute of 110 *centenaria* (11,000 pounds of gold). Having secured peace in the East at a tremendous cost, Justinian then turned westward, intent on a complete reconquest of the former Western Roman Empire.

> For there is nothing stabler nor more fortunate or admirable than a State which has copious supplies of soldiers who are trained. For it is not fine raiment or stores of gold, silver and gems that bend our enemies to respect or support; they are kept down solely by fear of our arms.
>
> Vegetius, *De Re Militari*

Back in Constantinople, Belisarius was eventually cleared of blame for defeat in the East. The following year, alongside Narses the eunuch and Mundus the Gepid, Belisarius was instrumental in putting down the bloody Nika Riots, which climaxed with the slaughter of over 30,000 rebels in the hippodrome. As the Emperor owed Belisarius his throne and probably his life, and because military victories legitimized Imperial authority, he now entrusted the general with a large-scale expedition against the Vandal kingdom in North Africa.

Given command of probably the most effective and skilled Roman force seen in the West in centuries, Belisarius landed close to Carthage, while 5,000 Vandal warriors under Tzanon were away, fighting in Sardinia. Belisarius' 16,000-man army was composed of 10,000 infantry and 3,000 cavalry from the *comitatenses* (elite) field army and *foederati*, 600 Huns and 400 Herule mounted archers, and 1,500 mounted *bucellarii* (elite household cavalry) of his own retinue. They travelled from the Bosphorus to North Africa on 500 transports, escorted by ninety-two *dromons* (oared warships discharging incendiary Greek fire).

> Belisarius is remarkable because of two features: first, the extraordinarily slender resources with which he undertook these far-reaching campaigns; second, his consistent use of the tactical defensive. There is no parallel in history for such a series of conquests by abstention from attack! And it may seem all the more strange since they were carried out by an army that was based on the mobile arm and mainly composed of cavalry.
> Basil H. Liddell Hart, *The Strategy of Indirect Approach*

Belisarius defeated the scattered Vandal forces sent to stop his advance at Ad Decimum and on 14 September 533 he entered Carthage. In December, Gelimer, King of the Vandals and Alans, was forced to surrender after being defeated a second time at Tricamarum. The capture of Hippo Regius ended the campaign.

The Vandal War marked the beginning of Justinian's campaigns of reconquest. After Belisarius' return to Constantinople the Emperor, reviving the customs of Ancient Rome, awarded him a triumph. The general paraded through the streets of the capital, displaying the rich and exotic spoils of war along with his captives. The people were enchanted; a truly charismatic Roman hero had arisen.

After his general had easily secured northern Africa, Justinian dispatched a new naval expedition under Belisarius, this time to retake Italy from the Ostrogoths. With a meagre force of just 7,500 men under his command, Belisarius first captured Sicily, then crossed into Italy in 536, while Mundus pinned down the Goths in Dalmatia. Belisarius entered Rome unopposed, as the Gothic garrison had fled the Eternal City. He then brilliantly defended Rome, besieged by King Witigis, for an entire year (March 537 to March 538). Throughout the siege, his wife Antonina organized relief efforts from the military harbour of Ostia.

Taking the offensive once more with only a few thousand troops, Belisarius marched north. He besieged and reconquered walled cities one after the other, even though he faced an unexpected Frankish invasion. Belisarius would use tactical defence, followed by counter-attack, his best asset in every battle being his mobile Hunnish horse-archers. He showed benevolence towards soldiers and civilians alike, controlled his troops by maintaining a high level of discipline, but had to deal with insubordinate officers.

> Belisarius had developed a new-style tactical instrument with which he knew that he might count on beating much superior numbers, provided that he could induce his opponents to attack him under conditions that suited his tactics. For that purpose his lack of numbers, when not too marked, was an asset, especially when coupled with an audaciously direct strategic offensive. His strategy was

thus more psychological then logistical. He knew how to provoke the barbarian armies of the West into indulging their natural instinct for direct assault.

Basil H. Liddell Hart, *The Strategy of Indirect Approach*

Consistently faced by superior numbers, Belisarius had no option other than to adapt, in order to become a master of asymmetric warfare. Some of Belisarius' tactics to weaken and defeat numerically greater foes were summed up by a ninth century Byzantine military engineer known as the Naval Syrian Magister:

> We should not advance into battle before the enemy have become inferior to us in some respect. This can be brought about if we fall upon them when they may be weary from just having finished a long march or one through rocky and hilly country. We can also fall upon them when they are in disorder, for example, setting up their tents or taking them down. The best time is when the enemy have broken up their units owing to a lack of supplies or some other reason. Then we can attack those detachments one at a time.

> This is what Belisarius used to do. When the enemy force was so large that he was unable to face up to it, he would destroy the provisions in the area before they appeared. Need for supplies would force the enemy to separate their units from one another and march along in several different groups and then he would defeat each unit by itself.

Syrianus Magister, *Strategikon* or *Military Compendium*

By 540 Belisarius had secured the surrender of King Witigis and his capital Ravenna. As he now held most of Italy, the Goths bowed to his superiority and offered him the title of Roman Emperor of the West:

> After deliberating among themselves, all the best of the Goths decided to declare Belisarius Emperor of the West. And sending to him secretly, they begged him to assume the royal power; for upon this condition, they declared, they would follow him gladly.

Procopius of Caesarea, *History of the Wars*, Book VI

At first, Belisarius pretended to accept, but eventually he prudently rejected their proposition. Alarmed, Justinian summoned Belisarius home and sent him to the eastern borders. As a popular general was always a potential competitor for the throne, the Emperor would never trust him again. The following year, Belisarius checked an invasion of Byzantine territories by Sassanid King Khosrow I.

While the plague was devastating the entire Mediterranean world, the Goths led by the formidable King Totila retook much of Italy. In Constantinople upwards of

300,000 people may have succumbed to the dreaded sickness. Belisarius, sent back to Italy seriously under-supplied and having to use his own funds, was unable to achieve a decisive victory. In 546 Rome was sacked by Totila; Belisarius, encamped at Portus and awaiting reinforcements, had been unable to relieve the city. He did retake Rome the following spring, but the beleaguered city soon changed hands again, and Belisarius was recalled to the 'Mother of Cities'. With a powerful army of 35,000 men, Imperial Chamberlain Narses eventually crushed the Franks and Alemanni at the Battle of Capua and completed the second Byzantine reconquest of the Italian peninsula (554 AD).

Owing to court intrigues and Justinian's growing suspicions, Belisarius had fallen out of favour. He retired from public life and went to live in his estate at Rufinianae in Chalcedon. In 559, when a Bulgar incursion led by Khan Zabergan threatened Constantinople, Justinian summoned Belisarius back into service. With only 300 retired veterans and untrained civilians, Belisarius frightened the invaders away by a series of clever stratagems.

After a lifetime of outstanding service to the Empire, Belisarius was nonetheless arrested and imprisoned on trumped-up charges of corruption. In 562 he was eventually pardoned by Justinian and partially restored to his former position. In 565 the Emperor and his most talented general died within a few months of each other. Three years later, the Lombards, allied with the Saxons, launched their conquest of Italy. In the eleventh century visitors could still contemplate a gilded statue of Belisarius outside the Great Palace beside a statue of Justin I and a cross erected by Justinian.

Achievements

Steadfastly loyal to the service of a resurgent Byzantine Empire, Belisarius was an authentic genius, a resourceful tactician who understood how to seize every opportunity. An outstanding leader, he earned the respect of both his troops and his adversaries, whom he treated with humanity. He was, however, plagued by insubordination and the target of envious rival officers and courtiers, Justinian himself being jealous and distrustful of his immense popularity. Belisarius' conquests against overwhelming odds brought the Byzantine Empire to its greatest territorial extent. Owing to his phenomenal achievements in different theatres, despite having access to limited resources and manpower, the conqueror of Carthage, Rome and Ravenna is regarded as one of the greatest generals in military history, an assessment shared by T.E.Lawrence 'of Arabia', who considered the virtuous Thracian one of three 'first-class Roman generals in history', together with Scipio Africanus and Gaius Julius Caesar. North Africa would remain under Byzantine control until the Muslim invasion of 698 AD, while in southern Italy Byzantine authority held out for half a millennium, until the Norman conquest of 1071.

Khalid Al-Hariri of Basra, 7th Maqāmāt, 1237. (*Bibliothèque Nationale de France*)

Chapter 10

KHALID IBN AL-WALID
'The Sword of Islam'

You should convert to Islam, and then you will be safe, for if you don't, you should know that I have come to you with an army of men that love death, as you love life.

Khālid ibn al-Walīd to the Sassanids before the Battle of
al-Qādisiyyah, November 636

Khālid ibn al-Walīd rose to become Supreme Commander of all the early Arab armies. He was noted for his personal bravery, his ruthlessness and his brilliant tactics, commanding the forces of Medina under Muhammad and the forces of his immediate successors of the Rashidun Caliphate, Abu Bakr (632–4) and Umar ibn Khattab (634–44). Khālid's long list of strategic achievements include the conquest of the Arabian peninsula during the Ridda Wars (632–3), followed by Sassanid Mesopotamia and Byzantine Syria (632–636). He is also remembered for his decisive victories at Yamamah, Ullais, Firaz and al-Qādisiyyah, and his tactical successes at Walaja and Yarmouk. His victories contributed greatly to the early Jihadic expansion.

Abū Sulaymān Khālid ibn al-Walīd ibn al-Mughīrah al-Makhzūmī (c.585–642) was a companion of the prophet Muhammad. After Khālid's conversion to Islam (c.627), it was under his military leadership that Arabia, for the first time in history, was united as a single political entity, the Caliphate. Commanding the forces of the initial Islamic state, Khālid was victorious in numerous battles against the Byzantines and the Sassanids, as well as rival Arab tribes, at a time when decades of warfare had exhausted both the Byzantines and the Persians.

At the Battle of Mu'tah (September 629), after three Muslim leaders had been killed fighting the Byzantines and Ghassanids (Christian Arabs), the command was given to Khālid ibn al-Walid, and he succeeded in saving the rest of the force by retreating to Medina. In January 630, sent by Muhammad to the lower Tihamah to find the Banu Jadhimah tribe and force them to convert, he tricked them in surrendering and executed them in cold blood, even those who had accepted Islam.

During the Mesopotamian campaign of 633, marching northward along the Euphrates, Khālid's army defeated the Sassanids in five consecutive encounters: at the Battles of Chains, of the Blood River (Ullais), at Walaja and Muzayyah, before defeating a local coalition of Sassanid-Byzantine and Christian Arab forces at the Battle of Firaz, a border town between the two old empires (January 634).

> We attacked them with mounted troops, and they saw the darkness of death around those leafy gardens. By morning they said we were a people who had swarmed over the fertile country from rugged Arabia.
>
> Al-Qa'qa' bin Amr, Commander of Khālid's army in
> Mesopotamia, from Ibn Kathīr's *The Beginning and the End*

In May 634 Caliph Abu Bakr appointed Khālid to command the 8,000-strong army leaving for the Syrian campaign, declaring, 'By Allah, I shall destroy the Romans and the friends of Satan with Khālid Ibn Al Walid!' Damascus surrendered in September of that year. The inhabitants were allowed to leave the city in peace, but six days later, Khālid fell on the refugees heading for Antioch, securing rich booty and taking thousands of captives. By 635 Palestine, Jordan and southern Syria, with the exception of Jerusalem and Caesarea, were all in Muslim hands.

After Abu Bakr's death in August 634, Umar his successor appointed Abu Ubaidah as the official Commander-in-Chief of the Muslim armies, although the companion of Prophet Muhammad continued to rely heavily on Khālid's military expertise during the next four campaigns. As Khālid was the architect and mastermind of most of the early Muslim military strategy, he was also the pioneer of almost every major tactic during the early Islamic conquests.

Until Khālid, the Arabs were basically light cavalry skirmishers and raiders. After exhausting the less mobile enemy units, Khālid would launch his cavalry at their flanks, employing a pincer movement as he did at Firaz. He used a double-envelopment manoeuvre against the numerically superior Persian army at the Battle of Walaja, and at Emesa in 636 he raised the siege, faked a withdrawal, then encircled the garrison that had sallied out and left no one alive. At the Battle of al-Qādisiyyah in November of the same year, his lieutenant Al-Qa'qa' bin Amr came up against Sassanid war elephants. He disguised his horses as monsters to scare the pachyderms, and they turned and fled from the battlefield in terror.

After victory at the Battle of Ajnadayn in 634, Khālid organized a force of 4,000 horsemen from his army of Mesopotamia which became known as his Mobile Guard (*Tulai'a Mutaharrika*). He kept this elite light cavalry under his direct command as a reserve for use in battle as required. The remainder of his forces were all camel-mounted, allowing them to cross vast expanses of desert in a matter of days, raiding deep inside enemy territory and taking their troops and garrisons by surprise. On the march, early Islamic armies were divided into a vanguard, preceded by a large unit of scouts, followed by the centre and the rear, while the rearguard detachment prevented any enemy from attacking or harassing the column.

Khālid's ability to command, motivate and lead from the front endeared him to his men. According to contemporary sources, he would often engage in single combat against his chief opponent. In May 633, at the Battle of the Blood River in Mesopotamia, Khālid killed the Christian Arab tribal leader Abdul-Aswad in a duel. At Marj-ud-Debaj in September 634 he allegedly killed the Byzantine Thomas, leader of Damascus' survivors and the Emperor Heraclius' son-in-law. At the siege of Emesa (Homs) in Syria in March 636 Khālid again killed a Byzantine commander in single combat. The purpose of these duels was to reduce the morale of the opposing army and damage its command by killing as many champions and generals as possible.

The decisive Muslim victory against the Byzantines was achieved at the key Battle of Yarmouk (August 636). In March of that year, Muslim light horsemen had intercepted a Byzantine convoy and prisoners were interrogated, providing critical information regarding the plans of Emperor Heraclius and the concentration of a large Byzantine army at Antioch. Recently allied with the young Sassanid Shah Yazdegerd III, Heraclius was intent on overwhelming the new Arab state before it became unstoppable. The Caliphate now faced a potential invasion on two fronts.

Khālid advised Abu Ubaidah to gather all the Muslim armies of the region at once. An urgent message was sent to Caliph Umar asking for reinforcements. Khālid then selected a battle site on a plain east of the Yarmouk River, the ideal location for the deployment of his cavalry, while the 6,000-strong reinforcements sent by the Caliph arrived on the scene. The Byzantine army still outnumbered the Arabs by two to one, but its contingents and leaders were disunited. At the end of a gruelling six-day battle, Khālid managed to trap the retreating Byzantine forces in a steep ravine by stealthily capturing their only escape route, the bridge across the deep gorges of Wadi-ur-Ruqqad situated at their rear. In the carnage that ensued, the Muslims took no prisoners.

In the aftermath, the Rashidun Caliphate annexed the whole Levant, then conquered Jerusalem and Antioch in 637. Yarmouk, in fact, ended Byzantine Christian domination of the Levant once and for all. In the east, in March 637, the Sassanid capital of Ctesiphon had also fallen to general Saʻd ibn Abī Waqqās, and Shah Yazdegerd III was on the run. By 639 Byzantium had lost Armenia and Mesopotamia. As chronicler Ioannis Zonaras wrote, from that time on 'the race of the Ishmaelites did not cease from invading and plundering the entire territory of the Romans.'

Khālid put the emphasis on annihilating his foes, giving no mercy to enemy combatants. At the Battle of Ullais (or Blood River), he tricked the Persians and their Arab allies into surrendering, promising he would spare their lives. Then, according to Al-Tabari, he had every prisoner beheaded. Under Khālid's command, the aftermath of every battle climaxed with a mass slaughter of prisoners to avoid the logistic burden of dealing with large numbers of captives. Women and young children who constituted part of the booty were usually spared and enslaved.

In 638, at the zenith of his career, with the morale of the Muslim armies at an all-time high, Khālid was abruptly dismissed from military service. Umar had already appointed Abu Ubaidah as Commander-in-Chief to replace him, although Khālid's record of service was flawless. The general, charged with misappropriation by the Caliph, was forced back to Medina under guard to answer these allegations. Treated 'like dirt' by the supreme ruler of Islam, he would remain particularly bitter for the rest of his days:

> Do you see a space of the span of a hand on my leg, chest, arm which is not covered by some scar of the wound of a sword or an arrow or a lance? I have sought martyrdom in a hundred battles. Why could I not have died in battle?
> Khālid to a friend, a few days before his death

Allegedly, when the 'Sword of Islam' died in 642 AD, Caliph Umar eventually expressed remorse for the rash dismissal of his most formidable general. Umar himself was assassinated two years later by a Persian slave, a former soldier who had been captured at the Battle of al-Qādisiyyah. Khālid was entombed in a mausoleum at Emesa (Homs) in Syria which became a centre of pilgrimage. When Timur invaded Syria in 1400 he sacked Aleppo and Damascus but spared Homs from destruction because it contained the mausoleum of Khālid, whom the Turco-Mongol conqueror held in high regard.

Achievements

Tradition records that Khālid ibn al-Walīd fought around a hundred battles and skirmishes during his relatively brief ten years of supreme command over the nascent Muslim forces or as Abu-Ubaidah's lieutenant. Never defeated, he remains one of the most efficient, if ruthless, military commanders in history. He would use surprise, audacity and brute force to achieve success. His victory over the superior Byzantine forces at Yarmouk is considered one of the most decisive battles of all time. By 642, at the time of his demise, Alexandria of Egypt had fallen; within 25 years of Muhammad's death, largely owing to Khālid's victorious campaigns, Islam had conquered lands stretching from Carthage to northern India, and from the Red Sea to the Caucasus Mountains. This would be one of the largest empires the world had ever seen. To this day, Khālid ibn al-Walīd is considered one of the greatest heroes of the Islamic world, a powerful symbol of Arab nationalism.

Charles de Steuben, Battle of Poitiers, Palais de Versailles. (*Wikimedia Commons*)

Chapter 11

CHARLES MARTEL, 'THE HAMMER'
Commander of the Frankish Kingdom

While Abd al-Raḥmān was pursuing Eudes, he decided to despoil Tours by destroying its palaces and burning its churches. It is then that he found himself face to face with the lord of Austrasia, Charles, a mighty warrior from his youth, and trained in all the occasions of arms. After each side had tormented the other with raids for almost seven days, they finally prepared their battle lines and fought fiercely. The northern peoples remained as immobile as a wall, holding together like a glacier in the cold regions. In the blink of an eye, they annihilated the Arabs with the sword.

Mozarabic Chronicle, 754

Charles Martel united and ruled the *Regnum Francorum* (Kingdom of the Franks) from 718 until his death. As its uncontested military and political leader, he consolidated and extended the kingdom, spending a quarter of a century campaigning almost every year against all of its enemies, both within and outside the realm. In 732 Charles decisively defeated a large-scale Saracen invasion of Gaul, then reconquered lands from the Umayyads, halting Islam's expansion in Western Europe and elevating the Frankish kingdom to the status of the bulwark of Christendom. This epoch-making event ranks as a pivotal moment in the history of western civilization. Charles was the creator of the Carolingian military machine, the founder of the first knightly order, and the instigator of European feudalism.

Charles 'Martel' ('Hammer' in old French), c.688–741 AD, was the illegitimate son of Austrasian (eastern Frankish sub-kingdom) *maior domus* (Mayor of the Palace) Pepin (Pippin) II of Herstal and his second wife Alpaida. In 687, after his victory at the Battle of Tertry over the western kingdom of Neustria, Pepin had taken the title 'Duke and Prince of the Franks' (*Dux et Princeps Francorum*) to signify his extended authority. Being illegitimate, Charles Martel was entirely neglected in his father's will: Pepin had named as heir his grandson Theudoald. When Pepin died, an intense civil war broke out, and Charles campaigned against Ragenfried, the Mayor of the Palace of Neustria (north-western Frankish sub-kingdom) and Burgundy, and against his stepmother, Plectrude.

By 724 Neustria was subdued. From then, as sole Mayor of the Palace, Charles restored a centralized government to Francia, which still had a king, but one who reigned in name only. The *Dux et Princeps Francorum* now took overall command of the armies of the kingdom, in addition to his administrative duties as Mayor of the Palace.

Charles launched a series of annual military campaigns that re-established the Franks as the undisputed masters of Gaul. He made vassal-states of the Duchy of Bavaria (724–6), the territory of the Alamanni and Frisia (734). He also compelled some of the Saxon tribes to recognize Frankish supremacy. Boniface of Wessex's religious campaign of destruction against Germanic pagan sites in Thurigia and the northern regions aided Charles' offensives, although the Saxons' full assimilation and conversion to Christianity would only be concluded by his grandson Charlemagne.

At the same time, there was a growing threat on the south-western borders of the Regnum Francorum. The rapid seventh-century Muslim conquest of the Levant and North Africa had resulted in the permanent imposition by force of Islamic culture and religion on a previously Christian base. In 711 the Visigothic kingdom fell to the Muslim conquerors in a single battle on the Rio Barbate. In the early decades of the eighth century Islamic forces were flooding into Europe through the Iberian peninsula, threatening Frankish and Burgundian territory and raiding it with ever-increasing ferocity. The Iberian Saracens added Berber light horsemen to the heavy Arab cavalry to create a formidable army.

Al-Samh ibn Malik al-Khawlani, the governor of Al-Andalus, built up a powerful invasion force from Umayyad territories to conquer the Duchy of Aquitaine in south-west Gaul. In 721 he besieged Toulouse, Aquitaine's most important city. Duke Eudes of Aquitaine immediately left to seek assistance from Charles Martel, but the 'Hammer' preferred to wait and see rather than help his southern rival. Eudes returned three months later with Aquitanian and Frankish troops and attacked the Umayyad invasion force on 9 June. Arab historians agree that the Battle of Toulouse was a total disaster for them, and Eudes was hailed as champion of Christianity by the Pope. Charles, involved in military campaigns in the east, steered clear of the political and military developments in south-west Gaul for another decade.

In 725 the Wali of Al-Andalus, Anbasa ibn Suhaym Al-Kalbi, took Carcassonne, invaded Burgundy and sacked Autun. In 732 a Saracen army landed in Provence and marched north following the River Rhône, killing and pillaging in every village, town and city in its path. In October 732 another Umayyad army, led by Governor of Cordoba Abd al-Raḥmān al-Ghafiqi, invaded Aquitaine once more. The old Duke Eudes, who was defeated near Bordeaux by the Arab cavalry, again appealed for assistance to the powerful Frankish Mayor of the Palace. After Bordeaux was taken and sacked by the Saracens, this time Charles responded. Only the Frankish kingdom stood a chance of halting the Arab onslaught.

Marching back thousands of kilometres from the Danube, Charles formed a coalition of 30,000 Franks, Burgundians and warriors from Aquitaine. Moving his army with haste over the mountains and avoiding open roads, he escaped detection until he positioned his men on a high wooded plateau, carefully selecting the battlefield and denying the plains to the highly mobile Muslim light cavalry.

Al-Ghafiqi met Eudes' and Charles' allied forces between the cities of Tours and Poitiers, and the battle lasted seven days in October. Wave after wave of Muslim cavalry crashed into the Frankish heavy infantry armed with long spears and were shattered. Duke Eudes set fire to the Cordovan camp, sparking confusion and wreaking havoc among the enemy's rearguard. The superiority of Frankish armour, comprising chain mail, helmets and shields, and the discipline of the Frankish warriors, were the decisive elements in the sweeping Christian victory. Al-Ghafiqi was killed in the melee, and the Umayyad army withdrew in confusion.

The Muslims planned to go to Tours to destroy the Church of St Martin, the city, and the whole country. Then came against them the glorious Prince

Charles, at the head of his whole force. He drew up his host, and he fought as fiercely as the hungry wolf falls upon the stag. By the grace of Our Lord, he wrought a great slaughter upon the enemies of the Christian Faith, so that – as history bears witness – he slew in that battle 300,000 men, likewise their king by name Abderrahman. Then was he first called 'Martel,' for as a hammer of iron, of steel, and of every other metal, even so he dashed and smote in the battle all his enemies. And what was the greatest marvel of all, he only lost in that battle 1,500 men.

Chronicles of Saint Denis

After his crucial victory at Tours, Charles resolutely took the offensive against the Saracens, campaigning in Aquitaine, Septimania and Provence, driving the invaders from the fortresses of Agde, Beziers, Maguelonne, Avignon and Aix and crushing Islamic forces gathered at Nimes and Narbonne (734–41). The string of defeats that Charles inflicted on the Saracens was decisive, effectively halting the northward advance of Islam, signalling the end of their *razzias* (raids), and ultimately preserving Christianity in Western Europe.

Charles was known for his swift troop movements and renowned for his unpredictability. He had the ability to surprise opponents by moving his armies far further and faster than they expected. A brilliant tactician, he was able, even in the heat of battle, to adapt his moves to his foe's forces and tactics.

Charles was a prominent reformer and a talented organizer. Having probably adopted the idea of the stirrup from the Avars, he is credited with its introduction to the Carolingian army, creating a powerful force of heavy cavalry to counter the Saracens. In exchange for an oath of loyalty, Charles supported and rewarded his magnates with land, a 'fief', often confiscated from the Church, and in return they would provide fighting men for his armies each year. This new relationship between the ruler of Francia and his vassals was at the heart of what would become known as feudalism. The elite cavalry of his bodyguard became the first members of the Knightly Order of the Genet.

After consolidating the *Regnum Francorum* and establishing it as the most powerful political and military entity since the Roman Empire, Charles died on 22 October 741 in the Picardy region of France. He was buried near Paris in the church of the Abbey of St Denis, the necropolis of the Kings of France since Clovis I.

Achievements

To Edward Gibbon, the historian of Rome's decline, Charles Martel was 'the paramount prince of his age'. Though the Frankish Mayor of the Palace had chosen not to take the title of king, he rose to become the absolute ruler of virtually all of today's continental Western Europe north of the Pyrenees. Only some Saxon tribes, Lombardy, and the *Marca Hispanica* south of the Pyrenees were significant additions to the Frankish realm after his death. After Charles' victory at Tours, the stature of the Carolingian family was so immense that his son, Pepin III 'the Short', was able to overthrow the last Merovingian king and assume the throne of the Franks in 751. Charles was a giant of the early Middle Ages, the progenitor of the Carolingian line of Frankish rulers and the grandfather of Charlemagne, who would extend the Frankish realms to include most of Western Europe, becoming the first Emperor in the West since the fall of Rome.

Giuseppe Patania, Roger I receiving the keys of Palermo, 1830, Palazzo dei Normanni, Palermo. (*Wikimedia Commons*)

Chapter 12

ROBERT GUISCARD
The Norman 'Terror of the World'

This Robert was a Norman by birth, of obscure origin, with an overbearing character and a thoroughly villainous mind; he was a brave fighter, very cunning in his assaults on the wealth and power of great men; in achieving his aims absolutely inexorable.

Anna Komnene, *The Alexiad* (1969 translation)

Robert Guiscard was one the most successful military leaders of all time, and the most remarkable of the Norman adventurers who conquered southern Italy. Through their string of victorious campaigns against the Lombard princes, the Pope, the Saracens, the Holy Roman Emperor, the Byzantine Emperor and the Venetians, Robert and his swashbuckling brothers established themselves as firm masters of the *Mezzogiorno* (southern Italy) and Sicily. They founded an opulent, multi-ethnic kingdom that rapidly evolved into a key European power.

Robert Guiscard ('the Cunning') de Hauteville (c.1015–85) was the sixth of the twelve sons of Tancrède de Hauteville, a petty lord from western Normandy. In the wake of the Quarrel-Drengot brothers, who founded the Norman County of Aversa in 1029, Robert would join his elder brothers Guillaume Bras-de-Fer (Iron-Arm), Drogon (Drogo) and Onfroi (Humphrey) in Apulia, where the first Normans were serving as mercenaries either for the Lombard princes or the Byzantine Catepanate (military region).

Aversa, the first permanent establishment of the Normans outside the Duchy of Normandy, became the base from which they would forge a state in Sicily and Italy. By 1042 Guillaume Bras-de-Fer was recognized by the Prince of Salerno Guaimario IV as Count of Apulia. After Guillaume's death four years later, Drogon took over, further expanding Norman territory. In 1047 Drogon captured Benevento, and the Holy Roman Emperor Heinrich III 'the Pious', who came to the *Mezzogiorno* to demand homage from the southern princes, invested him with the territories recently conquered. Drogon, now a vassal of the Empire, titled himself 'Duke and Master of Italy, Count of the Normans of all Apulia and Calabria'.

That same year, according to Anna Komnene, the daughter of Emperor Alexios I Komnenos, Robert left Normandy with only five knights and thirty men on foot to reunite with Drogon and Onfroi in search of wealth and glory. When this band of restless young warriors arrived in southern Italy, Drogon settled Robert in a fief next to Cosenza, Calabria.

The Byzantine princess has left us with a striking description of the ambitious Norman adventurer:

> He was a man of immense stature, surpassing even the biggest men; he had a ruddy complexion, fair hair, broad shoulders, eyes that all but shot out sparks of fire. In a well-built man one looks for breadth here and slimness there; in him all was admirably well-proportioned and elegant. Thus, from head to foot, the man was graceful. Homer remarked of Achilles that when he shouted his hearers had the impression of a multitude in uproar, but Robert's bellow, so they say, put tens of thousands to flight. With such endowments of fortune and nature and soul, he was, as you would expect, no man's slave, owing obedience to nobody in all the world.
>
> *Anna Komnene, The Alexiad* (1969 translation)

While still just a robber baron, Robert took as his first wife the daughter of the Lombard nobleman Gulielmus Mascabeles, but the two men eventually quarrelled. When they met, in a field surrounded by hills, Robert invited Gulielmus to dismount in order to negotiate a peace. The Lombard obliged, not knowing that Robert had in fact hidden his men in ambush behind the hills:

> Robert jumped on his horse, quickly donned his helmet, seized his spear, and brandished it fiercely and sheltering himself behind his shield, turned round, and struck one of Gulielmus' men such a blow with his spear that he yielded up his life on the spot. In the meantime, he held back the rush of his father-in-law's cavalry, and checked the relief they were bringing. Mascabeles was taken bound and a prisoner of war to the very fortress which he had given as wedding gift to Robert at the time he betrothed his daughter to him.
>
> Anna Komnene, *The Alexiad* (1928 translation)

Robert and his brothers undertook the conquest of the southern Italian peninsula, exploiting local weaknesses and divisions, gradually driving out Lombards and Byzantines by brute force as well as tactical shrewdness. In August 1051, when Drogon was assassinated, victim of a Byzantine conspiracy, his younger brother Onfroi replaced him. By that time, Robert's prowess had already marked him out as a formidable and crafty warlord.

Pope Leo IX was also alarmed by the Normans' growing ambitions. In June 1053 he attacked them with his force of Swabian mercenaries, together with a large Lombard coalition, only to be thoroughly defeated at the Battle of Civitate by Onfroi and the Hauteville and the Drengot brothers, all banded together for the occasion. The humiliated pope remained a hostage at Benevento for months before being released. This forced the Papacy to acknowledge the Norman leader's authority in Italy.

A later Pope, Nicholaus II (1059–61), resolved instead to ally with the powerful Norman warlords and redirect them against the enemies of Christendom. He invested Robert Guiscard with the duchies of Apulia, Calabria and the yet-to-be-conquered island of Sicily, in return for oaths of fealty and the promise of assistance. With papal endorsement, the Hauteville brothers launched their invasion of the Emirate of Sicily in 1060.

The Normans first stormed and captured Messina, then fought their way across northern Sicily. They captured the Saracen capital of Palermo ten years later, in January 1072, after a six-month siege. Robert Guiscard, as suzerain, then officially invested Roger as Count of Sicily. Robert retained Palermo, half of Messina and the north-east portion of the island. When Noto, the last Saracen stronghold, fell in February 1091, the Normans were left in complete control of Sicily.

The two brothers established an amicable arrangement: Robert was left as ruler of southern Italy, and Roger would keep Sicily. When Bari was captured by Guiscard in April 1071, Byzantine authority finally came to an end in Italy, five centuries after Belisarius' reconquest. Guiscard and the Count of Aversa Richard Drengot then besieged Salerno, which fell in May 1077. The surrender of Prince Gisulfo II signalled the end of the last Lombard state in Italy, together with the unification of the entire southern peninsula under Norman rule. Salerno became the capital of Robert Guiscard's 'Duchy of Apulia, Calabria, and Sicily'.

Following the completion of their conquest of southern Italy and most of Sicily by 1072, Robert Guiscard and his brothers saw no reason to stop, since Byzantium itself looked ripe for conquest. In May 1081 Robert Guiscard and his son Bohemond of Taranto crossed the Adriatic with 15,000 battle-hardened soldiers, including 1,500 Norman heavy cavalry. They first captured Corfu, then landed at Dyrrhachium in Illyria. Unfortunately for Robert Guiscard, however, his fleet was soundly defeated by the Venetian and Byzantine allied navies, leaving him no choice but to press on with the siege of Dyrrhachium.

While Robert's camp was struck by disease, in October Emperor Alexios I arrived at the head of a coalition army of 25,000 men made up of Byzantine troops and mercenaries (Franks, Turks, Anglo-Saxon Varangians and 7,000 Seljuk Turk auxiliaries), reinforced by King of Serbia Konstantin Bodin's troops. At once Alexios and Konstantin Bodin attacked Guiscard's army from the rear, the feared Varangians spearheading the assault:

> The English whom they call Varangians had requested the emperor that they form the vanguard, for these men enjoy being in the forefront. They started the battle by making a fierce attack in two columns, and at first the situation was very unfavourable for our men. But one of our squadrons attacked them on their unprotected flank and this gallant attack forced them, wounded and terrified by the assault, to flee towards the church of St Nicholas which was nearby. Looking to save their lives, some of them, indeed as many as could fit in, entered the church, while others from this great multitude clambered onto the roof which then collapsed under their weight, thus hurling them on top of those down below. In the crush both groups were suffocated. Seeing the Varangians, in whom his chief hope of victory lay, totally defeated and our pursuing forces resolutely advancing against him, the emperor was terrified and chose flight rather than battle. The entire Greek army, abandoning its tents and all its other equipment, fled, with every man trying to outdo the other in their haste to run away.
>
> Goffredo Malaterra, *The Deeds of Count Roger of Calabria and Sicily and of Duke Robert Guiscard, his brother*

A combination of battle experience and superior leadership by Guiscard, his wife Sichelgaita of Salerno and his son Bohemond had won the day against Alexios' much larger coalition. The close ranks of Norman heavy cavalry, with their couched lances, smashed through the elite Varangian Guard and trampled the Anglo-Saxon mercenaries. The Byzantine camp fell into the hands of the Normans, and a wounded Alexios fled the battlefield, barely escaping with his life.

In February 1082 Dyrrhachium, defended by Venetians and Albanians, fell when an Amalfitan citizen opened the gates to the Normans. Guiscard's army then proceeded to take most of northern Greece without encountering much resistance.

At that time, learning that Holy Roman Emperor Heinrich IV was at the gates of Rome, Guiscard left Bohemond in command in Greece with a portion of the Norman forces and rushed back to Italy to assist Pope Gregorius VII. On 21 March 1084 the Emperor entered Rome and enthroned his own Pope as Clemens III, before returning to Germany. Robert Guiscard had no difficulty in retaking Rome in May. In the process, his army of 30,000 men, including mostly Muslim auxiliaries, sacked the Eternal City for three consecutive days.

A liberated Pope Gregorius VII was compelled to withdraw to the castle of Salerno, where he passed away in May 1085. Robert, who had returned to fight the Byzantines in the Ionian Sea, died of fever during the siege of Cephalonia on 17 July 1085. He was buried next to his brothers at Venosa (Basilicata), in the Hauteville mausoleum, situated in the abbey church of the Most Holy Trinity.

> Robert died in the twenty-fifth year of his reign as duke and at the age of seventy. The Emperor, on hearing of Robert's sudden death, was greatly relieved by having such a burden lifted from his shoulders.
>
> Anna Komnene, *The Alexiad* (1928 translation)

Achievements

A brilliant strategist, an inspirational leader and a competent statesman, at his death in 1085 the former young adventurer from Normandy had become Duke of Apulia and Calabria, Prince of Salerno and Suzerain of Sicily. Robert established a permanent Norman presence in southern Italy, replacing Lombard and Byzantine rule with Norman hegemony. Guiscard remains the hero and main founder of the Norman Kingdom of Italy. His nephew Roger II would unite Sicily, the Hauteville territories on the mainland and coastal areas of Ifriqiya (parts of today's Libya, Tunisia and Algeria) in c.1140 into a single powerful and prosperous kingdom, known as the Kingdom of Sicily, Apulia and Calabria. Although it would be ruled by a number of dynasties through the centuries (Hohenstaufen, Angevin, Aragon, Habsburgs, Bourbons), the Kingdom of Sicily would last until the unification of Italy in 1860.

Battle of the Kalka River, miniature from Russian Medieval Chronicles.

Chapter 13

SUBOTAI 'THE VALIANT'
Genghis Khan's strategist

Jamuqa said, 'My sworn friend Temüdjin has been feeding "four hounds" on human flesh, leashing them with iron chains. They are the ones approaching in pursuit of our patrol. Those "four hounds", their foreheads are of hardened copper, they have chisels for snouts, and awls for tongues. With hearts of iron, and swords for whips, they advance feeding on dew and riding on the wind. On the day of killing, they eat human flesh, on the day of battles, they make human flesh their provisions. Loosed from their iron chains – which had surely restrained them! – they are now full of joy and are approaching. Who are those "four hounds"? They are Jebe and Qubilai, Jelme and Sübe'etei.'

Jamuqa, on Genghis Khan's 'Four Hounds',
Secret History of the Mongols

Very few leaders in history can match Subotai's phenomenal achievements as one of the world's greatest strategists and field commanders. As one of Genghis Khan's 'four hounds' (alongside Jelme, Jebe and Kublai), he supervised campaigns across the whole of Eurasia, from south-eastern Asia to Central Europe. Subotai's conquests made the Mongol Empire the largest land empire in history, and his strategies and tactics are studied in military academies to this day.

Subotai (also written 'Sube'etei', c.1175–1248) was born in central Mongolia. A member of the Uriankhai clan, as a teenager he joined the Mongol leader Temüjin along with his older brother (or cousin) Jelme. The *Secret History of the Mongols* tells how Jebe and Subotai were appointed as the first *Örlögs Baghatur* (Valiant Knights) of the unified army of the steppes forged by the great Khan.

> On the day of battle, with such men before me, I could rest assured!
>
> Genghis Khan, on his *Örlögs Baghatur*

From a very young age, Subotai participated in all of Temüjin's military campaigns, and owing to a system of promotion based on merit, he became one of his closest and most trusted companions. In his first commands, Subotai was usually paired with Jebe (d. 1224), who held seniority, but within a decade he had risen to become an officer (*tümen-ü noyan*) in command of one of four *tümens* (units of 10,000 men) of Genghis' vanguard.

> I send you to cross high mountain passes and to ford wide rivers; mindful of the distance you have to cover, you must spare the army mounts before they become too lean and you must save your provisions before they come to an end.
>
> Gengis Khan to Subotai in 1205, *Secret History of the Mongols*

Subotai fought in the wars of unification of the Mongol plains (1190s–1206), the conquest of central Asia, including the subjugation of the Sunni Muslim Khwarazmian Empire (1217–21), the conquest of Western Xia and the Jin Dynasty in Manchuria and China (1205–34), the long-distance raid that reached the Black Sea and culminated in the utter defeat of the Rus' and Cumans at the Battle of the Kalka River (1223), and the famous full-scale attack on Europe that brought the Kievan Rus' principalities into subjection and crushed the Poles and the Hungarians (1237–42).

> With one stroke a world which billowed with fertility was laid desolate, and the regions thereof became a desert, and the greater part of the living, dead,

and their skin and bones crumbling dust, and the mighty were humbled and immersed in the calamities of perdition.

'Ala-ad-Din 'Ata-Malik Juvayni, *History of the World-Conqueror*

Subotai always took the field to supervise operations in person. In many instances, including against the Georgians (1220) and at the Battle of the Kalka River (Kalchik River, May 1223), he adopted the traditional tactic of the feigned retreat used by the nomadic peoples of the steppes. For nine days he retreated with a handful of cavalry in order to lure his enemies into a carefully set ambush. Then Subotai ordered a massed charge of his heavy cavalry against the disorganized Rus' and Cuman forces. The Rus' led by Mstislav III of Kiev were forced to surrender, and Subotai, Jebe and the other Mongol officers celebrated their victory with a banquet set on the bodies of the Russian princes, who were slowly crushed to death.

And they were all thrown into confusion, there was a terrible and savage slaughter. And Mstislav, Knyaz of Kiev, seeing this evil, never moved at all from his position; for he had taken stand on a hill above the river Kalka, and the place was stony, and there he set up a stockade of posts about him and fought with them from out of this stockade for three days. The Tartars took the stockade and slaughtered the people, and there they fell dead. And having taken the Knyazes they suffocated them having put them under boards, and themselves took seat on the top to have dinner. And thus they ended their lives.

Chronicle of Novgorod, AD 1224

Subotai was a master of rapid troop movement and distant troop coordination; he would fall on his enemies before word could reach them that he was coming. Campaigns would only be launched after the thorough compilation and analysis of information from many intelligence sources. For example, Subotai and Batu spent an entire year scouting central Europe before coordinating the annihilation of the Polish and Hungarian armies in the two separate Battles of Legnica and Mohi, which took place just two days apart in April 1241.

Like Genghis Khan, Subotai would use terror and massacre to crush resistance, creating a wave of fear and panic that spread far and wide. Deceit was often used too: during the 1220–1 invasion of the Caucasus, Jebe and Subotai carried a large cross on their front line. The Georgians were confused and caught off guard, believing this was the arrival of a Christian army of unknown origin, since the Mongols had just devastated the Muslim Khwarazmian Empire.

Beyond the rivers you will perhaps lose courage, but continue to advance. In the same way, beyond the mountains you will perhaps lose heart, but think of nothing else apart from your mission . . . If you constantly think that even though We are out of sight it is as if We were visible, and even though We are far it is as if We were near, you will also be protected by Heaven Above.

Gengis Khan to Subotai in 1205, Secret History of the Mongols

From the 1210s Genghis Khan's campaigns were planned at the strategic level by Subotai. The planning was often done by Jebe, Subotai and a staff which comprised multi-ethnic experts from Mongolia but also from the Chinese and Muslim lands. After Genghis Khan's death, his son Ögedei Khan left the military planning and oversight to his younger brother Tolui and to Subotai. As well as working with a clear command structure, they were supported by experienced subordinate commanders who could be trusted to operate independently. Each commander selected his own junior officers. From top to bottom, every man knew his role and the task assigned to him. Banner signals were employed when silence was part of the battle plan.

Operating in distant, hostile territory, most of the time outnumbered, Subotai almost always emerged victorious, with one exception. From 1229 to 1231 Emperor Aizong of Jin scored three consecutive victories over the Mongol armies at Dachangyuan, Weizhou, and Daohuigu. Ögedei and Subotai's relationship became strained as Subotai was blamed for the defeats, but Tolui intervened in his favour, and Subotai soon redeemed himself with renewed success.

They hunt and practise archery, for they are all, big and little, excellent archers, and their children begin as soon as they are two or three years old to ride and manage horses and to gallop on them, and they are given bows to suit their stature and taught to shoot them.

Giovanni di Plano Carpini, The Story of the Mongols

The Mongols' riding and archery skills, along with their remarkable endurance, made them exceptional warriors. As they mostly wore leather armour, or in the best case Persian hauberk (chain mail), they tended to avoid hand-to-hand fighting to minimize casualties, sending prisoners and non-Mongol troops into battle first.

No one kingdom or province is able to resist the Tartars; because they use soldiers out of every country of their dominions. If the neighbouring province to that which they invade will not aid them, they waste it, and with the inhabitants, whom they take with them, they proceed to fight against the other province. They place their captives in the front of the battle, and if they fight not courageously they put them to the sword.

Giovanni di Plano Carpini, The Story of the Mongols

They would attack their adversaries with a long-range barrage of arrows, before closing in for the kill. No Mongol wounded were left behind, and if Mongol soldiers were lost as a result of careless orders, their commander could be punished. While maintaining strict discipline, Subotai took great care of the men under his command and asked them to overcome any challenge.

> Making this a matter of law, see to it that you seize and beat any man who breaks them. Any man I know who ignores my decree, have him brought back to stand before me. Any man I don't know who ignores this decree, just cut them down on the spot.
>
> Genghis Khan to Subotai, *Secret History of the Mongols*

Genghis Khan and his successors appointed crown princes as the nominal commanders of military operations, while real authority rested with the field commanders such as Subotai. In the campaign against Rus' and the West, Batu, Genghis' grandson, was the nominal commander, but Subotai was the real power behind the scenes, since he planned the campaigns and directed the battles. This often led to friction, with Subotai and Batu frequently clashing. During the Battle of Mohi Subotai refused to obey an order to withdraw, even implying that Batu had lost his courage and good judgement. Güyük and Büri also accused Batu of incompetence. Subotai was eventually recognized as the mastermind of Mongol victories in the West. As the *History of Yuan* records, 'Everything that was achieved then was due to Subotai's merit.'

Further expansion in Western Europe was halted by the death of Ögedei Khan. Batu returned at Karakorum to take part in the *kurultai* (Imperial Assembly) and the election of the new Great Khan. Subotai remained behind with just a few thousand men. Once Güyük (Ögedei's son) had been confirmed in power he appointed Subotai to command the planned attack on the Song dynasty, despite the fact that Subotai was then about seventy years old. Subotai would not continue his campaigns in Europe because of the political rivalry and enmity between Güyük and Batu.

Subotai's invasion of Hungary, Poland, Austria and Dalmatia in 1241–2 had alerted Latin Christendom. The threat of the Mongols caused so much concern that Pope Gregorius IX called for a Crusade in response. In March 1245, his successor Innocentius IV put the case on the agenda of the Ecumenical Council in Lyon. Two pairs of delegates were at once dispatched to the East from Lyon. The Franciscans Giovanni di Plano Carpini and Friar Benedykt from Poland left Europe in 1245 to inquire as to the Mongols' future intentions and to convince them to cease their attacks on the Latin West. A second mission, carrying the same message, left at roughly the same period with Dominicans Ascelino di Cremona and Simon de Saint-Quentin.

A third mission was conducted by Guillaume de Rubrouck, who also travelled overland from France to Sarai and Karakorum in 1253–5. All of these diplomatic delegations attempted to forge an alliance with the khans, as well as bringing them to the Catholic faith. In response to the Franciscan and Dominican delegations, Güyük demanded the submission of the Pope and every ruler of Europe, summoning them to his capital in order to swear allegiance to him! Two Mongol envoys, Aïbäg and Särgis, travelled to Lyon, where they met Innocentius in 1248, bringing the Great Khan's reply written in Persian and Middle Turkish:

> Through the power of God, all empires from the rising of the sun to its setting have been given to us and we own them. You must in person come with your kings, all together, without exception, to render us service and pay us homage. Only then will we acknowledge your submission. And if you do not follow the order of God, and go against our orders, we will know you as our enemy.
>
> Letter from Güyük Khan to Pope Innocentius IV, November 1246

That same year, Subotai returned to the Mongolian heartland, where he died. The death of Mongke Khan a decade later would mark the beginning of the dissolution of the Mongol *Ulus* (nation) into five entities: the Jochid Khanate, the Yuan Dynasty, the Ögedei Khanate, the Chagatai Khanate and the Ilkhanids. Subotai's children would take the field in the campaigns against the Song Dynasty, and his grandson Aju was appointed as Kublai's trusted chancellor.

Achievements

A master of deception, large-scale movements, speed, surprise and the decisive outmanoeuvring of his opponents, Genghis Khan's ruthless 'hound' was tactically brilliant and innovative. Using his unmatched leadership and coordination skills, according to Basil Liddell Hart, Subotai overran thirty-two nations and won sixty-five battles, playing no small part in creating the gigantic Mongol Empire, the largest land empire in world history. He remains the only commander able to conquer all of Russia and Eastern Europe. Subotai pioneered command and control tactics which later inspired the Soviet Deep Battle doctrine. His son Uriyangkhadai and his grandson Aju would also prove to be accomplished commanders. Subotai's strategies and tactics are studied in military academies to this day. Because of this rare combination of leadership skills and long-lasting legacy, Subotai ranks as one of the greatest underrated generals in history.

Pavel Korin, Aleksandr Nevsky, 1942, State Tretyakov Gallery, Moscow.

Chapter 14

ALEKSANDR 'NEVSKY'
Hero of Russia

Prince Aleksandr with the men of Novgorod and with his brother Andrey and
the men of the Lower country went in the winter in great strength against the
land of the Chud people, against the Germans. Prince Aleksandr and all the
men of Novgorod drew up their forces by Lake Peipus at Uzmen by the Raven's
Rock; and the Germans and Chud men rode at them driving themselves like
a wedge through their army; and there was a great slaughter of Germans and
Chud men. God helped Prince Aleksandr. And the Germans fell there and the
Chud men gave shoulder, and pursuing them fought with them on the ice. And
there fell of the Chud men a countless number; and of the Germans 400, and
50 they took with their hands and brought to Novgorod. And they fought on
5 April, on a Saturday, the Commemoration Day of the Holy Martyr Theodulus.

Chronicle of Novgorod

Few historical characters are as illustrious as Aleksandr Nevsky, a heroic thirteenth-century Prince of Novgorod and Kiev, Grand Duke of Vladimir, who halted the eastward drive of the Swedes and Germans. By defeating the Swedish invasion force at the confluence of the Rivers Izhora and Neva in 1240 he won the epithet 'Nevsky' ('of the Neva'). From this moment and until his death in 1263, Aleksandr dominated Novgorod. He saved the Republic a second time by routing the Livonian Order at the Battle of Lake Peipus. To avoid the total destruction of what remained of Kievan Rus', Aleksandr and his brothers became vassals of the Mongols, who imposed their domination for the next 240 years. To this day, Aleksandr Nevsky remains Russia's favourite historical figure and an icon of the nation's popular culture.

Aleksandr Yaroslavitch (1221–63), son of Grand Prince Yaroslav II of Vladimir, came from the Vladimir-Suzdal branch of the Rurik dynasty. In 1236, the Republic of Novgorod's wealthy merchants summoned the young noble to become their electoral prince (*Knyaz*), the military leader who would defend their north-western frontiers. This was a huge responsibility for a mere adolescent although, as the proverbial saying in medieval Russia had it, 'Who can stand against God and the Great Novgorod?'

Concurrently, Aleksandr's princely house faced another, even more dramatic challenge: after a first invasion in 1223, the Mongols (called 'Tatars' in Russia) were heading west again. Batu Khan and Subotai invaded Russia in 1237 with 40,000 horsemen. The Cumans, the Bulgars and the Alans had submitted to the Mongols, and Yuri II, Grand Prince of Vladimir, Yaroslavl's elder brother, was crushed at the Battle of the Sit River (March 1238). The cities of Ryazan, Moscow, Vladimir, Suzdal and Tver, as well as countless towns and villages, were devastated by Batu's divisions. Kiev, the mother of all Rus' towns, fell in December 1240:

> Batyj approached Kiev in great force; [he came] with a mighty host of soldiers and surrounded the city. It was encircled by the Tatars and a close siege began. Batyj pitched camp outside the city while his men besieged it. And one could not hear anything as a result of the great din [caused by] his screeching carts, countless bleating camels and neighing herds of horses. And the land of Rus' became filled with soldiers.
>
> *Galician-Volynian Chronicle*

Only north-westerly principalities such as Pskov, Smolensk and Novgorod survived the onslaught. Given the overwhelming military superiority of the Mongols, neither Yaroslav nor his son Aleksandr and his younger brothers attempted to resist. Prince Yaroslav and his relatives took the fateful and controversial decision to pay tribute in money and furs, officially acknowledging the double suzerainty of the Khagan-Emperor and of the Golden Horde in order to preserve their lands from utter destruction.

On the northern border, the Scandinavians, probably commanded by Birger Magnusson (1210–66), a magnate of the Folkung family and future Jarl of Sweden, were attempting to expand into Rus' and convert the Slavs to Roman Catholicism. The 20-year-old prince at the head of his *druzhina* (retinue) won his first important victory on the bank of the Neva River over the Swedish invasion force on 15 July 1240. According to the *Novgorodian Chronicle*, the northern warriors landed at the confluence of the Rivers Izhora and Neva and attempted to block Novgorod's route to the Baltic Sea. Aleksandr and his army attacked the invaders and defeated them, and Birger sailed back to Finland with the Swedish survivors. With the Battle of the Neva, Aleksandr had gained his eponymous triumph, and northern Rus' had been saved from a full-scale invasion.

> Aleksandr with the men of Novgorod and of Ladoga did not delay at all; he went against them and defeated them ... And there was a great slaughter of Svei. And having loaded two vessels with their best men got away first to sea; and the rest of them having dug a pit they threw [the dead] into it without number; and many others were wounded; and the same night without waiting for the light they went away in shame. And Knyaz Aleksandr with the men of Novgorod and of Ladoga all came back in health to their own country, preserved by God and St Sophia, and through the prayers of all the saints.
>
> *Chronicle of Novgorod*

Nonetheless, a few months later, the Novgorodians expelled the young prince for interfering in their affairs, and the Republic at once petitioned Yaroslav II for another commander. Andrey, Aleksandr's younger brother, was sent to Novgorod, only to leave it several months later. When their lands came under attack by the Livonian Order, Yaroslav again sent Andrey with several units to assist.

Intent on taking advantage of Novgorod's weakness in the wake of the Mongol and Swedish invasions, the Livonian knights and their Estonian allies occupied Pskov, Izborsk and Koporye. After retaking Pskov, in 1242 Andrey joined his Suzdalian forces with Aleksandr's for the final showdown in the celebrated 'Battle on the Ice'. Aleksandr's and Andrey's troops faced the Livonian heavy cavalry and Estonian infantry led by the Magister of the Order Hermann I von Buxthoeven. Nevsky met his adversaries on the ice of Lake Peipus and defeated them on 5 April 1242. The threat from the crusaders had been dealt with, the German *Drang nach Osten* had been halted, Russian Orthodoxy saved.

In 1243 Yaroslav, now the senior Prince of Rus', was summoned by Batu Khan to Sarai on the Volga, capital of his *ulus* (nation), to pay homage and deliver his pledge of loyalty. Two years later, he was summoned at Karakorum by Töregene Khatun, regent of the Mongol Empire, to renew his patent of rule (*yarlik*). Yaroslav attended the Great *Kurultai* (Imperial assembly) but, according to Giovanni da

Pian del Carpine, he was poisoned in its aftermath. Following the death of his father, in 1249 Aleksandr became the new Prince of 'Kiev and the entire Russian Land' (*Trinity and Laurentian Chronicles*).

In 1252, internecine struggles culminated in Aleksandr's ousting of his younger brothers Alexey and Yaroslav III from Vladimir, with Mongol military support. Aleksandr travelled to Karakorum in order to be installed as Grand Duke of Vladimir by the new Khagan, Möngke Khan:

> When Möngke Khan held the Great *Kurultai* for the second time, they deliberated together concerning the extirpation and subjugation of all the remaining rebels; and it was decided to seize the lands of the Bulghar, the As and the Rus, which bordered on the camping grounds of Batu; for they had not completely submitted being deluded by the size of their territory.
>
> 'Ata-Malik Juvayni, *History of the World-Conqueror*

Mongol agents began taking censuses in the Rus' principalities, and in 1259 their tax-collectors and census-takers arrived in Novgorod, provoking an uprising. Aleksandr punished the leaders of the revolt severely, cutting off noses and gouging out eyes, then forced the city to submit to the census and taxation to avoid Mongol retaliation. Tax collectors were also killed at Vladimir, Suzdal, Rostov, Pereyaslavl and Yaroslavl, but Aleksandr succeeded in averting reprisals by journeying to Sarai and imploring the mercy of Berke Khan, Batu's brother and successor. Metropolitan Kirill was allowed to establish a bishopric in Sarai; Aleksandr also obtained an exemption for Russians from a draft. Owing to Aleksandr Nevsky, Novgorod remained the only Russian state to escape full Mongol subjugation.

Aleksandr died, possibly poisoned, in November 1263 while returning from Sarai. For the next two centuries, all of the Rus' states, including Novgorod, Smolensk, Galich and Pskov, remained under nominal Mongol rule. According to the Russian Orthodox Church, Aleksandr had made a fateful choice between the East and the West in favour of the East, thus preserving the Orthodox faith from Catholic influence.

In 1381 Aleksandr was elevated to the status of a local saint, and he was canonized by the Russian Orthodox Church in 1547. He became one of Russia's key historical characters. When Peter the Great founded St Petersburg in 1703 on the recently conquered shores of the Neva, he picked Aleksandr as patron saint of his new capital. By decree of the Tsar, in 1724 his relics were solemnly translated from Vladimir to St Petersburg and entombed in a massive silver sarcophagus within the Aleksandr Nevsky Monastery.

By the end of the seventeenth century, fifteen biographies had already been written about the prince of Novgorod. With Sergei Eisenstein's epic film of 1938, Aleksandr Nevsky came to the forefront of Russian popular culture just before the outbreak of the Second World War. 'Sergei, you are a true Bolshevik!' Joseph Stalin is said to have declared to Eisenstein, clapping him on the back, after viewing the film. Once Germany invaded the USSR in 1941, Nevsky was used extensively in Stalinist propaganda to rally the Russian people and inspire them to fight for their homeland.

Achievements

Facing invasions from both Asia and Western Europe, Aleksandr Nevsky rose to become one of the thirteenth century's great military commanders. As his reputation grew in the telling, he became a powerful symbol, a legendary saint-hero, the protector of Russia against crusaders and Tatars. Nevsky served as an intermediary between the khans and the Rus', ensuring the survival of the principalities as vassal states of the great Mongol Empire, and allowing the Orthodox Church to preserve its role through the sombre era of the 'Tatar Yoke'. Alhough a controversial strategy, Nevsky remained loyal to the Mongols in order to protect Russian Orthodoxy from Western inroads. His son Daniil was the ancestor of all the Grand Dukes of Moscow. As a princely warrior-saint, Aleksandr Nevsky remained an important patron of St Petersburg and the Romanov dynasty throughout the duration of the Russian empire. May 2021 marked the 800th anniversary of his birth, an event duly celebrated throughout Russia, where he retains his status as a national symbol.

Charles-Philippe Larivière, Battle of Cocherel, 1839, Palais de Versailles. (*Wikimedia Commons*)

Chapter 15

BERTRAND DU GUESCLIN
Hero of the Hundred Years' War

On Wednesday, the second day of October, the King of France made Constable a Breton knight named Bertrand Du Guesclin, renowned for his valour. His lineage was more modest than that of his predecessor, but by his prowess he had acquired many lands and lordships: in France, the County of Longueville, which the King of France had given him, and in Castile, a great many lands awarded by King Henrique.

Chancellor Pierre d'Orgemont, *Grandes Chroniques de France*, 1378

Du Guesclin is the most illustrious French knight and mercenary warlord of the early Hundred Years War. Participating in countless sieges and achieving fame by his feats in tournaments, his guerrilla tactics against the English in Brittany, his victory at Cocherel and his Spanish adventures, du Guesclin rose to become Marshal of the Kingdom, the 'Good Constable' who expelled the English from France. This folk hero started his military career with the capture of the Castle of Fougeray, and his life ended while he was besieging the castle of Châteauneuf-de-Randon in Gévaudan, twenty-six years later. His military prowess altered the course of the Hundred Years' War.

Born into a modest Breton knightly family, Bertrand du Guesclin (c.1320–80) was, according to the chronicles, massively built and physically robust, although short in stature and hideous in appearance. At an early age he became a jousting champion, being only seventeen when he participated in his first tournament, defeating fifteen knights. Thereafter, his fame spread far and wide. In battle, du Guesclin's weapon of choice was the battleaxe, which he wielded with great dexterity.

During the War of the Breton Succession (1341–64), du Guesclin served under Charles de Blois who was supported by Philippe VI of France, while Jean II de Montfort was backed by Edward III of England. With a handful of daring companions the young Bertrand conducted a cunning guerrilla war, constantly harassing the Anglo-Breton forces before seeking refuge in the neighbouring forests. This earned him the nickname 'the Black Mastiff of Brocéliande'. With thirty fellow Bretons, whose vanguard he disguised as loggers, in 1354 he took the castle of Grand-Fougeray. Knighted shortly after, from then on he would use the motto *Dat virtus quod forma negat* – 'courage gives what beauty denies'.

The first half of the fourteenth century saw the arrival of gunpowder in Western Europe and its rapid diffusion. Primitive guns were used in Italy in the 1320s–30s, and their presence was attested at the siege of Cividale del Friuli in 1331. Crude *pot-de-fer* designs were later used at the battle of Sluys (1340), and even earlier by Philippe VI's Admiral Hugues Quieret during his raids on English coastal cities in 1338, including the sack of Southampton. In March/April of the following year French royal troops used artillery against the English at the siege of Puyguilhem (Perigord). According to Froissart, in 1340, during the siege of Le Quesnoy, the locals defended their city walls against French Marshal de Mirepoix with guns and bombards (an early cannon). By the 1340s there was no turning back, and the proliferation of guns was inevitable. In 1346 King Edward III would use artillery on the battlefield of Crécy, mostly 'to cause panic'. Firearms started to transform medieval warfare.

Du Guesclin recognized the value and potential of these new weapons, at least initially for psychological effect, and used artillery from the 1350s during siege operations. In 1356–7, for nine months, du Guesclin held the city of Rennes against Henry of Grosmont, 1st Duke of Lancaster. He also fought a number of duels against Englishmen, including Sir Thomas of Canterbury during the Siege of Dinan, defeating all his opponents. He used scorched earth tactics against the invasion of Edward III, who besieged many cities but failed to take any except Caen.

Entering the service of the Dauphin Charles V 'the Wise' of France, du Guesclin won the Battle of Cocherel against the superior coalition forces of Navarrese, English and Gascons led by King Carlos II 'the Bad' of Navarre and Captal de Buch (May 1364). Du Guesclin feigned a retreat, inducing his enemies to abandon their strong defensive positions on a hill to pursue the French and Bretons. He then dispatched 200 heavy horsemen under his lieutenant Eustache de la Houssaye against the flank of the English archers and sent the coalition army into disarray. This brilliant victory forced Carlos II to sign a peace treaty with his cousin Charles V, who was crowned King of France three days later at Rheims.

> The king raised his hands to heaven and gave thanks to God for the good victory that He had given him. In Rheims, where defeat was feared, it was indescribable enthusiasm when a herald brought the news.
>
> Christine de Pisan, *Livre des fais et bonnes meurs du sage Roy Charles V*

At the Battle of Auray (September 1364), Charles de Blois was killed and his army routed. Du Guesclin, after breaking his weapons, was forced to surrender to the Constable of Aquitaine Sir John Chandos. This English victory put an end to the War of Succession. Although Jean IV de Montfort was recognized as King of Brittany, he would later pay allegiance to the French crown. Ransomed by Charles V for 100,000 francs, in 1366 du Guesclin persuaded the leaders of the 'free companies', who had been pillaging France since the Treaty of Brétigny, to join him in a Spanish expedition to support Count Enrique of Trastámara against his half-brother Pedro I of Castile. Du Guesclin, with Guillaume Boitel, his faithful companion and leader of his vanguard, captured Magallón, Briviesca and eventually the capital Burgos.

Pedro and Edward the Black Prince surprised Enrique's less numerous army at Nájera, where the English used field artillery (1367). Although du Guesclin and his vanguard once again put on a show of valour, many Castilian units defected. Henrique managed to escape to safety, and the Black Prince, affected by dysentery, withdrew his support for Pedro and left for Aquitaine. Du Guesclin and Henrique de Trastámara then routed Pedro at the decisive Battle of Montiel and killed him in an ensuing scuffle in which du Guesclin had to intervene to give Henrique the upper hand (March 1369). Henrique was proclaimed king in Calahorra, and Castile became a firm ally of the French crown. For his services, du Guesclin was made Duke of Molina and Count of Soria.

> Do not forget what I have repeated to you a thousand times, that in whatever country you wage war, the clergy, women, children, and even the people, are not your enemies.
>
> Du Guesclin to his companions and soldiers

Recalled by Charles the Wise, du Guesclin, now aged fifty, was appointed Constable of France. Together, the King and his main general chose a strategy of attrition, extending the fighting to every region still in enemy hands. The newly-appointed Constable crushed Sir Robert Knolles at the Battles of Pontvallain and Vaas (1370). Thereafter, du Guesclin reconquered all of Maine and Anjou, put the English garrisons to flight and captured a great number of knights who attempted to flee to England. According to the historian Alexander Gillespie, the Pontvallain campaign 'destroyed the reputation of the English on the battlefield.'

In June 1372, while du Guesclin was laying siege to La Rochelle, the Franco-Castilian fleet commanded by Ambrosio Boccanegra annihilated the English fleet, sinking or taking all their ships. More than 400 English knights and 8,000 soldiers were captured. In the following months du Guesclin defeated the English once more at the Battle of Chizé, then recaptured the Poitou, Saintonge and Angoumois regions from the enemy. Now master of the Channel, in coordination with Castilian naval power, he organized destructive landings on English coastal settlements in retaliation for English *chevauchées* (cavalry raids).

During the siege of Saint-Sauveur-le-Vicomte in Normandy (Sir John Chandos' castle), Admiral Jean de Vienne fielded no fewer than thirty-two guns firing a variety of ammunition such as bolts, metal and stone balls (1375). Two years later, the Duke of Burgundy Philippe 'the Bold', ally of King Charles V, brought his mighty artillery train to the Siege of Odruik held by the English. Some of the heaviest ordnance could discharge projectiles weighing as much as 90kg. As the battered walls were eventually breached by the concentration of artillery fire, the garrison surrendered.

Firearms were the greatest military innovation of the late medieval period. Philippe the Bold's victory had a huge impact on siege warfare, since it demonstrated that high stone walls could not withstand the repeated impact of cannonballs. Military architecture would have to undergo its own revolution in order to adapt to this threat. The Siege of Odruik heralded the dawn of a new era. Soldier-diplomat Andrea Redusio described the guns used by the Venetians to assault the castle of Quero situated along the Piave River (1376):

> The Bombard is a very strong iron weapon with a wide tube in the front, in which a round stone of the size of the tube is placed, and having a chamber joined to it at its rear end. That which is joined at the rear is more or less twice the size of the tube, but narrower. In it is placed a black powder made of

saltpetre, sulphur, and willow charcoal through the opening of the chamber against its mouth. This opening is then closed with a wooden tampion which is pressed in, and when the round stone has been inserted and arranged against its mouth, fire is applied through a smaller opening in the chamber, and by the great force of the lit powder, the stone is discharged with great impetus. And when these bombards belched forth their stones, men thought that God was thundering from above.

Andrea Redusio, *Chronicon Tarvisinum*, 1420s

Du Guesclin spent his remaining years leading expeditions against scattered English forces and mercenary bands. In July 1380, while on campaign in Languedoc and besieging the castle of Châteauneuf-de-Randon, he died after drinking contaminated water. By then, the only cities still in English hands were Brest, Bayonne, Bordeaux and Calais.

Acknowledging the merits of his Constable, in an unprecedented move, Charles V had du Guesclin's remains buried in the royal basilica of Saint-Denis, among the Kings of France, at the very foot of the tomb he had prepared for himself. Weakened by tuberculosis, the King passed away just a month later. Charles V 'The Wise' and du Guesclin, through their concerted military and political strategy, had set France on the road to reunification, its standing army under direct royal control. The kingdom had been given the foundations of a modern state.

Achievements

Du Guesclin possessed many of the skills of a great captain. His companions and soldiers, who had the utmost confidence in his abilities, followed him in every adventure. Steadfastly loyal to the king, he was an able tactician and a disciplined soldier. Under his supervision, the French royal army was able to turn the tide of the Hundred Years' War. By the end of Charles V's reign in 1380, Constable du Guesclin had reconquered most of the territories ceded to the English by the Treaty of Brétigny twenty years earlier. Du Guesclin is considered a medieval national hero of France, an almost legendary figure as significant as Jeanne d'Arc or Marshal de Boucicaut.

Paolo Uccello, John Hawkwood, Duomo of Florence. (*Wikimedia Commons*)

Chapter 16

JOHN HAWKWOOD
Mercenary and *Condottiero*

Two Franciscan monks encounter a mercenary captain near his fortress of Montecchio. 'May God grant you peace,' the monks say, their standard greeting. 'And may God take away your alms,' replies the mercenary. Shocked by such insolence, the monks demand explanation. 'Don't you know that I live by war,' said the mercenary, 'and peace would destroy me? And as I live by war, so you live by alms.' And so he managed his affairs so well that there was little peace in Italy in his times.

Franco Sacchetti on Hawkwood, *Il Trecentonovelle*

Hailing from Essex, Sir John Hawkwood, who fought in the Hundred Years' War, was a mercenary captain who became a legend in his own time. After the Peace of Brétigny left thousands of soldiers unemployed, he achieved notoriety as the unscrupulous leader of the redoubtable White Company that roamed Italy, and he even served as King Richard II's ambassador. Leaving behind him a trail of terror and destruction, the swashbuckling English mercenary rose to become a key actor in fourteenth-century Italy, torn as it was by constant internecine warfare, shifting alliances and convoluted politics.

The second son of a minor Essex landowner, John Hawkwood (c. 1323–94) chose a soldier's career, serving as a captain of the Black Prince in France during the reign of Edward III. It has been supposed that he participated as an archer in the Battles of Crécy (1346) and Poitiers (1356). The King probably knighted him in the course of the war.

After the Treaty of Brétigny temporarily ended the first phase of the Hundred Years' War (1360), Hawkwood soon became the leader of a free company of unemployed mercenaries who opted to remain and continued to pillage the defenceless French villages and countryside. According to Jean Froissart, who called him 'Jean Hacconde', Hawkwood 'was a seasoned knight, renowned in the Italian marches where he performed many great deeds of arms'.

In order to remove them from southern France, Pope Innocentius VI had no choice but to hire these marauders, sending them across the Alps to fight in the active war zone of northern Italy. At the time, the Italian cities, between wars and episodes of plague, exercised little control over their own territories, which were periodically invaded by enemies, brigands and a plethora of rampaging bands whose leaders were often *condottieri* (mercenary captains). Between contracts, these mercenaries took to preying on the countryside, artificially generating demand for their own 'protection' services. Wedged between Papal territories and the Republic of Florence, the city-state of Siena was ransacked no fewer than thirty-seven times between 1342 and 1399.

> What are so many foreign swords doing here? Why is the verdant earth covered with the blood of barbarians? Nature provided well for us when she placed the shield of the Alps between us and the German frenzy, but blind greed clashing with its own good has now so contrived as to cause sores on the healthy body.
>
> Francesco Petrarca, *My Italy*, c.1344

In 1363 Hawkwood joined the 'Great Company of English and Germans', better known as the 'White Company'. This mercenary band founded by the German Albert Stertz grew into an army of 6,000 unemployed soldiers of fortune from the four corners of Europe: English, Germans, French, Hungarians and Italians. Hawkwood was elected Captain General of the Company in January 1364. The

White Company was hired by the Republic of Pisa to fight against Florence, alongside Anneken von Bongard's company.

> At this period, there was in Tuscany a right valiant English knight, called sir John Hawkwood, who had there performed many most gallant deeds of arms; he had left France at the conclusion of the peace of Bretigny, and was at that time a poor knight, who thought it would not be of any advantage to him to return home; but when he saw, that by that treaties, all men at armes would be forced to leave France, he put himself at the head of those free companions called late-comers, and marched into Burgundy. Several such companions, composed of English, Gascons, Bretons, Germans, and men from every nation, were collected there. Hawkwood was one of the principal leaders.
>
> Froissart, *Chronicles*, Book II

The White Company's leader drew on his own experience of Welsh longbow tactics developed by the English to achieve victory at Dupplin Moor (1332), Halidon Hill (1333), Crécy and Poitiers against the Scots and the French. Choice of terrain was paramount: marshy or muddy ground in front of the archers' well prepared positions on a hillside considerably slowed down the Scottish schiltrons (spearmen) or the elite French heavy cavalry. Volleys of arrows fired by vast numbers of archers (a trained longbowman could shoot ten to twelve accurate arrows a minute) would disrupt the assailants' charge before they could reach the defensive pits, caltrops (spikes) and stakes, only to be shot at point-blank range by the well-entrenched English longbowmen supported by their men-at-arms. Head-on frontal assaults of this sort were, of course, suicidal. Wounded and exhausted riders and their horses were literally festooned with arrows. Though the famed Welsh warbow had a draw weight of somewhere around 80–150lbs, its arrows could hardly penetrate steel plate armour, even at close range; but the knights' mounts were more vulnerable, as were the sergeants, men-at-arms and hired mercenaries wearing chainmail or lower quality armour.

> You have often given me good proof of your courage and your loyalty. In many fierce tempests of war you have shown that you are not degenerate sons, but of the same blood as those men under the leadership of my father and my ancestors as kings of England found no task impossible, no place forbiddingly impassable, no mountain too high to climb, no tower too strong to capture, no army unbeatable, no armed enemy formidable.
>
> Edward the Black Prince to his longbowmen before the Battle of Poitiers, 1356, in *Chronicle of Geoffrey le Baker*

Longbow-armed yeomen had a fatal weakness, though: caught in the open, without sufficient support from men-at-arms or cavalry, they could be systematically cut to pieces; this was the fate they suffered against Marshal de Beaujeu at Ardres (1351), and against du Guesclin at Cocherel (1364), Pontvallain (1370) and Chizé (1373). In set-piece battles, natural barriers such as rivers, hilly terrain and woods were essential to prevent being outflanked or attacked from the rear. When properly employed under the right conditions, longbows remained the premier distance weapons dominating Western European battlefields until the advent of effective firearms in the 1450s.

Hawkwood and his lieutenants Richard Ramsey, John Berwick and John Clifford became famous for the rapidity of their deployment, made possible by the lighter armour and equipment of their men, for their handling of infantry, and for the discipline of their troops. Hawkwood would feign retreat and then use ambushes to surprise his adversaries. Using integrated battle plans, the suppressive fire of his longbowmen would be used to support dismounted men-at-arms and cavalry. Many of Hawkwood's successes can also be attributed to the superior training and experience of his lieutenants and their troops.

Between 1372 and 1378 Hawkwood and his soldiers of fortune alternately served Pope Gregorius XI or Milan. In March 1376 his Company looted Faenza, killing and raping without hindrance. Hawkwood himself ran his sword through a young nun who was being fought over by two of his men. He then sold the city to the Lord of Milan Bernabó Visconti for 20,000 florins. In February 1377, hired by Gregorius, Hawkwood's White Company took part in the notorious massacre of some 5,000 to 7,000 inhabitants of Cesena in Romagna. This horrendous bloodbath lasted three days. In May, his marriage to Donnina, the illegitimate daughter of Bernabó Visconti, the infamous 'Scourge of Lumbardye', came with a considerable dowry of rich properties in that region.

According to Geoffrey Chaucer, who probably met him several times, Hawkwood was nothing but a 'cold-blooded, professional soldier'. Edward de Berkeley's and Chaucer's 1378 voyage to Italy involved an attempt to recruit Hawkwood (on Visconti's payroll at the time) to the service of the new English King Richard II, an offer the mercenary declined. That same year, Hawkwood was appointed Captain General of Florence, receiving 1,200 florins a year, although the White Company would also fight for other clients when their services were not required by the Florentine republic. Milan, Bologna, Pisa, Lucca, Faenza, Siena, Rimini, Perugia, Ravenna, Naples, Savoia, Verona, Bologna, Venice . . . every city, and every village in between, was marked by the fire and sword of Hawkwood's passing.

In 1381 King Richard II appointed him ambassador to Pope Urbanus VI and Charles II of Durazzo. The English monarch favoured Urbanus and Charles against the French-backed Pope Clement VII in Avignon. Hawkwood then quarrelled with his father-in-law, the Lord of Milan, and the Republic of Florence paid extortionate amounts to buy him off. The following year, he sold lands bestowed upon him by the pope in Romagna and bought estates near Florence.

In 1383 he founded another mercenary band, the Company of the Rose, with Richard Ramsey and Giovanni d'Azzo Degli Ulbadini. The following year, Hawkwood appropriated the castle of Montecchio Vesponi from the territory of Arezzo, turning it into one of his residences.

By 1385 Sir John was over sixty years old, with extensive landholdings in both Italy and England. Most of his duties under Florence were defensive, and he had not fought in a major battle for over a decade. However, in the winter of 1385–6 war broke out between Padua and Verona, and Hawkwood would lead the Paduan forces under the nominal command of Francesco Novello di Carrara.

Brave knights, if it were possible to fight the enemy in the open field, truly I know you would be victorious. But seeing the manner in which they are fortified there it is impossible that they can be taken by force and defeated by us; but it is impossible to stay here, since we cannot survive but for a few days, and those in great necessity, we must beat the enemy with cleverness.

Hawkwood's address to his soldiers before the Battle of Castagnaro in Piero Giovanni di Minerbetti's *Cronica volgare*

The most important engagement in the war was the Battle of Castagnaro, on 11 March 1387, probably Hawkwood's greatest victory. During the battle, Hawkwood saw that the Veronese left flank was exposed and ordered his men to advance. He harassed their flanks with his 600 longbowmen and further weakened them with cavalry charges that he led in person, securing victory for his men and their Paduan allies. Galeazzo and Andrea Gatari's *Cronaca Carrarese* claimed that 4,620 fighting men were captured. The Veronese had brought three organ guns, but they failed to break the Paduan formation. These engineering marvels were seized, along with the Veronese baggage train.

In the following years Hawkwood and his men continued their rampage across Italy. In March 1390 the Republic of Florence, which had formed an alliance against the new Duke of Milan Gian Galeazzo Visconti, welcomed him like a prince, rewarding him with the former Bishop of Parma's palace, an increased annual pension and a dowry of 2,000 gold florins for each of his three daughters Janet, Catherine and Anne. The old *condottiero* became an honorary and distinguished Florentine citizen. He finally retired from all active military service in August 1392.

In early 1394, in preparation for his return to England to spend his last years, a weary Hawkwood started liquidating his Italian properties for 6,000 gold florins, but he died in March at the age of seventy-one before his plan to travel back to his homeland could be carried out. He was given a sumptuous funeral by the Florentine republic; the cortege passed through the city, and he was entombed in the cathedral of Santa Maria del Fiore.

A few months later, King Richard II petitioned Florence for the return of Hawkwood's remains, as he had done for Robert de Vere, Duke of Ireland. Sir John's large fresco portrait on horseback, still visible in the Duomo of Florence, was created by Paolo Uccello in 1436. It stands between the monument dedicated to *condottiero* Niccolò da Tolentino and a painting of Dante Alighieri, the poet of the Divine Comedy. The Latin inscription translates as:

> This is John Hawkwood, English knight, esteemed the most cautious and expert general of his time.

Achievements

John Hawkwood was one of the most ruthless mercenaries of the fourteenth century. A master of extortion, he moved with ease in the shifting world of the Italian city-states' wars and politics, sometimes working as an emissary between conflicting parties. Self-serving, talented and dangerously crafty, the leader of the White Company and the Company of the Rose earned a fortune and immense estates by renting his services to the highest bidder. In their quest for plunder and riches, the soldiers of fortune of his companies left behind a path of destruction, sparing neither civilians nor holy places. Known as 'Giovanni Acuto' in the peninsula, he was the most sought-after mercenary captain of his time: every prince, every Italian republic and beyond, competed to hire his services at one time or another. Florence, in particular, honoured and remembered her most capable *condottiero*. He probably inspired the saying, 'An Italianized Englishman is the Devil Incarnate.' Terry Jones has even speculated that Geoffrey Chaucer based his character of the Knight in the *Canterbury Tales* on the very imperfect Hawkwood himself.

Jan Matejko, Battle of Grunwald (detail), 1878, Muzeum Narodowe w Warszawie, Warsaw. (*Wikimedia Commons*)

Chapter 17

JAN ŽIŽKA
Leader of the 'Warriors of God',
national hero of Bohemia

Žižka, the one whom no mortal hand could destroy, was extinguished by the finger of God. As he lay ill he was asked where he wished to be buried after his death. He ordered that his body be flayed, the flesh discarded for the birds and animals, and a drum be fashioned from his skin. With this drum in the lead they should go to war. The enemies would turn to flight as soon as they heard its voice.
Enea Silvio Piccolomini, *Historia Bohemica*

In early fifteenth-century Bohemia, what started as a local popular religious upheaval became a full-fledged revolution. The execution of reformer Jan Hus, followed by successive attempts to crush his followers, forced the Bohemians to defend themselves. The success of the Hussite movement against more numerous Catholic foes was in large part due to the military genius of Jan Žižka of Trocnow and his immediate successors. His highly disciplined army of commoners, calling themselves the 'Warriors of God', threw back five successive crusades blessed by Pope Martinus V and raided as far as the Baltic Sea. Although little known beyond Central Europe, the leader of the Hussite armies used ground-breaking weapons and tactics and never lost a military engagement.

In July 1415 at the Council of Constance, convened to end the Great Schism (with three papal claimants), reformers Jan Hus and Jerome of Prague were burnt at the stake as heretics, despite the fact that they had been granted formal protection by Emperor Sigismund of Luxembourg. Hus' death triggered a revolt among his followers. On 30 July 1419, a mob of Utraquists (moderate Hussite reformers) led by the monk Jan Želivský descended on the new town hall of Prague, threw King Wenceslaus IV of Bohemia's representatives out of a window and hacked them to pieces. This dramatic event became known as the First Defenestration of Prague. Jan Žižka of Trocnow and Kalicha (c.1360–1424) was born into an aristocratic family of Trocnow (near present-day Borovany). He lost his left eye at the age of ten or twelve, earning the nickname 'One-eyed Žižka'. According to Polish chronicler Jan Długosz, in 1409–11 Žižka fought as a mercenary for Polish King Władysław II Jagiełło, who defeated the Teutonic knights at the Battle of Tannenberg. According to Vavřinec of Březová, Žižka played an active part in the First Defenestration of Prague.

The revolt that had begun in the Kingdom of Bohemia quickly spread throughout the remaining lands of the Bohemian Crown, including Moravia and Silesia. Fighting erupted after King Wenceslaus died, shortly after the infamous defenestration. Churches and monasteries were destroyed, and church property was seized by the rebel Hussite nobility. In March 1420 Pope Martinus V issued a bull calling upon Catholics to take up arms against the Hussites. The bull *Omnium plasmatoris domini* was promulgated by Fernando de Palacios, Bishop of Lugo, at the imperial diet in Breslau, launching the anti-Hussite crusades.

Three Imperial campaigns and five crusades against the Hussites under the papal aegis would end in failure. In the early 1420s and again in 1431 mass expeditions invaded Bohemia from the north-east, from the south-west or from the north. In the late 1420s, Sigismund, heir to the Kingdom of Bohemia, preferred what he called 'daily warfare' waged on the Bavarian and Saxon borderland.

King Sigismund was an overt persecutor of the truth, but for their part the Táborites [Hussites] were more cruel: between them they lit the fires which reduced almost to nothing the noble and bountiful land of Bohemia.

Vavřinec of Březová, *Historia Hussitica*

To successfully counter the large numbers of German knights and other better equipped mercenaries facing them, Žižka and his Hussites would use cumbersome but modified horse-drawn wagons. Žižka came up with a method of rapidly deploying a defensive wagon laager (*vozová hradba* in Czech, *wagenburg* in German). The men were trained to quickly set up a defensive system of wagons linked by iron chains, sheltering the horses inside and taking up defensive positions.

In December 1419 at the Battle of Nekmíř, Žižka repelled the attack of a superior Bohemian royalist force by forming for the first time a protective mobile wagon fort and using hand guns. Žižka's Hussites also pioneered the use of light field artillery mounted on the wagons, fielding various pieces of ordnance such as the *houfnice* (which gives the English term 'howitzer'), the heavier *tarasnice* (falconet) and the *bombarda* (mortar).

In the spring of 1420 radical Hussites founded the fortified camp of Tábor, which grew to house a population of 3,000 people. Four captains were elected, one of whom was Jan Žižka, leader of the 'Warriors of God'. With military experience acquired fighting the German knights, Žižka set out to build an army made up of townsmen and peasants, instituting military discipline into these untrained and poorly equipped soldiers. Once trained, and fired by nationalist and religious zeal, the Taborites would prove superior to the undisciplined feudal levies opposed to them.

The early use of gunpowder and innovative tactics helped Žižka's commoners beat off attacks by larger forces of mounted knights. The heavy wooden walls of the Hussite wagons, preferably deployed on high ground, offered excellent protection. Within the enclosure of the *wagenburg*, hand-gunners and crossbowmen were supported by infantrymen using spears, pikes, even farmers' scythes, to defend the gaps and strike at the enemy horses from below. Ideally, each wagon would have its own sergeant, two armed drivers, two hand-gunners, six crossbowmen, four flailmen, four halberdiers and two pavisiers (spearmen with large shields). Initially, light firearms called *píšťala* played only a supporting role in the defence of the wagon wall. Counter-attacks were carried out by infantry armed with cold steel, and by charges of light cavalry.

Following another victory at Sudoměř in March 1420, where his Hussites had been outnumbered five to one, Žižka ordered the mass manufacture of improved war wagons. In December 1421, at the Battle of Kutná Hora, Žižka was forced to use his war wagons offensively. By then, wounded by an arrow and having already lost his right eye, Žižka had become completely blind. Since his 12,000 Hussites were hopelessly outnumbered and surrounded by the 50,000 crusaders led by Sigismund, Žižka organized his wagons in columns during the night in order to execute a tactical retreat. At five o'clock in the morning, at full speed and with all guns blazing, the wagon columns smashed through Sigismund's lines, allowing the Taborites to break free from their encirclement.

Shortly after the New Year, Žižka set out again for Kutná Hora, and on 6 January he appeared about 6–7 km from the town near the village of Nebovidy, taking by surprise a troop of Hungarian mercenaries and defeating them. The Battle of Kutná Hora was one of the earliest instances of firearms being used in tactical offensive operations, although the Ghent militia had used gunpowder weapons in attack in 1382 at the Battle of Beverhoutsveld. From 1422 firearms progressively became the primary long-range weapons of the Hussites. The Diet also instituted a law to call to arms every able man to defend the homeland in case of invasion.

In the aftermath of the victory at Kutná Hora, the local silver mines fell under the control of the Taborites, providing critical finance for the Hussite cause. As this was a holy war, it was assumed by all that God would be on the side of the virtuous, and in July 1423, Žižka issued his famed Regulations of War (*vojenský Ĝád*) enforcing draconian discipline on his own people:

Brother Žižka and the other nobles, captains, knights, squires, citizens, craftsmen, and peasants named above, and all the communities will, with the help of God and of the commonwealth, punish all disorders by banishment, by flogging, slaying, decapitating, hanging, whipping, burning, drowning and by all other punishments which are befitting according to God's law, with exceptions of no one, whether of male or female sex. If we observe and fulfil the salutary articles written above the Lord God will be with us with His holy grace and help; for it befits the warriors of God to live in a truly Christian fashion.

Regulations of War, Article XII

After defeating his enemies (including some dissidents) at Habry, Horice, and Malesov, Žižka the Blind died of the plague at Přibyslav on 11 October 1424, while he was planning an invasion of Moravia held by Sigismund's partisans. According to future Pope Enea Silvio Piccolomini (Pius II), Žižka's dying wish was to have his skin used to make drums so that he might continue to lead his troops even after death!

In the following years, Hussite armies led by Prokop the Bald continued to prevail, even invading Silesia and Saxony (1425–6) and later Hungary, Silesia, and Saxony again (1428–30). Exploiting war-weariness and divisions between the radicals (Taborites and Orphans) and moderates (Ultraquists and Calixtines), Emperor Sigismund eventually defeated the extremist Hussites at the Battle of Lipany in May 1434. He would finally enter Prague as King of Bohemia two years later. The moderate Hussites survived, however. They were allowed to practise their religion until the outbreak of the Thirty Years' War in 1618, by which time most Czechs had become Protestants.

Achievements

One-eyed at the start, blind at the end, Jan Žižka is responsible for the phenomenal success of Hussite armies, which routed every Papal and Imperial invasion attempt. Under Žižka's ingenious command, the increasingly disciplined and trained Hussites made extensive use of early hand-held firearms, as well as wagon forts which were revolutionary for the time, consistently defeating numerically superior professional forces. The tactic was soon adopted by others: war wagons in the armies of János Hunyadi were used to great effect against the Ottomans in the 1440s. The Muscovites and Cossacks, who called them *'gulyay-gorod'* and later *'tabor'*, were still employing these medieval tanks against the Crimean Tatars as late as the seventeenth century. Žižka has gone down in history as a great military tactician, famous for his radical and decisive leadership, and today he is celebrated as a national hero by the Czechs.

Gentile Bellini, Mehmet II, c.1480, National Gallery, London.
(*The Yorck Project/Wikimedia Commons*)

Chapter 18

SULTAN MEHMET II
'The Grand Turk',
conqueror of Constantinople

On the fifth of the month of April 1453, one hour after daybreak, Sultan Mehmet came before Constantinople with about 160,000 men. On the seventh, he moved with a great part of his forces to within about a quarter of a mile of the walls, and they spread in a line along the whole length of the city walls, which was six miles.

Niccolò Barbaro, *Diary*

Sultan of the Ottoman Empire from 1444 to 1481, at the age of twenty-one Mehmet conquered Constantinople, bringing the Byzantine Empire to an end. He took to the field every year, leading twenty-five campaigns in person. He upgraded the mighty Ottoman war machine, greatly extended the boundaries of the Ottoman possessions in both Anatolia and Europe and sent expeditions as far as northern Italy. Three popes would call for unsuccessful crusades against the 'Grand Turk', Europe's most powerful and most feared ruler.

As a child, Mehmet (1432–81) was educated by the famous scholar Akshamsaddin of Damascus. According to Ottoman historians, the young Prince learned Persian, Arabic, ancient Greek and Italian. He became well versed in engineering, arithmetic, history, astronomy, geography, philosophy and poetry. Akshamsaddin would remain Mehmet's tutor and close advisor until his death in 1459.

At the age of twelve Mehmet II became Sultan for the first time when his father Murad II abdicated. However, he was forced to step down after only two years because of a revolt by the Janissaries (elite household servants of the Sultan) instigated by Grand Vizier Çandarlı Halil Pasha. Humiliated, Mehmet took up residence at Manisa (Magnesia), the usual training ground for crown princes. In 1458 and 1450 he gained practical military experience when he joined his father's campaigns against Skanderberg's Albania.

Mehmet ascended the throne once more in February 1451 after his father's death. Soon after, the young man had to deal with Karamanid attacks on Ottoman lands in Eastern Anatolia. Emperor Konstantinos XI of Byzantium, attempting to use this situation to the Empire's advantage, decided to attempt a risky strategy of disruption. A great-grandson of Ottoman Sultan Bayezid I, Orhan Çelebi, was living as a hostage in Constantinople. Other than Mehmet II, Orhan was the only claimant to the throne. Murad II had previously agreed to pay annually 300,000 *aspers* (small silver coins) for Orhan to be kept at Constantinople, but Konstantinos XI now asked for a doubling of Orhan's allowance; otherwise he would release him, potentially sparking an Ottoman civil war.

The threat of releasing Orhan gave Mehmet the pretext to concentrate all his energy and resources on seizing Constantinople, his *Kızıl Elma* ('Red Apple'). The young ruler, who needed to establish his authority and prove himself in the eyes of senior Ottoman officers, realized that his ultimate goal must be the conquest of the 'Queen of Cities'. In the middle of the fifteenth century the Byzantine capital's population had declined to some 50,000 inhabitants. An isolated bastion, Constantinople had been surrounded by Ottoman-held territories for decades.

Mehmet began his preparations at once by assembling a formidable fighting force on land and sea. In April 1452 he inaugurated the construction of the castle of Rumeli Hisarı on the Bosphorus to prevent any maritime relief reaching the Byzantine capital. In order to face the anticipated onslaught, Konstantinos XI enacted the formal union of the Roman Catholic and Orthodox churches in a ceremony held at Santa Sophia on 12 December. But it was too little, too late, and very few reinforcements would come from the West. At the time, France and England were still fighting their Hundred Years' War. Constantine's city was about to be hit by a storm.

> I can cast a cannon of bronze with the capacity of the stone you want. I have examined the walls of the city in great detail. I can shatter to dust not only these walls with the stones from my gun, but the very walls of Babylon itself!
>
> Orban of Brasov to Mehmet II

By the time he began to besiege Constantinople, Mehmet possessed huge cannons to batter the walls and doors of the city, much to the consternation of its defenders. While Mehmet still preferred to field colossal guns as a matter of prestige, in Western Europe, Burgundy and France in particular, the tendency had been to develop smaller, much more mobile ordnance to be used both for siege warfare and on the battlefield. To shatter the English at the Battle of Castillon in July 1453, the brothers Jean and Gaspard Bureau had used no fewer than 300 fast, mobile field guns on wheeled carriages, in conjunction with lighter firearms.

Just a few days earlier, 2,200km from the last battlefield of the Hundred Years War, Hungarian engineer Orban of Brasov had delivered to the Sultan the largest cannon ever built. Named the 'Basilica', the nearly 9-metre-long, 32-ton, 750mm bronze bombard cast in two parts and assembled after transportation, required seventy oxen to drag it. It was a formidable psychological weapon: hurling a 600kg granite cannonball, with an effective range of 1.5km, the Basilica could punch holes through the city walls. However, it took forever to cool it, repair any cracks and reload, so its rate of fire was no more than eight shots a day. In January, at Adrianople, Orban's bombard had passed its primary trials in the presence of the awestruck Sultan. On 2 April 1453, Mehmet's army of 80,000 men, assisted by large numbers of irregulars, the usual medieval trebuchets (compound machines throwing projectiles), and the most powerful heavy siege artillery ever assembled (fourteen very large guns and fifty-six smaller ones) laid siege to the city. The Basilica was placed among the four batteries in front of Mehmet's pavilion on Maltepe Hill, facing the St Romanus Gate. Reportedly, its tremendous blast caused women to faint inside the city. The Basilica now displayed its gargantuan firepower:

> And the stone, borne with enormous force and velocity, hit the wall, which it immediately shook and knocked down, and was itself broken into many fragments and scattered, hurling the pieces everywhere and killing those who happened to be nearby. Sometimes it demolished a whole section, and sometimes a half-section, and sometimes a larger or smaller section of a tower or turret or battlement, there was no part of the wall strong enough

or resistant enough or thick enough to be able to withstand it, or to wholly resist such force and such a blow of the stone cannonball.

Michael Kritovoulos of Imbros, History of Mehmet II

However, Orban's supergun eventually blew up at the end of the siege, killing its crew and its inventor. On the sea side, the entrance to the Golden Horn was barred by the giant 750-metre long iron Great Chain, resting on eight pyramidal floating pontoons. Each massive iron link weighted more than half a ton. After two failed attempts at breaking the Chain, to bypass this marvel of early medieval engineering Mehmet's pioneers built a sliding rail of greased wooden logs across the steep hill of Galata, behind the semi-autonomous neutral Genoese colony of Pera. On 22 April seventy-two light galleys were hauled overland, then slid downhill and launched into the harbour, behind the Chain. All the while, the *mehter* (Ottoman military bands) were playing their war tunes. Not only did this manoeuvre utterly demoralize the defenders, it enabled Amza Bey's sailors and marines to attack the city's low sea walls on the Golden Horn, while their main force assaulted the land walls. After fifty-five days of a siege punctuated by continuous night and day bombardment, Mehmet launched the final all-out attack:

> One hour before daybreak, the Sultan had his great cannon fired, and the shot landed in the repairs which we had made and knocked them down to the ground. We Christians now were very frightened, and the Emperor had the tocsin sounded through the whole city. The defenders all began to take flight, and all abandoned their posts at once and went rushing towards the harbour in the hope of escaping in the ships and the galleys. Then the second wave followed the first and went rushing about the city, and anyone they found they put to the scimitar, women and men, old and young, of any condition. This butchery lasted from sunrise, when the Turks entered the city, until midday, and anyone whom they found was put to the scimitar in their rage. Those of our merchants who escaped hid themselves in underground places, and when the first mad slaughter was over, they were found by the Turks and were all taken and sold as slaves. The blood flowed in the city like rainwater in the gutters after a sudden storm, and the corpses of Turks and Christians were thrown into the Dardanelles, where they floated out to sea like melons along a canal.

Niccolò Barbaro, Diary

Despite a desperate defence of the crumbling Theodosian walls by the massively outnumbered Christian forces (c.7,000 men, including Venetian and Genoese volunteers), the decrepit city of Constantinople fell on 29 May 1453, spelling the end of the Byzantine Empire. The Genoese *Podestà* (chief magistrate) Angelo Giovanni Lomellino then surrendered Pera on 1 June. As for the martyred city of Constantine, after three days of chaotic plunder, slaughter and rape, with most of the survivors taken captive, the young Sultan finally called for a return to discipline:

> On the third day after the fall of our city, the Sultan celebrated his victory with a great, joyful triumph. He issued a proclamation: the citizens of all ages who had managed to escape detection were to leave their hiding places throughout the city and come out into the open, as they were to remain free. He further declared the restoration of houses and property to those who had abandoned our city before the siege, if they returned home, they would be treated according to their rank and religion, as if nothing had changed.
>
> George Sphrantzes. *The Fall of the Byzantine Empire*

Since he had overcome the Queen of Cities, Mehmet took the title of *Fatih* ('Conqueror'). As a revenge for past humiliations, one of Mehmet's first acts after his victory was to have Grand Vizier Çandarlı Halil Pasha executed. He then assumed the title of *Kayser-i-Rum* (Caesar of Rome) and moved his capital from Edirne to Constantinople. In 1459 he ordered the construction of the *Yeni Saray* (New Palace, now known as Topkapı) on the Seraglio Point. This palace would serve as the main residence of the sultans, their harems and the court until the mid-nineteenth century. The *Divan* (Imperial Council) met in a dedicated building in the second courtyard. According to the humanist Georgios of Trebizond, as master of Constantinople, Mehmet could even claim overlordship over the entire world.

> There has never been a man nor will there ever be one to whom God has granted a greater opportunity for sole dominion of the world than He has granted to Your Mightiness. Neither Cyrus nor Alexander nor Caesar nor Constantine was given as much. I arrived at this opinion immediately after I heard how God bestowed Constantinople on you.
>
> Georgios of Trebizond's letter to Mehmet II, 1466

Mehmet's army was the most disciplined and feared military force of its time, due to its high level of organization, logistical capability and possession of elite troops in the form of the Janissary corps and the *Sipahi* household cavalry. The 6,000 crack *yeniçeri* ('new soldiers') at the time of the siege were the most important of the troops grouped under the title *kapıkulu* (elite household servants of the Sultan). Neither freemen nor ordinary slaves, they were considered an elite section of both the Ottoman military and of society. The infamous *devşirme* system required a yearly quota of non-Muslim boys from the ages of six to fourteen to be forcibly enrolled, converted, indoctrinated and schooled. The musket first appeared in the Ottoman Empire during Mehmet's rule, and the Janissaries, originally trained as highly-skilled archers, would make the new firearm their weapon of choice. At the peak of its power in the early eighteenth century the Ottoman army would field as many as 80,000 Janissaries against the Holy Roman Empire.

The arrival of gunpowder weapons resulted in the construction by the Ottomans of bastionned geometric strongholds situated at strategic sites. The fortress of *Rumeli Hisarı* (Castle of Rumelia), built by Mehmet in 1451–2 on the European shore of the Bosphorus in only twenty weeks, was equipped with heavy artillery. It stood just 850m from its counterpart *Anadolu Hisarı* (Castle of Anatolia), erected in 1394 by Mehmet's great-grandfather Bayezid I at the narrowest part of the strait.

When a Venetian ship attempted to sail past the castles she was sunk, her captured crew of thirty were beheaded and her captain Antonio Rizzo impaled on a stake. After the conquest of the Byzantine capital, Mehmet had new foundries built in Istanbul, the most famous of which is the *Tophane-i Amire* which, under the leadership of Münir Ali, continued to produce impressive bronze siege cannons with a gauge of 600–1,000mm.

Mehmet had the Imperial shipyard constructed across the Golden Horn, and the new ships built there would soon contest Venetian and Genoese naval supremacy. Constantinople became the main base of the nascent Ottoman Navy:

> It is believed that he [Mehmet] is preparing a new fleet from scratch, since he intends to make all the islands of the Aegean archipelago subject to him or to destroy them if he can. For his heart swells with pride and he boasts that he has equalled or surpassed the deeds of Alexander of Macedon. He also threatens that he will attempt to do what Alexander never did, push into Italy and the regions of the West with his arms and might and see whether fortune shall favour him there as it has throughout the East. This is why all Christian kings and princes should turn their minds to some sort of alliance.
>
> Letter of the Order of St John to the Margrave of
> Brandenburg, Rhodes, 30 June 1453

Following the conquest of the Byzantine capital, the over-ambitious Mehmet went on to invade Serbia, the Duchy of Athens (1458), the Despotate of Morea (1460), the Empire of Trebizond (1461), Bosnia, Albania, Rumelia, Wallachia, Moldavia and Crimea, as well as wresting eastern regions of Anatolia from the Karaminds. Most of the Balkans were incorporated into the Ottoman state, and Ottoman raids in the 1460s and 1470s reached as far as Styria and Carinthia, the Habsburgs' southern Austrian lands. Concurrently, he waged war against Venice for sixteen years, seizing most of the Serenissima's possessions in the Aegean

(1463–79). Mehmet's capture of the powerful Venetian fortress of Negroponte (1470) spread further terror, as it signalled to the West that Turkish naval power was now able to threaten the entire eastern Mediterranean and beyond.

After taking Negroponte, Mehmet rode eastward across Anatolia to face the Serenissima's allies in the Orient, the Aq Qoyunlu's Turkoman Confederation. The great Battle of Otluk Beli in August 1473 provided a show of overwhelming Ottoman firepower against Emir Uzun Hassan's forces equipped with bows and arrows. The Turkomans' cavalry, no match for the Ottoman cannons and handguns, was decimated, suffering 30,000 to 50,000 casualties in the space of just a few hours. Uzun Hasan himself barely escaped from the carnage. Ottoman supremacy over Anatolia would not be contested again.

With the capture of Constantinople, the conquest of the last Genoese cities in the Crimea (1475) and the vassalization of the Tatars, the control of territories on all its shores turned the Black Sea into an Ottoman lake. It also signalled the end of Genoese commercial dominance. The Sultan then entitled himself 'Ruler of the Two Lands [Rumelia and Anatolia] and the Two Seas [the Aegean and Black Seas]'. Only Belgrade (1456), Scutari (1474) and Rhodes (1480) were able to repel Mehmet's assaults.

The end of Mehmet's reign marked the beginning of Ottoman maritime expansion in the western Mediterranean. After Venice was forced to hand over Scutari in 1479, Albania came under Ottoman control. From there, in the summer of 1480, while Grand Admiral Mesih Pasha was leading 70,000 men in an ultimately failed attempt to conquer Rhodes, Gedik Ahmed Pasha's force of 20,000 had more success with the capture of Otranto in Italy. According to historical accounts, 12,000 inhabitants were killed and a further 5,000 enslaved, including victims from the territories of the Salentine peninsula around the city. Otranto was to be used as an Ottoman bridgehead for further operations against Naples, and possibly Rome itself. For a time, Pope Sixtus IV considered evacuating the Eternal City to take refuge in Avignon.

> If so many conquests have been achieved during the thirty years of his reign . . . just imagine what will be accomplished in the next thirty! It is not at all difficult for God to unite the whole world under a single person!
> Grand Vizier Karamanî Mehmed Pasha, 1480

In the fall of 1479, a year after the conclusion of the Ottoman-Venetian War, at the request of the Sultan himself, the celebrated painter Gentile Bellini was sent by Venice to Constantinople. Acting as a kind of 'cultural ambassador' of the Serenissima, Bellini painted Mehmet's portrait. The naturalistic painting, dated November 1480, is in the National Gallery in London. Bellini included three golden crowns on each upper side of the picture, probably symbolizing the Sultan's dominion over Anatolia, Constantinople and the European Byzantine territories, and Trebizond.

While on his way to the East for a new military campaign, Mehmet, already in poor health, died on 4 May 1481, possibly poisoned at the instigation of the Halvetî dervishes and his eldest son Bayezıd II. He was buried in a tomb within the Fatih mosque complex in Constantinople.

Achievements

Mehmet II attained mythical status during his own lifetime. An outstanding strategist and resourceful tactician, while still a young man he planned the operations of the Siege of Constantinople, mobilizing all his forces and coming up with innovative tactics. He foresaw the need for a new navy and more efficient artillery. His reign saw the Sublime State turn into a formidable Empire. Leading twenty-five military campaigns in person, and overwhelming most of his adversaries, Mehmet expanded the Ottoman domains from 880,000 to over 2.2 million square kilometres with control over the 'Two Lands' and the 'Two Seas' and ruling a population of c.10 million. Under Mehmet II the Empire developed into the dominant force in Eastern Europe and the Middle East. The conqueror of Constantinople gave the Ottoman Empire its heartland, and institutions that would remain unchanged until the nineteenth century. He is an icon to Turks today and a hero throughout the wider Muslim world. Every year, Istanbul commemorates its conquest by Mehmet II with celebrations and festivities.

Andrea Mantegna, Matthias Corvinus, fifteenth century, Budapesti Történeti Múzeum, Budapest. (*Wikimedia Commons*)

Chapter 19

MATTHIAS CORVINUS
The warrior 'Raven King'

Hand-gunners are set behind the shield-bearers at the start of the battle, before the armies engage, in defence. Nearly all of the infantry and the arquebusiers are surrounded by armoured soldiers and shield-bearers, as if they were standing behind a bastion. The large shields set together in a circle present the appearance of a fort and are similar to a wall in whose defence the infantry and all those among them fight almost as if from behind bastion walls or ramparts and at the given moment break out from it.

Matthias Corvinus, letter to Gabriele Rangoni,
Bishop of Eger, 1481

One of the most exceptional monarchs of the fifteenth century, King Matthias Hunyadi, nicknamed 'Corvinus' (from the raven on his family's coat of arms), the 'Warrior King' and 'the Just', elevated Hungary to a great European political and military power. His famed Black Army was one of the most efficient of its time. Enjoying full support from the Papacy, Hungary under his rule constituted an effective, though short-lived, 'Bulwark of Christendom', acting as a major deterrent to Ottoman expansion westward for more than half a century. Matthias, also on a collision course with the Holy Roman Empire, triumphed against Friedrich III, when the humiliated and destitute Emperor was forced out of his own capital, in which Matthias settled. Also famous for his patronage of literature, sciences and art, by the end of his rule Matthias Corvinus was the undisputed master of a Renaissance Empire, home to a multi-ethnic population estimated at five million.

Matthias Hunyadi (1440–90) was the son of the 'White Knight' János Hunyadi, the national hero of Transylvania, who had waged war against Mehmet II, fending off the Sultan's attacks on Belgrade (1456). On the death of his father in January 1458, a faction of the Hungarian Diet elected Matthias as King, believing the 15-year-old nobleman could be easily controlled. The youthful King would have to face two powerful and expanding neighbouring states: the Holy Roman Empire and the Ottoman Turks.

Opponents of Matthias had proclaimed as King the Holy Roman Emperor Friedrich III, who held the crown of St Stephen. Matthias, soon to be known as 'The Just', proved an able military leader and crushed the rebel magnates, capturing many of his rivals. Vlad III 'Dracul', the prince of Wallachia, who petitioned for his intervention against the Ottomans, was also detained. After the intervention of Pope Pius II, Emperor Friedrich returned the crown of St Stephen in return for the colossal sum of 80,000 gold florins. On 24 March 1464 Matthias could finally be crowned King of Hungary at Székesfehérvár.

Under his rule, Buda would become a centre of Renaissance art and scholarship. After his marriage to Beatrice of Naples in 1476, the scholars, artists, poets and architects who flocked to his court glorified his patronage. Inside the rebuilt and enlarged palace of Buda, two rooms with golden ceilings housed the *Bibliotheca Corviniana*, one of the largest libraries in Europe at the time. The Hungarian capital became the first centre of the Renaissance north of the Alps.

Matthias raised a powerful army of mercenaries known as the 'Black Army' or 'Black Legion' (*Fekete Sereg)*, probably because of the darkened steel armour they wore. The colour was the result of a chemical process to prevent it from rusting that turned the steel a shade of dark blue. In later centuries this process would be known as 'blueing'. The Black Army became the core of the forces the King could mobilize in case of war and it was led by capable commanders like the Voivode (governor) of Transylvania István Báthory, Lovro of Ilok, Pál Kinizsi, František

Hag and Blaž the Magyar. The ranks were filled by Serbs, Bohemians, Moravians, Germans, Poles and later Hungarians. Alongside the Ottoman corps of Janissaries, and the *Compagnies d'Ordonnance* created by Charles VII of France in 1445, it was one of the few European standing armies of the fifteenth century. From 1466 Matthias used this army almost exclusively in his campaigns on Hungary's western frontier. Unruly and often rebellious like most medieval mercenary troops, the Black Army would be disbanded in 1492 after Matthias' death.

The size of the mercenary contingents varied depending on the objective and the available funds. For his 1470 campaign, Matthias set out from Trenčín to Moravia with a newly-manned Black Army of 12,000 men, but he fought his 1474 Silesian campaign with only 10,000. The forces Matthias raised for the 1479 campaign were assembled from various regions: 16,000 soldiers came from Bohemia, Silesia and Moravia, 14,000 from Hungary, and another 16,000 were Transylvanian Székely cavalrymen armed with lances and bows. The artillery train was manned by eighty master gunners with an assortment of weapons transported on wagons: 6,000 handguns of various types, thirty 32-pounder heavy guns, eight siege bombards and ten mortars. One third of these forces fought against the Turks at the Battle of Breadfield that year.

According to Antonio Bonfini, Corvinus' court historian, at the review held at Wiener Neustadt in 1487 the Black Army at its peak, operating against Emperor Friedrich III, consisted of 28,000 men: 20,000 horsemen, heavy and light cavalry (hussars), and 8,000 infantry, 2,000 of them using hand-guns. Crossbowmen and hand-gunners would either be protected by a large pavise (shield) held by a servant, or take cover in the wagons used as mobile fortresses on the battlefield – the *wagenburg*, the famed Hussite tactic perfected by Jan Žižka.

Firearms, first introduced to Hungary c.1380, were still dangerously unreliable at the end of the fifteenth century. They often proved more hazardous to their daredevil servants than to the targets they were aimed at. During the siege of Głogów in September 1488, a huge Hungarian bombard exploded after firing fourteen rounds. Soon afterwards, another lighter weapon blew up also. From the numerous recovered fragments of broken barrels in and around castles besieged by Matthias' armies, catastrophic explosions seem to have been a rather common occurrence.

Mining and smelting was concentrated in the north of the kingdom, and towns provided the armies with food, artillery and gunpowder. Under the protection of St Barbara, the guilds of Prague or the Saxon towns of Transylvania, including Brașov (Kronstadt), were among the prominent manufacturers of guns and ammunition. Gun makers also dealt with maintenance and repairs.

The Bohemian King Jiří left a garrison of several thousand men strong in the town of Třebíč lead by his son Viktorin and Václav Vlček from Čenov. The Hungarian king Matthias besieged them. Duke Viktorin sallied out of the city to fight the Hungarian king but the duke could not resist him and, together with his force, had to retreat. The Hungarian king stormed the city and burned it down.

> Václav Vlček of Čenov, 1468, in Šimek Frantińek,
> *Staré letopisy české*, 1937

Completely neglecting the southern frontier during his reign, Matthias was mostly concerned with western expansion at the expense of the Czechs and Austrians. At the time of his Bohemian Crusade, also called the Second Hussite War (1468–9), he led campaigns against his former ally, the excommunicated Hussite King Jiří of Poděbrad. To check the Hussite style of warfare, with which Matthias and his generals were particularly familiar (even his father János had adopted their tactics), the Hungarians deployed field artillery and cavalry to disrupt their adversaries, denying them the time needed to take up their defensive positions. Matthias was eventually crowned King of Bohemia at Olomouc on 3 May 1469. He then waged war against King of Poland Kazimierz IV, ordering raids into Opavian Silesia and Lesser Poland in 1474:

> Meanwhile King Matthias, seeking an excuse to provoke the king of Poland, has equipped the Duke of Zagan to fight Wielkopolska. The Duke assembles 4,000 Silesian troops, many of whom are just tanners, tailors, cobblers, and other artisans, and with them some of Wrocław's guns, made available on Matthias' orders, fords the Oder below Scinawa. Then, since King Casimir as is his habit, is prevaricating and doing nothing, for he considers the matter unimportant, the Duke is able to use the bridge as well as the ford, and so penetrates into Wschowa where he attacks the town.
>
> *Annals of Jan Długosz*

In retaliation, at the end of the year, Jagiellonian (Polish royal) armies invaded Silesia and besieged Breslau, until a peace agreement was reached between the belligerents in December.

From the time of his election in August 1471, Pope Sixtus IV had favoured renewed crusading efforts to unite Christendom and contain the Turks. Although Matthias responded that he was more than willing to fight the Infidels, he claimed that Friedrich III's impending threat to his western frontier prevented him from turning his arms against Mehmet II. Thus, in sharp contrast to his father, Matthias never led a large-scale crusade against the Ottomans, although he garnered the Papal subsidies intended to finance the campaigns against the 'most infidel Turks' (250,000 ducats were expected in 1480, a crucial year when the Papacy called for another crusade). A truce signed in 1468 with Mehmet II was renewed in 1470 and again two years later.

Then, in April 1473, in a controversial move, Matthias dispatched two envoys to Constantinople offering military alliance and assistance in exchange for

Serbia and Bosnia being transferred to Hungarian suzerainty. These negotiations eventually failed, however. At the time, Mehmet's Grand Vizier and Admiral were engaged in a bitter war against Venetian maritime power in southern Greece and the Aegean, while the Sultan marched in person against the Serenissima's allies in the Orient, the Aq Qoyunlu's Turkoman Confederation on the Empire's eastern borders.

Matthias did his best to avoid direct confrontation, which was probably the best posture to adopt against the might of the Ottoman war machine, although his troops met the Turks in several small-scale border skirmishes in Serbia and Transylvania. In July 1476, after Mehmet II's victory at Valea Albă (White Valley) against Prince Ștefan III cel Mare (Stephen the Great), the arrival of a fresh Hungarian army commanded by István Báthory persuaded the Sultan to retreat from Moldavia. For his relatively limited efforts against the Turks, Matthias was then awarded the title of 'Invincible and most Magnificent Defender and Champion of the Catholic faith' by Pope Sixtus IV. The Pontiff was evidently in desperate need of a hero.

The most important encounter took place in October 1479, when an Ottoman-Wallachian raiding party was annihilated at the Battle of Breadfield by István Báthory and Pál Kinizsi. The following year, Matthias instituted two new defensive buffer banats (military frontier territories), Jajce and Srebernik, in reconquered Bosnian territory, and garrisoned their border fortresses. The two parallel lines of castles and fortifications stretching from the Adriatic to the Lower Danube would serve their purpose until Süleyman I the Magnificent's massive invasions of the 1520s.

In open war from 1478 against his arch-enemy Emperor Friedrich III, and in reality dedicating most of his energy to securing the Imperial crown for himself, Matthias finally conquered Vienna on 1 June 1485, after a 4-month siege. Adorned in shining parade armour, he rode into the city on his finest horse. Matthias had, ironically, accused the Emperor of secretly negotiating with the Turks and breaking the peace. In the immediate aftermath of his victory, Matthias moved his court to the newly occupied city, proclaiming himself Duke of Austria (1486–90). Vienna became, for a few years, the capital of the Hungarian kingdom. After Wiener Neustadt also fell to the Hungarian army in 1487, Friedrich was forced to seek refuge in Linz. Meanwhile, Maximilian of Habsburg, Friedrich's son, had inherited the title of King of the Romans.

This almost constant state of warfare on two fronts came at a tremendous cost. The burden of Matthias's splendid court, his mercenary army, river navy, new constructions and artillery mainly fell on the serf households who paid most of the ordinary and extraordinary taxes, amounting to two thirds of annual revenue. The Royal Treasury also collected from the monopolies on salt, mining and minting, and from the towns. The Dubnic Chronicle (written at Varad in 1476) stated that 'widows and orphans' were cursing the King. In 1470 the bishop of Pécs and poet Jannus Pannonius, once the 'pride of the court', in his pamphlet entitled 'Pleading with Mars for Peace', could not find words harsh enough to criticize Matthias' hunger for power in the West. The pacifist Pannonius bestowed on his former patron acerbic epithets such as 'enemy of the peace', 'drunk on human blood', 'author of terror', 'waster of ploughland, destroyer of towns, the world's depopulator, filler of Hell', etc. In October 1471 a plot to overthrow Matthias and replace him with St Kazimierz, son of the Polish King, failed. Matthias' crackdown on the conspirators was merciless.

After his death from natural causes in April 1490, Matthias was laid to rest in the Nagyboldogasszony Basilica of Székesfehérvár, where the Hungarian kings were crowned and buried. By the time the magnates assembled the Diet to elect a successor, four candidates had laid claim to the throne: Matthias' illegitimate son János 'Corvinus', Maximilian of Habsburg, Władysław Jagiellon (who had the support of senior military commanders István Báthory and Pál Kinizsi), and Jan Albrecht. The War of the Hungarian Succession soon broke out, and the disintegration of the kingdom inevitably followed.

Matthias' former enemies would exert posthumous revenge shortly thereafter. Maximilian recruited an army of mercenaries with a loan from the Fuggers of Augsburg, reoccupied all of Austria and Vienna in August 1490, then took Székesfehérvár and ransacked and desecrated the basilica's royal graves on 17 November. In 1543 the Ottomans took the city and also looted the basilica, further desecrating the tombs, before converting it into a mosque. By then, even his 2,000-volume legendary *Bibliotheca Corviniana* had been looted by the Turks when Buda had fallen. Only the legend of the Raven King would live on.

Achievements

The 32-year reign of Matthias Corvinus marked the apex of medieval Hungary's power. He dealt firmly with the noble factions and imposed strong, centralized royal authority. At the time of his death, his realm stretched from the Adriatic to the Black Sea. Matthias' famous Black Army, one of the earliest professional standing armies in medieval Europe, was one of the most powerful forces on the continent. Aware of his limitations, Matthias maintained a largely peaceful *modus vivendi* with the Turks, but his policies slowed down Ottoman expansion to the west. Without a legitimate heir, his conquests fell apart within months of his death, and his famed Black Army was disbanded due to lack of funds. During the centuries of foreign occupation by Ottoman and Habsburg rule his name became a rallying symbol of the once-mighty and independent kingdom. Matthias Corvinus is one of the most renowned figures of Hungarian history, and in Hungarian folk tales he is often depicted travelling through the countryside in disguise, dispensing justice on behalf of the oppressed.

Part III

THE EARLY MODERN ERA

Anonymous painter, Francisco de Almeida, Museu Nacional de Arte Antiga, Lisbon.
(*Wikimedia Commons*)

Chapter 20

DOM FRANCISCO DE ALMEIDA
First Viceroy of the Portuguese Indies

All our strength be at sea, let us stop appropriating the land. The ancient traditions of conquest, the empire over Kings so far away do not suit us. We destroy the new people (Arabs, Afghans, Ethiopians, Turks) and settle among the old and natural ones of these lands and coast: then we will go further ...

Francisco de Almeida's letter to King Manuel I
of Portugal, 1505

Francisco de Almeida was a Portuguese soldier, admiral and explorer, first Viceroy of the Portuguese Indies and founder of the *Estado da Índia*. Under his leadership, the Portuguese set about breaking the monopoly which Mamlûks and Venetians had enjoyed for centuries in trade with Asia. Victorious over a powerful coalition of local rulers allied with the Ottomans and Mamlûks, Almeida established long-lasting Lusitanian naval supremacy in the Arabian Sea. As founder of the Portuguese State of India, he played no small part in the creation of the world's first global empire.

A member of the powerful family of the Counts of Abrantes, Franciso de Almeida (c.1450–1510) began his military career at an early age. In 1476 he took part in the Battle of Toro and he achieved fame during the wars against the Moors and in the Castilian conquest of Granada (1492). In 1505 King Manuel I, establishing the Portuguese *Estado da Índia* (ensemble of Portuguese outposts from the cape of Good Hope to Japan), appointed navigator Tristão da Cunha first Viceroy of the Portuguese Indies for a three-year term, but when da Cunha fell ill, Dom Francisco de Almeida was chosen to replace him.

The Portuguese crown had already sent six armadas to India. Since Vasco da Gama had opened a direct sea route to India in 1498, Almeida's predecessors had forged local alliances and established 'factories' (trading posts) in Cochin, Cannanore and Quilon. Taking advantage of the rivalry between the Maharajah of Cochin and the Zamorin of Calicut, the Portuguese had been welcomed at Cochin, where they were allowed to build Fort Manuel in 1503 and establish the first European settlement in India. The following year, Duarte Pacheco Pereira defended Fort Manuel successfully, repelling the forces of the Zamorin of Calicut.

By early 1505 King Manuel had determined that the Portuguese would no longer undertake the long *Carreira da Índia* (India run) merely to trade for the five 'glorious' spices (black pepper, cinnamon, cloves, mace and nutmeg). During his three-year term, Almeida was expected to considerably expand Portugal's royal monopoly in the East with the establishment of a Christian state under the crown's authority. He was tasked to spread Catholicism, make local alliances and even launch a Holy War to outflank the Ottomans.

On 25 March 1505 Almeida left Lisbon as Captain-Major of the seventh India Armada, an impressive fleet of twelve dark-hulled ocean-going *naus* (carracks) and square-rigged caravels, followed by a second squadron under Manuel Paçanha and a third led by Pêro de Anaia.

Almeida's ships had many distinctive features that gave them an edge over rival navies of the time, in particular their seaworthiness, stability, advanced rigging and the artillery they carried. Portugal had become the world leader in naval ordnance. New Portuguese ship designs incorporated square gun ports, and they mounted long-range falconets, together with a large number of anti-personnel swivel guns. King Manuel's nation was, in fact, leading a naval warfare revolution. Breaking away from medieval tactics and hand-to-hand combat on the decks, Portuguese carracks could keep superior numbers of enemy vessels at bay, sinking them with their firepower alone. One of Almeida's lead ships, the 400-ton *nau Flor do Mar* commanded by João da Nova, had a complement of 500 men and carried no fewer than fifty guns.

After doubling the Cape of Good Hope, Almeida conquered Kilwa, on the present-day Tanzanian coast, where he built Fort Sant' Iago. He then captured and looted Mombasa and seized the port of Sofala, collecting tribute along the way. On 22 October 1505 he landed in India and settled at Cochin. The local Kolathiri Rajah allowed Almeida to build a fort at Cannanore in Kerala, and Gonçalo Gil Barbosa laid its foundation stone. The construction of the wooden Fort Santo Ângelo, protected by palisades, was completed in a matter of days. Its first Captain, Lourenço Britto, was in command of a garrison of 150 Portuguese soldiers. The fort was rebuilt in stone just in time to withstand a brutal siege in 1507 by the allied forces of a new local Rajah and the Zamorin of Calicut.

Almeida focused on western India, in particular the Sultanate of Gujarat, and he had to battle to counter the Mamlûks in the Indian Ocean to ensure Portuguese predominance. In the following months he promoted the first exploration of Ceylon, the Maldives and Madagascar, erecting a series of fortified outposts. A commercial treaty was also concluded with Malacca. During the same period, the eighth India Armada led by Tristão da Cunha and Afonso de Albuquerque conquered Socotra, Ormuz and Muscat in the Persian Gulf, before relieving Lourenço Britto's garrison at Cannanore.

In March 1508 Mamlûk Admiral Amir Husain Al-Kurdi, along with Malik Ayyaz of the Gujarati sultanate, attacked a Portuguese squadron in the harbour of Chaul, resulting in the defeat of the Portuguese and the death of Almeida's only son Lourenço. Concurrently, Afonso de Albuquerque landed in India with the eighth India Armada, carrying written orders to replace Almeida. Instead of complying with the King's decree, Almeida had Albuquerque imprisoned in Fort Santo Ângelo and remained in command.

To avenge his son's death, a grieving Almeida took to the sea with fifteen carracks and caravels, supported by two galleys and one brigantine. He first attacked the seaport of Dabul, laid waste to the city and massacred every living being, not only its population, but also every animal. Then, on 3 February 1509, he annihilated the Mamlûk-Gujarat-Calicut combined fleet in the port of Diu. Almeida's flagship in that battle was the still-in-commission *Flor do Mar*. Superior Portuguese ship design, artillery and masterful tactics ensured a crushing victory; Almeida did not lose a single warship, while all of his adversaries' 200 vessels were sunk or captured. The treatment of the Mamlûk prisoners by the Portuguese was beyond brutal: some were hanged, others were burned alive or tied to the mouth of cannons and blown to pieces.

In the aftermath, both the Egyptians and Ottomans would abandon the Indian Ocean to the Portuguese. For *Comandante* Saturnino Monteiro, author of *Batalhas e Combates da Marinha Portuguesa* in eight volumes, the 'glorious' Battle of Diu represented the most important event in the entire history of the Portuguese navy.

With the arrival of Marshal Fernando Coutinho in November 1509, Almeida recognized Albuquerque as his successor and finally set sail for Portugal. On his return trip, in March 1510, Almeida and sixty-four of his men were killed in a battle with Khoïkhoï and Xhosa tribesmen at the mouth of the Salt River (Table Bay). His body was later retrieved by other crewmen and buried in haste on the beach. For contemporary historian Damião de Góis, the Viceroy's tragic fate was a divine punishment for 'Almeida's cruelty when he executed the prisoners captured at the great victory of Diu'.

Achievements

Considered one of Portugal's greatest heroes of the Age of Exploration, Almeida ruthlessly asserted Portuguese supremacy in the Arabian Sea, laying the foundation of the first global Empire. A farsighted colonial administrator, Almeida founded a string of fortified coastal settlements in East Africa, the Persian Gulf and western India in order to control maritime trade. After the Battle of Diu, considered one of the most decisive battles in history, Portuguese monopoly of the lucrative spice trade would not be contested until the arrival of the Dutch East India Company a century later. In November 1510 Albuquerque would seize Goa from the Bijapur Sultanate, and this outpost would become the new capital of the *Estado da Índia*. Goa's territory, the centre of the propagation of Christianity in Asia, would remain in Portuguese hands for four and a half centuries, until its annexation by India in 1961.

El Gran Capitan: Federico de Madrazo, Battle of Cerignola (detail), 1835. Museo del Prado, Madrid. (*Wikimedia Commons*)

Chapter 21

GONZALO FERNANDEZ DE CORDOBA
'The Great Captain'

When Gonzalo Fernández arrived at the camp of King Fernando, everyone had the utmost respect for him, as he had gained the esteem of the soldiers of the various nations assembled there. They considered he was nothing like the other Captains, that he was superior to all of them. Since then, as if they had agreed upon it in common consent, they began to call him the Great Captain.

Jerónimo Zurita, *Historia del rey Don Fernando el Católico*

Gonzalo Fernández de Córdoba was a Castilian Captain-General who fought the Portuguese, the Moors, the French and the Turks in the War of the Castilian

Succession (1475–9) and took part in the Conquest of Granada (1491–2), the Italian Wars (1494–1504) and the Second Ottoman-Venetian War (1500). He is remembered as the founder and reformer of the Spanish army of the Catholic Kings, creating the *coronelía*, precursor of the *tercio*, the elite military unit that would dominate the battlefields of Europe for the next 150 years.

Gonzalo Fernández (1453–1515) was the second son of Pedro Fernández de Córdoba, Count of Aguilar. He and his older brother Alfonso grew up in Córdoba. At the age of thirteen Gonzalo was sent to the court of Castile to serve as a page, first to Prince Alfonso, later in the retinue of Princess Isabel, the future queen. Gonzalo and Isabel being of about the same age, this was the start of a lifelong close relationship.

Gonzalo began his military career in the War of the Castilian Succession, a conflict between Isabel (Henrique IV's half-sister) and Juana (daughter of the deceased King). Gonzalo experienced his baptism of fire at the Battle of Albuera against the Portuguese (1479). Afterwards, he participated in the conquest of the Nasrid emirate of Granada (1482–91), taking part in the sieges of Tájara, Íllora, Montefrío and Loja. Gonzalo was well versed in Arabic and, trusting in his diplomatic abilities, Isabel appointed him one of the two commissioners for the negotiation of the Treaty of Granada with Emir Abu Abdallah Muhammad XII.

During the First Italian War, in which the Habsburgs and Valois battled for control of the Italian peninsula, Gonzalo was dispatched to Naples by King Fernando II of Aragon with 6,000 men to support Ferrante II's attempt to reconquer his capital from the French. The Battle of Seminara, fought in Calabria in June 1495, ended in a crushing French victory over the Spaniards and Neapolitans. Charles VIII's army had used a combination of *gendarmes* (heavy cavalry) and Swiss pikemen (and halberdiers) who made short work of the lighter Italian and Spanish units. Later on, faced by the threat of a large coalition, Charles marched back to France almost unopposed (July 1495). He would not be the last French monarch to attempt to enforce his claim to the Kingdom of Naples, the so-called Angevin inheritance.

> A Macedonian Phalanx was nothing else than a battalion of Swiss is today, who have all their strength and power in their pikes.
>
> Niccolò Machiavelli, *The Art of War*.

Seminara would be Gonzalo Fernández's only defeat, and a severe wake-up call. Realizing that he could not match the sheer shock power of the *gendarmes* and Swiss pikes, Fernández de Córdoba came up with a revolutionary pike-and-shot military unit in which pikemen and swordsmen were combined with long-range weapons, acting in support of one another. Early on, companies of mixed units inspired by ancient Roman military formations were called *coronelías*, each led by a *coronel* (colonel). A *coronelía* was composed of twelve companies, with ten companies made up of 200 pikemen, 100 arquebusiers (soldiers using heavy matchlock hand-guns) and crossbowmen, and 200 *rodeleros*, and two companies of pikemen only. *Rodeleros* (swordsmen with bucklers) were employed to disrupt enemy pike formations. Over time, the *coronelía* evolved to include these three types of unit in roughly equal numbers.

> The *tercios*, although they were instituted in imitation of the legions, can only be compared to them in few things, they have only half the number of men, they formerly amounted to three thousand soldiers, for which they were called *tercios* and not legions.
>
> Sancho de Londoño, *El Discurso Sobre La Forma De Reduzir La Disciplina Militar*, 1589

The early sixteenth-century *tercio* ('third') was composed of one-third pikemen, one-third swordsmen and one-third arquebusiers and crossbowmen, all acting in strict cooperation. Their size varied over time, with a typical *tercio* consisting of around 3,000 men organized into companies of 300. The fifty-nine rows of pikemen occupied a large hollow square of about 55m by 60m, the arquebusiers being stationed at each corner. Pikemen protected the arquebusiers from enemy cavalry, while the gunners aimed at opposing pike squares. By the 1530s the *rodeleros* and crossbowmen would become obsolete; as gunpowder weapons evolved rapidly and became more reliable, their number steadily increased.

In battle, the *tercios* were manoeuvrable and capable of extensive skirmishing. They were an impressive sight, like a hedgehog fortress on the move. As standing units, they developed outstanding cohesion and very strong *esprit de corps*. Their flag, emblem and pride of each company, was held at the centre of the block of pikemen. Strict discipline was enforced, and training by companies was introduced. With the *tercios*, the Spanish armies would become the dominant force in Europe and beyond for a century and a half, defeating their enemies in countless battles and sieges (mostly in Flanders and Italy) and acquiring a reputation for invincibility that would last until the end of the Thirty Years' War.

In October 1500, appointed Captain-General of the Spanish armies fighting alongside the Venetians during the Second Ottoman-Venetian War, Fernández de Córdoba directed the siege of the Castle of San Giorgio in Cephalonia that ended with the capture of the island's chief fortress. His force included Spaniards, Venetians, Italians and even Frenchmen. This achievement was the only Christian victory in an otherwise disastrous war against the Turks.

In the meantime, Louis XII, Charles VIII's successor, had reiterated the French claim to Naples. Based upon the agreement of the secret Treaty of Granada (signed in November 1500), Charles XII partitioned the kingdom with King Fernando of Aragon. Both armies seized Naples in August 1501, ousting the titular King Federico I, only to then quarrel over the spoils.

Fernández de Córdoba, by then already called 'El Gran Capitan' by the Spanish soldiers, had increased the number of arquebusiers among his troops. He knew how to fight the enemy on his chosen ground, on his own terms. At the Battle of Cerignola (April 1503), during the Third Italian War, his artillery and gunmen, protected behind a ditch and strong field fortifications, repelled the fierce assaults of the Swiss pikemen and the French heavy cavalry. The engagement ended in a bloodbath, with 3,000 enemy dead. Cerignola was the first battle won almost solely by volleys from gunpowder weapons.

> Would to heaven that this accursed engine had never been invented. I had not then received those wounds which I now languish under, neither had so many valiant men been slain for the most part by pitiful fellows, and the greatest cowards; poltroons that had not dared to look those men in the face at hand, which at distance they lay dead with their confounded bullets.
>
> Blaise de Montluc, *Commentaires*

At Garigliano on 28 December 1503, the Great Captain, along with seasoned *condottieri* Bartolomeo d'Alviano and Prospero Colonna, crossed the river on a pontoon bridge during the night, taking by surprise King Louis XII's troops and his Italian allies under Ludovico II of Saluzzo. The French and their allies retreated to Gaeta, and Louis XII was forced to abandon Naples. In January 1504 the French king withdrew to Lombardy, putting an end to the Third Italian War. The Spanish victory at Garigliano inaugurated the Habsburg domination of southern Italy that would last until 1735. In 1505 the Treaty of Blois established that the title King of Naples would be reserved for Fernando's grandson, the future Holy Roman Emperor Carlos V.

Once the Third Italian War was over, Fernández de Córdoba was appointed Vice-King of Naples. After the death of his patron Queen Isabel of Castile, the Great Captain fell from grace. Accused of venality and the desire to seize the crown of Naples for himself, King Fernando of Aragon recalled the famed soldier to Spain. The Great Captain retired to Loja, where he would fill the position of governor of the city, under constant royal scrutiny, until his death from malaria a decade later.

Achievements

With Isabel la Católica's support, Fernández de Córdoba became a general of international prestige, known as the 'Great Captain'. A pioneer of early modern warfare, he undertook the complete reorganization of the Spanish military, transforming it from a medieval to a modern form, relying increasingly on pike-and-shot formations and using state-of-the-art gunpowder weapons. Owing to the Great Captain's tactical brilliance, in the space of only two decades the nature of warfare had evolved dramatically and Spain had become dominant in Europe. The sixteenth century would mark the peak of Spanish power, the so-called Golden Age, when Spain rose to become one of the most powerful nations in the world.

Hernán Cortés, a copy by José Salomé Pina, Museo del Prado, Madrid. (*Wikimedia Commons*)

Chapter 22

HERNÁN CORTÉS
Conqueror of the Aztec Empire

As soon as the brigantines were completed and launched into the canal, I reviewed our whole force, and enjoined much on the Spaniards to observe and comply with the orders I should give them in conducting the war with as great strictness as possible; and that they should take fresh courage and spirits, since they saw that Our Lord was leading us to victory over our enemies; and that they should consider especially, that we were fighting in behalf and for the spread of our faith, and to reduce to your Majesty's service the lands and provinces that had rebelled; a consideration which should inspire them with courage and zeal to conquer or die.

Hernán Cortés, third letter to Holy Roman Emperor and
King of Spain Carlos V, 15 May 1522

In April 1519, Conquistador Hernán Cortés, accompanied by a few hundred Spanish soldiers, landed on the shores of Mexico in search of fame and fortune. Although he had no prior military experience, Cortés would now face Aztec King Moctezuma II, a living god who ruled over the 21 million subjects of Mesoamerica's most powerful empire. Through shrewdness, boldness, duplicity, diplomacy and superior military technology, in less than two years of some of the most ruthless campaigns ever waged in history, Cortés managed to subdue the Aztecs, devastate their capital Tenochtitlan and bring large parts of Central America completely under Spanish control. To this day he remains a highly controversial figure in the Spanish conquest of the Americas.

Hernán Cortés Monroy Pizarro Altamirano (1485–1547) was born in Medellín, in the province of Estremadura. He came from a lesser *hidalgo* (gentry) family. According to Francisco López de Gómara, at the age of fourteen Cortés was sent to the University of Salamanca, where he studied for two years. In 1504 the 19-year-old Hernán travelled to the island of Hispaniola in search of opportunity. He served there as a colonial notary until 1511, when he joined Diego Velázquez de Cuéllar in the conquest of Cuba, an expedition which encountered little resistance from the natives.

> Gold is a metal most excellent above all others and of gold treasures are formed, and he who has it makes and accomplishes whatever he wishes in the world and finally uses it to send souls into Paradise.
> Cristoforo Colombo's letter from Jamaica to the Catholic
> Monarchs of Spain, 7 July 1503

Following Juan de Grijalva's 1518 expedition to Yucatán, Diego Velázquez authorized Hernán Cortés to conduct an exploratory expedition of Mexico. However, mistrusting Cortés, Velázquez soon cancelled the expedition. Disobeying direct orders, Cortés departed for Mexico anyway. From then on, sponsored by landowners including his own father, Cortés would claim to act on behalf of King Carlos I of Spain (V of the Holy Roman Empire), but in reality he answered to no one.

Cortés sailed from Santiago de Cuba in February 1519 with eleven ships, 508 soldiers, about 100 sailors, thirty-two crossbowmen, thirteen arquebusiers, six light cannons and sixteen horses. Along the way, he recruited the shipwrecked Jerónimo de Aguilar as well as an enslaved Nahua woman known as 'La Malinche', or 'Doña Marina' after her conversion to Roman Catholicism. These two proved a critical asset since they spoke indigenous languages, enabling the would-be conquistador to communicate with the people he was about to encounter:

> As Doña Marina proved herself such an excellent woman and good interpreter throughout the wars in New Spain, Tlaxcala and Mexico, Cortés always took

her with him. Doña Marina knew the language of Coatzacoalcos, which is that common to Mexico, and she knew the language of Tabasco, as did also Jerónimo de Aguilar, who spoke the language of Yucatan and Tabasco, which is one and the same. So that these two could understand one another clearly, and Aguilar translated into Castilian for Cortés.

Bernal Díaz del Castillo, *Historia verdadera de la conquista de la Nueva España*

Cortés made allies of some of the indigenous peoples he came across, and hostile groups like the Tlaxcalan and Cholulan warriors were crushed in a display of overwhelming Spanish military superiority. Before marching on Tenochtitlan, the Aztec capital and home to ruler Moctezuma II, in one of the boldest moves in military history Cortés burned all his ships to prevent his men from turning back.

Tenochtitlan, which the Spaniards called the 'City of Dreams', was built on Lake Texcoco. With a population of 150,000, it was one of the largest cities in the world at the time. After being received with great honour and given quarters in the palace of former emperor Axayacatl, Cortés proceeded to take Moctezuma hostage, while his men plundered the city searching frantically for gold and jewels.

Forced to leave Tenochtitlan briefly, to face Pánfilo de Narváez who had landed in Mexico with an army to arrest him, Cortés placed his lieutenant Pedro de Alvarado in charge. During Cortés' absence, relations between the Spaniards and their hosts deteriorated rapidly, the ruthless Alvarado leading a massacre of unarmed Aztec elites attending a religious festival in the Great Temple. Upon Cortés' return, Moctezuma was killed by his own people as the outraged Aztecs rose up on a massive scale. Cortés and his men had to fight their way out of Tenochtitlan, suffering heavy losses during the episode known as the *Noche Triste* (30 June/1 July 1520).

It is incalculable how much our people suffered, as well Spaniards as our Indian allies of Tascaltecal, nearly all of whom perished, together with many native Spaniards and horses, besides the loss of all the gold, jewels, cotton cloth, and many other things we had brought away, including the artillery.

Hernán Cortés, second letter to Holy Roman Emperor and King of Spain Carlos V, 30 October 1520

The surviving Castilians and their Tlaxcalan allies promptly rallied behind Cortés, inflicting a crushing defeat on 20,000 Aztecs at the Battle of Otumba a week later. Aztec numerical superiority and weapons proved no match for Spanish tactics, armour, firearms and cavalry. Cortés led the mounted charge himself with five other captains, aiming directly at the leader of the Aztecs; when the latter was killed, his troops were thrown into total disarray.

Cortés then began the systematic conquest of what would become Mexico. He blockaded and laid siege to Tenochtitlan with an army of 100,000, only 1 per cent of whom were Spaniards, the others being indigenous allies. The Spaniards wore down the defenders of Tenochtitlan in a protracted, ferocious siege, taking control of the lake with thirteen armed sloops and cutting off the capital from the outside world. Spanish military operations were aided by an outbreak of smallpox which weakened and killed many of the city's defenders, including their new emperor, Cuitláhuac. Finally, in August 1521, some 60,000 starving Aztecs surrendered. The Aztec capital lay in ruins, and what was left was razed to the ground. By then, most of the tribes of Central Mexico had submitted to Spanish rule.

> The inhabitants fought with resolute valour. On both sides of the street there was an immense multitude who attacked us in a courageous manner from the terraces: but when a number of our archers and musketeers arrived, and we discharged the two cannons so as to rake the street, we did them great mischief.
>
> Hernán Cortés, third letter to Holy Roman Emperor and
> King of Spain Carlos V, 15 May 1522

Despite his stunning successes, Cortés faced plenty of challenges to his authority from rivals both in Spain and in the Americas. In the following years he sent exploratory expeditions to Honduras and to the Baja California peninsula. Under mounting pressure from his adversaries, in 1528 he travelled back to Spain, to be received at Toledo by Carlos V, who honoured him by creating him Marqués del Valle de Oaxaca but did not appoint him as Governor of New Spain.

In 1541 Cortés finally retired to Spain, arriving in time to participate in the expedition against Algiers at the end of the year. The last years of his life were spent seeking recognition for his achievements. Immensely wealthy but disaffected, his past glory obscured by the treasures being brought back at that time from Peru, Cortés died in Castile in December 1547 at the age of sixty-two.

> Cortés killed and Cortés won, he conquered – as they say – many nations, he plundered and stacked gold in Spain and became the Marquis del Valle. His only concern was to find means to achieve his goals: to tyrannize and plunder all, great or small, right or wrong.
>
> De Las Casas, *History of the Indies*, Book III

Achievements

An authentic military genius, the ambitious and ruthless Cortés was quick to grasp how to use the weaknesses of the Mexica Alliance to subjugate Moctezuma II and his forces, resulting in the Mesoamerican empire's sudden and total collapse. Cortés skilfully forged alliances with tributaries who resented the Mexicas' domination. Close cooperation with the Tlaxcalans above all proved to be one of the keys to ultimate Spanish victory. A once mighty civilization, the Aztec Empire was left in ruins after the Spaniards razed Tenochtitlan and waves of infectious disease had taken their toll. An estimated 200,000 Aztecs had perished. Modern-day Mexico City is built upon the ruins of ancient temples and valuable Aztec sites. A 2kg gold bar, lost by the conquistadors during the *Noche Triste*, was uncovered in 1981 on the site of a previous canal. The unfolding of the conquest of Mexico remains one of the most fascinating and tragic events in human history. With it, the Spaniards gained access to the Pacific Ocean, finally achieving Columbus' original goal of reaching Asia by sailing west. Out of the immense new territories under its control the Spanish crown would extort fabulous wealth, providing the funding for its Golden Century. As for Cortés, by virtue of his contribution to the enlargement of the Spanish empire, he is still regarded as one of Spain's greatest historical figures.

Haydar Reis Nigari, Barbarossa, Topkapı Sarayı, Istanbul. (*Wikimedia Commons*)

Chapter 23

KHAYR AL-DIN 'BARBAROSSA'
Pirate-Admiral of the Ottoman navy

The supremacy of Turkey at sea dates from Kheir-ed-Din's first winter in the dockyards of Constantinople. Before he took charge the Turks, apart from a few corsairs, knew nothing of the seaman's art. Inspiring his men with his own marvellous energy, he laid out sixty-one galleys during the winter, and was able to take to the sea with a fleet of eighty-four vessels in the spring.

Jean de Chesneau, *Le Voyage de Monsieur d'Aramon dans le Levant,* 1547

In the sixteenth century, at the time of the epic struggle between the Ottoman Empire and the Habsburg monarchy for the control of the Mediterranean, four brothers-turned-pirates seized Algiers. Their leadership and the promise of infinite booty attracted a multitude of zealous *ghāzī* (Muslim warrior against Infidels) adventurers willing to serve under their command. From their North African base of operations, Mediterranean shipping routes from Spain to Egypt, and every harbour and island in between, came under the constant threat of their destructive raids. The last surviving brother, nicknamed Barbarossa from the ginger colour of his hair and beard, came to Süleyman the Magnificent's attention. Honoured with lands, titles and the overall command of the Ottoman fleet, he rose to become an infamous scourge of Christendom whose name spelled terror in the hearts of many peoples. With a fleet built under his own supervision Barbarossa defeated the Holy League sent against him at Preveza, establishing the joint dominance of the Ottomans and the Barbary pirates.

Khizr (1475-1546) was the son of Yakup Ağa, a *sipahi* (fief-holding provincial heavy cavalry officer) who had settled in Mytilene after the conquest of the island by the Ottomans (1462), and a Greek widow. Four sons were born of that union: Ishak, Oruç, Khizr and Ilyas. Early on, the brothers turned pirate, targeting Christian shipping. Ilyas was killed in a naval encounter with the Knights of St John, while Oruç was captured and remained three years a prisoner.

In 1504 Oruç and Khizr struck an important deal with the Sultan of the Hafsid dynasty, Abu Abdallah Muhammad IV al-Mutawakkil. The Sultan allowed the brothers to operate from the port of La Goulette (Tunis) in exchange for a third of all loot they captured. The brothers later established their base of operation at Djerba, before moving to Algiers (1516), where they established their own rule.

In the earlier years the brothers employed only free Turks or Muslims as oarsmen on their galleys and galliots (small fast galleys), in contrast to the Christian policy of using slaves. Everyone onboard was a fighting man eager for battle and spoils. But this changed as the number of their captives increased. They raided countless islands and coastal settlements from Spain to the Aegean, their fame and success attracting an increasing number of *ghāzī* warriors to their ranks.

In the Mediterranean, and especially in the Aegean archipelago, where the summers generally see calm seas and the shore is never too distant, galleys retained an essential role. Speed and manoeuvrability were their main assets. Their average speed was 3 knots, the maximum speed being 12 knots under sail and 6 knots under oars. Light Barbary galleys carried one or two masts with a lateen sail. With three culverins (long-barrelled cannons) mounted in the prow, they could even tackle heavy carracks, while staying outside their enemy's angle of fire. Their guns could be used as long-range weapons, and to attack an enemy vessel, they would close in, fire all their guns, then attempt to grapple and board. This is what took place at the Battle of Preveza when, after the wind suddenly dropped, the becalmed Christian galleons became easy prey to Barbarossa's mobile galleys.

Galleys were slim, low-lying warships: the rowers sat only one metre above the waterline. North African light galleys typically used only eighteen to twenty-four benches. Galliots were even smaller vessels, with just sixteen benches. Life was beyond miserable for the enslaved oarsmen, prisoners captured at sea or during coastal raids. Three men lived chained in a tight compartment, pulling a single oar. Space was cramped, the labour back-breaking. Few survived more than a couple of years of the harsh treatment, dehumanization, hunger, thirst, sunburn, exposure and injuries. They risked being wounded or killed when their galley went into action, or drowned in a storm. As they were shackled to their bench they could neither take shelter, nor escape if their ship went down.

In 1518 Oruç and Ishak were killed fighting the Spaniards and the local sultan's troops at the Battle of Tlemcen. Khizr, the last surviving son, who temporarily withdrew from Algiers, would become know as 'Khayr al-Dīn' (Defender of the Faith), the most famous Barbary pirate of all time. With Spain's military presence increasing on the coast of North Africa, Barbarossa sent an envoy to Ottoman Sultan Selim the Grim. In 1519, in exchange for his allegiance, he was granted the title of *beylerbey* ('commander of commanders'), becoming the Sultan's vassal and chief corsair.

In 1529 Barbarossa finally secured Algiers and drove the Spanish garrison from the Peñón fort. Barbarossa and his successors would use Algiers as a major base to launch raids from the Barbary Coast. That same year, Sultan Süleyman I laid siege to Vienna with 100,000 men for three weeks, but eventually failed to take the Imperial capital when the rain and cold came early, hampering operations which were already beset by a lack of supplies and shortage of heavy artillery.

In December 1533 Barbarossa was summoned by Süleyman I to Topkapı Palace. As an expert in naval matters, he was appointed Grand Admiral (*Kapudan-i derya*) of the Ottoman fleet by the Sultan, who ordered him to take the Spanish protectorate of Tunis. As one of the Sultan's trusted advisors, member of the Council (*Divan-ı Hümayun*) and in charge of the naval rearmament programme, Barbarossa was also given the government (and revenues) of the *Sanjak* (province) of Rhodes, Negroponte (Euboea) and Chios in the Aegean Sea.

After supervising the building of a new fleet at the Arsenal of Constantinople, during the campaign of 1534, in order to conceal his real main objective, Barbarossa led 100 galleys (manned by Christian slave oarsmen) and 25,000 soldiers to the mouth of the Tiber, causing panic in Rome. He raided Italian settlements and towns with total impunity, looting, killing or enslaving the local populations at Cetraro and San Lucido in Calabria, and Sperlonga and Fondi in Latium, where he attempted to kidnap the young noblewoman Giulia Gonzaga for the Sultan's harem, as she was reputed the most beautiful woman in Italy. From there he quickly headed south under oar and sail, landed near Tunis on 16 August and captured the city.

> After these victories, [Barbarossa] set off towards the west and anchored at the port of Bizerta. From there, he arrived with a propitious wind at the port

of Tunis on the sixth day of the victorious month of Safer in the year 941. Emir Hasan did not comply with the imperial order of the sultan, did not welcome the soldiers of Islam, and escaped the city of Tunis. The people of the city of Tunis and the rulers and notables of the castles and countries of that land obeyed and handed over the keys in a manner worthy of the Sultan. Thus, the lands of Tunis became part of the protected [Ottoman] domains.

Bostan Çelebi, *Süleymannâme*, 1547

From Tunis, Barbarossa threatened the island of Malta, which had been recently granted to the Order of St John. That same year of 1534, Süleyman I captured Tabriz and Baghdad from the Safavids. Ottoman power was at its zenith, and no kingdom or empire seemed able to halt the expansion of the Turks, either on land or at sea. Emperor Carlos V, Don Álvaro de Bazán and Genoese Admiral Andrea Doria at once organized a massive counter-offensive, mobilizing 400 ships carrying 600 guns and 30,000 soldiers and retaking Tunis in June 1535. The giant ironclad Maltese carrack *Sainte-Anne,* together with the Portuguese galleon *São João Baptista*, nicknamed *Botafogo* ('setting it on fire'), delivered a powerful artillery barrage that silenced La Goulette's batteries at the entrance of the bay. The *Botafogo* broke the harbour's chain, Barbarossa's fleet of eighty ships was captured and the hard-pressed King of the Seas fled to Algiers to fight another day.

I undertook this enterprise with the intention of subduing Barbarossa and his corsairs for the harms they have done to our Kingdoms and Christendom, most of which had been carried out on the galleys, galliots and fustas [small light galleys] which had been captured in La Goleta.

Letter of Carlos V to Ambassador Lope de Soria, 29 June 1535

This Christian success provided a strong incentive for the Sublime Porte (the Ottoman government) to enter into a formal if unlikely alliance with France, thus initiating a long period of cooperation between the two states. The Franco-Ottoman alliance was officially established in February 1536 with a series of *ahdname* ('capitulations') granted by Sultan Süleyman the Magnificent to King François I. The two sides, united by their rivalry with the Habsburgs, exchanged intelligence, cooperated militarily and attempted to develop a common strategy. A French contingent participated in Barbarossa's siege of Corfu in 1537 while François I was marching into northern Italy. Barbarossa's new fleet was later invited to winter in Toulon in 1543 and 1544 after the Siege of Nice, conducted jointly with the French Royal troops of François de Bourbon, Comte d'Enghien.

In September 1538, owing to their superior tactical manoeuvring, Barbarossa and his lieutenants Turgut Reys (Dragut) and Sinan Reis defeated the larger joint fleet of the Holy League commanded by Andrea Doria at the Battle of Preveza, near the site of the first-century BC Battle of Actium. After losing galleys and galleons without being able to reply, during the following night Andrea Doria retreated, pressed hard by Barbarossa's fleet. The Battle of Preveza is considered the greatest Turkish naval victory in history, marking the beginning of Ottoman supremacy in the eastern Mediterranean. Barbarossa's prestige was at its highest.

> After this demonstration of fear from the Christians, the Turks became more audacious during the following night. Getting close to our vessels, they started discharging their guns against them, and were fired upon in return, producing so much noise, explosions and smoke, that nothing else than the continuous roar and the screams of the men could be heard. This horrible spectacle seemed like a depiction of Hell.
>
> Giacomo Bosio describing the end of the Battle of Preveza,
> *Dell'istoria della sacra Religione*, volume III

The following year, Barbarossa captured most of the remaining Latin outposts in the Ionian and Aegean Seas and took Castelnuovo in Albania after a protracted siege, slaughtering the survivors of the gallant Spanish garrison. Although Emperor Carlos V attempted to capture Algiers in the fall of 1541, the expedition ended in utter disaster after a gale wreaked havoc on the Spanish ships. The city was defended by Barbarossa's deputy Hadım Hassan Ağa. Many Spaniards who had already landed were left stranded, 150 ships were lost and 18,000 men killed. Carlos V himself barely managed to escape from the tragedy. A few weeks earlier, Süleyman at the head of a large host had defeated another Imperial army in Hungary, after which, using deceit, he captured Buda, Matthias Corvinus' former capital. The Ottoman war machine appeared unstoppable.

In the Mediterranean, islands and entire coastal areas were left depopulated, after the survivors of pillaging raids were carried off to be sold as slaves. To avenge the loss of Tunis, Barbarossa took 6,000 captives in Menorca in September 1535 after hoisting a Spanish flag to gain access to the harbour at night. The whole population of the Venetian islands of Cerigo (Cythera) and Tinos, as well as the 6,000 women and children of Aegina, were also enslaved (1537). In June 1543 he landed at the head of 12,000 men at Reggio in Calabria. The old pirate only spared the city and its inhabitants because of his unanticipated infatuation with the 18-year-old Flavia Gaetani, the governor's daughter, sailing away with her.

The following year, the scourge of the Christians raided Tuscany, then the carnage followed the same pattern at Ischia, Pouzzoles, Procida and Lipari, before he landed again in Calabria. From there, Barbarossa sailed to Istanbul, his ships loaded with tens of thousands of captives destined to be sold in the slave markets of the Ottoman capital. With so many Christian slaves available in Algiers, Smyrna and Istanbul, their value dropped to an all-time low. It was said that one could acquire a slave for the price of an onion!

After a highly successful life of raiding, having accumulated a fortune and faithfully served Süleyman I, the formidable ruler of Algiers retired, spending his last months dictating his memoirs. In 1546 Barbarossa died peacefully in his seaside palace at Constantinople. His tomb, built by Sinan the Grand Architect, stands in the centre of Beşiktaş, on the European shore of the Bosphorus. Bala Hatun, one of his wives, was entombed at his side. The Grand Admiral's epitaph reads:

> This is the tomb of the Conqueror of Algiers and Tunis, the fervent soldier of God, the veteran Captain Khayr al-Dīn, may God rest his soul.

Achievements

By the time he retired in 1545, Barbarossa's campaigns had consolidated an Ottoman supremacy over the eastern Mediterranean which would last until the Battle of Lepanto in 1571. Under Süleyman I the Ottoman Empire reached the zenith of its political and military power. Ruthless raiders and expert seamen, perfectly acquainted with the sea, its winds and shorelines, Khayr al-Dīn and his brothers terrorized the Mediterranean for decades, enslaving populations by the hundreds of thousands. No Christian ship, harbour or coastal area was safe during their reign of plunder and bloodshed. They were the first *beylerbeys* of Algiers, the fortified city that became the chief seat of the Barbary pirates, a threat to European shipping that lasted until the nineteenth century. The 'King of the Seas' Khayr al-Dīn Barbarossa is considered a national hero in Turkey, and is one of the greatest military leaders in the history of the Ottoman Empire.

Marcus Gheeraerts the Younger, Francis Drake, 1591, National Maritime Museum, Greenwich, London. (*Wikimedia Commons*)

Chapter 24

FRANCIS DRAKE
Elizabeth I's most famous privateer

Although he had not been brought up a soldier by profession, his Queen gave him appointments as Commander-in-Chief of her forces, and employed him in positions of trust and honour. In his profession as a seaman he was one of the most outstanding mariners the world had ever seen: in sailing around it, only Magellan preceded him.

Francisco Caro de Torres, *Relacion de los servicios de Don Alonso de Sotomayor*, 1620

Francis Drake was the most daring and successful of the English 'sea dogs' who raided the West Indies and the Spanish Main. He was also an explorer who led the second naval expedition to circumnavigate the world, returning home with Spanish treasures. In the middle of the sixteenth century England was a relatively impoverished country compared to the vast Spanish Empire, but '*El Draque*' proved to be a thorn in the side of the Spaniards for years. The corsair was elevated to the status of national hero by heading off the Spanish Armada; Drake's successes brought him immense wealth and fame; and his attacks on Spanish ports and shipping lanes transformed his private war into an epic struggle between Protestant England and Catholic Spain.

Francis Drake (1540–96) was one of the twelve sons of a Protestant pastor from Devon. At sea from the age of just thirteen with his second cousin John Hawkins, Drake began as a cabin boy on the first English slaving voyages from Africa to the New World. It was during another voyage with family members in 1568 that Drake first came up against the Spanish, at San Juan de Ulua, Mexico, where a surprise attack nearly cost Hawkins and Drake their lives. From this incident Drake acquired a deep hatred of the Spaniards and their religion.

> If there be cause, we will be devils rather than men.
> Francis Drake to the Spaniards, 1571

By 1572, with the two ships *Swan* and *Pascha* manned by seventy young sailors, he was carrying out raids on the New World's Spanish towns. Since the conquest of Mexico by Cortés and the Inca Empire by the conquistador's second cousin Pizarro, the Spanish Main had been famed for its phenomenal wealth in precious metals. Earl J. Hamilton has estimated that Spain imported 181 tons of gold and 16,000 tons of silver from the mines of Peru, New Granada and New Spain between 1521 and 1660. The Spanish crown retained a fifth ('*quint*') of the value of all bullion. Since the 1530s, countless adventurers had been drawn to the New World, lured by fantastical tales of the mythical *El Dorado*.

At first, Drake's enterprise encountered severe setbacks. In July 1572 he tried to capture Nombre de Dios by surprise but was repelled, losing his two young brothers John and Joseph, together with a third of his crew, to Spanish action and yellow fever. In April 1573 Drake received critical intelligence from *Cimarrones* (escaped slaves) and forged an alliance with them. This improved his odds dramatically. Guided through the jungle by the *Cimarrones*, Drake's thirty-one remaining companions, joined by seventy French Huguenots led by famous cartographer-explorer Guillaume Le Testu, ambushed a mule-train travelling on the trans-isthmic *Camino Real* road from Old Panama to Nombre de Dios (in other words, from the Pacific to the Caribbean). The buccaneers were able to eliminate the forty-five armed guards and capture 190 mules, and although they were not able to take the silver, they carried away some 100,000 pesos in gold.

> There was a certaine English man name Francis Drake . . . he came to the sound
> of Dariene, and hauing conference with certaine Negros which were fled from

their masters of Panama, and Nombre de Dios, the Negros did tell him, that certaine Mules came laden with gold and siluer from Panama to Nombre de Dios, who in companie of these Negros went thereupon on land, and stayed in the way where the treasure should come with a hundred shot, and so tooke two companies of mules, which came onely with their driuers mistrusting nothing.

Lopez de Vaz in Richard Hakluyt's
The Principal Navigations, 1589

Between 1577 and 1580 Drake sailed the world on the 80-ton *Pelican*, a race-built galleon. He raided Spanish treasure ships and claimed land for the Queen of England along the way. He attacked ships in the Cape Verde Islands, sailed down the coast of South America, passed through the Strait of Magellan amid storms, then headed north into the Pacific Ocean, where raids were carried out against Spanish colonial settlements such as Valparaiso. More treasure ships were captured, but the voyage's richest prize was taken off the coast of Peru, the *Nuestra Senora de la Concepćion* literally laden with gold and silver. All of Drake's discoveries above latitude 48° contained in his journal were suppressed by Queen Elizabeth I and kept secret.

The *Pelican*, renamed the *Golden Hind*, crossed the Pacific in sixty-eight days. Drake spent some time in the Indonesian archipelago establishing commercial contacts, then crossed the Indian Ocean, rounded the Cape of Good Hope and finally headed for home. In all, he had raided six coastal settlements and captured thirteen ships, returning in triumph to Plymouth in September 1580. Although there were was no official public celebration, Queen Elizabeth I was delighted to learn that her half-share of the loot surpassed the rest of the crown's income for that entire year!

Seven months later, on 4 April 1581, Drake was duly knighted on board the *Golden Hind* by French diplomat Monsieur de Marchaumont in the Queen's presence, thereby rewarding the national hero's magnificent feat of navigation. Public knowledge of the circumnavigation would only become available to a wider public years later, the first published narrative by Hakluyt dating from 1589. This 'secret' voyage had, however, triggered the curiosity of statesmen, scholars and scientists, including Geert de Kremer, the greatest cartographer of the era, better known as Mercator.

Your letter afforded me great pleasure because of the dispatch about the new English voyage, on which you had previously sent me a report. I am persuaded that there can be no reason for so carefully concealing the course followed during this voyage, nor for putting out differing accounts of the route taken and the areas visited, other than that they must have found very wealthy regions never yet discovered by Europeans, not even by those who have sailed the Ocean on the Indies voyages. That huge treasure in silver and precious stones which they pretend they secured through plunder is, in any case, an argument for me to suspect this. This voyage was reported to me in confidence, so keep secret the fact that you know anything about it.

Gerard Mercator to Abraham Ortelius,

12 December 1580

The damage Drake had done to Spanish interests was significant, and it greatly affected their prestige. When King Felipe II complained about the acts of piracy and the depredations committed by Drake and her other 'sea dogs', Elizabeth claimed she had no knowledge of their actions. To the Spanish Ambassador, Don Bernardino de Mendoza, she observed of Drake: 'The gentleman careth not if I disavow him.' In 1585 the Queen sent Drake back to the New World, raiding to divert King Felipe's attentions from his war against the Dutch rebels (the Eighty Years' War). This time, he led twenty-five ships against the Spanish settlements in the Caribbean. First, he sacked the ports of Santo Domingo and Cartagena. Then, in June 1586, his men sacked and burned the town of St Augustine, leaving nothing but ruins behind them:

> On the 6th instant Francis Drake arrived at this port with forty-two sail, twenty-three being large vessels and nineteen pinnaces, frigates and shallops. At dawn on the 7th he landed 500 men and with seven large pinnaces sought me forthwith in the fort. With 80 men I had in the fort I resisted him until nearly midday. In view of my resistance he sent to the ships which lay outside the bar for reinforcements, and in nine vessels landed some 2,000 men and planted four pieces of artillery among certain sand dunes near the fort, with which he began to batter it. I retired as best I could, to protect my women and children (more than 200 persons). Having occupied the fort, the enemy took and sacked the town and burned the church with its images and crosses, and cut down the fruit trees, which were numerous and good. He burned the fort and carried off the artillery and munitions and food supplies. We are all left with the clothes we stood in, and in the open country with a little munition which was hidden. We are without food of any sort except six hogsheads of flour which will last twenty days at half a pound per head.
>
> Pedro Menéndez Marqués to the President of the House of
>
> Trade, San Agustin, June 17, 1586

On 19 April 1587 Sir Francis Drake entered the harbour of Cadiz and led a 'preemptive' strike on the Spanish fleet, burning thirty-seven ships and their supplies and causing the planned Spanish attack on England to be postponed for over a year. Drake referred to this raid as 'Singeing the King of Spain's beard'. He returned to England, serving as Vice-Admiral of the English fleet under Lord Howard of Effingham when it fought off the Spanish 'Armada Invincible' (1588). His attacks on Spanish shipping and settlements had been one of the contributing factors to Felipe deciding to launch his invasion of England. The Duke of Medina Sidonia's fleet of 130 ships was supposed to link up with the Duke of Parma Alessandro Farnese's 16,000 men in Zeeland and provide support for their crossing of the Channel to invade England.

Drake and Howard prepared eight fireships to send into the Spanish fleet at Calais to break their formation and to force them out to sea. The next day (6 August 1588), Drake participated in the Battle of Gravelines where, owing to superior numbers, greater manoeuvrability and the longer range of their culverins, the English galleons succeded in provoking the Spanish while staying out of range. Amid the exchange of cannon fire, according to Martin Frobisher, Drake was more interested in gaining booty than actually fighting. During the pursuit, in true privateering fashion, he broke formation in order to board and capture a struggling Spanish ship, the *Nuestra Señora del Rosario*, putting the English squadron at risk by doing so. Strong currents and southerly winds then scattered the Spanish Armada, forcing their heavy galleons into the North Sea. Elizabethan England had been saved from invasion.

On fridaye last, upon good consideracion we lefte the army of Spagne so farre to the northewardes, as they could neither recover England nor Scotland. And within three daies after we were entertayned with a great storme, considering the tyme of the yere, the which storme, in many of our judgmentes hath not a litle annoyedd the enemies army. If the wind hinder it not, I think they are forced to Denmark, & that for diverce causes. Certain it is that manie of their people were sick and not a fewe killed, there shippes, sailes ropes & mastes needeth great reperations for that they had all felt of your Majestie's force.

> Sir Francis Drake to Queen Elizabeth, 8 August 1588

The following year, the English 'Counter-Armada', led by Drake as Admiral and Sir John Norreys, failed to drive home the advantage England had won by the scattering of the Spanish Armada. In May 1589 the mighty fleet of 150 English and Dutch warships, transporting 25,000 soldiers, attempted to secure the surrender of the port city of La Coruña, only protected by its antiquated thirteenth-century walls.

When Juan Pacheco de Toledo, Marquis de Cerralbo, Governor and Captain General of Galicia, refused to surrender, the English landed some guns and thousands of soldiers. The Marquis de Cerralbo assembled 1,500 men (militia, soldiers, sailors and civilians) and managed to hold the city for two weeks, before the English re-embarked and sailed away, having only taken the lower suburbs, losing 1,300 men in the process (another 1,000 had deserted). By July 1589 the expeditionary force was back in English harbours, having lost a third of its ships and 15,000 men. Arguably, the campaign was an even greater disaster than the Spanish had suffered in the loss of their Armada a year earlier. This resounding Spanish victory marked a revival of Felipe II's naval power through the next decade.

Drake's last voyage, organized with John Hawkins, was another fiasco. In 1595 he failed to conquer the port of Las Palmas, and following a disastrous campaign against Don Alonso de Sotomayor on the Spanish Main, he failed to take San Juan de Puerto Rico. Hawkins died in November 1595. After burying two of his brothers on an island in Panama, Drake also passed away, probably from dysentery, on 27 January 1596. Clad in full battle armour, his body was allegedly buried at sea, two nautical miles off Portobello's cove, in a lead-lined casket that no one has been able to locate to this day. When word of his death reached Europe, Spain was relieved, but all England mourned her hero.

Two years later (1598), while visiting London, German lawyer Paul Hentzner was appreciative of Drake's deeds and reputation:

> The English are good sailors and better pirates, cunning, treacherous, and thievish . . . Upon taking the air down the [Thames] river, the first thing that struck us was the ship of that noble pirate, Sir Francis Drake, in which he is said to have surrounded this globe of earth.
>
> Paul Hentzner, in Sir Robert Naunton's *Travels in England*,
> 1892

For nearly a century the *Golden Hind* remained in an earth-filled dry dock at Deptford as a tourist attraction, but her hull was neglected and allowed to rot. The remains of the second ship to circumnavigate the world were then buried *in situ* and forgotten.

Achievements

Sir Francis Drake was an outstanding seaman, an audacious and charismatic privateer who became a legendary figure of the Tudor period. His almost 3-year long circumnavigation, still shrouded in mystery, was harrowing, skilful, wittily recorded and, most of all, lucky. 'A man of great practise and rare resolution' according to navigator John Davis, Drake inspired great national pride. As he made England realize her potential at sea, the whole nation was emboldened to stand up to mighty Spain. Towards the end of his life, luck, or divine favour, finally abandoned the English adventurer. His last fateful expeditions against La Coruña and the Spanish Main were nothing short of disastrous, and Drake lost his life in the latter. Nevertheless, the era of Drake and Hawkins marked the emergence of England as a major maritime nation, with her navy and shipbuilding capacity increasing rapidly, and the defeat of the Spanish Armada established the Virgin Queen's reputation as a tenacious and capable monarch. During this 'Golden Age', Elizabeth's sea captains brought wealth and heralded English expansion overseas, laying the foundation of a global empire that would last three centuries.

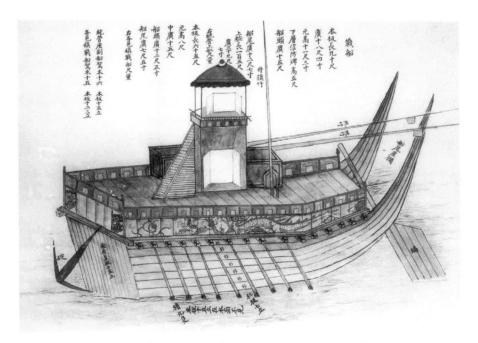

A panokseon warship. (*Korea Naval Academy Museum*)

Chapter 25

ADMIRAL YI SUN-SIN
The legendary saviour of Chosŏn Korea

Calling my Staff Officers and all ships' Captains, I gave the following instruction: 'According to the principles of strategy, he who seeks his death shall live, he who seeks his life shall die. If one defender stands on watch at a strong gateway he may drive terror deep into the heart of the enemy coming by the ten thousand. You Captains are expected to strictly obey my orders. If you do not, even the least error shall not be pardoned, but shall be severely punished by Martial Law.

Admiral Yi Sun-sin, *War Diary,* on the eve of the Battle of
Myeongnyang

Yi Sun-sin is the most revered admiral in Korean history, and rightfully so. Despite not being versed in naval matters, during the Chosŏn Dynasty this provincial naval commander rose to save Korea by defending his homeland against the Japanese invasion in the conflict known as the Imjin War. Although Korean forces lost most of their land battles, Yi won every one of his twenty-six naval engagements in the Yellow and the Southern Seas against the Japanese, even when vastly outnumbered, and without losing a single ship in action. Yi's extraordinary victories foiled the Japanese invasion plans and ensured Chosŏn Korea's survival.

> I will build a fast ship and tell Korea that they should come to Japan to greet the Emperor. If no one comes from Korea [to greet the Emperor,] I will inform them that I will conquer them next year. I shall take control over China during our lifetime. If [Korea or China] look down on me, it will be difficult work.
>
> Toyotomi Hideyoshi to his first wife Kitanomandokoro,
> Higo, 1587

The brutal Imjin War was triggered by Japanese Regent Toyotomi Hideyoshi's limitless ambition to conquer nothing less than all of China, a feat which would be achieved by marching through Korea, a tributary state of the Ming dynasty. Understandably, King Sŏnjo of Chosŏn, as a loyal vassal of the Wanli Emperor, refused to allow the Japanese to pass through his country in order to invade the 'Celestial Empire'. The over-confident Hideyoshi never attempted to dissimulate his intentions:

> My object is to enter China, to spread the customs of our country to the four hundred and more provinces of that nation, and to establish there the government of our imperial city even unto all the ages.
>
> Toyotomi Hideyoshi to Korean envoys, 1589, in Yu
> Sŏngnyong, *The Book of Corrections*

On 13 April 1592 Hideyoshi started a large-scale Asian war by unleashing a formidable force of 160,000 battle-hardened warriors (a quarter of them arquebusiers using *Tanegashimas*, or matchlock guns), supported by 1,000 ships. The expedition and its logistics having been planned since 1586, it was no wonder that in a matter of only twenty days the Japanese were able to steamroll the Koreans' land forces, conquering all the lands between Busan and Hanseong (Seoul). At this point Hideyoshi expected to bring about a swift and total victory:

> So far, we have occupied many castles in Korea. To the Korean capital, it will take about twenty days from the port we just took over. I have already sent

many soldiers to take over the capital of Korea. So, before soon, we should be able to get the capital. I will get more ships and will send the rest of the soldiers. I shall obtain the capital of China, and send people to welcome you. I will get the capital of Korea for sure, and I myself will be there shortly.

Toyotomi Hideyoshi to his first wife Kitanomandokoro,
Nagoya, 1593

However, the Japanese warlord's expectations were about to be shattered by an authentic naval genius. Yi Sun-sin (1545–98) of the Deoksu Yi clan was a military officer who reached senior rank relatively late in his career. After experiencing success against the Jurchens in 1583, he had been stripped of his rank and for many years remained unemployed by the state, before in early 1591 being appointed Commander of the Left Jeolla Province's Naval District. Realizing that the Japanese were not bluffing, he embarked on local ship-building and naval reforms to meet the impending threat from a unified Japan under Hideyoshi. Concurrently, Yi subjected his men to intensive training that included archery, the use of artillery and the deployment of a wide variety of naval manoeuvres and formations.

The Koreans were outnumbered, but the Wanli Emperor of the Ming dynasty hesitated to send help to Chosŏn while still occupied with quelling a rebellion in Ningxia. However, Yi could count on a secret weapon, the *geobukseon* ('turtle ship'). Following earlier designs, officer Na Dae-yong created a new kind of warship and under Yi's command began constructing them in secret in Jeolla's harbours. The first *geobukseon* was launched on 27 March 1592, two months before the siege of Busan which ended with the scuttling of Admiral Bak Hong's Korean fleet.

Powered by eighty oarsmen, with fifty soldiers on the upper deck, the 35m-long turtle ship had a spiked superstructure, making boarding impossible. Built from sturdy pine and reinforced with heavy timbers, it was armed with twelve guns firing through gunports along each side, effectively keeping the Japanese ships at bay while shattering them with artillery fire. It was also capable of launching a variety of rockets. A good-luck dragon's head protruding from the bow housed a large cannon or ejected sulphur and saltpetre-burning smoke. Fast, extremely well armed, impossible to board, the Japanese had nothing that could match the geobukseon. Yi, now in effect a naval commander, would put them to good use:

Foreseeing the Japanese invasion, I had a turtle ship made with a dragon's head, from whose mouth we could fire cannons, and with iron spikes on its back to pierce the enemy's feet when they tried to board. Because it is in the shape of a turtle, our men can look out from inside, but the enemy cannot look in from outside. It moves so swiftly that it can plunge into the midst of even many hundreds of enemy vessel in any weather to attack them with cannonballs and fire throwers.

Yi Sun-sin, *War Diary*

The backbone of the Chosŏn navy were strong, oar- and sail-propelled 25–30m long vessels called *panokseons*, but Na Dae-yong eventually built six to eight turtle ships which could tip the scales in battle. Used as breakthrough weapons, they would penetrate deep into enemy formations, unleashing a hail of cannonballs in every direction and aimed principally at disabling the Japanese flagship.

Yi Sun-sin's navy also made good use of multiple rocket launchers called *Hwachas*, capable of firing a barrage of up to 100 rocket-propelled fire-arrows or spears in a matter of seconds after a single master fuse was lit. Although the Koreans did not have individual firearms, guns and *Hwachas* had been used onboard Chosŏn warships for two hundred years to repel Wokou pirates. 'Heaven cannons', the heaviest type of ordnance produced in Korea, had a diameter of 140mm and weighed 300kg. Yi's ships normally used lighter guns and mortars mounted on wooden carriages.

Korean ships formed a line or performed elaborate manoeuvres to make the most of their long-distance firepower, rather than using grappling and boarding tactics like the Japanese. At close range, their guns discharged deadly buckshot or canister, and their archers fired arrows. Yi himself would shoot arrows from his command platform in the thick of battle. If boarded, Korean sailors defended the *panokseons'* open upper deck with spears and swords.

In May 1592, at the Battle of Okpo, Yi Sun-sin and Admiral Won Gyun's fleet destroyed twenty-six Japanese transport ships. It was the first naval battle of the Imjin War and Yi's first victory against the Japanese fleet of Tōdō Takatora. A month later, at Sacheon, Yi destroyed Kurushima Michiyuki's fleet using a turtle ship for the first time.

Because our country has long been at peace, our soldiers are weak and fearful and if a sudden crisis should occur, it is doubtful they could withstand the enemy.

Ŏ Hŭimun, *Swaemirok* (A refugee's record), 1591–1601

While Yi had given a stunning demonstration of his skill in naval warfare, Chosŏn Minister of War Sin Rip attempted to halt the Japanese at the Choryeong Pass. Sin Rip's forces, consisting of mounted archers without portable firearms, were ill-prepared to face Konishi Yukinaga's foot soldiers equipped with arquebuses and discharging continuous volleys at them. The face-off ended in carnage: 8,000 Koreans died that day, including Sin Rip, who committed suicide in the wake of his catastrophic failure.

The road to the capital now lay open, and the Chosŏn Gyeongbokgung Palace was soon burned to the ground by the invading forces. King Sŏnjo (1552–1608) fled to Ŭiju, on the banks of the Yalu River at the northern border with Ming China. The entire peninsula was devastated, crops were destroyed, a large portion of the population was displaced and 100,000 artisans were forcibly removed to Japan. In every part of the country wandering refugees suffered from looting, widespread famine and disease. Yi took it on himself to accommodate hundreds of starving refugees at his naval station, providing them with shelter and food. In July Konishi captured Pyongyang after routing an utterly demoralized Chosŏn army.

Under the bright moon in Hansan Island, in deep agony with a sword at my side.

Poem by Yi Sun-sin

Then, when everything seemed lost for Korea, the Battles of Hansan Island and Angolpo in August turned the tide of the war. Using a 'Crane Wing' formation, Yi managed to sink or capture fifty-nine Japanese ships while losing none. In a brilliant nine-week naval campaign consisting of fifteen engagements, Yi, the Admiral of the Jeolla Navy, destroyed the enemy's battle fleets and transports, critically impairing Japanese logistics and their ability to reinforce their land army in Korea. While Yi's navy was blocking supplies, 42,000 Ming troops under General Li Rusong began pushing the Japanese southward, retaking Pyongyang and Hanseong (January–February 1593). The military situation had been stabilized.

In September Yi attacked Busan harbour using a 'Long Snake' formation, destroying 130 Japanese ships without losing one. Hideyoshi's dream of invading China had been wrecked by Yi Sun-sin's masterful and inspirational leadership, and the Japanese were forced to agree to peace negotiations.

Five years later, Hideyoshi attempted a second invasion of Korea. Meanwhile, because of political intrigue, Yi had been arrested by his own sovereign and tortured. Following this ignominious treatment, the King went so far as to demote him to the rank of private soldier, in order to humiliate him further. In August 1597 Tōdō Takatora thoroughly defeated the less experienced Admiral Won Gyun at the Battle of Chilchonryang. The entire 200-ship Chosŏn Navy was destroyed in the seven-day battle. Only Bae Seol's squadron of thirteen warships escaped the disaster, and none of these were turtle ships.

Reinstated in haste by King Sŏnjo, despite being physically broken, the steadfastly loyal Yi had to instil hope and discipline in the remnant of his force to accomplish the impossible. Gathering his last men, Yi famously declared: 'According to the principles of strategy, he who seeks his death shall live, he who seeks his life shall die!' These dauntless words would change the fate of the nation. In a letter to the King, Yi expressed his determination to continue fighting to the very end, still displaying admirable confidence and patriotism:

> Your humble servant still commands no fewer than twelve ships. If I engage the enemy fleet with resolute effort, even now, as I believe, they can be driven back. The total decommissioning of our navy would not only please the enemy, but would open up for him the sea route along the coast of Chungchong Province, enabling him to sail up the Han River itself, which is my heart's greatest fear. Even though our navy is small, I promise you that as long as I live, the enemy cannot despise us.
>
> Yi Sun-sin, *War Diary*

Yi carefully chose where to make his last stand against the Japanese: in the Myeongnyang Straits, between Jindo Island and the mainland, where tidal forces make the current reverse direction every three hours. In the 'Roaring Channel', in October 1597, Yi achieved a staggering victory. Although he was outnumbered ten to one, with his thirteen battered *panokseons* firing roundshot or tightly-packed 2.5cm canister, Yi managed to destroy thirty-one enemy ships while damaging another ninety-one, forcing the Japanese to withdraw. As the current changed direction, the Japanese ships smashed into each other. In 2012, some 8.6cm and 9.8cm stone cannonballs were discovered at the bottom of the straits where the battle had taken place. The calibre indicates that these were fired by Yi's Jeolla navy.

The Battle of Noryang in December 1598 ended the war. A Ming-Chosŏn force of 150 ships, led by Yi Sun-sin and Admiral Chen Lin, destroyed or captured half of the 500 Japanese ships commanded by Shimazu Yoshihiro. Yi, who was wounded during the engagement, died while the battle was still raging, declaring:

> Do not weep, do not announce my death. Keep beating the drum, blow the trumpet, wave the flag for advance. We are still fighting. Finish the enemy to the last one.

Following the death of Toyotomi Hideyoshi in September, Japan was torn by a bloody war of succession. After the Battle of Noryang, the Council of Five Elders led by Tokugawa Ieyasu ordered the last Japanese units under Konishi Yukinaga to evacuate the Korean peninsula. Later, the Tokugawa shogunate would not only prohibit any further military expeditions to the Asian mainland, but also closed Japan to nearly all foreigners for 214 years.

The memory of the legendary Korean admiral lives on at the Hyunchungsa Shrine in Asan. Built in 1606, the shrine is home to two giant swords (197cm long and weighing 5.4kg) forged in 1594 that belonged to Yi, along with other swords offered by the Wanli Emperor, spears, fire-arrows, Yi's *War Diary* and a scale model of one of his iconic turtle ships.

Achievements

Although his bravery and tactical brilliance are little known to the Western world, Yi is remembered as Korea's saintly hero, and is one of the greatest military leaders in history. His heroic deeds, unyielding loyalty and sacrifices on behalf of his nation earned him the posthumous title of 'Lord of Loyalty and Chivalry'. Despite receiving no support from the central government, the campaigns of Yi, who literally ruled the sea, were pivotal in restoring hope and thwarting the Japanese invasion, which had the ultimate aim of conquering not just Korea, but Ming China as well. The Battle of Myeongnyang, fought against overwhelming odds, ended in a remarkable victory unparalleled in the annals of naval warfare. According to Togo Heihachiro, Admiral of the Japanese Imperial fleet during the Russo-Japanese War of 1904–5, Yi Sun-sin simply had no equal, while Admiral George Alexander Ballard compared him favourably to Nelson. Considering his enormous impact on Korean and Asian history, the undefeated Yi is undoubtedly the most underrated naval commander of all time. To the Korean people to this day he is a larger-than-life figure, a role model and their ultimate God of War.

Govardhan, Akbar, c.1630, Metropolitan Museum of Art, New York. (*Wikimedia Commons*)

Chapter 26

AKBAR
The greatest Mughal Emperor

Guns are wonderful locks for protecting the august edifice of the State, and befitting keys for the door of conquest. With the exception of Turkey, there is perhaps no country which in its guns has more means of securing the government than this. His Majesty looks upon the care bestowed on the efficiency of this branch as one of the higher objects of a King, and therefore devotes to it much of his time.

Grand Vizier Abu'l-Fazl, *Akbarnama*

Akbar I was the third and greatest of the Mughal emperors. During his 49-year reign he consolidated and expanded the frontiers of his domain. Through military campaigns and diplomacy he conquered Bihar, the Afghan kingdom of Bengal,

Malwa, Gujarat, Kashmir, Sind, parts of Orissa, and the Deccan Plateau, gradually extending the Empire to include all of the Indian subcontinent, from Afghanistan in the north to the Godavari basin in the south, and ruling over an estimated 115 million subjects, some 20 per cent of the world population at the time.

Abū al-Fatḥ Jalāl al-Dīn Muḥammad Akbar (1542–1605), better known as Akbar ('The Great' in Arabic), was the grandson of Babur 'The Tiger', founder of the Mughal Empire. In 1556, following the accidental death of his father Humāyūn, Akbar ascended the throne at the age of thirteen. At first, his guardian, the trusted regent Bairam Khan, helped the young Emperor expand and consolidate Mughal domains in India, and Akbar assumed full authority four years later. The young dynasty spent his entire youth fighting and hunting, which turned him into a daring and fearless warlord, eager to lead the charge in battle.

His first military campaigns were launched against the Afghans and the neighbouring kingdoms of Malwa and Gondwana, and were also aimed at suppressing the rebellion of his younger brother Mírza Muhammad Hakim, ruler of Kabul (1561–6). During the conquest of Gujarat in 1572, the young Emperor pursued the Timurid Prince Ibráhím Husain Mírza, who was attempting to flee Baroda. At the head of forty of his most trusted companions, Akbar did not wait for reinforcements, deciding instead to cross the Mahi River and attack the enemy camp.

> The Emperor held a council, and Jalal Khan urged that, as their own forces had not come up, and the enemy was in great strength, it was inexpedient to fight by day and they should either wait for reinforcements, or fall upon the enemy by night. But this sensible and prudent counsel did not please the Emperor, who said it was unworthy of brave warriors, and that it was advisable to make a dashing attack at once. 'Let each one of us,' said he, 'single out his adversary and bring him down.' Trusting in Heaven they went on their course, till they came in sight of Sarnal. His Majesty went on a little in advance, to the bank of the Mahindari to arrange his men. He gave orders for them to buckle on their armour, and when he thus prepared for the assault, he had not with him more than forty men.
>
> Abu'l-Fazl, *Akbarnama*

Akbar recklessly forded the river and, surrounded by enemy horsemen, was only saved by the timely intervention of his bodyguards. The conquest of Gujarat extended the Empire's frontiers to the Arabian Sea. The Emperor could now contemplate the ocean for the first time. In 1573, during his siege of Surat, Akbar met a delegation of Portuguese from Goa led by Antonio Cabral. The Mughal Emperor would maintain friendly relationships with the Portuguese of the *Estado da India*. The newly-conquered Province of Gujarat, and Surat its major port, would represent an enormous source of wealth for Akbar. In order to enjoy commercial rights, the Portuguese and Dutch trading companies were compelled to make large tributary payments to the Emperor.

After Gujarat, new military campaigns were launched in the east against Bihar, Bengal and Orissa (1570–85). During the same period Akbar also had to face new revolts instigated by his brother Mírza Muhammad Hakim (1580–1).

Akbar progressively developed and professionalized the formidable Mughal military machine. Since the reign of Babur, the Mughal Sultanate had become, along with the Safavids and the Ottomans, one of the 'Islamic Gunpowder Empires'. With the technical assistance of Ottoman and Portuguese gunsmiths, Akbar's reign saw the introduction of numerous innovations in fortifications and siege warfare, a great variety of guns firing brass round shots or explosive shells, and the widespread use of matchlock muskets by the infantry from the 1570s. At the Battle of Haldighati in June 1576, Mughal infantry armed with matchlock muskets repelled a charge by the Rajput of Mewar's elephants. In general, Mughal victories in set-piece battles were won by a combination of mounted archers and infantry equipped with firearms, supported by field artillery.

During the siege of Chittor (1568), the key to central Rajasthan, Akbar gave a demonstration of his personal marksmanship when he shot down Rajput commander Jaimal Rathore with his favourite musket, known as *Sangram* ('Struggle' in Hindi):

At this time His Majesty perceived that a person clothed in a cuirass known as the thousand nails which is a mark of chieftainship among them, came to the breach and superintended the proceedings. His Majesty took his gun *Sangram*, which is one of the special guns, and aimed it at him. To Shuja'at Khahn and Rajah Bhagwant Das he said that, from the pleasure and lightness of hand such as he experienced when he had hit a beast of prey, he inferred that he had hit the man. And in fact on the morning when the breeze of victory and dominion arose, it was ascertained that the Emperor's musket had reached Jaimal, the governor of the fort, and had at once destroyed both him and the fort.

Abu'l-Fazl, *Akbarnama*

Mughal artillery, from super-heavy siege cannons and mortars to lighter field artillery and rockets in metal casings, was far superior to anything that could be deployed by other regional powers. Those 'weapons of mass destruction' were conceived to instil terror in the ranks of the enemy. At the siege of Ranthambore Fort in 1567–8 Akbar brought to bear giant cannons designed by Persian engineer Sayyed Mír Fathullāh Shīrāzī. One heavy siege mortar used during that siege reportedly fired a 3,000lb projectile! The local Rajah, recognizing the futility of resistance, submitted and bowed to the Mughal Emperor. Akbar himself designed gun carriages and also tested muskets and other types of firearm regularly. Swivel guns were mounted onto carts, others were placed on the back of camels and elephants:

> Some elephants are trained to carry guns on their backs. When the black powder is ignited and the gun is discharged with a thunderous roar, the elephant does not become in the slightest terrified or unmanageable. The King directed that fifty elephants thus trained and armed should bring up the rear of the advancing army.
>
> Antonio Montserrate, *Commentary of Father Monserrate, on his Journey to the Court of Akbar*

Akbar's armed forces, which peaked at c.300,000 men, was reorganized into four branches: navy, cavalry, infantry and artillery. Cavalry, the prominent branch, was mostly made up of mounted archers but also included elephants. Generals were expected to direct battles from the vantage point of a *howdah*. Female elephants towed heavy siege guns and carried the baggage, males were trained to fight in the melee, tearing apart enemy foot soldiers. A corps of 12,000 musketeers served in the Imperial Guard, together with a same number of cavalry. According to the Catalan Antonio Montserrate, for the 1581 campaign against his brother Mírza Hakim, Akbar assembled 50,000 cavalry, 500 war elephants, 28 field guns, and an unnumbered host on foot.

Every officer and military governor was appointed by Akbar's court. With the implementation of the *Mansabdari* system (1571), every official of the state from highest to the lowest was paid by the imperial department of the army. The system of ranking determined their civil and military duties. Officers were graded from commanders of ten men to commanders of 5,000, higher ranks being allotted to the Emperor's own blood relatives and tribesmen with the rank of 25,000.

In his capital city of Agra, Akbar built the powerful 'Red Fort' alongside the Yamuna River. Made of bricks and red sandstone, it took eight years to construct, under the superintendence of Qasim Khan Mir Barr-u-Bahr. The 22m-high inner walls, punctuated at regular intervals by massive bastions, are surrounded by a lower enclosure and a moat. The semi-circular walls encompass a circumference of some 2.5km. The Red Fort, part military fort, part imperial residence, became the repository for all the wealth of one of the most extensive empires of the Early Modern era.

> The king, in his wisdom, understood the spirit of the age, and shaped his plans accordingly.
>
> Abu'l-Fazl, *Akbarnama*

Although he remained illiterate, Akbar established a fairly efficient centralized and unified administration throughout his culturally diverse empire. Military and civil service was open to candidates from all backgrounds. Implementing policies of religious tolerance, the Emperor assumed a near-divine status, proclaiming himself as acting as a universal agent of God. Rajput princes were allowed to keep their ancestral lands providing they acknowledged his supremacy, paid tribute, supplied troops and concluded marriage alliances with the Emperor, measures that helped to secure their lasting loyalty. In any case, to prevent any attempt on his life Akbar was armed at all time and was always accompanied by a sizeable squad of trusted bodyguards.

In spite of his very heterodox attitude towards the religion of Muhammad, Akbar has not yet been assassinated. He has an acute insight, and shows much wise foresight both in avoiding dangers and in seizing favourable opportunities for carrying out his designs. His court is always thronged with multitudes of men of every type, though especially with the nobles, whom he commands to come from their provinces and reside at court for a certain period each year. When he goes outside the palace, he is surrounded and followed by these nobles and a strong body-guard. He is very fond of carrying a European sword and dagger. He is never without arms; and is always surrounded, even within his private apartments, by a body-guard of about twenty men, variously armed. He himself can ride and control elephants, camels, and horses.

Antonio Montserrate, *Commentary of Father Monserrate, on his Journey to the Court of Akbar*

During the last two decades of his reign, Akbar launched campaigns in the north-west. Qandahar was seized from the Persian Safavids, as well as the Kashmir and Kabul. Khandesh and parts of Ahmadnagar were also annexed to the Empire. Akbar's last military campaign was the siege of Asirgarh Fort, the 'Key of the Deccan', which he captured using deception in January 1601.

In October 1605, Akbar died of dysentery at Agra. He was sixty-three. Before expiring, the Emperor appointed his estranged son Salim (later known as Jahangir) as his successor. Akbar was buried outside of Agra at Sikandra. His armour, shield and elegantly decorated helmet are on display at the CSMVS Museum in Mumbai.

Achievements

Although he never learned to read or write, Akbar, a most capable ruler and commander, grasped the importance of diplomacy and the decisive use of military innovations to consolidate and expand his realm. The Mughal Empire tripled in size and wealth, and Akbar came to rule over a significant portion of the world population of that time. Effective administration and applied gunpowder technology served as the pillars of Mughal power, which reached its height under Akbar. His policies provided the Mughals with a firm footing for the next century and a half. Owing to his remarkable achievements, Akbar is regarded as one of history's greatest warrior-kings. In 1984 his monumental Agra Fort was designated a UNESCO World Heritage site. Under Aurangzeb (1658–1707), the Mughal empire would reach the peak of its military and economic power, but also its greatest geographical extent, before entering a phase of instability.

Kanō Tan'yū, Tokugawa Ieyasu (detail), seventeenth century, Osaka Castle keep.
(*Wikimedia Commons*)

Chapter 27

TOKUGAWA IEYASU
Unifier of Japan and founder of the last Shogunate

Evil-doers and bandits were vanquished and the entire realm submitted to
Lord Ieyasu, praising the establishment of peace and extolling his martial
virtue. May this glorious era that he founded continue for ten thousands
upon ten thousands of generations, coeval with Heaven and Earth.

Hayashi Gahō, Tokugawa historian and
rector of Shōhei-kō, 1652

At the end of the sixteenth century, three leading Japanese warlords contributed to
the unification of Honshû and Kyushu under a single feudal military government.
From 1573 Oda Nobunaga showed the way, fighting incessantly to bring down
the powerful *daimyō* (lords). Toyomi Hideyoshi completed the unification, and

Tokugawa Ieyasu, a trusted aide to Hideyoshi, put in place the *bakufu* (shogunate) after his victory at the Battle of Sekigahara in October 1600, ending the chaos and civil wars of the *Sengoku-jidai* or 'Warring States' period. Participating in some ninety battles, Tokugawa Ieyasu, who started as a child hostage for a clan that was almost wiped out, ended as the uncontested *Shōgun* of a re-unified Japanese archipelago.

The feudal military dictatorship known as *bakufu* was instituted by Minamoto no Yoritomo in 1192, with its headquarters at Kyoto, not far from the Imperial residence. In the *shogunate* system the emperor remained the spiritual leader who appointed the *Shōgun*, but it was the latter who wielded real military and political power. As the centuries went by, the *bakufu*'s powers expanded, becoming the effective ruling institution of Japan. The later era of the Ashikaga Shogunate (1338–1573) witnessed the rise of increasingly powerful *daimyō*, regional lords ruling over their domains almost independently of Kyoto. During a century of upheaval, the *bakufu* struggled and failed to bring the warring *daimyō* back under control.

In August 1573 Oda Nobunaga overthrew the fifteenth *Shōgun* Ashikaga Yoshiaki, abolished the Muromachi Shogunate and launched a war of conquest to re-unify a fragmented Japan by force from his base at Azuchi-yama. In 1582 he was at the height of his power, already controlling most of Honshû, when the infamous Honnō-ji temple 'incident' took place. Betrayed by his own retainer Akechi Mitsuhide and surrounded, Nobunaga was forced to commit *seppuku* rather than die in the flames of the temple. Mitsuhide was quickly defeated by Toyotomi Hideyoshi, who regained control of the Oda holdings and extended them. However, even when Hideyoshi came to rule over a mostly unified Japan, he could not become *Shōgun* because he was descended from peasant stock. Two failed invasions of Korea set the process of unification back, and the Japanese islands once again found themselves in turmoil by the end of Hideyoshi's life in 1598.

Shortly before Hideyoshi's death, he entrusted his vassal Ieyasu, a prominent member of the Council of the Five Elders, with the regency, until his 5-year-old son Toyotomi Hideyori came of age. But Ieyasu made short work of the young prince and his faction, and as Ieyasu claimed descent from the powerful Seiwa Genji line of the Japanese Minamoto clan, he could pretend to the *bakufu*.

Tokugawa Ieyasu (1543–1616), the first son of a minor *daimyō*, was born in Mikawa Province. At the age of six he was sent as a hostage, first to the Oda clan in neighbouring Owari Province, and later to the *daimyō* Imagawa Yoshimoto of Suruga and Tōtōmi provinces at Sunpu. Early on, his father was murdered by his own vassals, and the family's land was appropriated by the Imagawa clan.

In 1560, Yoshimoto lost his life fighting Oda Nobunaga at the Battle of Okehazama. Ieyasu, pledging fealty to the new strongman, was able become the *daimyō* of the entire Mikawa province by 1565. He would provide Nobugana with precious support, serving by his side at the Battle of Anegawa in 1570. Ieyasu gradually increased his holdings, conquering Takeda lands upon the death of Takeda Shingen in 1573, and displaying an unwavering loyalty to his lord Nobunaga, to the point of having his own chief consort executed and ordering his eldest son Nobuyasu to commit *seppuku*.

At Nobunaga's sudden death in 1582, Toyotomi Hideyoshi became his successor, being awarded the rank of Grand Chancellor of the State by Emperor Go-Yozei. He and Ieyasu initially fought indirectly against each other, then made peace in 1585, Ieyasu eventually agreeing to become his vassal. After the destruction of the Hōjō clan at Odawara (1590), Hideyoshi offered Ieyasu lordship over eight Kantō provinces. Edo (renamed Tokyo in 1868) became Ieyasu's main base. The Edo castle grounds, extended considerably over the next decades, served as the *Shōgun*'s and his successors' residence. Ieyasu carefully abstained from sending his forces to take part in the invasion of Shikoku and Kyūshū and in the Korean campaigns (1592–8).

Following Hideyoshi's death, administrator Ishida Mitsunari and Councillor Mōri Terumoto formed an alliance against Ieyasu's growing power, garnering a large supporting group of noble loyalists to reassert the Toyotomi clan's authority. At the decisive Battle of Sekigahara on 21 October 1600, a total of 170,000 men fought to determine the future of Japan. Ieyasu sealed victory in only six hours when many Western Army *daimyō* switched sides in the heat of battle. The defeated Mitsunari was later beheaded in Kyoto.

Sekigahara cemented Ieyasu's place as sole ruler of Japan. In the aftermath of battle he redistributed the lands and fiefs of the participants, rewarding those who had fought on his side, punishing and exiling ninety-three *daimyō* who had taken up arms against him. Strategic areas, including Edo and Osaka, remained under direct Tokugawa control or were entrusted to Ieyasu's most trusted allies. On 24 March 1603 Emperor Go-Yozei granted Tokugawa Ieyasu the title of *Sei-i Taishōgun*, making him the de facto leader of Japan.

According to legend, even the ascetic Kaguyō Tōbutsu, founder of the Edo-period Mount Fuji worship, praised the bringer of the Great Peace (*taihei*) and the return of order in Japan in his first sermon:

Ieyasu is winning the land not for himself, but for the sake of all the people. As *Shōgun*, Ieyasu will be the fountainhead of all things.

Gotaigyō no maki, 1620

The Tokugawa Shogunate would face a last military challenge in the person of Toyotomi Hideyori, son and designated heir of Toyotomi Hideyoshi, whom Ieyasu had dispossessed. In 1614 Toyotomi, now a 21-year-old warlord with ample support, was gathering forces of *rōnin* (vagrant samurai without a master) and enemies of the shogunate in his fief of Osaka. The 72-year-old unifier of Japan would besiege the castle of Osaka twice. At the end of the Summer Siege of 1615, Hideyori and his mother committed *seppuku* on 5 June, bringing to an end the final major uprising against Tokugawa rule.

With numerous allies and vassals, Ieyasu controlled thousands of castles and was in overall command of armies numbering hundreds of thousands of soldiers, giving him total military supremacy over the country. His four most effective samurai generals, Ii Naomasa, Sakakibara Yasumasa, Sakai Tadatsugu and Honda Tadakatsu, were nicknamed the Four Heavenly Kings.

During the Azuchi-Monoyama and early Edo periods, Japanese warfare was revolutionized. In the year when Ieyasu was born, a Chinese junk had brought to Tanegashima island a couple of 'barbarian' (Portuguese) traders, who sold two Goa-made snap matchlock arquebuses to Lord Tokitaka. The new thundering weapons, called *teppô* by the Japanese, spread rapidly to nearby Kyushu. In less than a year these firearms were being produced by iron workers not only at Tanegashima, but also at Negoro, Sakai and Kunitomo.

> One shot from this object can make a mountain of silver crumble and break through a wall of iron. Someone with aggression in mind toward a neighbouring country would lose his life instantly when hit. Needless to say, this also holds for the deer that ravage the rice just planted. The many ways this object can be used in the world cannot possibly be counted.
>
> Confucian scholar Nanpo Bunshi to Lord Tanegashima Hisatoki, *Teppôki (The Record of the Musket)*, 1606

Nicknamed *Tanegashimas*, some local copies of the two Portuguese arquebuses were probably first used in January 1544 during the invasion of Yakushima island. *Tanegashima* gunners and spear-wielding conscripted *Ashigaru* infantry soon replaced mounted soldiers armed with bow and sword. At the Battle of Nagashino in 1575, Lord Oda Nobugana had brought 3,000 arquebusiers, who contributed to the defeat of the famous Takeda cavalry.

Ashigaru infantry, trained for mass-formation manoeuvres, wore distinctive uniforms which fostered *esprit de corps* and discipline. Saltpetre was imported from China or India to produce local gunpowder. An alternative to saltpetre, potassium nitrate, was produced locally. In the late sixteenth century the manufacture of breech-loading *Furankihō* swivel guns, also *taihō* and *harakan* heavier types, was developed in Sakai, Kyoto and Tosa. After the setbacks suffered in Korea against Admiral Yi Sun-sin's navy, use of cannons briefly took hold in Japanese warfare.

At the Battle of Sekigahara and the Siege of Fushimi Castle in the same year, Ieyasu fielded some of the nineteen bronze cannons taken from William Adams' ship, the *Leifde*. Adams would also direct the construction of the nation's first light galleons. In the following years, Ieyasu bought some long-range ordnance (culverins and sakers) from the Dutch and English to use during the sieges of Osaka (1614–15). Plenty of Japanese-made firearms were also produced for the sieges of Sakai, Kunitomo and Hino.

In the eighteenth year of the same era, Hideyori rebelled at Osaka. In the early winter, the forces from Edo and Sunpu reached Settsu province. Over and over again cannon (*ishibiya*) and hundreds of small firearms (*kozutsu*) were allocated to the Osaka Campaign. All together, muskets and cannon numbered 20,000 pieces. The foot soldiers had their orders: to conquer the strong fortress.

Kunitomo teppôki Chronicle, 1633

It was the first time that cannons had been properly used in the siege of a castle in Japan. After the Siege of Osaka and during the long-lasting period of peace that followed, artillery became irrelevant, and its development remained essentially at a standstill in the archipelago. From 1607 guns could only be manufactured in the seventy-three foundries of Nagahama under licence from the *bakufu*. The four Kunitomo master gunsmiths were ordered to resettle at Sunpu when Ieyasu retired there. Later on, production of firearms was halted altogether in order to weaken the *daimyō*, and they soon fell into disuse in the Japanese islands.

After barely two years of rule, Ieyasu turned the nominal title of *shōgun* over to his third son, Tokugawa Hidetada and retired to his castle at Sunpu, although he retained most decision-making powers. On 1 June 1616 Ieyasu died at Sunpu, probably of syphilis. He was seventy-three years old.

Look upon the wrath of thy enemy, If thou only knowest what it is to conquer, and knowest not what it is to be defeated, woe unto thee, it will fare ill with thee. Find fault within thyself, rather than with others.

Tokugawa Ieyasu's will

Achievements

Nobunaga started the process of national re-unification, and Hideyoshi carried it forward, but the hereditary shogunate was ultimately founded in 1603 when Ieyasu was granted the title of *shōgun* by the Emperor. The new *bakufu* meticulously established a centralized power structure, with absolute supremacy over the powerful *daimyō*, initiating the Edo period that brought much-needed stability to Japan. As the seat of the shogunate, Edo, the future Tokyo, flourished. Ieyasu laid the foundations of a family dynasty that would rule a pacified country for the next 265 years. He even arranged for his deification after his death. Ieyasu established relations with the Spanish authorities in Manila and the Dutch and English East India Companies, although under his grandson Japan would gradually isolate itself from foreign influence. By virtue of his numerous awe-inspiring achievements, Tokugawa Ieyasu remains one of Japan's most revered figures.

Ferdinand Bol, Michiel de Ruyter, 1667, Rijksmuseum, Amsterdam. (*Wikimedia Commons*)

Chapter 28

MICHIEL DE RUYTER
'The Lion of the Seas'

No King will heed our warnings, no Court will pay our claims,
Our King and Court for their disport do sell the very Thames!
For, now De Ruyter's topsails, off naked Chatham show.
We dare not meet him with our fleet – and this the Dutchmen know!
Rudyard Kipling, *The Dutch in the Medway*, 1911

Nicknamed the 'Terror of the Ocean' by his adversaries, de Ruyter is the most illustrious admiral of the Dutch Golden Age. In the seventeenth century the Dutch Republic, the world's dominant trading nation, was at war for sixty years because of commercial and maritime rivalry. Although the Dutch had the largest fleet in Europe, they would face England, a maritime power on the rise, allied with Portugal, Sweden and later, Louis XIV's France. The navy of the Republic had to protect overseas shipping lanes, but also repel any invasion of Dutch territory. Revered as saviour of his nation, de Ruyter would become the most celebrated of Dutch seamen. A prime theoretician of modern sea warfare, de Ruyter is considered one of the most able commanders of the seventeenth century.

The son of a sailor, Michiel Michielszoon (1607–76) was born in Zeeland; he would not use the name 'Michiel Adriaenszoon de Ruyter' before the 1640s. Starting his career at the age of nine as a ship's boy, by the age of thirty Michiel had worked his way up to captain and accumulated wealth in the service of Vlissingen-based Cornelius and Adrian Lampsins, owners of a fleet of 300 merchantmen. While Adrian Lampsins was on the board of Directors of the mighty *Verenigde Oostindische Compagnie* (United East India Company, or VOC), his brother Cornelius was a Director of the *Geoktrooieerde Westindische Compagnie* (West India Company, or GWC) organized similarly. De Ruyter's patrons exerted considerable economic and political influence over the Republic's overseas policies in the four corners of the globe.

Two years after the granting of a charter to the English East India Company by Queen Elizabeth, in March 1602 the Dutch States-General supported the formation of the world's first global conglomerate, the VOC, which was listed on Amsterdam's stock exchange. Launched with an initial capital of 6.4 million guilders, the conglomerate expanded rapidly. At its peak in the 1660s–70s, it employed 50,000 people, including 10,000 soldiers, and operated 200 ships from the busy ports of the North Sea to the exotic Japanese islands, sailing between Company posts established on the shores of Africa, Persia, India, Indonesia, Vietnam, Formosa and Japan.

> East of the Cape of Good Hope and beyond the Straits of Magellan, representatives of the Company shall be authorized to enter into commitments and enter into contracts with princes and rulers in the name of the States General of the United Netherlands or the country's Government in order to build fortifications and strongholds. They may appoint governors, keep armed forces, install judicial officers and officers.
>
> Charter of the VOC granted by the States-General,
> 20 March 1602

The growing economic power of the Republic came primarily from its commerce in the Baltic Sea and its monopoly on the spice trade with the East Indies (Indonesia) and Ceylon, as it gradually ousted its Portuguese competitors in Asia.

In 1641 Malacca was captured from the Portuguese, and in 1667 the Treaty of Breda ending the Second Anglo-Dutch War gave sole control over the precious nutmeg trade to the VOC. The Company's activities were not limited to the monopoly on spice, for it also dominated the intra-Asian trade network of key commodities, acting as an intermediary and supplying regional markets with its own fleet.

Authorized by its charter to deploy troops and wage 'spice wars' if necessary, the Company was in permanent conflict with Portugal, Spain and multiple local powers. The Dutch, aware of the Portuguese presence in Japan since the publication of Jan van Linschoten's famous *Itinerario* (1596), received *Shōgun* Tokugawa Ieyasu's official permission to open a trading post at Hirado in 1609. From the island of Hirado large amounts of silver and other precious metals were carried away by the Dutch in exchange for Chinese silk, textiles, porcelain and sugar. Hirado was also a prominent naval base for opportunistic privateering operations against Ming and Portuguese shipping, before a base in Formosa was secured. By 1639 the Dutch were the only European traders allowed in Japan, and two years later the *bakufu* ordered them to resettle at Dejima in Nagasaki Bay.

In Mughal India since the time of Akbar, the VOC, through its trading post at Surat, had brought spices, Japanese gold, silver and copper to purchase Indian silk, cotton and textiles. The immense profits accumulated by the VOC, and by the much less successful GWC in West Africa and Brazil, established Dutch economic and maritime dominance centred on Amsterdam. By the 1670s, with 6,000 ships, the Dutch merchant navy amounted to half of the entire European tonnage.

The workhorses of the VOC were the large armed merchant ships known as East Indiamen, carrying twenty to thirty guns and escorted by the Company's men o'war that regularly embarked a detachment of forty to fifty soldiers. VOC vessels were built and commissioned by each of the Chambers at the Admiralty provincial arsenals, including Texel, Middleburg, Enkhuizen, Delftshaven and Amsterdam.

After serving as Rear-Admiral of the Zeeland Admiralty and briefly assisting Portugal against Spain as part of the Restoration War (1641), for the next decade de Ruyter remained on active duty in the merchant navy on board his own ship, the 400-ton *De Salamander*. At the outset of the First Anglo-Dutch War (1652–4), a 'purely commercial war' (Sir George Clark) provoked by the clash of interests between the two nations, he accepted a naval command from the Zeeland Admiralty. With the rank of Commodore, he served with distinction under Maarten Tromp, who was killed at the Battle of Scheveningen. De Ruyter first gained recognition as a skilled tactician and energetic leader with his victory at the Battle of Plymouth against General-at-Sea George Ayscue (August 1652).

We immediately made sail towards them, and met them about four o'clock.
It proved to be Admiral Sir George Ayscue with his English squadron.

A determined fight ensued between us. We sailed with all our ships twice right through their fleet, so that the enemy drew off. Both sides were much damaged, but our men fought with great bravery, though some of the ships came off very badly. Thanks be to God for granting that the enemy was put to flight, although they were forty-five ships strong and in great force.

Commodore De Ruyter's log on the *Neptunus*, August 1652

After the peace with England, as Vice-Admiral of the Admiralty of Amsterdam, de Ruyter took part in several actions against Sweden in the Baltic and against Barbary pirates in the Mediterranean. It was at this time that England captured New Amsterdam from the Dutch West India Company and renamed it 'New York'. At the end of 1664 de Ruyter recaptured GWC trading posts from the English in West Africa and then sailed to America to raid their colonies, from Barbados in the Caribbean to Newfoundland in Canada. These expeditions further boosted his fame at home and abroad.

After the devastating defeat at the Battle of Lowestoft, when the Dutch Navy lost sixteen ships and 4,000 men (June 1665), Grand Pensionary Johan de Witt replaced the deceased Lieutenant-Admiral Jacob van Wassenaer with de Ruyter. This led to bitter rivalry with Lieutenant-Admiral Cornelis Tromp, a political enemy of de Witt. De Ruyter's blaming Admiral Tromp for defeat in the St James's Day Battle the following year resulted in Tromp's resignation from the Navy until 1673, when the two commanders were reconciled.

The lesson learned by both belligerents from previous engagements was that only men o'war able to carry sixty or more heavy guns could make a difference in the battles to come. De Ruyter worked closely with Johan de Witt to expand the Dutch Navy, introducing new, larger and better-armed purpose-built warships (instead of relying on converted armed merchantmen or hired VOC ships), and improving their organization. In two years, ten new three-deckers armed with 75–84 guns were commissioned. The flagship of the Republic, the 1,600-ton Rotterdam-built *De Zeven Provinciën*, was fitted with eighty bronze guns, including twenty-eight 36-pounder muzzle-loaders on the primary gun deck that packed a tremendous punch (capable of piercing a metre of oak at 400m) and had an effective range of 1.6km. Fireships were also used by both sides, with mixed results.

Until then, the favoured Dutch tactic was to engage in an undisciplined melee, individual ships boarding and attempting to capture their opponents, then leaving the battle with their prizes. With de Ruyter, the single-line-ahead battle formation, requiring strict fleet discipline, became the standard Dutch tactic in the new Fighting Instructions approved by the States-General in August 1665. The fleet was divided into three squadrons, each with a clear chain of command. Signalling was improved, with forty-four flag signals becoming the standard, and the principle of concentrating superior force against part of the enemy fleet was adopted. Faulty captains were put on trial, some were executed and others were cashiered.

Finally, in December 1665, the *Regiment de Marine* was founded and placed under the command of Colonel Willem Joseph Baron Van Ghent tot Drakenburgh and Lieutenant Colonel François Palm. Companies of these sea-going soldiers were deployed aboard every ship. From the outset, the Dutch *Mariniers* were trained in ship-boarding and amphibious warfare.

These reforms soon paid off. During the rest of the Second Anglo-Dutch War (1665–7) de Ruyter's 'New Navy' achieved victories at the Four Days Battle (June 1666) and in the audacious raid on the Medway (June 1667). De Ruyter's fleet navigated the treacherous shoals and sandbanks of the Thames estuary and the Medway, broke the chain across the river and attacked the large English ships anchored at the Chatham yard. Spearheaded by Van Ghent's *Mariniers*, the Dutch burned thirteen English ships of the line and captured two, including the *Royal Charles*, flagship of the English navy. Only the *Royal Sovereign* survived because she was at Plymouth at the time.

> All our hearts do now ake; for the newes is true, that the Dutch have broke the chaine and burned our ships, and particularly 'The Royal Charles', other particulars I know not, but most sad to be sure. And, the truth is, I do fear so much that the whole kingdom is undone.
>
> Diary of Navy Board Secretary Samuel Pepys, 12 June, 1667

The Raid on the Medway, considered to be one of the most embarrassing defeats in English history, accelerated the progress of Anglo-Dutch peace negotiations that had begun at Breda in April 1667. Joost van den Vondel wrote a poem in which he hailed de Ruyter as 'The Lion of the Seas on the Thames'. Yet it was the Admiral's performance in the Third Anglo-Dutch War (1672–4), during the French invasion of the Low Countries, that is considered his greatest achievement.

On land, with the handicap of its geographical position, the situation had become critical for the Dutch Republic. At sea, De Ruyter literally saved the United Provinces from utter destruction by cornering more powerful Anglo-French fleets in four decisive naval battles. De Ruyter would tolerate no talk of capitulation and declared he would, if necessary, take the fleet overseas to continue the fight. His friend and ally Johan De Witt was murdered in August 1672 with Cornelis Tromp's involvement, but the new *Stadhouder* Willem III kept De Ruyter as Commander-in-Chief with the rank of Lieutenant-Admiral-General.

De Ruyter's victories over Anglo-French forces off Solebay, where Van Ghent was killed on the deck of the *Dolfijn* while attacking HMS *Royal James* (1672), at the Battles of Schooneveld and at Texel (1673) turned the tide of war. At the most critical time the Dutch managed, owing to de Ruyter's tactical brilliance, to inflict so much damage on the French and English fleets in Dutch territorial waters that their invasion was called off.

> They returned fire with all their guns abaft the mainmast, shooting us to pieces, dismounting our guns and tearing up the rigging. There were scores of dead and wounded, among them Admiral Van Ghent. He was standing close to the mainmast where he fell dead, when a cannon ball shot away his leg just above the knee, in addition to four or five major wounds in the chest and abdomen and other shrapnel wounds. He fell forward with three or for sailors as well as the commander Jan Claasz.
>
> Captain Michiel Kindt, *Dolfijn* ship's logbook

By then widely considered the most talented admiral of his day, in 1675 de Ruyter was sent with a fleet to the Mediterranean to assist the Spanish against French Admiral Abraham Duquesne. At the hard-fought Battle of Augusta off Sicily, De Ruyter was mortally wounded when a cannonball struck him in the leg (22 April 1676). Cornelis Tromp was appointed his successor as Supreme Commander.

De Ruyter's body was embalmed and returned home on the *Eendracht*. As a sign of respect, by order of King Louis XIV, French coastal batteries fired salutes as the ship sailed by. The Sun King even lamented, 'He was a formidable enemy, however we ought to lament his loss; this man did honour to humanity.' In March 1677 de Ruyter received a solemn state funeral in Amsterdam with an entire nation mourning the fallen hero. Entombed in the Nieuwe Kerk, the Latin inscription engraved with golden letters on his monument that occupies the space of the main altar reads:

Intaminatis Fulget Honouribus (He shines in untarnished honour)

Achievements

A superb naval tactician, leader and reformer, de Ruyter is considered one of the most important national heroes of the Netherlands. Under his leadership, the Dutch Navy became the most powerful in the world. When the economy and even the very survival of the Dutch Republic was under threat, the United Provinces' most brilliant successes against England and France were mostly due to de Ruyter's tactical prowess and superior seamanship. He was considered a strict but fair captain who took good care of his crews. Amid fierce battles, de Ruyter avoided unnecessary risks. His victories at sea during the three Anglo-Dutch Wars (1652–74) saved the Dutch Republic and ensured its independence. Since the eighteenth century nine warships of the Royal Netherlands Navy have been named after him.

Shivaji in the 1680s, Department of Oriental Manuscripts and Printed Books, British Museum. (*Wikimedia Commons*)

Chapter 29

SHIVAJI BHONSLE 'THE GREAT'
Founder of the Maratha Empire

Sevagi [Shivaji] possessed all the qualities of command . . . In personal activity he exceeded all generals of whom there is record; for no partisan appropriated to service ever traversed as much ground as he at the head of armies. He met every emergency of peril, howsoever sudden and extreme, with instant discernment and unshaken fortitude, the ablest of his officers acquiesced to the imminent superiority of his genius, and the boast of the soldier was to have seen Sevagi charging sword in hand.

Robert Orme, *Historical Fragments of the Mogul Empire*, 1782

Shivaji was a warrior-lord of the Bhonsle clan who founded the Maratha Empire in 1674. Leading the movement to free the Marathas, using guerrilla warfare against the last Deccan sultanates and Mughal emperor Aurangzeb, Shivaji founded an independent, viable Maratha state, mostly at the expense of the Bijapur Sultanate. He created a navy and successfully defended his new kingdom against foreign threats. Uniting his people into one nation, Shivaji is considered the greatest Indian of the Early Modern Era.

Shivaji (1630–80) was descended from a line of prominent nobles. At the time, India was under Muslim rule: the Mughals in the north and the Muslim sultans of Golconda and Bijapur in the south. The whole Deccan was torn by civil wars, disorder and anarchy. Raised at Pune, at the age of twelve Shivaji came to Bangalore with his mother Jijabai. They had been summoned by his father Shahaji Raje, then a *jāgīrdār* (landholder official of the state) of the Bijapur ruler. Shahaji developed Bangalore as the southern military headquarters of the Adil Shahi sultans.

A born leader, at the age of sixteen the young Shivaji, from his *jagir* (estate) assigned in the Pune region (which consisted of 3–4 provinces), began his uprising against Bijapur by organizing bands of the hardy Mavales and waging guerrilla warfare. Between 1646 and 1658 Shivaji captured Bijapuri strongholds in the Desh and the Konkan regions one after the other, carving out from the declining sultanate an enclave that was the genesis of the Maratha state. The emphasis was on mobility: Shivaji made good use of light infantry and light cavalry in the mountainous regions of Maharashtra. He also set up a network of spies and informants under the leadership of Bahirji Naik Jadhav. During all this time, Shahaji did not support his son's actions.

> Prince Shivaji did not lack information from his secret intelligence, which he had all over India. He made little of all these preparations and plans against him, and like a second Alexander told his soldiers that the more his enemies had of luxury, splendid appointments, and gorgeous trappings, the less courage they would have, and that he preferred to see his men covered with iron and steel, which are the true ornaments of every soldier
>
> Abbé Carré, *Travels in India and in the Near East*, 1672–4

The Bijapur government was unable to respond adequately as it was already dealing with Mughal incursions and internal divisions. With the relative consolidation of Sultan Ali Adil Shah II's authority, General Afzal Khan was sent to deal with Shivaji at the head of a 12,000-strong army. In November 1659 the two leaders agreed to meet face-to-face, and Afzal Khan, who demanded Shivaji's submission to the Sultan, was killed by Shivaji's entourage. A much larger Maratha force, concealed in the forest, then emerged and annihilated the Bijapuris at the Battle of Pratapgad. Within fifteen days, a quarter of Bijapur territory fell to Shivaji's forces.

Shivaji also invaded Mughal territories in the Deccan, which brought him into direct conflict with Aurangzeb, last of the great Mughals. In early 1660 Aurangzeb sent out his trusted maternal uncle and general Shaista Khan, who marched against Aurangabad and seized Pune, the centre of Shivaji's domains (10 May 1660). In January 1664, making use of his nascent sea power, Shivaji sacked the prosperous port city of Surat on the western coast, its riches providing additional revenue for the war effort. During the looting of the commercial district Shivaji spared the warehouses of the English, Dutch and French East India Companies to avoid retaliation by the European naval powers.

> After he had committed many cruelties, haveing destroyed 2/3 parts of the Towne with fier, and cutt of several heads and hands, at night, hee [Shivaji] having notice of some forces that were acomeing against him, having sufficiently enriched himselfe, having by report carried away with him about a million and a halfe of mony (Suratt not having been soe rich not in many years before), hee departed with the curses of many undone people. This unhapy disaster did obstruct all our buisnesse, wee being forced to lay aside all buisnesse, having spared most part of our men.
>
> Captain Nicholas Millett, logbook of the East India Company's *Loyal Merchant*, Surat, 6 January 1664

Aurangzeb retaliated with a huge army led by veteran Rajput general Jai Singh. Shivaji was forced to sign the humiliating Treaty of Purandar in June 1665, by which he surrendered twenty-three forts and agreed to enrol in the Mughal imperial service as a retainer. Shivaji only kept seventeen strongholds, including Raigad. In June 1666 he was summoned to Aurangzeb's court in Agra with his 9-year-old son Sambhaji. There they were kept in confinement for a month, but Shivaji managed to organize a famous escape by bribing the guards in Aurangzeb's absence.

> Sevagi [Shivaji] in this invasion reduced all the coast, from Rajapore, to the island of Bardez which belonged to the Portugueze, and was separared only by the harbour from the city and island of Goa. The city was not a little alarmed by the neighbourhood of Sevagi's operations, which greatly distressed their trade, and markets: nevertheless, not attacked, they refrained from acting offensively: for the sword of their ancient valour, had long cankered in its spoils.
>
> Robert Orme, *Historical Fragments of the Mogul Empire*, 1782

Shivaji realized he could only become the leader of the Marathas if he was the figurehead of a genuinely separate political entity. He definitely broke with the

Mughals by raiding Surat in 1669 for the second time. During the following years, he expanded his power in the western coastal lands and in the south. On 6 June 1674, Shivaji crowned himself *Chhatrapati* (Monarch) of his realm at the Raigad fortress, which became the capital of the new sovereign state of the Marathas. Moropant Trimbak Pingle was appointed as the first *Peshwa* (Prime Minister). Shivaji set the stage for a centralized state in which the King held the final authority; without his sanction no minister, military commander, or clerk could put any design or plan into action.

> Prince Shivaji, from being a simple minister of state in the kingdom of Bijapur, has risen today to such high fortune and grandeur that all the other Indian powers tremble before him. He had become master of the best part of this kingdom, namely its coasts and maritime frontiers. He had pillaged and sacked the richest towns of his king, the Mughal; he had taken the strongest places of the country; and no rivers, mountains, or forts, had yet been able to stem the progress of his enterprises and plans. Finally, if these ravages and continual successes were not opposed, he would become the most powerful king in the Orient.
>
> Abbé Carré, *Travels in India and in the Near East,* 1672–4

The homogeneous Maratha army under Shivaji consisted of men drawn mainly from Maharashtra, and it was commanded by a regular cadre of officers. Shivaji made sure his soldiers were paid punctually, sometimes in cash, but more often in kind, and he enforced discipline through military regulations. Prime Minister Moropant played an important role in planning for the defence and maintenance of a territory that would eventually encompass some 250 military forts (350 according to British East India Company's historiographer Robert Orme):

> Nothing was spared which might contribute to the internal defence of his country. Regular fortifications well armed and garrisoned barred the opened approaches; every pass was commanded by forts, and in the closer defiles, every steep and overhanging rock was occupied as a station to roll down great masses of stone, which made their way to the bottom, and became the most effectual annoyance to the labouring march of cavalry, elephants and carriages. It is said that he left 350 of these posts in the Concan alone.
>
> Robert Orme, *Historical Fragments of the Mogul Empire,* 1782

Shivaji's chief military architect was Hiroji Indulkar, who supervised the work on many of these forts. Raigad fortress's natural defences were further strengthened by ramparts of black basalt that follow the undulation at the edge of the cliffs.

The two main gates were both flanked by circular bastions. Sindhudurg fort in the Arabian Sea, built in 1664–8, served as the headquarters of the Maratha Navy.

> The [Raigad] fort is quite strong from all four sides. The cliffs on the four sides are straight as if chiselled and as high as one and a half a length of a village. Grass does not grow on these cliffs even in the rainy season. It is all a single rock from top to bottom. Seeing this, Maharaj was very happy and said this fort should be finalized for the capital of the throne.
>
> *Sabhasad Bakhar*, 1697

In the middle of the 1650s Shivaji, one of the few rulers in Indian history to care about maritime affairs, had begun the creation of a naval force. Coastal fortifications were built during his reign for the repair, storage and shelter of warships. Two fleets were organized, one under the command of Admiral Mainak Bhandari, the other under Daulet Khan. Although the sailors were mostly enlisted native Konkanis, the fleets were commanded by experienced European and Siddi mercenaries. Towards the end of Shivaji's reign, the Maratha Navy numbered an astounding 400 vessels, primarily *grabs* (light frigates) and *gallivats* (galiots).

The last years of Shivaji's life were spent extending and consolidating his new state. The warrior king died of dysentery on 4 April 1680, leaving a large but vulnerably located kingdom. A period of instability followed, as Aurangzeb launched an attack that led to a bitter 27-year-long conflict. The death of Aurangzeb in 1707 ended the war and marked the beginning of the decline of the Mughal Empire. The Maratha Empire would reach its zenith under *Peshwa* Baji Rao I (1720–40).

Achievements

A visionary and astute tactician, the former vassal of the Sultan of Bijapur was a source of hope for his people as he united them against their Muslim rulers, forging a distinct national identity. The decline of Islamic power in the Deccan started with Shivaji, who became a mighty symbol of Hindu resistance and self-rule (*Swarajya*). His coronation heralded a new era in the history of Early Modern India. Under his successors, the Maratha Empire would cover one third of the subcontinent and dominate the political scene in India until the early nineteenth century. Shivaji is considered the father of the Indian Navy and a national hero, one of the greatest figures in Indian history, especially in the State of Maharashtra, where he has acquired almost godlike status. In April 2021, fourteen of Shivaji's forts of the Maharashtra, including Raigad, were submitted to the Tentative List of UNESCO World Heritage sites.

Justus van Egmont, Grand Condé, 1650s, Musée Condé, Chantilly. (*René-Gabriel Ojeda/RMN-Grand Palais*)

Chapter 30

THE GRAND CONDÉ
Louis XIV's master tactician

It was he who, with his cavalry, attacked this hitherto invincible Spanish infantry, as strong, as compact as the ancient and esteemed phalanx. Respect for the Spanish armies in Europe turned to the French armies, which had not for a hundred years won such a famous battle.

Voltaire, *The Age of Louis XIV*

Louis II de Bourbon, Duc d'Enghien and Prince de Condé, better known by his nickname of 'Grand Condé' (1621-1686), was a legendary figure of 'the Great

Century'. His victory at the age of twenty-one against the Army of Flanders at Rocroi spelled the swansong of the *tercios* and brought him international fame. A cousin of the 'Sun King' Louis XIV, he led the *Fronde* aristocratic uprising (1648–53) against the crown; but later, pardoned by Louis, he became one of the King's most trusted generals, helping to turn France's army into the most powerful and efficient military machine of the Early Modern Era. Condé's military genius and his string of victories altered the course of history and consolidated his reputation as one of the greatest commanders who ever lived.

Sixteenth- and seventeenth-century Europe was dominated by the unequal struggle between the Habsburg 'universal monarchs' and the weakened Bourbon House of France, a cadet branch of the Capetian dynasty. The Habsburgs ruled over the mighty Spanish Empire 'on which the sun never set' and the Holy Roman Empire. In Europe, the senior and junior branches ruled the Low Countries, Franche-Comté, large swathes of Italy and Germany, Spain, Sicily and Sardinia, Austria and Royal Hungary.

On its northern and eastern flank, France thus shared a continuous 1,000km land border with Habsburg dominions from the North Sea to the territory of Milan. On its southern flank, the 450km between the Atlantic Ocean and the Mediterranean offered another route for Spanish expansion, completing the Habsburg encirclement and making France particularly vulnerable to invasion by its great rival from all sides. France was unable to challenge Habsburg power at sea either, lacking a navy until the end of Louis XIII's reign (1601–43). The 72-gun *La Couronne*, the first large French ocean-going warship, was only commissioned in 1637. Built with Dutch technical assistance, it had to be equipped with Swedish ordnance.

France was gradually emerging from the eight consecutive civil wars and series of Spanish invasions that had devastated the kingdom for almost half a century. The bitter Wars of Religion had deeply divided the population, ravaged the country and caused two million deaths. Under the feeble King Louis XIII, the slowly recovering nation still faced renewed Huguenot (Calvinist French Protestant) rebellions. Louis' prime minister, the unshakeable Cardinal Richelieu (1585–1642), was instrumental in redirecting the Thirty Years' War from a religious conflict between Catholics and Protestants to a war of independence against Habsburg hegemony; this meant siding with Protestant nations allowing a pacified France to emerge eventually as a rising power.

When Louis XIII died on 14 May 1643, the 4-year-old Louis Dieudonné became king under the shared regency of the Queen Mother Ana of Austria and the prudent Cardinal Mazarin, Richelieu's successor. This supreme authority over the kingdom in the hands of a Spanish princess and an Italian clergyman was vehemently contested by the nobility, leading to political unrest. Seizing the opportunity, Spanish Captain General Dom Francisco de Melo, who had crushed a French army the previous year, again invaded northern France from the Spanish Netherlands with 25,000 men. This time, de Melo intended to take Paris.

Louis II de Bourbon, Duc d'Enghien (1621–86) was the son of Henri II, 3rd Prince de Condé, a prominent member of King Louis XIII's court belonging to a cadet branch of the Bourbons. His participation in the Siege of Arras in 1640 as a volunteer was the full extent of his military experience when, in April 1643, Cardinal Mazarin gave him nominal command of the 20,000-strong Army of Picardy to halt the Spanish invasion. The disgruntled 62-year-old Marshal de l'Hospital was supposed to exercise actual command and rein in the young Duke's youthful impetuosity.

Enghien could rely on the military expertise of two veteran officers serving as his lieutenants. The Huguenot *Mestre de Camp Général* of the cavalry Jean de Gassion, who was called 'La Guerre' (the War) by Richelieu, had fought in the Swedish army until the death of King Gustav II Adolf at Lützen in 1632. With the Swedes he had learned to direct the sheer shock power of cavalry charging with sword in hand, instead of the caracole tactics practised since the 1540s by the Imperial *reiters* ('Black Riders' equipped with three-quarter armour) armed with a pair of wheellock pistols. Lieutenant General Claude de Létouf, Baron de Sirot, commander of the French reserves, was an even more seasoned cavalier, having served in the armies of Maurits of Nassau, Carlo Emanuele I of Savoy, Albrecht von Wallenstein and Gustav Adolf, the most prominent commanders of the Thirty Years' War.

Innovations in infantry tactics by the Habsburg armies, and later to a greater extent by the Dutch and the Swedes between the 1560s and the 1640s, had transformed infantry warfare as well. To maximize firepower, the proportion of musketeers in linear formation delivering continuous salvo fire by rotation had increased compared to the pikemen. Improving on the Dutch tactics, Gustav Adolf's battalions were the first to use regimental artillery and triple-rank salvo fire. This evolution came about through improved gunpowder, better discipline and systematic drill, which included weapons training and a reloading process broken down into a specific number of steps, enabling an average rate of fire of one shot per minute. Though smoothbore matchlock muskets were becoming more reliable, their recoil was massive and their aiming imprecise at best. The effective range remained limited at about 120 to 200 metres, depending on the angle of fire and amount and quality of gunpowder, but also on the bore and windage.

The *tercios* were still considered almost invincible, however. Although they had been checked by Maurits of Nassau at Nieuwpoort forty-three years earlier in a hard-fought battle, Spanish *tercios viejos* had crushed the 'modern' Swedish army at Nördlingen in 1634. Combining a force of armoured pikemen and the shots of the musketeers, operating in conjunction with field artillery, the *tercios* remained the tool of Spanish domination in Europe and beyond in the first half of the seventeenth century, though by the time of Rocroi in 1643, as they had dwindled to c. 1,500 – 2,000 men per formation, *tercios* basically meant regiments in the Habsburg armies.

In order to instil courage in troops that were about to challenge the formidable *tercios*, the young Duc d'Enghien gave an inspirational talk, witnessed at first hand by Pierre Lenet, son of a Parliament President:

> Before daybreak, the Duke was on horseback, and as soon as the sun set up, he passed in front of all the battalions and squadrons of his army; to the officers and the soldiers he demonstrated the greatness of the action they were about to begin for the service of the King and for the glory of his State, of which the safety in the present conjuncture depended on their courage; that he hoped that their bravery would reassure so many peoples afraid of the enterprise of a powerful enemy, the defeat of which would fill them with honour and fortune. His liveliness, the obvious joy on his face, and his good appearance animated marvellously his harangue.
>
> *Mémoires de Pierre Lenet*

To face Dom Francisco de Melo's superior numbers at Rocroi on 19 May, the French infantry was drawn up in two lines, with Sirot's 4,000 men kept in reserve. While Marshal de l'Hospital was in command of the left flank, Enghien and Gassion commanded the right. The impetuous Duke compensated for his numerical inferiority by speed of manoeuvre and by making extensive use of Jean de Gassion's heavy cavalry, routing his opponents' own mounted forces before falling on the slow-moving *tercios*' rear and attacking the veteran infantry regiments from all sides.

The Army of Flanders suffered 15,000 casualties, including *Maestre de Campo* Paul-Bernard de Fontaine, and lost 250 flags and 18 guns. A victory of this magnitude against the legendary *tercios* had not been seen since the Battle of Ceresole in 1544, when François de Bourbon, Comte d'Enghien (a great-uncle of our hero), had routed a joint Imperial-Spanish army. In the aftermath of the battle, the young Duke credited the success to the valour of his lieutenant:

> Monsieur, I dispatched Mr de la Moussaie [François de Goyon, baron of Nogent] to the Court to bring the news to the King of the success of this battle. I address you personally imploring you to recognize the services of Mr de Gassion on this occasion with the nomination of Marshal of France. I can assure you that he deserves the principal honour of this combat.
>
> Louis de Bourbon, letter to Cardinal Mazarin, 19 May 1643

Gassion was duly promoted Marshal of France, and Enghien was sent by the Queen-Regent Ana of Austria and Cardinal Mazarin to the Rhine, alongside the more experienced Vicomte de Turenne. At Montijo that year, the Portuguese fought a drawn battle against the Spaniards under the command of the Marquis of Torrecuso, although both sides claimed the victory.

In August 1644 Enghien, Turenne and Gassion defeated the Imperial forces and Bavarians led by Field Marshal Franz von Mercy at Freiburg. The same commanders won the second Battle of Nördlingen in 1645 (when Mercy was killed by a musket ball), and they took Philipsburg. In October 1646 Enghien captured the city of Dunkirk with Gassion, Dutch Admiral Marteen Tromp and 3,000 foot soldiers sent by the Queen of Poland Louise-Marie de Gonzague-Nevers. In December, on the death of his father, he became the 4th Prince de Condé, inheriting massive estates and an immense fortune.

The following spring, Cardinal Mazarin sent him to Catalonia to aid the rebellion against the Spanish crown, before recalling him to Flanders. The Prince de Condé won another stunning victory at Lens (19/20 August 1648), which would be the last major battle of the Thirty Years' War. Gassion 'La Guerre' had been killed during the Siege of Lens by a musket ball in the head a few months earlier. He was only thirty-four. Condé's, Turenne's and Gassion's successes contributed to the signing of the Peace of Westphalia.

It's a miracle of God that in this occasion M the Prince [of Condé] was spared, being even more exposed than ever before, and I believe that says it all.
Marshal of Grammont to Cardinal Mazarin after the Battle of Lens, 21 August 1648

Meanwhile in France, the civil war known as *La Fronde* had broken out between Cardinal Mazarin and the high nobility. The Grand Condé's fame and past victories actually posed a growing threat to the throne. The two most prominent soldiers of France were now in opposition to one another: Turenne, as the defender of Queen Ana, was the only commander who could match Condé. The Prince, in turn, led the rebellion of the nobility opposed to Mazarin and the Queen. Condé, who until then had been the Spaniards' worst nightmare, now switched sides, taking command of King Felipe IV's armies against the Regency. For this act of treason, he was sentenced to death *in absentia*. The young King Louis proclaimed that he would personally hunt him down and bring him to justice.

The French King [Louis XIV] is going to Flanders with two armies accompanied by all of his Kingdom's nobility. He is determined to hunt down Condé to kill or arrest him. God save him [Condé] from an enemy so powerful and from any betrayal, we would miss him, for his courage, and for the intelligence his receives from his many contacts.
Jerónimo de Barrionuevo, *Avisos*, 9 June 1655

Turenne eventually ended the *Fronde* with his victory over Condé at the Battle of the Faubourg St Antoine (1652), but the war against Spain dragged on. Condé and Don Juan José of Austria prevailed at Valenciennes in 1656 against Turenne, but this would be the last victory of a Spanish army against France. Two years later at the Battle of the Dunes (1658), the Franco-English coalition led by Turenne, Major General Thomas Morgan and Sir William Lockhart defeated the Anglo-Franco-Spanish alliance led by Don Juan José of Austria, the Duke of York and the Grand Condé. Allegiance to one's nation of birth was not yet well established at the time.

> Notwithstanding the advice which the Prince of Condé had given, Don Juan was positive in his first resolution. The prince, not without great indignation, consented; and drew up his troops in the place they desired; and quickly saw all come to pass that he had foretold. The English foot under Lockhart charged the Spanish foot, broke and routed them; after which there was not much more resistance on that side, the Spanish Horse doing no better than their foot . . . The day being thus lost, with a greater rout and confusion than loss of men, Don Juan and the Marquis of Carracena were contented to think better of the Prince of Condé's advice, by which they preserved the best part of the Army.
>
> Edward Hyde, 1st Earl of Clarendon, *The History of the Rebellion*

With the Peace of the Pyrenees in 1659, France ended the dominance of the Habsburgs in Europe. The young Louis XIV had triumphed over a declining Spain and the Holy Roman Empire, and France became predominant in Western Europe. French armies had regained the pre-eminence on the battlefield they had lost to the Habsburgs since the Battle of Cerignola in 1503. In terms of territorial gains, the Bourbon monarchy received parts of Flanders in the north and northern Catalonia in the south.

The Grand Condé was allowed back to France after the peace, meaning that he could gradually return to the battlefield in the service of his cousin the King. In 1668 Condé was tasked with conquering the Spanish-held Franche-Comté. In just three weeks he took the region of Artois, with the three cities of Besançon, Dôle, and Gray that had been heavily fortified under Emperor Carlos V.

Finally pardoned completely and restored to Louis XIV's favour, Condé was given overall command of the army tasked to invade Holland alongside Turenne (1672). Some of his regiments would experiment with the first plug bayonets, a weapon that would further revolutionize infantry tactics, leading to the disappearance of the pikes three decades later. King Charles II of England followed the French example: one regiment of dragoons was issued with bayonets that same year. Though wounded at the crossing of the Rhine near Arnhem, Condé nevertheless went on to defend Alsace from Imperial forces. After the evacuation of the United Provinces, he fended off a larger Imperial, Spanish and Dutch army under the command of William III of Orange at the particularly bloody Battle of Seneffe in the Spanish Netherlands (1674), then forced the Allies to abandon the siege of Oudenarde.

Following Turenne's death at Salzbach in July 1675, Condé assumed command of the French troops in the Rhineland. There he confronted Field Marshal Raimondo Montecuccoli, Austria's foremost commander, in a war of manoeuvre. This was Montecuccoli's and Condé's last campaign, as both generals retired thereafter.

Garlanded with glory, 'Monsieur le Prince' spent the rest of his life in his luxurious Château de Chantilly where, at his sumptuous court, he entertained the most illustrious artists and brilliant minds of his time. When Condé died at Fontainebleau in December 1686 at the age of sixty-five, Louis XIV lamented, 'I have just lost the greatest man of my kingdom!', while William III of Orange, his former adversary, declared to his entourage, 'The greatest man in Europe has just died!'

Achievements

At Rocroi and Lens Condé annihilated the *tercios*, marking the end of Spain's military ascendancy in Europe. Thanks to Condé's victories, France was in a position to dictate the Treaties of Westphalia which ended the Thirty Years' War in 1648. Bold and impetuous, Condé was regarded as an expert in the deployment of cavalry. Both Condé and Turenne were masters of movement, making full use of combined infantry and cavalry, often leaving their artillery behind in order to proceed with greater speed. As warfare increasingly became a matter of firepower, Turenne and Condé were closely associated with the post-1648 development of linear infantry tactics. After Condé retired, Louis XIV came to favour positional warfare, ushering in a period where siege and manoeuvre came to dominate military tactics. With Condé, who was regarded as both the greatest hero and best general of his time, the Bourbons had ended the Hasburgs' dominance.

Giovanni Carboncino, Francesco Morosini, c.1688, Museo Correr, Venice. (*Author*)

Chapter 31

FRANCESCO MOROSINI
Venetian God of War

Morosini is a tall, well-built man, particularly witty, astute as the devil, skilful, firm and vigorous, never unsettled by anything that happens. I have observed him in several encounters where a less able man than him would have been disconcerted. His majestic countenance allied with his great resolution have always pulled him out of every situation. On the day of our sortie, the confusion with which we came back into the city [of Candia] did not surprise him a bit.

Memoirs of Captain Pierre Domenisse, 1669

A towering figure of the European seventeenth century, Venetian admiral Francesco Morosini was undefeated until his very last battle, after fifty-five years of active service and countless battles against the Ottomans on land and at sea. Appointed four times Captain General of the Venetian forces and crowned Doge of the Republic while still on campaign, Morosini defended the mighty fortified city of Candia during the last phase of what became the longest siege in history. Recalled to active duty at the age of sixty-six, he then reconquered the Peloponnese from the Ottomans in four remarkable military campaigns. Scourge of the Turks, uncontested master of the Adriatic and the Aegean seas, Morosini is still considered a Venetian and Italian national hero.

Francesco Morosini (1618–94), of ancient Venetian patrician lineage, started his naval career at the age of eighteen on board the galley of his cousin Petro Badoer, the Captain of Candia's guard. Candia (present-day Heraklion) was the capital of the 'Kingdom of Crete', a prized Venetian possession since the Fourth Crusade. Even before the loss of Cyprus in 1571, the fortifications of Crete had been significantly upgraded by some of the most prestigious military architects of the Renaissance, including Giulio Savorgnan and Michele Sanmicheli. Together with Malta and Corfu, these state-of-the-art fortresses were considered the strongest and most advanced in the Mediterranean. Morosini experienced his baptism of fire during a Venetian expedition against Valona in Albania and fought in the War of Castro (1642–4) against the forces of Pope Urbanus VII.

Naval warfare had evolved since the days of Khayr al-Dīn Barbarossa a century earlier. Galleys and galiots were still the mainstay of any navy in the Mediterranean, but by the middle of the seventeenth century men-o'-war, packing much greater firepower, had turned into the ultimate artillery platforms. In November 1665, off Chios, a single two-decker warship under the command of the Order of Saint John's Chevaliers d'Hocquincourt and Tourville was able to repel the attack of no fewer than thirty-four Ottoman galleys. The battle raged for five hours. At close range, the ship's guns discharged devastating canister shots, and the crew also made good use of hand grenades and muskets to keep the Turks at bay, preventing them from boarding. When the wind picked up, the battered Maltese ship, finally able to manoeuvre, simply sailed away, leaving behind 600 dead Turks. Interestingly, some of their assailants had still been using bows and arrows, along with more modern matchlock muskets.

Immediately after this one-sided battle with far-reaching consequences, Venice started to build its own ships of the line in the *Arsenale* shipyard and armouries. Since building and maintaining a fleet was so costly, the Senate had usually rented private Dutch, French or English armed merchantmen with their crews when needed. The 68-gun *Giove Fulminante*, the first ship of the line built by the Republic, was commissioned in 1667. Since the Battle of Lepanto in 1571, the Venetian navy had also been employing galleasses. Powered by both oars and sails, these hybrid warships carrying up to sixty guns of all calibres had been used as breakthrough weapons. The Spaniards soon began to build their own, as did the Ottomans, who named this peculiar type of warship '*mahonne*'.

The young Francesco was in active service when Ottoman Grand Vizier Silahdar Yusuf Pasha landed 60,000 men by surprise on the island of Crete in June 1645. Venice was caught off guard; a long period of peace since 1573 meant that its military was unprepared to withstand an invasion of this magnitude. In a matter of weeks, the fortified city of Canea fell, followed by Retimno the next year. Morosini spent the subsequent two decades constantly on the front line, on land or at sea, in command of the squadrons of galleys and galleasses attempting to intercept and destroy Ottoman convoys before they could bring more supplies and reinforcements to their armies in Crete.

In 1656 Morosini was appointed governor of the island (or of the part of it still in Venetian hands by that time), and the following year, he was promoted to Captain General for the first time, in charge of all the *Serenissima*'s forces (navy and army) in the Levant. In 1666 he was appointed Captain General for the second time. In the course of the next three years, Morosini defended Candia with such ability that he became a living legend, both in Christian Europe and among his enemies the Turks.

> This General, always a Venetian Noble, is created by the Senate in times of war, to command the Fleet of the Republic. His power is so absolute over other Generals & Captains that he appears to be a Dictator or even a Sovereign rather than a subject during the three years of his Command. His authority does not only extend to the Fleet, but also to all the Ports, all the Isles, & all the Fortresses, where they receive his orders without flinching.
>
> Amelot de la Houssaie,
> *Histoire du Gouvernement de Venice*, 1676

The last phase of the siege witnessed experimentation with and refinement of techniques in bombardment, defence, approaches, trenches and tunnelling for underground mining and counter-mining. Thousands of volunteers and hundreds of military engineers flocked from all over Europe to fight the Turks on the bastions of Candia and to learn or improve their knowledge of siege warfare. Many of them, such as Georg Rimpler, would later serve during the Siege of Vienna and the subsequent campaigns against the Turks in Central Europe and the Balkans (1683–99). In August 1669, after the evacuation of Louis XIV's soldiers, only 3,600 men remained to defend Candia against the 60,000 Turks of Grand Vizier Köprülü Fazıl Ahmed Pasha's invasion force. In the end, Morosini was forced to surrender what was left of the city, having long since earned the respect of the Turks, who had come to fear his very name. Morosini had become a sort of dreaded, almost supernatural figure. The Grand Vizier allowed the garrison and inhabitants to leave the smouldering ruins of Candia peacefully with whatever they could carry and with full military honours. The Ottomans had lost 150,000–200,000 men in conquering the mighty bastionned city, the Venetians had lost 30,000, including a quarter of their entire male nobility.

> Thus we fought great battles, but these, compared to the Battle of Candia, were only easy walks and pleasure gardens of Aspôzi. In the 1,700 kingdoms since Adam's fall on earth, there has never been nor will ever be again such a great battle as the one of Candia.
>
> Evliya Çelebi, *Seyâhatnâme*, seventeenth century

Surviving the merciless War of Candia, Francesco Morosini rose to become the undisputed master of amphibious warfare in the Eastern Mediterranean. One of the most striking examples of his skill was his 1659 raid on Çeşme, at the heart of the Ottoman domains. He first ordered the landing of Venetian troops led by the Chevalier Michel de Grémonville close to the city walls; then, when the Turks sallied out to meet them, Morosini forced his way into the harbour of Çeşme, mounted a second landing with his marines and captured the city from within.

Enjoying total maritime supremacy throughout the conflict, Morosini coordinated a large number of landings and raids on the shores of the Aegean under cover of his naval artillery. He would proceed in the same manner during the following Morean War (1684–99), using an elaborate and extensive system of spies to gather vital intelligence, creating diversions to deceive the Turks, then landing where he was least expected. These tactics ensured the smooth capture of Preveza and Santa Maura (1684), Calamata and Coron (1685), Modon, Navarino and Napoli di Romania (1686) and Patras, Corinth and Athens (1687), among others forts, cities and outposts.

> So that in three days we had landed in the face of the enemy, beaten his Army, made ourselves masters of two cities and two castles, with all their cannons and ammunition, and every house full of goods, and a country as luxuriant and abundant as our Italy.
>
> Count Francesco Arrighetti, July 1687

When in 1683 the *Serenissima* joined the Holy League to fight against the Ottomans (the first time that Venice had actually declared war on the Turks!), the Senate did not hesitate long before recalling Morosini to active duty, appointing him Captain General for the third time. With an army of 10,000–15,000 men, made up of infantry and cavalry regiments recruited from Italians, Germans, French and Dalmatians, and supported by a fleet of some fifty ships (ships of the line, galleasses and galleys), Morosini expelled the Turks from the Peloponnese (Greece) in four awe-inspiring campaigns.

After having spent all the years of my life through the afflictions of War, and the hazards of the Sea, with determination, I will now search to acquire, through the dangers and the bloodshed, successes and military Triumphs, spending the rest of my days enhancing the glory of the Most Serene Republic. To achieve victory, I implore both the mighty hand of the Lord and the blessing of the Motherland.

Dispatch of Captain General Francesco Morosini to the
Venetian Senate, June 1684

Using a large galley called '*bastarda*' as his flagship, Morosini coordinated the fleets and the 'landing army' (*Armata da sbarco* in Venetian) led by foreign seasoned *condottieri* such as the Swedish Count Otto Wilhelm von Königsmark and Saxon Baron Heinrich Adam von Steinau, who regularly defeated the *seraskers'* (provisional provincial military commanders) provincial forces on the battlefield. The Turks typically disposed their troops in a crescent (*Hilal*) formation reminiscent of nomadic hunting parties, with the *Janissaries* at the centre and their fast-moving horsemen on both wings, systematically attempting to envelop their adversaries. The obvious weakness of this traditional disposition was that Europeans had come to expect it and had therefore devised tactics to counter it effectively. Nor, since the early sixteenth century, had they fallen for the Ottoman tactic of feigned retreats.

Italian and *Otramontani* (German and French) regiments fully equipped with matchlock muskets were drawn up in two lines, while cavalry regiments made up of Croats and dragoons were distributed on the flanks. A few men were tasked to carry the *chevaux de frise* (portable 'hedgehogs' projecting long wooden spears), setting these devices in front and on the flanks of the first ranks. These portable defences provided effective protection against the *Sipahi* cavalry. Interspersed among the infantry's first line were light field guns, positioned to provide longer-range firepower. Musketeers were ordered to hold their fire until the Turks approached within pistol range.

Morosini's generals would use heights, rivers, swamps or the shoreline to prevent any outflanking of their solid, slow-moving, firing fortress that the more numerous Ottomans, equipped with less artillery, were not able to challenge. After the Ottoman artillery had fired a couple of times, their *Sipahis* would charge the flanks, uselessly slashing at the *chevaux de frise*. The *Janissaries* would rush forward to assault the centre, only to be stopped dead by the *chevaux de frise* and the musketeers' double-rank volleys. After one or two attempts, the Turks would then retreat in confusion, abandoning the battlefield and leaving behind their dead, all the artillery and part of their camp.

Venice possessed a critical technological advantage in the form of its *Arsenale*, Europe's largest and most efficient military complex up to the Industrial Revolution. For the 1571 campaign leading to the decisive Battle of Lepanto, their skilled workers had built, equipped and launched 100 galleys in just fifty days. In 1685, Count Antonio San Felice Muttoni of Verona built two bomb ketches in the *Arsenale* such as the ones he had seen in action in Abraham Duquesne's French naval squadrons during the bombardments of Algiers (1682–3) and Genoa (1684). Engineer Sigismondo Alberghetti would call these mortars 'the most terrifying weapons in the world'. Concurrently, inventor Isaac Alemanno ('the German') devised a rapid-firing multi-barrel gun with an effective range of more than 200 metres. Morosini and his successors fielded these weapons during their Morean campaigns. Other groundbreaking gunpowder weapons were designed and tested during the war by outstanding engineers and gunsmiths such as the members of the Alberghetti dynasty.

The armies commanded by the Ottoman *seraskers* were routed on the battlefields of Preveza, Coron, Navarino, Calamata, Argos and Patras. Every fortress of the Peloponnese was either besieged and stormed or surrendered, one after the other. Morosini also took the Acropolis of Athens, an event mostly remembered for the destruction of the Parthenon. On 26 September 1687, an explosive shell launched by one of Antonio Muttoni's twenty-seven master gunners went through the roof of the old temple, detonating the barrels of gunpowder stored there and instantly killing 300 Turkish women and children who had taken refuge in the building.

Morosini's last campaign, aiming at the reconquest of Negroponte (Euboea) in the summer of 1688, ended in failure: While the Venetian army was decimated by an outbreak of plague, the Turks managed to keep their supply lines open. Recalled to Venice after his string of extraordinary victories, Morosini was given a hero's welcome upon his arrival in January 1690. He was crowned the 108th Doge of the Republic and awarded a ceremonial gilded silver sword blessed by Pope Alexander VIII in recognition of his contribution to the defence of Christendom.

The old soldier did not enjoy retirement for long, however. Finding him to be absolutely indispensable, in 1693 the Senate sent him back to the Levant to take overall command of the Venetian forces for the fourth time. In August of that year some senators considered asking Morosini to sail with the entire fleet to Constantinople and fire naval guns at the Sultan's capital and palace, in order to force the Ottomans out of the war.

Morosini died aged seventy-five in January 1694 from natural causes in Napoli di Romania, capital of the Venetian 'Kingdom of Morea' he had himself reconquered. He was first given a lavish military funeral by his own soldiers and sailors in Napoli di Romania, then his remains were brought home. The 'Peloponnesian' was buried in the central nave of San Stefano church in Venice, under a large circular bronze tombstone created by Antonio Gaspari and Filippo Parodi. Venice would mourn the loss of her greatest soldier and statesman until the forced dissolution of the Republic by Napoléon I in 1797.

Achievements

One of the most brilliant military leaders and tacticians of the 'iron century', Francesco Morosini was equally at ease in siege warfare, overseeing fleets in combat and tackling huge logistic issues, as he was in coordinating forces made up of officers and mercenaries from the four corners of Europe in land battles. Ambitious and fiercely devoted to the service of the Republic, Morosini proved extremely cunning and often ruthless. He was also capable of acting in the most chivalrous manner, never breaking truces or agreements he had made with his enemy. Undefeated in hundreds of battles, raids and skirmishes, except at Negroponte at the end of his career, Morosini embodied the Venetian Baroque era and brought military glory to the *Serenissima* as never before or since. To honour the memory of Venice's greatest seaman and Doge, the Military Naval Academy of Venice was named after him, as four ships of the Italian Navy have been since 1938. The 400th anniversary of his birth was duly celebrated in Venice, Italy and Greece throughout 2019 and 2020.

Jan Matejko, Jan Sobieski defeats the Turks at the Gates of Vienna (detail), Sobieski Room, Vatican Museums. (*Wikimedia Commons*)

Chapter 32

JAN III SOBIESKI
The Liberator of Vienna

God be blessed forever! He gave victory to our nation. He gave her a triumph never seen before in the past centuries. All the artillery, the whole camp of the Muslims, infinite riches have fallen into our hands. The surrounding fields are covered with the dead of the infidel army and the rest flee in confusion. The Vizier abandoned everything in his flight, keeping only his coat and his horse. All the troops performed their duty well. The governor of the city, Starhemberg, came to see me, hugged and kissed me and called me the saviour. I went inside two churches where the people kissed my hands, my feet, my clothes; others only touched me from afar, saying, 'Ah, let us kiss these victorious hands!'

Jan Sobieski to his wife, Queen Marie-Casimire,
13 September 1683

Jan Sobieski is probably the most famous military leader and monarch in the history of the Polish-Lithuanian Commonwealth. As a military leader of the crown, Sobieski made brilliant use of his superb cavalry, gaining successes against the Tatars and the Cossacks. He also clashed with the Ottomans and their vassals, defeating them at the Battles of Podhajce (1667), Chocim (1673) and Lwów (1674). Elected king in May 1674 by virtue of the immense prestige acquired by this string of victories, Sobieski's military career culminated in his decisive contribution to the Christian triumph at the Battle of Vienna in 1683, which rescued the Imperial capital and saved Austria from the Turks. This battle, at the high water mark of Turkish expansion, is widely recognized as the beginning of Ottoman territorial retreat from Europe.

Jan Sobieski (1629–96) was born at Olesko (in present-day Ukraine) to a prominent magnate family. His father Jakub was Voivode (high-level official in charge of a military region) of Ruthenia and Castellan of Kraków. His grandfather Stanisław Żółkiewski, Grand Hetman (Commander-in-Chief) of the Crown, had lost his life fighting the Turks at the Battle of Cecora (1620). After receiving an outstanding education, Jan and his older brother Marek travelled extensively through Western Europe. Sobieski began his military career in 1648 at the siege of Zamość alongside Marek. Initially the leader of his own troop of cavalry, Jan steadily rose through the ranks, while his brother fell victim to the Cossacks at the Batoh massacre (June 1652).

During the 'Deluge', when Karl X Gustav invaded Poland in 1655, Jan like many other noblemen first joined the Swedes against King Jan II Kazimierz Waza. In 1660, as standard-bearer of the Crown, he participated in the Cudnów campaign against the Russo-Cossacks. In October 1667 he avenged his brother by defeating a greatly superior force of Tatars and Cossacks at Podhajce. He was then promoted to Grand Crown Hetman, the highest military rank of the Polish-Lithuanian Commonwealth. In 1665 he married the crafty young French widow, Marie-Casimire-Louise de la Grange d'Arquien, lady-in-waiting to Marie-Louise de Gonzague-Nevers, Queen of Poland. Marie exercised overwhelming influence on her husband and Polish politics. During the short reign of King Michał I Korybut (1669–73) Sobieski won further victories over the Cossacks.

The peoples and armies of the Commonwealth put their faith in the icon of the Black Madonna of Częstochowa and the best shock cavalry of the Early Modern Era, their elite 'winged hussars'. Contrary to today's widespread belief, developments in battlefield tactics and firearms had not yet made plate armour obsolete. Clad in shining cuirasses, wearing leopard or tiger pelts over their shoulders and with large, whistling wings fastened to their backs, the winged hussars were a truly awesome sight. Nimble in action despite their armour, they were used alongside other heavy cavalry units such as *pancerny* wearing chainmail and German *Reiters*, or light units such as dragoons, Lithuanian Tartars and Cossacks. At the first Battle of Chocim (7 September 1621), 605 of these legendary horsemen with a company of *Reiters* fell upon the flank of 10,000 Ottoman *Sipahis* and *Janissaries* marching towards the Commonwealth's camp, routing them decisively.

> The Hussars are the first Gens d'Arms of the Kingdom and without contradiction the finest Cavalry in Europe, in respect of the Mien of the Men, the goodness of the Horses, and their Magnificent and Noble Apparel. They are reserved only for Battles and other Distinguished actions. They are composed of handsome Men, mounted on the finest Horses of the Kingdom, with divers other led-horses, richly caparisoned.
>
> Dalerac, *The Secret History of the Reign of John Sobieski the Third*, 1699

Members of the *Szlachta* (nobility), the 'companions' (*towarzysze*) were accompanied by retainers (*pocztowy*) armed with carbine and sword who fought by their side, protecting their lord to the last. The winged hussars were superb, highly trained riders. Their fast and powerful mounts, hybrids of ancient central European *tarpans* and Arabian or Tatar horses, were bred to sustain a gallop while carrying a heavy load – the Sarmatian knight, his armour and equipment.

The hussar's armour weighed an average of 15kg. It included a Hungarian-Turkish type of helmet and a breastplate, both of which provided effective protection against pistol or musket fire. The seventeenth century had witnessed the introduction of superior two-ply or even three-ply armour (and helmets) that could resist bullets, even when fired at close range. There were even accounts of hussar armour protecting its owner from cannon fire. In 1660, during the Cudnów campaign, the castellan of Połaniec Andrzej Prusinowski under the command of Prince Jerzy Lubomirski was struck by a cannon ball. His breastplate was profoundly dented but not penetrated. After recovering he would serve under Jan Sobieski from 1666 and live on until 1701.

The hussars' remarkable wings were made of wood and ostrich or eagle feathers, and fixed to the backplate or the saddle. The main armament of the hussar was his ultra-long cavalry lance known as *kopia*. It was surprisingly light (2–3kg) and partly hollow, made of fir and with a head of damascened steel. The lance was single-use, since it would break on impact, but as it was 5–6m long it effectively outreached the enemy's spears. A hussar's lance could pierce two or more opponents; the record, allegedly, was six Russians impaled in one thrust at the battle of Połonka (June 1660)! As secondary armament, the hussars would carry a pair of pistols, a sabre with an 85cm blade or a stabbing sword, and sometimes a battle-axe. Their adversaries might be able to discharge one or two volleys, but then they would be run through and trampled by the heavy cavalry charging them, massed in close ranks at impact. Usually, the enemy just broke and ran for their lives.

King Michał I passed away on 10 November 1673. The following day, Sobieski won a crushing victory over the Turks and their Wallachian vassals under Governor of Ochakov Sarı Hüseyin Paşa at the second Battle of Chocim in Bessarabia. After a 15-minute intensive artillery bombardment of the enemy positions, Sobieski personally led his *pancerny* cavalry in the storming of the fortified Turkish camp, while 1,200 winged hussars under Voivode Stanisław Jabłonowski penetrated the right flank and routed the *Sipahis*. As the only bridge over the icy Dniester collapsed under the weight of the Turks, their retreat was cut off. Most of their 30,000-man Ottoman army had been killed or captured by the end of the day; only 3,000 were able to flee before the destruction of the bridge.

> Many good men of our armies had perished in this hard-fought battle. More than half of the *kopias* [winged hussars units] are lost, and I realize that such brave men, as those from the Turkish side, had not existed for centuries, and that while being inside their camp, we were twice close to defeat.
>
> Jan Sobieski's address to his men the day after the Battle of Chocim, 12 November 1673

The second Battle of Chocim represented the greatest victory over the Ottoman Empire in Europe up to that time. From then on, the Turks nicknamed Sobieski the 'Lion of Chocim'. Sobieski's reputation was so great that he was easily elected King in May 1674 with the full support of France against the Habsburg candidate, Duke Charles V de Lorraine. The coronation ceremony took place two years later in Kraków cathedral.

> I don't pretend to rank the King of Poland among his Generals, because he is beyond comparison, and above all Encomiums and Titles, but we may without flattery adventure call him the Hero of the North.
>
> Dalerac, *The Secret History of the Reign of John Sobieski the Third*, 1699

In August 1675, while on campaign against the Turks and the Tatars in the plains of Ukraine, the King led the charge of 1,700 Polish winged hussars against 10,000 Tatars and routed them at the Battle of Lwów. The war with the Ottomans and their vassal Khan Selim I Giray ended with the Treaty of Żurawno in October 1676.

Sobieski, for a long time attached to the French faction, eventually concluded an alliance with Holy Roman Emperor Leopold I against the Turks, who posed a mortal threat to both nations. In January 1683 the *Seym* (Diet) approved the treaty: Leopold committed to mobilize 60,000 men, the Commonwealth 40,000. The Imperial forces would fight in Hungary, while the Poles desired to reconquer

Kamieniec in Podolia and were looking toward further conquests in Ukraine. The Alliance of the Holy League was formalized in Rome with Pope Innocentius XI's blessing. It thus became the fourteenth Crusade officially sanctioned by the Papacy.

> It is better to fight on foreign soil, eating foreign bread, in assistance of all of the Empire's forces, not only the Emperor himself, than to defend ourselves, while eating our own bread when all our friends and neighbors have left us if we don't give them a hasty rescue!
>
> Letter of Jan Sobieski to Field Hetman of the Crown
> Mikołaj Sieniawski. Częstochowa, 25 July 1683

When a huge Ottoman force of 150,000 men led by Grand Vizier Kara Mustafa approached Vienna in the summer of 1683, Sobieski rallied 20,000 Poles in haste and marched from Kraków. At the end of August, Sobieski and Charles de Lorraine, Commander of the Imperial army and his former rival for the throne of Poland, met at Oberhollabrunn. The final order of battle was established and the nominal leadership of the entire multinational force was entrusted to Jan Sobieski, who was by far the more experienced commander in fighting the Turks, but each prince was to exercise authority over his own troops on the battlefield.

The tactic adopted was straightforward: the allies would come down the slopes of the Kahlenberg hill in a linear battle formation to steamroll the Ottoman units facing them. On the right wing, the Poles were divided into three corps: King Jan III Sobieski in the centre (with his 16-year-old son Jakub Ludwik), Sieniawski on his left flank, and Jablonowski on his right. The Polish forces mostly consisted of cavalry, their 15,000 horsemen divided into *pancerny*, light cavalry and the 2,670 elite winged hussars who would act as tip of the spear of the entire allied force.

> Warriors and friends! Yonder, in the plain are our enemies, greater in numbers, indeed, than at Chocim, when we trod them underfoot. We have to fight them on a foreign soil; but we fight for our own country; and under the walls of Vienna, we are defending those of Warsaw and Cracow. We have to save, today, not a single city, but the whole of Christendom; of which, Vienna is the bulwark. The war is a holy one. There is a blessing on our arms; and a crown of glory for him who falls. Follow me! The time has come for the young to win their spurs!
>
> Jan Sobieski's address to his troops before the Battle of
> Vienna, Karl August Schimmer, *Wiens Belagerungen*, 1845

The battle started before all the units were fully deployed. At 4.00 am on 12 September 1683 the Ottomans attacked, seeking to interfere with the deployment of the

Holy League's regiments. The Germans were the first to strike, when Charles de Lorraine moved forward with the Imperial army on the left and the other Holy Roman Imperial forces in the centre. In the early afternoon, a large battle started on the other side of the field as the Polish infantry advanced on the Ottoman left flank. The Ottomans found themselves in a desperate position, caught between the Polish and Imperial forces. Charles de Lorraine and Jan Sobieski both decided on their own account to resume the offensive and finish off the enemy.

Long expected by both Imperials and Poles, the winged hussars moved to the front lines. At around 6.00 pm Sobieski ordered the cavalry to attack in four groups, three from the Commonwealth and one from the Holy Roman Empire. Eighteen thousand horsemen rode down the hill in what remains one of the largest cavalry charges in history. The winged hussars spearheaded the action, battering the Ottoman ranks. At that point, the Grand Vizier retreated to his headquarters in the main camp; by then, many Ottomans were already leaving the battlefield.

> The Victory which the King of Poland has obtained over the Infidels is so great and so complete that past Ages can scarce parallel the fame; and perhaps future Ages will never see any thing like it. All its Circumstances are as profitable to Christendom in general, and to the Empire in particular, as glorious to the Monarch.
>
> Dalerac, *The Secret History of the Reign of John Sobieski the Third*, 1699

The allied cavalry headed straight for the Ottoman camp and Kara Mustafa's fabulously rich pavilion, while the Viennese garrison led by Count Ernst Rüdiger von Starhemberg sallied out to join the fray. The booty was immense: 25,000 Ottoman tents and pavilions, 9,000 wagons, 10,000 oxen, 5,000 camels, 300 guns. Fifty thousand Turks were killed during the siege and the climactic battle. Following the customary looting of the enemy's baggage train, Sobieski entered Vienna in triumph, hailed by a cheering crowd. He attended a Mass in the Augustinian Church, where he had the Te Deum sung, much to the surprise of the Imperial officers who were already beginning to find the presence of the King of Poland rather inconvenient.

> There was a man sent from God whose name was John . . .
>
> Sermon given in Vienna's Cathedral, the day after the liberation of the city, 13 September 1683

With the Ottoman army in Hungary in total disarray, the lifting of the siege was followed by a successful late summer campaign. The tide had turned, paving the way for the liberation of Central Europe after centuries of Islamic occupation.

The following years proved somewhat anticlimactic for Sobieski and the Polish armies. The Moldavian campaigns of 1684–6 and 1691 achieved little. Weakened by ill health, the Crusader-King resigned his personal command and entrusted it to Hetman Stanislaw Jablonowski.

The Commonwealth would recover Kamieniec in Podolia with the Treaty of Karlowitz (1699), but by then Sobieski was no more. The king, who had suffered from poor health his all life, died on 17 June 1696, 'having fainted, as the ascites [fluid build-up in the abdomen] was already approaching the heart' (Kazimierz Sarnecki). He was buried where he had been crowned, at Kraków, in Wawel Cathedral. The death of the warrior-king was a profound national tragedy. An heroic legend in his own time, Sobieski rapidly became the focus of a patriotic cult perpetuated to this day as a part of Poles' collective heritage.

Achievements

Jan Sobieski, whom Clausewitz considered one of the greatest generals of all time, is numbered among the outstanding military leaders and statesmen in Polish history. He mastered combined-arms tactics using different types of cavalry, infantry and artillery, on both a strategic and a tactical scale. The Battle of Kahlenberg is considered one of the most decisive in world history. Had the Holy League coalition armies lost, the Sultan would have dominated central Europe unchallenged. The defeat of the Turks at Vienna has been hailed as Sobieski's finest hour, his greatest service to Europe, the moment when his legendary winged hussars saved Christendom. His reign also marked the last moments of glory for the Commonwealth, as the Habsburg Monarchy became the dominant power in the region. The lasting fame of the winged hussars contributed to the development of light *uhlan* units in the eighteenth century and the resurgence of lancers during the Napoleonic Wars.

Vauban, portrait attributed to François de Troy, Palais de Versailles. (*Gérard Blot/RMN–Grand Palais*)

Chapter 33

MARQUIS DE VAUBAN
Europe's foremost military engineer

This was his main goal, the preservation of his men. Not only the interest of war, but also his natural humanity made them dear to him. He always sacrificed to them the brilliance of a more prompt conquest and the glory, and resisted the impatience of the Generals. Thus the soldiers obeyed him with complete devotion, animated less by the extreme confidence they had in his capacity, than by the certainty and gratitude of being spared as much as could be.

Eulogy of Vauban by Fontenelle, 1708

Vauban was the leading military engineer of the Early Modern Era and one of the mainstays of French military strategy. During Louis XIV's 72-year-long reign

France was the dominant European power and fought five major wars. In an era when siege warfare dominated military campaigns, Vauban perfected methods of capturing cities that minimized both delay and casualties. His reputation was attested by the popular maxim of the time: 'Any city besieged by Vauban is taken, any city defended by Vauban is impregnable.' Vauban participated in some 140 battles and 50 sieges during his career. In charge of all the fortifications of the kingdom from 1678, he supervised hundreds of construction projects, giving France an 'iron belt' of formidable, state-of-the-art citadels that efficiently protected its borders against invasion.

Sébastien Le Preste de Vauban (1633–1707) was born into a modest provincial family. An orphan from a very young age, at seventeen the young Sébastien embarked on a military career, enlisting as a cadet in the regiment of the Prince of Condé, who was leading the *Fronde* rebellion of the high nobility against the Regency. In 1653, in consideration of the young officer's remarkable bravery, Cardinal Mazarin recruited him to the service of child-King Louis XIV.

Vauban would study engineering and the art of siege warfare under the Chevalier de Clerville (1610–77), the future Commissioner General of the Fortifications. After receiving his patent in 1655 at the age of twenty-two, Vauban was appointed engineer-in-chief at the siege of Gravelines in 1658. Twenty years later, he replaced his mentor the Chevalier de Clerville as Commissioner General of the Fortifications, after two decades devoted to the fortification of large cities in northern France, such as Dunkirk (1662) and Lille (1667). He was promoted to the rank of Lieutenant General in 1688.

It was in the early 1670s that Vauban, in order to protect the kingdom from invasion, came up with a radical new concept, envisaging French territory in the form of a geometric figure, easier to defend, that he named the '*Pré Carré*' (Square Meadow), since France was a traditionally rich and fertile nation.

> Seriously my Lord, His Majesty should consider making his 'Pré Carré'. This confusion of jumbled fortified places belonging to friends and foes displeases me; you are compelled to maintain three instead of one. Your peoples are tormented by that, the number of your defences is drastically increased, your forces much diminished.
>
> Vauban to Minister of War Marquis de Louvois,
> January 20, 1673

Vauban's building legacy would be nothing short of monumental: he designed, supervised, built or modernized a staggering 160 fortresses and citadels in France, as well as vast civil works. The expenditure on this huge fortification programme during Louis XIV's reign amounted to more than 154 million French pounds, the equivalent of the entire net revenue of the state in an unusually prosperous year (in 1706 the revenues only amounted to 50 million, while spending skyrocketed to 220 million). Versailles, the King's spectacular palace, cost about 81 million to build.

Bearing in mind that strategy is always determined by geography, Vauban planned and realized the Sun King's *Pré Carré*: a double line of fortified cities that protected the new borders of France against the Spanish Netherlands, but also defended the right bank of the Rhine, the Alps, the border with Spain and the coastal areas, including islands and harbours. Vauban built and improved bastionned fortifications at the four corners of the vast kingdom and beyond.

> Would you wish me to teach that a curtain wall is situated between two bastions, that a bastion is made up of an angle and two faces, etc? This is not my way. The art of fortifying isn't an amalgamation of rules and systems, it is based on common sense and experience.
>
> Vauban in Thomassin, *Mémoires sur la Fortification*, 1712.
> Manuscript in three vols, SHD, Vincennes

Vauban built on the theories of his predecessors, Jean Errard, Blaise de Pagan, Antoine de Ville and the Chevalier de Clerville, adapting his own innovative designs to each site. Using three successive systems, he constantly improved his fortifications and increased the number of outer works and their complexity, culminating in his 'third system', best illustrated by the ideal fortress of Neuf-Brisach (1702). In order to build, perfect and inspect his phenomenal stone heritage, but also to carry out diplomatic missions on behalf of the King, Vauban travelled an average of 4,000km a year on horseback, in every season and in all weathers, covering a total of 180,000km in forty years. During peacetime he also advised the Duke of Savoy on the defences of Turin, Verrue and Vercelli.

In an era when war of positions was predominant, according to Bernard Le Bouyer de Fontenelle, Vauban participated in no fewer than fifty-three sieges, including the capture of the major bastionned cities of Tournai, Douai, Lille, Maastricht, Mons, Ath, Besancon, Namur, Steinkerque, Luxembourg, Ghent and Ypres! Vauban's experience grew from his first siege at Sainte-Menehould during the Fronde in 1652 and throughout the wars of Louis XIV, until his last successful siege of Alt-Breisach during the War of the Spanish Succession in 1703. It was dangerous work: Vauban was injured eight times in the line of duty. At the siege of Montmedy, in 1657, he was the only engineer who was not killed. In 1669 he created the world's first professional corps of military engineers, establishing their methods of recruitment and training.

> Long sieges ruine armies; empty the purse, and most commonly it falleth out so, that it hindreth armies from better imployments; and after a long siege, though things fall out according to a commander's desire, he will have little reason to brag of his victory, when he vieweth his expences, his time, and his army. The malice of a great army is broken, and the force of it spent in a great siege.
>
> George Monck, Duke of Albemarle, *Observations upon Military and Political Considerations*, 1671

Vauban would revolutionize Early Modern siegecraft. He developed a 'scientific' method of attacking fortified places, 'burning more powder, shedding less blood'. Investment of a fortress would start with the building of circumvallation and contravallation lines, isolating the city from the outside world and preventing any relief from reaching it. This was followed by a systematic approach using parallel trenches set at precise distances.

Siege parallels had been used since the sixteenth century, but the practical experience gained at the siege of Candia (1649–69) by engineers from all over Europe enabled Vauban to bring the concept to perfection in thirteen days at Maastricht (1676). Three parallel trenches were dug concentric to the walls, one at 600m, another at 350m and the third near or on the glacis, with connecting zigzag assault trenches. The digging, mostly done at night, had to be conducted as silently as possible. Sappers were organized in squads of fifty men, each led by seasoned officers who had been given precise objectives.

Getting closer to the enemy's fortifications allowed the blowing up of the outer works using mines filled with powder kegs. Then artillery was moved in to blast the base of the walls at point-blank range, while mortars launching bombs provided indirect plunging fire. Simultaneous attacks, including diversions, were launched from various angles in order to dissimulate where the main attack would take place. At the siege of Philippsburg in 1688 Vauban innovated again by using ricochet fire technique for the first time, loading his siege guns with less powder and dismounting the enemy's guns. Philippsburg fell after twenty-three days, to the satisfaction of the King:

> You have known for a long time what I think of you and the confidence I have in your expertise as well as your affection; you may rest assured that I do not forget the services you have rendered; what you have done in Philippsburg is extremely pleasing to me.
>
> Louis XIV to Vauban, 8 November 1688

Once a breach had been made, it could be stormed by the infantry, although by that time, the defenders would have usually agreed to surrender. Depending on the number of bastions and outer works, but also the manpower and artillery available, it became theoretically possible to predict the duration of any given siege. At Maastricht, it was only thirteen days before governor Jacques de Fariaux asked to negotiate a surrender, even though the city had been defended by Menno Van Coehoorn, probably the best military engineer in Europe after Vauban, and his arch nemesis.

Vauban's rationalized systems thus saved numerous lives from prolonged siege operations, and avoided the slaughter involved in all-out assaults against strongly fortified positions. According to Saint-Simon, he was not only a military commander but also something of a humanitarian. Vauban was, he said,

> perhaps the most honourable and the most virtuous man of his century [as] no man was ever more meek, more obliging, more civil, more respectful protective to the point of miserliness of the lives of his men.
>
> Saint-Simon, *Mémoires*

The 14-day siege of Ath during the spring of 1697 was a textbook example of Vauban's skill and hailed by contemporaries as his masterpiece, the most efficient siege ever conducted, owing to its speed, low cost and few casualties (only 100 French soldiers were killed). This demonstration of French military might even convinced the Allies to negotiate an end to the Nine Years' War with the Peace of Ryswick (October 1697). Owing to the obvious superiority of Vauban's system, France's adversaries, in turn, were forced to adopt his methods.

On 18 February 1699 Vauban was made an honorary member of the French Academy of Sciences. He wrote essays on colonization, forestry, farming, religious and social matters, hydrography, and drew up proposals for a more equitable fiscal system. His writings established the renowned military engineer as a reformer and a precursor of the Enlightenment. He was eventually made a Marshal of France in 1703, the only military engineer to reach such a rank.

Vauban died from pneumonia on 30 March 1707 in Paris at the age of seventy-three. He would not witness the triumph of his *Pré Carré* when Marlborough and Prince Eugene of Savoy failed to break through his double barrier of fortifications even after taking Lille in 1708. Vauban's influence on subsequent generations of military engineers was both immense and long-lasting; he set the standard for both his disciples and his adversaries. In May 1808 Napoléon I ordered the remains of Vauban transferred to Les Invalides, final resting place of some of France's outstanding military heroes. He was entombed facing Turenne's own monument.

Achievements

Dedicating his entire life to the service of the state, Vauban's military achievements proved decisive in Louis XIV's wars. He was noted for his talent in the conduct of both offensive and defensive siege operations. He refined siege warfare, developing Early Modern fortification to its pinnacle of sophistication. During the most desperate phase of the War of the Spanish Succession in 1708–9, his *Pré Carré* saved France from an Allied invasion. His impact on fortifications and siegecraft was both long-lasting and global. His methodical system would remain the standard way of attacking strongpoints up to the mid-nineteenth century and the advent of rifled artillery. Some of his fortifications (e.g. Saint-Malo, Brest, Cherbourg) were still tough nuts to crack during the Second World War, withstanding heavy aerial bombardment. As testament to Vauban's lasting genius, twelve of his finest fortifications are on UNESCO's World Heritage List.

Mikael Dahl, Karl XII, 1710s, Nationalmuseum, Stockholm. (*Wikimedia Commons*)

Chapter 34

KARL XII
The 'Swedish Meteor'

All his actions are almost incredible. Perhaps he was the only man, and certainly he was the only King, who never showed weakness. His passion for glory, war and vengeance made him too little of a politician, without which none has ever been a conqueror. He was an extraordinary rather than a great man, and rather to be imitated than admired. But his life may be a lesson to kings and teach them that a peaceful and happy reign is more desirable than so much glory.

Voltaire, *History of Charles XII*

At the start of Karl XII's reign Sweden ruled over a large empire that his predecessors had carved out in the course of the Thirty Years War, with vast holdings in the

Baltic states and northern Germany. Karl XII was only seventeen when he faced a great alliance of enemy nations led by the formidable Peter the Great, the founder of modern Russia. Despite these overwhelming odds, under Karl's XII skilled military leadership the Carolean (*Karolinen*) army remained invincible until July 1709. The final showdown at Poltava dealt a mortal blow to Swedish prestige, and Karl XII's untimely death at Fredriksten a decade later would lead to the demise of the Swedish Empire.

Karl XII (1682–1718) succeeded his father Karl XI in 1697 at the age of fourteen. He thus became the absolute monarch of a warlike, expansionist nation of 2.5 million, reputed to be a European great power. Since early childhood Karl had been fascinated by stories of Caesar and Alexander the Great. When a great coalition was formed to mount a three-front assault on the Swedish *dominium maris baltici* (Swedish establishment of a Baltic Sea dominion) which the young king had just taken over, he set out from Stockholm in the summer of 1700 seeking similar glory on the battlefield.

With a disciplined army of 76,000 men and a powerful fleet of forty-three three-deckers, the young King of Sweden struck first. After only two months, following Karl's lightning campaign and his siege of Copenhagen, Denmark-Norway was forced to withdraw from the war in August 1700. Next, the Russian army was soundly defeated at the Battle of Narva, fought in a blizzard in November 1700. Karl, still only aged eighteen, bravely led his troops, who were outnumbered four to one. After a short bombardment of the Russian entrenchments with his thirty-seven field guns, Karl ordered his 10,000 men forward to storm the enemy positions, which were defended by no fewer than 40,000 Russians:

As soon as the cannon of the Swedes had made a breach in the entrenchments, they advanced with fixed bayonets, having the snow, which drove full in the face of the enemy, behind them. At the first discharge the King received a ball in the shoulder; but it was a spent ball which rested in the folds of his black cravat and did him no harm. His horse was killed under him, and it is said that the King leapt nimbly on another, exclaiming, 'These fellows make me take exercise.' Then he continued to advance and give orders with the same presence of mind as before. Within three hours the entrenchments were carried on all sides; the King chased the enemy's right as far as the river Narva with his left, if one may speak of 'chasing' when 4,000 men are in pursuit of nearly 50,000. The bridge broke under them as they fled; in a moment the river was full of dead bodies; the rest in despair returned to their camp . . .

Voltaire, *History of Charles XII*

This astonishing victory established the myth of Swedish invulnerability and Russian ineptitude. Thereafter, Karl marched the Swedish army into Poland with the intent of dethroning Polish King August II 'the Strong', Jan Sobieski's successor. This would take six campaigns throughout Poland and Saxony. As they were mostly opposed by numerically superior adversaries, the Carolean army's '*Gå På*' (Go To) tactics were relentlessly offensive. Field artillery provided cover as the cavalry and infantry deployed; the Lutheran chaplains kept morale high; the Swedish troops were both highly disciplined and fearless, drilled to attack with cold steel, considered more effective than lead at close quarters. The cavalry charged with drawn rapiers, and the infantry with fixed bayonets and pikes after firing only twice at point-blank range (40 and 20 paces). Horsemen would discharge their pistols only while in pursuit of a retreating enemy.

> Never have I seen such a combination of uncontrollable dash and perfectly controlled discipline, such soldiers and such subjects are not to be found the wide world over except in Sweden.
>
> Count Magnus Stenbock after the
> Battle of Gadebusch, December 1712

On 9 July 1701 Karl XII gave a demonstration of Swedish expertise in amphibious warfare with his crossing of the Düna River near Riga to attack the Russian and Saxon forces. Under cover of a smokescreen, a flotilla of 195 small vessels and gunboats transported the 6,000 Swedish troops across the 600m-wide river. Karl also utilized four massive purpose-built floating batteries, each holding twenty-five guns and fifteen howitzers, to cover the landings.

> The King of Sweden had great boats made, after a new model, so that the sides were far higher than ordinary, and could be let down and drawn up like a drawbridge. When raised they protected the troops they carried, and when let down they formed a bridge to land by. He also employed another artifice. Having noticed that the wind blew straight from the north, where his troops lay, to the south, where his enemies were encamped, he fired a large heap of wet straw, which spread a thick smoke over the river and prevented the Saxons from seeing his troops, or guessing at his actions. Under cover of this cloud he sent out boats filled with smoking straw, so that the cloud increased, and being right in the enemy's face, prevented them from knowing whether the King had started on the passage or not.
>
> Voltaire, *History of Charles XII*

The crossing, which took thirty minutes, was virtually unopposed. In the ensuing battle on the far bank of the river, the Swedes defeated the Russo-Saxon force under the Saxon *Generalfeldmarschall* Adam Heinrich von Steinau, former General *da Sbarco* of the Venetian Army in the Morea, who had defeated the Turks at Argos in 1695, and Russian Prince Anikita Repnin, a veteran of the Azov campaigns (1696–7).

Karl XII's victory over August's army forced the Polish-Saxon army to withdraw from Livonia, and Sweden secured Courland. The young King followed this up with an invasion of Poland, capturing Warsaw on 14 May 1702 and defeating the Polish-Saxon army a second time at the Battle of Kliszów in July. The 1,400 famed Polish winged hussars under the command of Hieronim Augustyn Lubomirski, a veteran of the Battles of Chocim and Vienna, were first halted by volleys from the Swedish infantry, before being routed by the Carolean cavalry. The Swedes captured August II's coffers filled with 12,000 riksdaler, forty-eight cannons and sixty flags, as well as much ammunition and many tents, including a luxurious Ottoman pavilion that August II's father Johann Georg III of Saxony had brought back from the spoils of the Battle of Vienna.

After the battle, Karl took Kraków, the medieval capital of Poland. The Swedish King defeated yet another of August's armies under the command of *Generalfeldmarschall* Steinau at the Battle of Pułtusk in the spring of 1703, then besieged and captured Toruń. Karl and his Field Marshal Carl Gustaf Rehnskiöld defeated the Russians, Poles, and Saxons at Grodno and Fraustadt (September 1706). Then Karl combined his forces with Rehnskiöld's as they occupied Silesia, meeting virtually no resistance. With the Treaty of Altranstädt in October 1706, Karl finally achieved his primary goal, crowning Stanisław Leszczyński as the new Polish King. A weakened Commonwealth was forced out of the conflict; only Peter the Great's Russia was left standing.

About this time the King of Sweden having dethroned King Augustus, and forced him to such a Peace as he was pleased to impose upon him, the Czar was left by himself in the War; and it being then rumour'd that his Swedish Majesty intended to march out of Saxony directly to Mosco, and force the Czar to a peace also, Orders were immediately given to fortifie the city of Mosco . . . For the King of Sweden, who marched out of Saxony with an Army of 36,000 chosen Men, might (as 'twas believed by Persons of the greatest Judgment in Affairs of that time) have then easily obliged the Czar to honourable conditions of Peace.

Captain John Perry, *The state of Russia under the present Czar*

After the rejection of a Russian peace offer in 1707, Karl spent much of the summer of 1708 in Lithuania awaiting supplies for his planned invasion of Russia. In September he decided to march down to Ukraine, where he expected to gain the support of the Cossack Hetman Ivan Mazepa. By this time Karl had total confidence in the superiority of his forces and in his own ability, having already routed his adversaries in eight major battles. The Swedish forces suffered a great deal during the abnormally cold winter of 1709, however, and they were regularly harassed by Russian units. As consequence, the Swedish army besieging Poltava was severely depleted by the time Peter the Great was ready to take the offensive.

A few days prior to the Battle of Poltava on 8 July, Karl XII was immobilized by a serious leg wound caused by a stray bullet and was unable to personally lead the Swedish forces. The starving Swedish army of 22,000–28,000 launched a major assault against Peter's 45,000 men, still finding the psychological strength to mount a frontal attack on their vastly superior enemy.

> The King is forced to keep to his bed of the wound he received in his left foot on the 17th [Julian calendar] but there being no apparent danger, His Majesty continues to give the necessary orders in the siege of Pultawa . . . We have had some probability to fight with his enemy who approach us nearer and nearer, which His Majesty's sickness has in a great measure made us defer. Though we speak but little of peace at present, yet here are but few among us who do not heartily wish for it, for the officers as well as the common soldiers begin to be tired of their continual fatigues.
>
> Captain James Jefferyes, *Letters to the Secretary of State*

Under the direct command of Field Marshal Rehnskiöld, the Caroleans, who only had four field guns at their disposal, attempted to storm the heavily fortified lines with fixed bayonets, but the attack failed. Poor organization and their inferior numbers ultimately led to a chaotic Swedish retreat, in which they suffered 6,901 dead or wounded and 2,760 captured. The Russian losses amounted to 1,345 dead and 3,290 wounded. Karl fled south with just 543 men and was forced into exile at Bender, in the Ottoman Empire. The remaining Swedish force of 14,000–17,000 under General Adam Ludwig Lewenhaupt surrendered at Perevolochna.

> Your Honour understood that the Svedes have had an entire defeat by Pultava; that 14:m (which by a mistake I thought were only 8:m) yielded themselves prisonners of warr, and that the King of Sweden made his escape over the Nieper with 2 or 3,000 as well officers and soldiers for Poland. This strange reverse of fortune has wholy chang'd the face of affairs in these parts.
>
> Captain James Jefferyes, *Letters to the Secretary of State*

The Swedish Empire had no army left in continental Europe to contest Russian attempts to reconquer their lost territories. In the aftermath of Karl's defeat, Frederik IV's Denmark-Norway, along with Saxony, Poland and Lithuania, all three ruled again by August the Strong, broke the earlier peace treaties, reversing the previous nine years of Swedish success. When George I of Great Britain, as Elector of Hanover, joined the fray with Hanover and Prussia in the summer of 1715, adding to the already long list of Sweden's enemies, Karl's military situation would only become more desperate; he now faced overwhelmingly superior numbers on both land and at sea.

By 1713 Karl was no longer welcome in the Ottoman Empire, and the *kalabalık* at Bender ended with the Swedish King and his entourage taken prisoner by the Turks. After his release, in 1714 Karl rode across half of Europe in just fifteen days, arriving in Stralsund in November to resume personal command of the nation and of the ongoing military operations.

> Their young husbands had died like heroes in battle. To gain peace and quiet, all of them took a male heart. It came to life in their breasts, thus they went to fight the country's enemy. And since he had given them all a kiss, they squeezed his blood out with bliss.
>
> Swedish military anthem, *Daily encouragement for God-fearing soldiers and faithful subjects*, 1716

The Swedish king tried to invade Norway twice, the first time in February 1716, to force Denmark–Norway into a separate peace. While inspecting trenches close to the perimeter of the fortress of Fredriksten in Norway on 11 December 1718, Karl was struck in the head by a large-calibre projectile and died instantly. He was only thirty-six years old.

> At this moment Mr Siquier and Mr Megret saw the King fall on the parapet, with a deep sigh; they came near, but he was already dead. A ball weighing half a pound had struck him on the right temple, leaving a hole large enough to turn three fingers in. His head had fallen over the parapet, his left eye was driven in and his right out of its socket; death had been instantaneous, but he had strength to put his hand to his sword, and lay in that posture.
>
> Voltaire, *History of Charles XII*

Despite frequent investigation, doubt remains as to whether the shot came from the besieged fortress or from Karl's own lines. Some theories suggest he had been murdered. Upon the King's death, the Swedish forces retreated, and the Great Northern War ended in 1721 with the total defeat of Sweden, leaving Imperial Russia as the dominant power in the Baltic and a major new force in European politics. Sweden's decline was blamed on the adventurous military ambitions of Karl XII and the continuous wars that dominated his reign. A new school of historians suggest, however, that events largely beyond the reach of Karl XII were to blame for the decline of Sweden.

> Charles XII, perhaps the most extraordinary man ever born, a hero who summed up in his personality all the great qualities of his ancestors, and whose only fault and only misfortune was that he carried them all to excess.
>
> Voltaire, *History of Charles XII*

Achievements

From the outset of the Great Northern War, Karl XII proved himself a born military leader, winning devastating victories over his adversaries with relentlessly offensive tactics. A daring commander, master of speed and deployment, he always seized the initiative. Karl XII's reputation as an invincible military leader would only end in the gruelling Russian campaign, after a long string of successes against a coalition of powerful enemies. Being ruled by a warrior-king proved a demographic disaster for Sweden: at the end of Karl's II reign, there were few men left between the ages of sixteen and sixty-five in the Swedish countryside. Poltava, the defining battle of the Great Northern War, and subsequent reverses marked the end of Sweden as Northern Europe's major power. It is said that in 1812 Napoléon I, while sitting in the Kremlin in Moscow and beginning to realize that his Russian adventure might not be turning out as well as he had expected, studied Voltaire's *History of Charles XII*.

Duke of Marlborough, painting attributed to Mikael Dahl, c. 1702,
National Army Museum, London.

Chapter 35

1st DUKE OF MARLBOROUGH
Britain's greatest commander

I take with pleasure this opportunity of doing justice to that great man,
whose faults I knew, whose virtues I admired; and whose memory, as the
greatest general and as the greatest minister that our country or perhaps any
other has produced, I honour.

> Henry St John, 1st Viscount Bolingbroke, *Letters on the Study*
> *and Use of History*, 1752

John Churchill was a prominent English courtier, statesman and field commander
who served four monarchs, from the Stuart Restoration of Charles II and James II,
to William III and Queen Anne. Created Earl of Marlborough by William III
of Orange, the peak of his spectacular military career lasted a decade, from his

appointment as Captain-General in 1702 to his ignominious dismissal in 1711. The reports of Marlborough's campaigns in Netherlands, southern Germany, northern France, and Bavaria brought him fame and fortune such as no previous English commander had enjoyed.

John Churchill (1650–1722), son of the influential Cavalier Colonel Winston Churchill, was born in Devon. In 1667 he received a commission in the Foot Guards and fought in the Dutch War with Louis XIV of France's mighty army, the paramount military force of the period. Then, rising from the position of a page at the Stuart court, he served the Duke of York through the 1670s and early 1680s, earning military and political advancement and being raised to the peerage as Lord Churchill. The Battle of Sedgemoor against the rebellion of the Duke of Monmouth in July 1685 was the first engagement in which he played a leading part.

Bedroom politics played a decisive role in Marlborough's rise to power. Churchill was the lover of Barbara Villiers, erstwhile mistress of Charles II, and his entree into the retinue of James II was facilitated by the King's relationship with Churchill's sister Arabella, with whom James had four children. Churchill also changed sides with alacrity: he owed his early career and his peerage to James II and yet, determined to remain on the winning side, deserted him in his hour of need in November 1688 and pledged his allegiance to the Prince of Orange. In return, William III rewarded Churchill by granting him the Earldom of Marlborough. John Churchill would come late to major military command. His Captain-Generalcy of 1702 had everything to do with the close relationship between his wife, Sarah Jennings, and Queen Anne. As her favourite, shortly after her accession to the throne in 1702, Anne also made him the first Duke of Marlborough.

In September 1701 the War of the Spanish Succession was undertaken by the Grand Alliance, formed by the United Provinces, England, Emperor Leopold I and Prussia, against King Louis XIV, in order to prevent the succession of his grandson Philippe d'Anjou to the throne of Spain. At the outset of hostilities, Marlborough was appointed overall Commander of the Grand Alliance in the Low Countries.

To relieve the pressure on Imperial forces after their defeat at the Battle of Höchstädt (September 1703), Marlborough's 20,000 men marched 400km in five weeks from the Moselle River to join forces with Prince Eugene of Savoy and the Margrave Ludwig von Baden in Germany. With the logistics of that march carefully organized and depots established along the route, the troops lacked neither supplies nor rest, each night's camp being prepared for them in advance. His men, who nicknamed Marlborough 'Corporal John', were thus fully fit to fight when they arrived at their final destination.

I have heard much of the English cavalry, and find it, indeed, to be the finest and best-appointed I have ever seen. Money, of which you have no want in England, can buy clothes and accoutrements; but nothing can purchase the spirit which I see in the looks of your men. It is an earnest of victory.

Prince Eugene to the Duke of Marlborough, June 1704, as cited in Winston Churchill's *Marlborough: His Life and Times*

Marlborough and Eugene then faced a Franco-Bavarian army commanded by the Duke of Tallard and Prince Elector Max Emanuel. The extent of the Allied victory at Blenheim on 13 August 1704, when the Franco-Bavarians suffered 30,000 casualties, forced Bavaria out of the war. This first decisive victory in a pitched battle over the mighty forces of Louis XIV was widely celebrated in Britain. The Dutch and the Princes of the Rhineland had, however, contributed considerably to the victory, and these allies were largely responsible for keeping the army properly supplied.

I have not time to say more, but to beg you will give my duty to the Queen and let her know her Army has had a glorious victory. Monsieur Talland and two other Generals are in my coach and I am following the rest: the bearer, my aide-de-camp, Colonel Parke, will give her an account of what has passed. I shall do it in a day or two, by another more at large.

Marlborough to his wife Sarah,
August 13, 1704

Allied efforts to exploit their victory in 1705 foundered on poor coordination and tactical disputes, forcing Marlborough to call off the campaign. In May 1706, however, he led an Allied force with Field Marshal Hendrik van Nassau Ouwerkerk at the Battle of Ramillies against the Duke de Villeroy and again prevailed. Marlborough made brilliant use of the terrain to move his troops and gain local superiority (something Villeroy failed to realize until it was too late). In the aftermath, the whole of Brabant fell to the Allies in just two weeks. Concurrently, with the Treaty and Acts of Union (1706–7), England and Scotland were politically integrated into a single kingdom known as Great Britain.

At the giant Battle of Oudenarde (July 1708), once again alongside Prince Eugene of Savoy and Field Marshal van Nassau Ouwerkerk, Marlborough executed a flanking manoeuvre, gaining the Allies a significant tactical and strategic advantage. The day ended with another victory, followed by the gruelling siege and capture of Lille, Vauban's 'Queen of the Citadels', defended by the able Marshal Boufflers. Prince Eugene was in charge of the siege operations, whilst Marlborough provided cover and prepared to fend off any relieving army.

It is impossible for me to expresse the uneasiness I suffer for the ill-conduct of the engineers at this siege, where I think everything goes wrong. It would be a cruel thing if, after what obliged the enemy to quit all thoughts of relieving the place by force, which they have done by repassing the Schell, we should faile of taking it by the ignorance of our engineers. Three times the troops recoiled from the dreadful carnage, and three times, resolute not to be outdone, they returned to the assault. On the fourth occasion, Eugene, almost desperate of success, himself led them on. 'Recollect,' said he, 'Hochstedt, Ramilies, and Oudenarde.'

Marlborough to the 1st Earl of Godolphin, Lannoy,
20 September 1708

The fall of Lille and Ghent to the Allies in December opened a corridor for the invasion of France. The following campaign ended with the Pyrrhic victory of Malplaquet (September 1709), at which the Allies suffered 24,000 casualties, while the Duke de Villars' smaller force only lost 6,000 men, the French even managing to withdraw in good order. Mons fell to the Grand Alliance in October, but the invasion of France had been prevented by Marshal Boufflers and Villars.

[We] attacked the Enemy in the wood with a great deal of courage and resolution but were received by the Enemy with as great bravery. Wee beat them from that post and they beat us back again with as great courage and resolution as wee had them . . . There was a great effusion of blood on both sides; the Armys fireing at each other bayonett to bayonett. And after came to stabb each other with their bayonets and several came so close that they knocked one another's brains out w'th the butt end of their firelocks.

Sergeant John Wilson about the Battle of Malplaquet,
The Journal of John Wilson

In the age of line tactics, British infantry regiments adopted platoon firing from the Dutch – a highly trained battalion would thus maintain a continuous fire effectively across its entire front. The French, for their part, opened fire by ranks in a deep formation. Marlborough's foot soldiers excelled in sustaining enemy fire while advancing to 30 metres. Then, after their point-blank volleys at only 5 metres had devastated the opposing ranks, they would charge home with bayonets.

Flintlock muskets replaced matchlocks during the war, and by 1702 all the Imperial regiments were equipped with the new muskets. The flintlock had numerous advantages over the matchlock and it was easier to reload, the process of loading the weapon being reduced from forty-four steps to only twenty-six. The rate of fire thus increased, and with cartridges replacing the bandolier, a trained infantryman was typically able to fire two to three shots per minute, a considerable increase in firepower. Steel ramrods would become standard issue in the Prussian regiments from 1718, leading to even quicker reloading.

The Marquis de Vauban had invented the revolutionary socket bayonet in December 1687. It became standard issue in Louis XIV's regiments as soon as early 1689, while Hugh Mackay's ring system was a byproduct of the Scottish government army's defeat at Killiecrankie in July of that same year. This development had the effect of making the *chevaux de frise* obsolete on the battlefield. From the 1703 campaign on, French regiments adopted bayonets using an efficient spring-loaded locking system which allowed men to reload and fire with the bayonet fixed on a flintlock musket. At the Battle of Speyerbach in November, Marshal Tallard defeated German troops when his infantry charged with locked socket bayonets, afterwards capturing Landau. That same year, pikemen disappeared altogether from the French regiments, allowing for greater tactical mobility.

> When this war started, some regiments had quit the pikes, the remainder always had a fifth of the soldiers armed with pikes; but by the winter of 1703–4 they were entirely given up, as were the muskets shortly afterwards. During this war the officers were armed with spontoons of eight feet in length; sergeants with halberds of six feet & half, and all the soldiers with flintlock muskets, with socket bayonets, to be able to fire with the bayonet at the end of the flintlock musket.
>
> Jacques-François de Chastenet de Puységur, *Art de la Guerre par principes et par règles*, 1748.

During the same period, the use of massed field artillery on the battlefield was steadily gaining ground. At Rocroi in 1643 Louis II de Bourbon had only twelve guns at his disposal; Turenne used sixty-four at the Battle of Arras (1654); at the Battle of Höchstädt (1703) ninety were deployed. The same number was used a year later at Blenheim by the Allies, but at Malplaquet Eugene and Marlborough lined up no fewer than 101 field guns to provide long-range barrage fire. Although Villars and Boufflers facing them had only eighty guns, Lieutenant General Saint-Hilaire's well-positioned batteries caused an appalling 5,000 casualties among the advancing Allies in the first thirty minutes of the battle, in particular at close range with the effective use of canister.

Meanwhile, their catastrophic defeat at Almansa by the Duke of Berwick (April 1707) had forced the British and Austrians to come up with a different grand strategy. The Allies had won battles, but they were unable to bring the war to a successful conclusion. The Sun King's armies had recovered from their previous string of defeats; more than ever, the French monarch would not concede any humiliating peace terms. Bourbon victories in the Hispanic peninsula had already secured the position of Philippe 'the Brave' as King of Spain. In Britain, the war was a huge financial drain and had become increasingly unpopular. It cost £1,000,000 a year to maintain the Army in continental Europe, the total burden of the war for Britain amounting to some £9,000,000 annually. Marlborough's bold grand strategy was critically hampered by lack of support both at home and from his allies.

This deteriorating situation further reduced Marlborough's and his wife's already waning influence with the queen. Sarah, who had fallen out of favour, was dismissed from the court. The anti-war Tory party won control of Parliament in 1710 and would force the Peace of Utrecht. That year, the campaign against Villars brought only a small success in the form of the capture of Bouchain.

In 1708 Graf Guido von Starhemberg had been appointed Supreme Commander of the Imperial forces in Spain. After his victories at Almenar and Zaragoza, together with James Stanhope, he occupied Madrid on 21 September 1710. In November, however, both Allied commanders were forced to leave the capital for lack of local support for the Habsburg pretender, since the population stood firmly behind Phillipe de Bourbon. Stanhope and Starhemberg were defeated by the Duke of Vendôme one after the other at the Battles of Brihuega and Villaviciosa (December 1710). Von Starhemberg had to pull back to Catalonia, while Archduke Karl returned to Austria to assume the Imperial crown after the death of his brother Joseph in April 1711.

The peninsular campaign was over, and the Hasburgs had definitively lost Spain. Marlborough, who had voiced his strong opposition to the peace, was replaced at the head of the Allied armies by the Duke of Ormond and charged with corruption by the House of Commons. The disgraced Duke would never lead an army again.

> In the ten campaigns he made . . . he never fought a battle which he did not gain, nor laid siege to a town which he did not take.
> Captain Robert Parker of the Royal Irish Regiment, 1747

At Denain, in July 1712, Marshal Claude Louis Hector de Villars' soldiers stormed the Dutch entrenchments and defeated a part of Prince Eugene's numerically superior army, pressing home their attack using bayonets. Reinforcements sent by Eugene were cut to pieces. Many defenders were killed, and the remaining Dutch infantry attempted to escape across the mill bridge, which collapsed during the retreat. Hundreds of Allied troops drowned in the Scheldt. The fall of Denain to Louis XIV's army was the turning point in the War of the Spanish Succession, enabling France to gain a more favourable peace.

Marlborough and his wife remained in exile in Europe from 1712 to 1714. The Duke eventually returned to favour under the House of Hanover, before his death from a stroke at his estate of Windsor Lodge in June 1722. His fame lived on in popular ballads and songs, and Sir Winston Churchill and Earl Spencer are both distant descendants of John and Sarah Churchill.

> And so God bless the Queen and Duke, and send a lasting peace,
> That Wars and foul Debare henceforth in all the World may cease.
> *A Happy Memorable Ballad on the Fight near Audenarde*, 1708

Achievements

Marlborough was England's outstanding general up to that time. According to Major General John Frederick Charles Fuller, 'Blenheim was the greatest battle won on foreign soil since Agincourt.' A brilliant soldier, skilful, opportunistic and deceptive, Marlborough also proved to be a talented military administrator and a superb organizer who excelled at logistics, battlefield tactics and siege warfare. Though early eighteenth-century warfare tended to rely on manoeuvre and methodical sieges, Marlborough also sought action through bold movement and decisive pitched battles. The concern he demonstrated for the well-being of his troops earned him the loyalty of his soldiers and the nickname 'Corporal John'. Marlborough's task was arduous: he was required to use authority and tact to hold together a large polyglot military coalition that suffered from conflicting aims, while dealing with significant political interference at home. Even if he did not achieve his ultimate goal of complete victory over the Bourbons, his triumphs on the battlefield turned Britain into a great European power.

Jacob van Schuppen, Eugene of Savoy, c.1720, Österreichische Galerie Belvedere, Vienna.
(*Wikimedia Commons*)

Chapter 36

PRINCE EUGENE OF SAVOY
Austria's 'noble knight'

From the age of twenty, he commanded the armies and fought the battles of Austria on all the fronts of the Empire. When he was not fighting the French, he was fighting the Turks. A colonel at twenty, a major-general at twenty-one, he was made a general of cavalry at twenty-six. He never married, and although he was a discerning patron of art, his only passion was warfare.

Winston Churchill, *Marlborough: His Life and Times*

Prince Eugene of Savoy, the 'noble knight', served under Emperors Leopold I, Joseph I, and Karl VI in the course of a military career spanning almost six decades, with effective participation in thirty campaigns. Champion of the struggle against the Ottomans in Central Europe, Eugene later successfully contained Louis XIV's forces in the Low Countries, Northern Italy, Germany, and the Palatinate, before returning east and inflicting a new string of decisive defeats on the Sultan's armies. Eugene was the most versatile and talented commander of his age and, according to Napoléon I, one of the greatest military commanders of all time.

Eugene of Savoy Carignano (1663–1736) was born in Paris. His father, Eugene Maurice of Savoy, was one of Louis XIV's generals. His mother, Olympia Mancini, was Cardinal Mazarin's niece, and Eugene grew up at the court of the Sun King. Initially groomed for the Church, instead, by the age of nineteen, Eugene had determined on a military career. Rejected by Louis XIV for service in the French armies, he escaped to Austria and transferred his loyalty to Emperor Leopold I.

Learning that his older brother Louis Julius had been killed by the Turks in a cavalry clash at Petronell, Eugene swore to avenge his death. Under the banner of the Duke Charles V de Lorraine, he arrived just in time to take part in the Battle of Kahlenberg that saved Vienna (1683). In the aftermath of this resounding victory he was given the rank of Colonel of a regiment of dragoons and fought against the Turks in the next four campaigns. During the Nine Years' War (1688–97), Eugene first served on the Rhine, then was sent to Piedmont-Savoy. At the Battle of Staffarda, the coalition of the Grand Alliance was defeated by Marshal Catinat, but in the spring of 1691 Eugene caused the siege of Coni to be raised and took possession of Carmagnola.

In June 1697 Eugene was finally given overall command of the Imperial army in Hungary. He was thirty-three years old, though already extremely experienced. Eugene found his soldiers to be in rather poor condition, but was quickly able to boost their morale. When told that he only had 31,142 men under his command, he reportedly replied, 'Thank you for this information. I am the 31,143rd, and soon we will be more!' The Imperial War Council gave him express orders to 'cover Peterwardein & the other fortresses along the Danube, without coming to a decisive battle, unless forced to do so'.

On the morning of 11 September 1697 Eugene learned that the Sultan's army had built a pontoon bridge over the Tisza near Zenta in northern Serbia. The Sultan and the cavalry had already crossed the river with part of the artillery train, but it would take longer for the infantry and baggage to follow. The young prince, who was expecting an attack on Peterwardein, decided to rush matters: by a forced march his army arrived in sight of the Ottoman camp protected by their *tábor* (wagons) in the late afternoon. Eugene did not hesitate, but led a frontal assault with the Prince de Commercy, while he sent Guidobald von Starhemberg to the flank of the Turkish encampment to cut off the enemy's retreat. When the Imperial artillery succeeded in disabling the floating bridge, thousands of *Janissaries* found themselves caught in a deadly trap. Enraged, they turned against the Grand Vizier and their officers, slaughtering them and sparing only their own *Aga* (top Ottoman military official, commander of the Janissary corps). The Imperial troops gave no quarter: by nightfall, 20,000 Turks had fallen in battle and 10,000 more had drowned while trying to swim the Tisza.

> It was six in the evening. The Turks, assaulted, and their entrenchments forced at every point, hurried in crowds to the bridge, and choked it up, so that they were obliged to throw themselves into the Teisse, where those who escaped drowning were killed. On every side was heard the cry of *Aman*! *Aman*! which signifies Quarter! At ten the slaughter still continued; I could take no more than 4,000 prisoners, for 20,000 were left dead on the field, and 10,000 were drowned. I did not lose a thousand men.
>
> Eugene of Savoy in Prince de Ligne,
> *The Life of Prince Eugene of Savoy*

The Grand Vizier and nearly fifty *pashas* were killed. The spoils of war were tremendous: the Vizier's war chest, 100 guns, 9,000 waggons, 60,000 camels, 700 horses, and no fewer than 423 banners. Prince Eugene's fame was definitely secured by this phenomenal success, inflicting on the Ottomans one of the most decisive defeats in the history of their Empire. The Turks started to nickname him the 'Dwarf Devil'.

> ZENTA [1697]. Whenever I call to mind the miserable confusion at that time, I cannot help being seized with a secret horror. There was then no safety, either from friend or foe, but, on the contrary, the greatest confusion imaginable. The Sultan lay hid three days in the town [Timişoara] unknown to all but the *Pasha*, while various reports flew through the whole camp of his being taken and betrayed by his subjects. The troops that had escaped, wandered up and down without discipline, and for hunger, plundered every one they met.
>
> Dimitrie Cantemir, *The History of the Growth and Decay of the Ottoman Empire*

Eugene was greeted in triumph by the citizens of Vienna on 17 November and honoured by the Emperor. Zenta was the last decisive step in forcing Sultan Mustafa II to sign the Treaty of Karlowitz (1699), ending Ottoman control over large parts of Central Europe and the Balkans.

In 1701, at the beginning of the War of the Spanish Succession, Eugene, who was given few resources, nevertheless gained the upper hand in Italy, outmanoeuvring Marshal Catinat and Marshal Villeroy and defeating them at Carpi and Chiari. In February 1702 Eugene took Cremona with a lightning raid, even capturing Villeroy. The following year, Leopold I appointed him President of the Imperial War Council. Eugene's celebrated partnership with the Duke of Marlborough secured resounding victories from 1704 to 1708 at Blenheim, Oudenarde and the Siege of Lille. The great march of 1704 to the Danube, actually conceived by Eugene, was executed triumphantly by Marlborough. It was a daring plan to withdraw the main allied force from the north to the south, from the Netherlands to Bavaria, but it paid off.

In 1706, as Imperial Commander in northern Italy, Eugene accomplished one of the most daring feats in Early Modern military history. In July-August his 42,000 men marched some 350km, crossing the Adige, the Canal Bianco and the Po, passing through the Venetian *Terraferma* which was feebly defended by the outnumbered forces of the *Serenissima* under Saxon General Steinau (who had just returned from the war against Karl XII of Sweden), and outflanking French defensive lines one after the other. Their goal was to come to the relief of the Duke of Savoy Vittorio Amedeo, whose capital, Turin, was besieged by the Duc d'Orléans (the future Regent of France).

During the Siege of Turin, the main attack under La Feuillade targeted the citadel. After three months of bloody operations (June–September), as Vauban had predicted, the bombardment had inflicted considerable damage, but the citadel remained largely intact. The besiegers were forced to withdraw by the timely arrival of Prince Eugene, who had outmanoeuvred the French Marshals. On 7 September he stormed their positions, winning an extraordinary victory. Marshal Ferdinand de Marsin was captured and died shortly afterward, and the entire French camp fell into the hands of the Imperial and German troops. Eugene's masterful campaign forced Louis XIV's armies to evacuate Italy.

The consequences of this victory were even greater than the triumph itself; and they deservedly place it among the most memorable battles which have occurred in modem times. The whole of Italy became the prize of the victor. The French troops on the north of the Peninsula hastened in dismay across the Alps; the fortresses they still held in Piedmont were all besieged and taken; the kingdom of Naples, cut off from all succour from France or Spain, by this victory by land, and by the English fleets by sea, was obliged to conclude a separate peace, and accept the Imperial government.

Archibald Alison, *The life of John, Duke of Marlborough*
with some account of his contemporaries

That same year, Marlborough had prevailed at Ramillies and captured most of the Spanish Netherlands. With Prince Eugene's success in northern Italy, the Allies had inflicted the greatest loss of territory and resources that Louis XIV would suffer during the entire War of the Spanish Succession. For the Allies, 1706 proved to be an *annus mirabilis*. Louis XIV sued for peace, but the Coalition demanded that the Sun King abandon Philippe V and collaborate with them to expel his own grandson from Spain. As Louis XIV rejected these humiliating conditions, the war dragged on until 1714.

After the Treaty of Rastatt, Eugene was named Governor of the Austrian Netherlands. When hostilities were renewed against the Ottomans, Eugene was again given command of the Imperial troops in Hungary. His reputation was consolidated in decisive victories at the Battle of Peterwardein, where Grand Vizier Damad Ali Pasha was killed and his army routed, then by the capture of Temesvár (1716). The following year, Eugene's 70,000-man army, laying siege to Belgrade, the gate of Central Europe, soon found itself threatened by the colossal 200,000-man Ottoman relief host of the new Grand Vizier Hacı Halil Pasha. The prospect of being able to escape from this giant trap appeared bleak.

> The whole of Europe was then occupied with the conduct of Prince Eugene; each reasoned about it in his own way, some accused him of temerity and recklessness for having engaged, a little too lightly, they said, between two fires; & to have put himself in a state of being able to get out of this strait only by a victory; the others praised his courage and his firmness, & relied on the resources of his genius, superior in effect to all difficulties. A famous French General could not help saying then, considering the situation this Prince had found himself in, that he was going to gamble the fate of the Empire on a throw of dice. M. le Prince Eugene had placed himself in the necessity of conquering or of dying when he had made the resolution to wait for the Turks.
>
> Thomas Amaulry, *Campagnes de M. le Prince Eugene en Hongrie*

Caught between the mighty Belgrade fortress and the Grand Vizier's innumerable forces, there was no escape: 'Either I will take Belgrade or the Turks will take me!' declared Eugene to his staff. But many of the Imperial troops were battle-hardened veterans of the War of the Spanish Succession, and at midnight on 16 August Eugene signalled the launch of a surprise offensive against the Turkish relief forces, 60,000 men marching through the fog against 200,000. On the left flank, Prince Alexander von Württemberg fell on the Turks with six infantry battalions. In the centre however, the *Janissaries* broke through the Imperial lines, and the Prince of Württemberg's troops had to be redeployed. Then the charge of the Austrian cuirassiers led by Eugene in person got the better of the *Sipahis*, who scattered and abandoned their infantry. The Grand Vizier fled for his life to Nissa, and around noon, the whole Ottoman camp fell into the hands of the victors, 30,000 Turks having been killed and 166 guns and mortars captured.

The Ottoman garrison of Belgrade then surrendered to Eugene on 16 August. Ten days later, the inept Hacı Halil Pasha was dismissed by the Sultan. Panic spread far and wide among Muslim and Turkish peoples in the Balkans as far as Edirne (Adrianople) and Istanbul.

> If I had been in charge when we won the Battle of Belgrade in 1717, I would have ordered my brave Germans to march against Constantinople, but the Prince Eugene would not consider this idea, and maybe it would not have succeeded.
>
> *Mémoires du Comte de Bonneval*

As for Eugene, his last two triumphal campaigns against the Turks inspired the famous folk song 'Prinz Eugen, der edle Ritter' (Prince Eugene, the noble knight). With the Peace of Passarowitz (1718) Austria obtained much new territory at the expense of the Ottoman Empire, including the Banat of Temesvár, Belgrade, northern Serbia and Wallachia. Under Eugene's military command, Austria reached its maximum expansion in the Balkans.

Throughout the 1720s, Eugene's influence and skilful diplomacy managed to secure powerful allies for the Emperor in his dynastic struggles against the Bourbons. In 1734, during the War of the Polish Succession, the 70-year-old Field Marshal was once more appointed Commander of the Army of the Rhine by Emperor Karl VI. He held Mainz against Marshal Berwick, then took the offensive until peace terms were reached. Returning to Vienna, Prince Eugene died at his Winter Palace on 21 April 1736. His magnificent three-day funeral ceremony, attended by huge crowds, was held in St Stephen's Cathedral. The Viennese mourned the loss of the *generalissimo* who had turned their city into the capital of a powerful multi-national empire.

The restless Eugene, who had demonstrated time and time again his remarkable bravery on the battlefield, was capable of grasping any tactical situation and taking rapid action. As he frequently exposed himself to danger, he was wounded many times. The Savoyard scarcely spent two years together without fighting. For more than fifty years, when he was not in Vienna, presiding over the Imperial War Council, he was on the march, in military camps or on the battlefield. Since he never married, Eugene was popularly styled 'Mars without a Venus'.

Indubitably, Prince Eugene deserves from a grateful world an appropriate monument since he was an example of virtue and courage, and we owe him even more for his protection than can be expressed in our gratitude . . .

Franciscus Peikhart, *Oratio funebris* [funeral oration] *in mortem serenissimi Principis Eugenii Francisci, e ducibus Sabaudiae et Pedemontii*, 1736

Achievements

Prince Eugene was the relentless adversary of the most powerful military machines of his day, the Ottoman forces and Louis XIV's armies. So outstanding were Eugene's talents and military genius that Napoléon I listed him among history's top seven generals, alongside Alexander the Great, Hannibal, Caesar and Friedrich the Great. While the Austrian monarchy faced severe peril on several fronts, Eugene helped to secure the Empire's western borders from French invasion, and he became the most important architect of central Europe's liberation after a century and a half of Ottoman occupation. His numerous resounding victories raised the reputation of the Imperial army to a point never achieved before. Eugene was also a great patron of the arts whose building legacy can still be admired in Vienna to this day.

Blas de Lezo, by an anonymous painter, 1735, Museo Naval, Madrid. (*Wikimedia Commons*)

Chapter 37

BLAS DE LEZO
The one-eyed, maimed and lame defender of Cartagena

Soldiers from mainland Spain and soldiers from American Spain, you have witnessed the ferocity and power of the enemy. In the Empire's darkest hour we are getting ready to give the final battle for Cartagena de Indias and ensure that the enemy does not pass. The keys of the Empire have been entrusted to us by the King, we will have to return them without the gates of this noble city having been profaned by the evil enemy!

Blas de Lezo to the defenders of Cartagena, 1741

Blas de Lezo is one of most famous Spanish military leaders of the eighteenth century. During his career he fought all the enemies of the Bourbons and the Spanish crown: the English, the Dutch, the Turks, Barbary pirates and untold numbers of privateers. Although suffering from multiple wounds and disabilities, this Basque naval officer served in the Mediterranean, the Pacific, the Atlantic, in mainland Europe, North Africa and on the Spanish Main. He achieved the status of national hero with his remarkable defence of Cartagena de Indias during the 1741 British invasion.

Don Blas de Lezo y Olavarrieta (1689–1741), was born in the harbour city of Pasajes in the Basque province of Guipúzcoa. At the age of twelve he joined the French Navy, the largest and most powerful of the time. Under the command of the Count de Toulouse he took part in the ferocious Battle of Vélez-Málaga (1704) during the War of the Spanish Succession, where the casualties amounted to some 6,000 killed or injured. The young man, seriously wounded by a cannon ball, had to have his left leg amputated below the knee. For the bravery he displayed during the battle, and in the subsequent surgery performed without anesthetics, the young sailor was promoted to the rank of Ensign. This would be but the first of his many wounds sustained in the line of duty.

Lezo participated in the relief of Peñíscola and Palermo attacked by the forces of Archduke Karl of Austria. In command of the four lightweight pinnaces *Renard*, *Lapin*, *Sanglier* and *Lièvre*, he managed to bring supplies to Maréchal de Tessé's forces besieging Barcelona (1706). At the siege of Toulon, the following year, he was one of Fort Sainte-Catherine's defenders. During the fighting he lost his left eye, and in 1713 he lost the use of his right arm after suffering a gunshot wound at the Siege of Barcelona. Aged twenty-five, he was already nicknamed 'medio hombre' (half-man), having lost one leg, one arm and one eye. In June 1715 he was part of the Bourbon fleet that recaptured Mallorca.

From 1720 to 1728 de Lezo was attached to the Viceroyalty of Peru, hunting down English and Dutch privateers and patrolling the 'South Seas' along the South American coastline. In August 1730 he was back in Cadiz and Sevilla for an audience with the King. In recognition of his services, Philippe (Felipe V) made him a member of the Orders of the Holy Spirit and of the Golden Fleece, the most prestigious chivalrous orders of the French and Spanish monarchies.

In 1731 State Secretary José Patiño y Rosales appointed him Admiral of the Mediterranean fleet. De Lezo took the offensive against the Republic of Genoa and exacted a tribute of 2 million pesos from the city after threatening it with a naval bombardment. One and a half million was destined for a new large-scale expedition against the Barbary coast, in which De Lezo served as second in command to Admiral Francisco Cornejo. The armada of 500 ships and a land force of 28,000 infantry and cavalry were placed under the overall command of Carrillo De Albornoz. In the summer of 1732, after landing under the cover of the naval guns, the Spanish army recaptured Oran and Mers el-Kebir from the Dey of Algiers and the Turks. Oran would remain under Spanish control until 1792.

In 1736 de Lezo was made Commander-in-Chief of the galleons of the Atlantic. A year later, he was appointed General Commander of Cartagena de Indias in the Viceroyalty of New Granada, on the coast of present-day Colombia. In 1739 Spain declared bankruptcy, and the Spanish Navy proved too small to support its vast worldwide empire when Britain initiated the War of Jenkins' Ear, called *La Guerra del Asiento* in Spanish.

> What might not be expected from Britain's Royal Navy riding (as it does) paramount of the Seas, capable too of transporting an Army sufficient to command the Enemy's Shores? When they [Navy and Army] are united, they carry with them the most formidable power. A Military, Naval, Littoral War, when wisely prepared and discreetly conducted is a terrible Sort of War. Happy for that People who are Sovereigns enough of the sea to put it in Execution! For it comes like Thunder and Lightning to some unprepared Part of the World.
>
> Colonel Thomas More Molyneux, *Conjunct Operations: or Expeditions that have been carried on jointly by the Fleet and Army*, 1759

On 22 November 1739 Vice Admiral Edward Vernon and General Thomas Wentworth first attacked the port of Portobello. Vernon was nicknamed 'Old Grog' by his sailors since he was in the habit of wearing a grogram cloth coat of silk and mohair. Portobello fell within 24 hours, as its inhabitants, unaware that Britain had declared war on Spain, were caught completely unprepared. The British occupied the town for three weeks before withdrawing, having first destroyed its fortifications, port and warehouses. This lightning success led to the naming of Portobello Road in London, as well as the first performance of the patriotic song *Rule, Britannia!* at Cliveden, Buckinghamshire, home of the Prince of Wales (August 1740).

> You have not only fulfill'd the Letter, but the Spirit of your Orders. Whatever was within your reach, you have made yourselves Master of, and the very Ruins behind us, shall, for many an Age, remain the Trophies of British Valour and Success.
>
> Admiral Vernon to his sailors

Reliably informed by Spanish and French intelligence that Cartagena, the jewel of the Indies, would be the next target of the British, de Lezo scrambled its defences. The Spanish garrison at Cartagena could only rely on 3,000 regulars and militia. De Lezo also had seven warships under his command. In March 1740 a first attempted landing by the British was beaten off by de Lezo, who did not hesitate to take the entire credit for this achievement:

Do not be surprised by my short letters, for I still lack time to rest, according to the occurrences that have burdened me, and especially the management of these dealings, and this fortified place, which the enemies would have undoubtedly conquered, as Portobello before, if I had not been in this Port as it is widely recognized, and it is still in the possession of the King today, owing to my care, and vigilance, compared to the abandonment in which the late Governor had left this place ...

> Blas de Lezo to Don Santiago de Irisarri, 21 May 1740

A year later, Vernon came back with a large combined naval and landing force: 28,000 British and Colonial American sailors and soldiers were transported by 130 ships escorted by 51 ships of the line. De Lezo, who had prepared his defences, used delaying tactics against the British and Colonists, standing firm with his seven warships, striking at the enemy and then falling back. He succeeded in halting the British fleet, first at Boca Chica and later in the harbour itself.

Your Majesty's Forces being in full possession of all the castles, Forts, and Batteries, for defending the Entrance into the Harbour of Carthagena, your Council of War took into Consideration what would be next advisable for them to proceed in.

> Vice Admiral Vernon to the Duke of Newcastle, 30 March 1741

At the end of March de Lezo scuttled his own ships to create a barrier at the entrance of the harbour and prevent the enemy entering the lagoon. When the Spanish had to abandon Fort San Luis, they created another gun battery called Albanicos. De Lezo's forces repelled amphibious assaults and attacks on the coast by ships, prolonging the siege until the arrival of the rainy season (May to November). By then, the last defenders had retreated to the Castillo San Felipe de Barajas, but the invaders were down to only 3,500 effective servicemen.

The admiral was a man of weak understanding, strong prejudices, boundless arrogance, and over-boiling passions; and the general, though he had some parts, was wholly defective in point of experience, confidence, and resolution.

> Tobias Smollett about Vice Admiral Vernon, *An Account of the Expedition Against Cartagena*

The whole expedition had indeed been shamefully mismanaged. The siege, which had lasted for sixty-seven days, ended with the British withdrawing having suffered 16,000 casualties, mostly from yellow fever and other tropical diseases. A total of fifty British ships were lost or abandoned for lack of crews. Of the 3,600 American colonists (initially under the command of Sir Alexander Spotswood, a veteran of the Blenheim campaign) who had volunteered for the expedition against the Spaniards, most died of yellow fever, dysentery or starvation; fewer than one in ten returned to the Colonies. Most of them had been used as pioneers during the siege, the English not trusting them in the front line since they were 'not esteemed fit for service' (Tobias Smollett).

> Stung by the reproaches of the Admiral, General Thomas Wentworth called a Council of his officers, and with their advice he attempted to carry Fort San Lazaro by storm. Twelve hundred men headed by General Guise, and guided by some Spanish deserters or peasants, who were either ignorant, or which is more likely, in the pay of the Spanish Governor whom they pretended to have left, marched boldly up to the foot of the fort. But the guides led them to the very strongest part of the fortifications; and what was worse, when they came to try the scaling ladders with which they were provided, they found them too short. This occasioned a fatal delay, and presently the brilliant morning of the tropics broke with its glaring light upon what had been intended for a nocturnal attack. They stood, under a terrible plunging fire, adjusting their ladders and fixing upon points where they might climb; and they did not yield an inch of ground, though every Spanish cannon and musket told upon and thinned their ranks.
>
> Tobias Smollett, *An Account of the*
> *Expedition Against Cartagena*

Following the retreat, Vernon sailed to Guantanamo Bay after sending a message to de Lezo promising he would come back to Cartagena to renew his attack. Allegedly, the *medio hombre* answered with heavy irony:

> To return to Cartagena, the King of England would need to build a larger squadron, since this one is so weakened that it can only be used to transport coal from Ireland to London.

Blas de Lezo's tenacious actions and tactics had saved Cartagena de Indias. Wounded again during the siege, the Spanish Navy's greatest hero eventually died from yellow fever four months after Vernon's withdrawal. Meanwhile, in Britain, commemorative medals showing de Lezo kneeling down and offering his sword in surrender had been struck prematurely. As for the British Vice Admiral, he would live on in memory for the watered-down ration of rum called 'grog'; sailors who drank too much of it became 'groggy'! Prime Minister Robert Walpole took the blame for the failure of the expedition, while Vernon's celebrated victory at Portobello ensured his lasting popularity at home.

De Lezo was entombed in the Dominican convent of Santo Domingo at Cartagena. In recognition of his distinguished service, in August 1760 the gallant defender of Cartagena received posthumously the hereditary title of Marquis of Ovieco:

> To reward the distinguished services rendered to the Crown during forty years by Lieutenant General of the Fleet Don Blas de Lezo, especially since his courage and admirable behaviour contributed to saving the famous fortified place of Cartagena de Indias, which was besieged by the English in the year one thousand seven hundred and forty, and from where they were expelled with much glory.

Achievements

By 1740 de Lezo had been maimed by four decades of campaigning, being one-eyed and lame, with limited use of one arm. He nevertheless accomplished his most difficult mission and achieved his greatest feat of arms against Vernon's formidable expedition. This remarkable victory consolidated Spain's hold over the Americas for the next seventy years. In Britain, however, news of the defeat at Cartagena was a significant factor in the downfall of Sir Robert Walpole. Upon his return to Virginia, George Washington's half-brother Lawrence named his plantation 'Mount Vernon' in the British Admiral's honour. Blas de Lezo y Olavarrieta would remain, along with sixteenth-century Captain General Álvaro de Bazán, the only undefeated naval commander in the history of Spain. Since 1885 the Spanish Navy has honoured the memory of Admiral de Lezo by giving his name to one of its ships.

Benjamin West, Robert Clive and Shah Alam, Treaty of Allahabad, 1818, British Library.
(*Wikimedia Commons*)

Chapter 38

ROBERT CLIVE
Founder of Britain's Indian Empire

The commander, who had to conduct the defence under circumstances so discouraging, was a young man of five and twenty, who had been bred a book-keeper. During fifty days the siege went on. During fifty days the young captain maintained the defence, with a firmness, vigilance, and ability which would have done honour to the oldest marshal in Europe.

Thomas Babington Macaulay on Clive during the Siege of
Arcot, *Lord Clive*, 1840

Robert Clive was a ruthless administrator, a cunning military officer and an ambitious empire builder who became the chief representative of the British East

India Company (EIC) in the subcontinent. Since the Company's Royal Charter of 1600 had authorized it to wage war, its military arm developed into a private armed force used as an instrument of geopolitical power and expansion. At its height, it ruled a territory larger than Britain and accounted for half of the world's trade. In the eighteenth century the Company became the dominant power in Bengal, the richest province of the Mughal Empire, centre of the worldwide muslin and silk trades. From 1741 the French under Governor General Joseph François Marquis de Dupleix allied with the Mughals to resist British expansion.

Robert Clive (1725–74) came to India in 1743 as a young clerk for the 'high and mighty, the noblest of exalted nobles, the chief of illustrious warriors', the EIC. After the fall of Madras to the French in 1746, Clive escaped and joined the EIC's army. In 1750 the Company had 3,000 regular soldiers; fifteen years later, it had a standing army of 26,000. In 1757 Clive adopted Governor General Dupleix's idea of the sepoy battalions used by the French East India Company since 1719. The EIC's sepoys were native Indian soldiers recruited in the Bombay and Madras Presidencies, armed, dressed and trained like British redcoats, but commanded by British officers.

As Captain of Fort St George, in August 1751 Clive seized the fort of Arcot in the Carnatic capital without a fight, after Nawab Chanda Sahib's garrison fled at the sight of his incoming forces.

> I am a most fortunate fellow, upon my march for Arcot the Moors took such a Pannick that they have left me in Possession of a Fort in the Midst of it, surrounded with a small Ditch, to-morrow I shall have 3 Months Provisions in the Place and nothing less than 300 Europeans with a Train of Battering cannon shall force me out of the Place.
>
> Robert Clive to Captain Rodolphus de Gingins,
> Arcot Fort, 2 September 1751

At the head of his 500 men, Clive then held out against the 4,000 men of a joint Indian-French counter-offensive led by Raza Sahib (the Nawab's son) that lasted fifty days, until relieved by British forces. Major Stringer Lawrence and Clive together then effected the relief of Trichinopoli, outmanoeuvring the besieging forces and compelling them to withdraw.

When Chanda Sahib was assassinated, Muhammad Ali, an ally of the British, replaced him as Nawab of the Carnatic. William Pitt, the Prime Minister, commanded Clive for his actions, calling him a 'heaven-born general'. Clive returned to Britain in 1753 as a national hero and a wealthy man. The following year, his formidable adversary, the Marquis de Dupleix, was recalled to France by the Directors of the French East India Company.

In 1757 Clive was back in India. As he assumed his new post of Deputy Governor of Fort St David at Cuddalore, the Nawab of Bengal, Siraj Ud Daulah, attacked and captured Calcutta, but the British retook the city after Clive's show of force against the Nawab's army. Threatened by the growing power of the British in Bengal, Siraj Ud Daulah then began negotiating with the French authorities. Now promoted to Colonel, Clive with Admiral Charles Watson attacked the French trading post of Chandernagore, which fell on 23 March 1757.

Since the Company's forces were badly outnumbered, Clive now began an intrigue to overthrow Siraj Ud Daulah. He convinced Mir Jafar, Siraj Ud Daulah's military commander, to betray his master in exchange for the nawabship. Consequently, at the Battle of Plassey on 23 June 1757, when Clive's army of 3,100 men clashed with Siraj Ud Daulah's 50,000 troops, the Company's forces emerged victorious after Mir Jafar's well-orchestrated defection. The victory owed more to treachery and bribes than to military prowess.

> Reinforced from the fleet, our army, amounting to 1,000 Europeans, and 2,000 sepoys, stood opposed to 20,000 horse, and 50,000 foot. In this situation, it was judged expedient to secure some of those chiefs in our interest, whom the nabob's violence had disgusted; and Meer Jaffier, being the most powerful, was chosen as a proper ally.
>
> Harry Verelst, A *View of the Rise, Progress, and Present State of the English Government in Bengal*

The betrayed Nawab was assassinated at Murshidabad, the Bengali capital, a few days later. The Comte d'Aché captured Cuddalore, but the French siege of Madras failed, while the British commander Sir Eyre Coote decisively defeated the Comte de Lally at the Battle of Wandiwash in 1760 and overran the French territory of the Northern Circars. Pondicherry, France's main outpost in India, fell to the British in 1761. By the Treaty of Paris (1763), France eventually retained five trading posts: Chandernagor, Pondicherry, Karikal, Mahé and Yanaon, but Britain ended the war as the dominant European power in India, well placed to take full advantage of the weakened Mughal Empire.

> National feeling was growing in strength; it had been kindled by Pitt, and fanned into a flame by a series of victories which were largely due to the inspiration of his lofty spirit. He had raised Great Britain from a low estate to a height such as it had never reached before. In India the victories of Clive and his generals were soon to be crowned by the fall of Pondicherry, and French and Dutch alike had already lost all chance of successfully opposing the advance of British rule by force of arms.
>
> William Hunt, *The Political History of England*

In the 1761 British General Election, Clive was elected a Tory Member of Parliament and elevated to the peerage as 'Baron Clive of Plassey, County Clare, in the Kingdom of Ireland', which provoked the caustic commentary from Horace Walpole that 'West Indian Nabobs and Conquerors' were taking over every borough. Following the victory of the Company's forces under Major Hector Munro at Buxar against Mughal Emperor Shah Alam II, who was captured, Clive returned to India for the third time, this time as Commander-in-Chief of the Company's civil and military forces.

On 12 August 1765, by the Treaty of Allahabad, Clive obtained an imperial *firman* (edict) from the coerced Shah Alam which gave the EIC the right to collect revenues in Bengal, Bihar and Orissa. This document served as the basis for British power in India, for the Company could now collect revenues from a population of 30 million.

> A business of such magnitude, as left neither pretence nor subterfuge, and which at any other time would have required the sending of wise ambassadors and able negotiators, as well as much parley and conference with the East India Company and the King of England, and much negotiation and contention with the ministers, was done and finished in less time than would usually have been taken up for the sale of a jack-ass, or a beast of burden, or a head of cattle.
>
> Ǧulām Husayn Khan, *Siyar-ul-Mutakherin*

In the province of Bihar, where the best opium in the East was grown, the Company quickly assumed monopoly control. Clive served twice as Governor of Bengal, and its tax burden was increased four times, while wages decreased and the Company's administrators failed to respond to droughts and floods. The collected taxes and customs duties were used to purchase Indian goods and export them to England. Clive, who never learned Persian and only understood a little Tamil, depended entirely upon interpreters and translators during his twelve years in India.

Clive also invested in diamonds, which he shipped home secretly for resale, and reinvested in the EIC itself, buying £100,000 worth of stock. After accumulating untold riches, he returned to Britain in 1767, purchasing a large estate in Surrey, where he built Claremont House. Clive the 'nabob' was envied by most of his contemporaries, but was also one of the most hated men in Britain. Horace Walpole, who loathed the *nouveau riche*, described him as a 'monster in assassination, usurpation and extortion'. Unsurprisingly, Clive was affected by bipolar disorder and opium addiction, as well as depression caused by criticism of his activities in India; he faced charges of embezzlement by Parliament and was held responsible for the Bengal famine of 1769–73 that caused an estimated

10 million deaths. According to the *Oxford Journal*, 'There were not people enough left alive to bury the dead' (23 March 1771).

> He considered himself as the general, not of the Crown, but of the Company. The Company had, by implication at least, authorised its agents to enrich themselves by means of the liberality of the native princes, and by other means still more objectionable. It was hardly to be expected that the servant should entertain stricter notions of his duty than were entertained by his masters. It was a very easy exercise of virtue to declaim in England against Clive's rapacity; but not one in a hundred of his accusers would have shown so much self-command in the treasury of Moorshedabad.
>
> Thomas Babington Macaulay, *Lord Clive*

Although Clive was officially cleared of these charges, King George III, 'while fully acknowledging Clive's services, thought him guilty of "rapine" and disapproved of his virtual acquittal.' Unable to cope with the physical and mental strain, 'Clive of India' eventually killed himself with a penknife on 22 November 1774. He was only forty-nine. Clive was buried without ceremony in an unmarked vault in the churchyard of the village of Morton Say, Shropshire.

> From his first visit to India dates the renown of the English arms in the East. Till he appeared, his countrymen were despised as mere pedlars, while the French were revered as a people formed for victory and command. His courage and capacity dissolved the charm. Nor must we forget that he was only twenty-five years old when he proved himself ripe for military command. This is a rare if not a singular distinction. It is true that Alexander, Condé, and Charles the Twelfth won great battles at a still earlier age but those princes were surrounded by veteran generals of distinguished skill, to whose suggestions must be attributed the victories of the Granicus, of Rocroi and of Narva. The only man, as far as we recollect, who at an equally early age ever gave equal proof of talents for war, was Napoléon Bonaparte.
>
> Thomas Babington Macaulay, *Lord Clive*

Achievements

In the middle of the eighteenth century Robert Clive became 'the richest self-made man in Europe' according to the *Oxford Journal*, estimated to be worth over £100 million in today's money thanks to his control of Bengal, one of the wealthiest regions in the world at the time. The former clerk had amazed everyone by his talent for organization, tactics and leadership. In everything he acted promptly and decisively. He almost single-handedly founded the Empire of British India, and built the sizeable army of the East India Company which became an empire within an empire. His victory at the Battle of Plassey was instrumental in establishing British power. Although Pondicherry and Chandernagore remained under French control until 1954, the French East India Company was abolished 20 years before the Revolution. The British Company would then monopolize trade from India for the next two centuries, ruling over large regions of the subcontinent, exercising huge military power and paving the way for the British Raj. According to some historians, the looting of Bengal even contributed to the Industrial Revolution in Britain. Today, the Clive Museum in Powis Castle (Welshpool) houses more than 1,000 Mughal items looted by Clive and his son Edward.

Charles Willson Peale, Nathaniel Greene, 1783.
(*Independence National Historical Park/Wikimedia Commons*)

Chapter 39

NATHANAEL GREENE
Washington's most trusted commander

We have struggled with innumerable difficulties, and they increase dayly.
My force and my Talents are unequal to the conflict. Without more effectual
support in the Southern States they must fall and I fear will lay a train to sap
the foundation of the Independence of the rest . . . We fight, get beat, rise,
and fight again. We have a bloody field; but little glory.

Nathanael Greene to the Marquis de La Fayette, 1 May 1781

Nathanael Greene was a Quaker autodidact from Rhode Island. Enjoying
lightning promotion, he was appointed General by the legislature of Rhode

Island and served his apprenticeship under George Washington at Boston, Long Island, New York, Valley Forge, Philadelphia, Trenton, Princeton and during the 'forage war'. He served Washington as his chief supply officer for most of the American War of Independence, becoming his master strategist, the most solid and dependable of his lieutenants. Greene's pragmatic, hit-and-run guerrilla warfare against Lieutenant General Cornwallis was decisive in winning the war.

Like most of the patriot commanders, Nathanael Greene (1742–86) had no formal military training. Before the war he ran his father's iron foundry in Rhode Island. His introduction to military strategy came shortly before the war through reading a variety of books on military history and treatises such as Caesar's *Commentaries on the Gallic War*, the *Mémoires* of Marshal Turenne and Maurice de Saxe's *Rêveries*. In 1770 the young patriot was elected to the local General Assembly, and four years later, as tensions between Britain and the Colonies mounted, Greene helped organize the Kentish Guards, a local militia, in which he only served as private because of his pronounced limp and asthma.

> I would make it a treason against the state to make any further remittances to Great Britain. We had as good begin in earnest first as last, for we have no alternative but to fight it out or be slaves.
>
> Nathanael Greene to Governor Samuel Ward,
> September 1775

In 1775 the state of Rhode Island raised three regiments and promoted Greene to Brigadier General to command them. In June, at the siege of Boston, he was made a Brigadier General of the Continental Army. He was then thirty-four years old and in the course of about a year had been promoted from private to Brigadier General, a meteoric rise if ever there was one!

> He came to us the rawest, most untutored being I ever met with, but in less than twelve months he was equal, in military knowledge, to any General officer in the army, and very superior to most of them.
>
> Henry Knox, on Greene

The Continental Army went into winter quarters at Valley Forge in December 1777. Their need for supplies of all kinds was evident from the beginning, and in order to secure enough food, Washington appointed Greene to look after the commissariat. In March 1778 he was convinced by Washington to accept the daunting responsibility of becoming the army's Quartermaster General.

When the weather and road conditions began to improve, Greene and his assistants succeeded in re-supplying the Continental troops with much-needed food and clothing.

> The public is much indebted for his judicious management and active exertions in his present department. When he entered upon it, he found it in a most confused, distracted and destitute state. This by his conduct and industry has undergone a very happy change.
>
> George Washington on Nathanael Greene, letter to the
> Continental Congress, 3 August 1778

After General Horatio Gates' humiliating defeat at Camden in August 1780, Greene became Commander of the Continental Army's southern wing. On paper, he had 2,500 men under his command, but in reality, only about 800 were fit for service. With these limited numbers, Greene was forced to engage in a strategy of avoidance and attrition against the British. Seconded by the seasoned Prussian Baron von Steuben and the fiery young French Marquis de La Fayette, and splitting his forces into widely separated groups, he improvised, reluctantly adopting guerrilla warfare, fighting skirmishes and driving Cornwallis to distraction with forced marches. Dividing his soldiers, he focused on preserving the field army, as he marauded across North Carolina, South Carolina and Virginia. Brigadier General Francis Marion's militiamen were all mounted, a fact which accounted for much of their success as against the redcoats and Loyalists.

> Let me conjure you, my countrymen, to fly to arms and repair to Head Quarters without loss of time and bring with you ten days' provision. You have every thing that is dear and valuable at stake; if you will not face the approaching danger your Country is inevitably lost. On the contrary if you repair to arms and confine yourselves to the duties of the field Lord Cornwallis must certainly be ruined. The Continental Army is marching with all possible dispatch from Peedee to this place. But without your aid their arrival will be of no consequence.
>
> Recruitment poster for Nathanael Greene's army, 1780

Lacking officers, men and supplies, but making the most of guerrilla tactics with his Continentals and militias, Greene was able to bleed Lieutenant General Charles Cornwallis's army in a series of small-scale tactical victories (Guilford Courthouse, 15 March 1781; Eutaw Springs, 8 September 1781), reducing the British chain of defensive forts in Georgia and South Carolina.

Sir, My letter to Congress a copy of which I enclose your Excellency will inform you of an unsuccessful action with Lord Cornwallis on the 15th. Our prospects were flattering; and had the North Carolinia Militia seconded the endeavors of their officers, victory was certain. But they left the most advantageous position I ever saw without scarcely firing a gun. None fired more than twice and very few more than once, and near one half not at all. The Virginia Militia behaved with great gallantry, and the success of the day seemed to be doubtful for a long time. The Action was long and severe.

Nathanael Greene to George Washington, in camp near
Guilford Court House, 18 March 1781

Cornwallis was compelled to move to Wilmington on the North Carolina coast to re-supply, allowing Greene to reclaim South Carolina. The British under the command of Lieutenant Colonel Francis Rawdon were expelled from most of the southern states, with the exception of areas around Charleston and Savannah. Eventually Cornwallis would take his fateful step into Virginia, seeking shelter in Yorktown. Greene never won a major battle, but he did not lose this crucial campaign. In just a year, and with virtually no outside material or manpower support, he had been able to revive the Revolutionaries' cause in the southern theatre. Greene, who was not involved in the Siege of Yorktown, remained at Charleston until August 1783, when he asked for leave from Congress which was granted as the assembly resolved

> That two pieces of the field ordnance taken from the British army at the Cowpens, Augusta, or Eutaw, be presented by the Commander-in-chief of the armies of the United States, to Major-general Greene, as a public testimonial of the wisdom, fortitude, and military skill which distinguished his command in the southern department, and of the eminent services which amidst complicated difficulties and dangers, and against an enemy greatly superior in numbers, he has successfully performed for his country; and that a memorandum be engraved on said pieces of ordnance, expressive of the substance of this resolution.

George Washington Greene, The Life of Nathanael Greene

After the war, as the South Carolina government had voted him a substantial reward for his services, he settled with his family on a plantation in Georgia. Greene, who had served brilliantly in the Continental Army during the entire war, died outside of Savannah of sunstroke in June 1786. He was only forty-three years old.

Achievements

Although he had no previous military experience and was self-taught, Nathanael Greene executed a textbook example of unconventional warfare in the Colonies. Using Fabian strategy, although he failed to defeat the British in pitched battle, the former militia private was responsible for winning the war in the southern theatre, earning a reputation as the prime strategist of the American Revolution. A talented administrator, a resourceful and innovative leader, Washington, who never lost faith in his abilities, considered him one of his most able and trusted commanders. Greene's remarkable contributions helped change the course of the American War of Independence.

La Fayette, portrait attributed to Louis Leopold Boilly, 1788, Palais de Versailles.
(*Wikimedia Commons*)

Chapter 40

MARQUIS DE LA FAYETTE
Hero of the American War of Independence

From the first moment I heard the name of America, I loved her; the second I knew she was fighting for freedom, I burned with the desire to shed my blood for her, and the moment I shall be able to serve her, at any time, or in any part of the world, will be the happiest of my life.

La Fayette to Henry Laurens, President of Congress, in camp near Warren, 23 September 1778

From 1777 to 1781 during the American Revolutionary War, the young Marquis de La Fayette served in the Continental Army with distinction and bravery, providing inspired leadership while securing vital resources from France. La Fayette's influence at the court of Louis XVI proved decisive, as the French government sent an army and a fleet to support the cause of the insurgents, changing the course of the war. Washington's trusted lieutenant dedicated his fortune, his valour and his heart to the cause of freedom as an American general. La Fayette was a key participant in the decisive campaign of Yorktown, culminating in the ultimate victory that led to Independence. The celebrated Marquis remained a lifelong advocate of political liberty.

Marie Joseph Paul Yves Roche Gilbert du Motier, Marquis de La Fayette (1757–1834), was born into a prominent military family of noble lineage in Chavaniac, France. In the 1790s he would joke about it to Madame de Pougens: 'I was baptized like a Spaniard, it isn't my fault'! La Fayette's father was killed fighting the British at the Battle of Minden (1759), and his mother and grandfather both died in 1770, leaving the young boy with a considerable fortune. He joined the Black Musketeers of the King the following year, and at the age of sixteen in 1773 he married 14-year-old Marie Adrienne Françoise de Noailles, daughter of another prominent French family.

Inspired by stories of his father's glorious death on the battlefield and the American colonists' struggle against the British crown, with childlike confidence he bought a merchant ship which he christened '*La Victoire*' and sailed to the Thirteen Colonies on 26 April 1777. He took with him a handful of close friends to fight as volunteers and a cargo of 6,000 muskets for the Georgia militia. Defying the orders of King Louis XVI, who did not wish to provoke Great Britain, the 19-year old Marquis eluded the authorities, crossed the Atlantic and arrived in Philadelphia – only to be initially rebuffed by Congress!

> The more desperate the cause, the greater need has it of my services; and, if Mr. Deane has no vessel for my passage, I shall purchase one for myself, and will traverse the ocean with a selected company of my own.
> John Quincy Adams, *Oration of the Life and Character of Gilbert Motier de Lafayette*, 31 December 1834

La Fayette was eventually awarded the honorary status of Major-General in the Continental Army on 31 July 1777, without pay. He received his baptism of fire during the Battle of Brandywine on 11 September 1777, when George Washington was defeated by William Howe. La Fayette was shot in the leg while trying to rally the retreating troops. Washington requested that Dr John Cochran, his personal physician, take special care of La Fayette, igniting a strong friendship between the two that lasted until Washington's death. The young man became Washington's beloved 'adopted son'.

> I am sorry to inform you that in this day's engagement we have been obliged to leave the enemy masters of the field. Unfortunately the intelligence received of the enemy's advancing up the Brandywine, and crossing at a Ford

about six miles above us, was uncertain and contradictory, notwithstanding all my pains to get the best. Our loss of men is not, I am persuaded, very considerable; I believe much less than the enemy's. Notwithstanding the misfortune of the day, I am happy to find the troops in good spirits; and I hope another time we shall compensate for the losses now sustained. The Marquis La Fayette was wounded in the leg, and General Woodford in the hand. Divers other officers were wounded, and some slain, but the numbers of either cannot now be ascertained.

George Washington to the Continental Congress,
11 September 1777

After two months' convalescence La Fayette returned to the field. He was given command of the division previously headed by Major General Adam Stephen and soon put his troops to good use. With 300 militiamen he surprised a force of Hessian *Jägers* (light infantry skirmishers and sharpshooters) and defeated them at the Battle of Gloucester. In December, La Fayette was given command of a division of Virginians. He spent the winter in Valley Forge with Washington, suffering along with the other Continental soldiers in the freezing, disease-ridden encampment. He supported Washington when the colonists' leader faced an internal threat from the Conway Cabal, a plot to drive him from his command. In March 1778, as France recognized American independence, the tide of war was about to turn.

> [At Valley Forge] there was often to be seen Lafayette, not yet turned of twenty-one, though a husband, a father, and a major-general; graver somewhat in his manners than strictly belonged either to his years or his country; and loved and trusted by all, by Washington and Greene especially.
>
> George Washington Greene, *The Life of Nathanael Greene*

In May 1778 La Fayette outwitted British Generals Henry Clinton and James Grant sent by Howe to capture him and his 2,400 men at his camp on Barren Hill, Pennsylvania. Their attempted pincer movement completely failed to ensnare La Fayette as the British left a large gap through which his army escaped, with the help of Oneida Natives. In June, Washington and La Fayette rallied the retreating Continental forces at Monmouth Courthouse to force a stalemate.

In January 1779 La Fayette departed for France. By March, Benjamin Franklin reported from Paris that he had become an excellent advocate for the insurgents' cause at the court of King Louis XVI. For his part, the Marquis was eager to return to the Colonies to fight alongside his mentor George Washington:

> What I want, My dear general, what would Make Me the happiest of Men, is to join Again American Colours, or to put under your orders a division of four or five thousand Country men of mine. American independancy is a

certain undoubtfull point, but I want that independancy to be aknowledged with advantageous Conditions—The whole, My dear General, Betwen us— For what concerns the Royal, ministerial, public good will towards America, I, an American citizen, am fully Satisfied with it, and I am sure the Alliance and friendship betwen Both Nations will be establish'd in Such a way as will last for ever.

La Fayette to George Washington, 13 June 1779

In March 1780 La Fayette returned to America on board the fast frigate *Hermione*. This time, the young Marquis returned as an official emissary of Louis XVI to George Washington, in order to announce that France was sending another squadron of 8,000 regulars in support of the independence of the Thirteen Colonies, a reinforcement which greatly boosted the insurgents' morale. Upon his return, La Fayette assumed increased military responsibility, helping to coordinate Vice-Admiral d'Estaing's campaign in Rhode Island. He defined the terms for the Comte de Rochambeau's arrival in 1780 and shuttled between the French and American commands.

Lord Cornwallis will not give up this Country without being soundly beaten. I wish our force was more competent to the business. But I am in hopes by little and little to reduce him in time. His troops are well found and fight with great obstinacy. I am very happy to hear the Marquis de la Fayette is coming to Virginia, tho' I am afraid from a hint in one of Baron Steubens letters, he will think himself injured in being superseded in the command. Could the Marquis join us at this moment, we should have a glorious campaign. It would put Lord Cornwallis and his whole army into our hands.

Nathanel Greene to George Washington, Camp near
Guilford Court House, 18 March 1781

As commander of the Virginia Continental forces in 1781, La Fayette shadowed Lieutenant General Cornwallis's army as it eventually moved back east towards Portsmouth, Virginia. He was instrumental in keeping Cornwallis pinned down at Yorktown, Virginia.

This devil Cornwallis is much wiser than the other generals with whom I have dealt. He inspires me with a sincere fear, and his name has greatly troubled my sleep. This campaign is a good school for me. God grant that the public does not pay for my lessons.

La Fayette, 9 July 1781

In early September La Fayette received reinforcements in the shape of the Marquis de St Simon's 3,200 men who had landed at Jamestown. Their army took up position in Williamsburg, waiting a week for the arrival of the further 4,500 French reinforcements led by Rochambeau and the 4,000 Continental troops commanded by Washington. In total, Louis XVI's France would expend more than a billion *livres* to support the American insurgents in their struggle for independence.

While the allies laid siege to the British camp, the Comte de Grasse defeated the British at the Battle of the Chesapeake. According to British naval historian Sir William M. James, Chesapeake was 'the decisive battle of the war'; its outcome was crucial to the successful Franco-American siege of Yorktown. Cornwallis was forced to surrender in the last major battle of the War of Independence, and La Fayette, proudly dressed in his uniform of Major-General in the Continental Army, witnessed the surrender of the British alongside his friend George Washington.

> The play is over, Monsieur le Comte; the fifth act has just ended. I was a bit uneasy during the first acts, but my heart keenly enjoyed the last one, and I have no less pleasure in congratulating you on the successful conclusion of our campaign.
> La Fayette to the Comte de Maurepas, 20 October 1781,
> after Lord Cornwallis's surrender at Yorktown

Recognized on both sides of the Atlantic as the 'Hero of Two Worlds', after returning with well-deserved laurels to France in December 1781, La Fayette continued to advocate the principles of liberty. He undertook the drafting of the first 'Declaration of the Rights of Man' and naturally became one of the leaders of the pre-revolutionary constitutional reforms in France.

Appointed Commandant-General of the National Guard of Paris on 15 July 1789, he managed to preserve public order by his sheer prestige and immense popularity. When La Fayette had the Bastille fortress, symbol of royal absolutism, dismantled, he sent its key to George Washington as a token of their friendship:

> Give me leave, My dear General, to present you With a picture of the Bastille just as it looked a few days after I Had ordered its demolition, with the Main Kea of that fortress of despotism—it is a tribute Which I owe as A Son to My Adoptive father, as an aid de Camp to My General, as a Missionary of liberty to its patriarch.
> Lafayette to Washington, Paris, 17 March 1790

During the French Revolutionary wars that followed, La Fayette initially fought the Austrians in 1792 as General of the Armée du Nord, but as a leader of the moderates he had to flee from France when the Revolution lapsed into the Reign of Terror. Captured by the Austrians, he languished for five years in prison at the Olomouc fortress, despite the efforts of the US Congress and President Washington to have him released. In November 1794 an escape attempt, organized by his American friend

Benjamin Huger, failed to rescue him, and La Fayette remained a prisoner, in chains, until September 1797. During the last two years of his captivity, his wife Adrienne, together with their two daughters Anastase and Virginie, resolved to share his fate, and Emperor Franz II allowed them to remain close to him in the fortress.

Almost three decades later, in 1824–5, La Fayette undertook a triumphal grand tour of the United States. The 'Hero of Two Worlds' had also regained prominence as a statesman in France before his death on 20 May 1834 at the age of seventy-six. When word of La Fayette's death reached the United States, the nation went into mourning. President Andrew Jackson ordered that the legendary Marquis receive the same funeral honours that President John Adams had ordered for George Washington in 1799.

> In the firmament of heaven that rolls over our heads there is, among the stars of the first magnitude, one so preeminent in splendor as, in the opinion of astronomers, to constitute a class by itself, so in the 1,400 years of the French monarchy, among the multitudes of great and mighty men which it has evolved, the name of Lafayette stands unrivalled in the solitude of glory . . . The name of Lafayette shall stand enrolled upon the annals of our race high on the list of the pure and disinterested benefactors of mankind.
>
> John Quincy Adams, *Oration of the Life and Character of Gilbert Motier de Lafayette*, 31 December 1834

Achievements

From the outset, the idealistic young Marquis de La Fayette had been determined to support the struggling colonists win their independence. In 1779–80 his securing of formal French support for the American cause was decisive. According to US author Larrie D. Ferreiro, 'The American Revolution had little chance of being won by the American colonists, if it had not been for the assistance of French and Spanish soldiers, money and weapons. France and Spain provided the Americans with what in today's dollars would be nearly $30 billion in financial assistance, as well as 90 per cent of all the guns the colonists used. The two nations also sent thousands of soldiers.' The charismatic aristocrat, who had never served in battle upon his arrival in America, ensured smooth cooperation between the insurgents and France through his integrity and diplomatic skills. As Major-General of the Continental Army, he demonstrated gallantry and tactical brilliance, harassing the enemy to keep Cornwallis's superior forces in check. La Fayette also commanded one third of Washington's Continental Army at the decisive siege of Yorktown. For his outstanding role in the American War of Independence, on 6 August 2002, the US Congress proclaimed him an honorary citizen.

Part IV

THE MODERN ERA UP TO THE COLD WAR

(1790 – 1991)

Antoine-Jean Gros, Joachim Murat at the Battle of Aboukir in July 1799, c.1807, Palais de Versailles, Google Art Project. (*Jean-Marc Manaï*)

Chapter 41

MARSHAL JOACHIM MURAT
Napoléon I's dashing cavalry commander

He was a brave man, no one was more so, but he was a fool. Murat was the best cavalry general in Europe. [At Waterloo] he would have given more impetuosity to the charges. Two or three battalions had to be broken in, and I believe Murat would have succeeded in doing so. Magnificent feathers surmounted his bonnet, sparkling with diamonds and embroidery; his entire costume was covered with gold. The enemy soldiers saw and admired only him. I cannot explain how he escaped death a thousand times. The enemies, and the Cossacks above all, uttered cries of joy when they saw him. Every day he engaged in some singular combat with them; he never returned without dyeing his sword with their blood. He was a real paladin. Murat and Ney were the two bravest men I have known. Murat's character was more noble, more frank.
Napoléon I in Las Cases, *Memorial of Saint Helena*, 1823

Joachim Murat was one of Napoléon I's most celebrated marshals, a dashing, boastful cavalry leader, famous for his insane bravery and flamboyant uniforms. From Italy to Russia, Napoléon's lieutenant participated in some 200 battles. He married Caroline, Napoléon's youngest sister, was one of the first men to be created Marshal of the Empire (1804), was granted the Grand Duchy of Berg (1806–8) and went on to be crowned King of Naples (1808–15), before losing it all after Napoléon's ultimate defeat.

The son of a wealthy innkeeper from southern France, Joachim Murat (1767–1815) was originally destined for an ecclesiastical career. Instead, he enlisted in the royal cavalry in 1787 and then won rapid promotion during the Revolutionary Wars. In October 1795, under the command of Brigadier-General Napoléon Bonaparte, he played a key role in suppressing a royalist insurrection in Paris. As Bonaparte's aide-de-camp during the campaign of Italy, he distinguished himself at Dego, Mondovi and Bassano (1796).

> I could fill up 10 volumes with the traits of bravery that I witnessed in every rank, from King Murat, to the simple fusilier . . . Murat, brave among the braves, always charged at the head of his cavalry and never returned without his sabre being bloodstained.
>
> Elzéar Blaze, *La Vie Militaire sous le Premier Empire*

At the Battle of Aboukir (25 July 1799) Murat led a cavalry charge against the Ottoman centre and captured the Turkish commander, Mustapha Bey, in single combat, during which the *Pasha* shot him at point blank range with a pistol. The bullet went through Murat's mouth, piercing both his cheeks, and he had to undergo an operation by the brilliant chief surgeon, Dominique Larrey. Thereafter he was forced to remain completely silent for twenty days. This bullet could have been fatal if Murat had not, at that precise moment, opened his mouth to scream, as usual, like a madman. 'It's the first time he ever opened it for a good purpose!' commented Napoléon.

On 18 Brumaire (9 November 1799), it was Murat's intervention that saved Napoléon's coup d'état, thanks to his grenadiers' storming of the Council of the Five Hundred. Murat's reward was the hand of Napoléon's youngest sister, the 17-year old Caroline, in January 1800. Napoléon, who was actually opposed to the union, did not attend the wedding. In June, at the Battle of Marengo, as a Divisional General, Murat helped win a hard-fought battle. He concluded the campaign against Bourbon-ruled Naples by imposing the Armistice of Foligno, which earned him a sabre of honour and his title of Marshal of the Empire in 1804.

During the 1805 Ulm campaign, Murat's squadrons covered 400 kilometres in just six day. He outflanked and routed the Austrians at Wertingen on 8 October.

Murat was given command of the entire right wing of the army, consisting of Ney's and Lannes' corps. At the Battle of Hollabrun on 16 November 1805, while Mikhail Kutuzov's army was in full retreat, Murat made the mistake of believing an armistice was about to be agreed. The ingenious Russian Field Marshal dispatched Ferdinand von Wintzingerode, Balgration and Dolgorouki to Murat in order to gain precious time, hinting that a peace treaty was about to be signed, and Murat ordered his troops to stand down. When Napoléon was informed, he was furious:

> I cannot find words to express my displeasure. You only command my vanguard and have no right to agree to an armistice without my orders. You will cost me the fruits of a campaign. End the armistice at once, and attack the enemy. Inform him that the general who has signed this has no power to make it, that only the Russian Emperor has the right, and that when the Russian Emperor ratifies this agreement, I will also ratify it. But it is only a ruse. March, destroy the Russian army! You are in a position to take his baggage and artillery.
>
> Napoléon to Murat, 16 November 1805

Murat, realizing that he had been deceived, informed Kutuzov that talks were over and resumed the offensive on the 16th. A month later, he pinned down the Austrian Army in Ulm, and then defeated the Austrian and Russian cavalry on the field of Austerlitz on 2 December 1805. In March 1806 Napoléon made him 'Grand Duke of Berg and Cleves'. At Jena, in October 1806, Murat completed the destruction of the Prussian Army, even capturing General Gebhard von Blücher at Lübeck:

> The whole [Prussian] hostile army is scattered, and it seems that they have not been assigned a rallying point, because all the generals have been wounded or killed. The highest praise goes to Your Majesty's cavalry that attacked yesterday alone, without infantry, a corps of about 10,000 infantry and three cavalry regiments, drove them from their position, captured their cannons and forced them to lock themselves in the fortress. Never have we seen such a rout, never was the terror so general; the officers openly declare that they no longer want to serve, all desert their flags and return home. I have been assured that if I march against them, they will lay down their arms.
>
> Murat to Napoléon, Iéna, 14 October 1806

Murat took part in the Polish Campaign and acquired immortal glory at the Battle of Eylau in February 1807. When the French Emperor pointed at the Russians and the Prussians and asked him, 'Will you let us be devoured by these people?' Murat responded by personally leading one of the largest cavalry charges in history. The 10,700 sabres of the Reserve Cavalry and the Guard Cavalry swept across the battlefield, smashing through the Russian lines and ultimately saving the day.

> The weather having cleared up, the Grand Duke of Berg [Murat], at the head of his cavalry, and supported by Marshal Bessières at the head of the Guard, turned the Saint-Hilaire division, and fell on the enemy army: a daring manoeuvre, if ever there was one. The enemy cavalry, which desired to oppose this manoeuvre, was overthrown; the massacre was horrible. Two lines of Russian infantry were broken; the third only resisted by positioning themselves against a wood. Squadrons of the Guard crossed the entire enemy army twice. This brilliant and unheard-of charge, which had overthrown more than twenty thousand infantry, and had forced them to abandon their artillery, would have immediately decided victory without the woods and some difficulties in the field.
>
> *Bulletin de la Grande Armée*, Preussich-Eylau, 9 February 1807

Regarded as 'brave among the brave' by Napoléon himself, Murat, even when he was a Marshal of France, would dismount and fight shoulder-to-shoulder with his men when required. At Eylau, Murat's finest hour, his gallant charge destroyed Russian attempts to break the weakened French centre. However, Murat was often carried away by his enthusiasm, which earned him the reputation of being rash and foolhardy. At the Battle of Heilsberg in June 1807 he threw himself with the 9,000 men of the Reserve Cavalry and Soult's infantry against Bennigsen's 80,000 well-entrenched Russians, suffering 10,000 casualties in the process. Only Lannes' timely arrival prevented the battle from ending in a French defeat. 'It would be better for us if he [Murat] was less brave and had a little more common sense', declared General Savary (Napoléon's aide-de-camp and Commandant of the Imperial Guard) on that occasion.

> At this moment the Grand Duke of Berg [Murat] came up to us; he came from our right rear, followed by his staff, passed at a gallop across our front, bending forward on his horse's neck, and as he passed at full speed by General Jean-Louis Espagne he flung at him one word alone which I heard, 'Charge!' This order, given without any further directions for an attack on sixty squadrons of picked men by fifteen unsupported squadrons, seemed to me difficult to understand . . . In case of a check we had no possible means of retreat, but the order was given and the thing had to be done.
>
> Colonel Aymar de Gonneville, *Recollections*

After taking Warsaw in November 1807, Murat was sent to Spain by the Emperor, who appointed him Commander of all French troops in the Peninsula. On 2 May 1808 Madrid rebelled against the French occupation; the uprising was put down brutally by Murat's elite Imperial Guard and Mamluk cavalry after the populace had lynched any Frenchman that they could get their hands on. Napoléon gave the Spanish throne to his brother Joseph and rewarded Murat with Joseph's former position as King of Naples.

In Naples, Murat and the ambitious Caroline carried out important modernizing reforms and public works. Murat also foresaw the unification of Italy, founding the influential Carbonari secret society, which would later play a major role in the *Risorgimento*. He also expelled Major Hudson Lowe's British troops from Capri.

On 4 September 1812, the army, still divided into three columns, set out from Gjatz and its environs. Murat had gone on a few leagues before. Ever since the arrival of Kutusof, troops of Cossacks had been incessantly hovering about the heads of our columns. Murat was exasperated at seeing his cavalry forced to deploy against so feeble an obstacle. On that day, from one of those first impulses worthy of the ages of chivalry, he dashed suddenly and alone towards their line, stopped short a few paces from them, and there, sword in hand, made a sign for them to retire, with an air and gesture so commanding, that these barbarians obeyed, and fell back in amazement.

Philippe Paul de Ségur, *History of the Expedition to Russia*

In 1812 Murat took part in the Grande Armée's fateful Russian campaign. On 5 September he began the Battle of Borodino with the Reserve Cavalry's attack on Konovnitsyne's horsemen. On the 7th Napoléon ordered Murat to take Latour-Maubourg's IV Cavalry Corps and strike at the enemy centre. At one point he found himself surrounded by enemies and barely managed to escape with his life:

Murat threw himself into the redoubt ... there he found only some unsteady soldiers whose courage had forsaken them, and running round the parapet in a state of the greatest panic. The presence of the king and his cries first restored confidence to a few. He himself seized a musket; with one hand he fought, with the other he elevated and waved his plume, calling to his men, and restoring them to their first valour by that authority which example gives. Scarcely had the king escaped this peril, when he ran into another; with the cavalry of Bruyère and Nansouty, he rushed upon the enemy, and by obstinate and repeated charges overthrew the Russian lines, pushed and drove them back on their centre, and, within an hour, completed the total defeat of their left wing.

Philippe Paul de Ségur, *History of the Expedition to Russia*

When Kutozov's Russians retreated from their positions in the smoke and confusion, Murat was one of the Marshals who advocated a final push by throwing in the Guard, a move Napoléon refused to authorize. On the battlefield 58,000 men lay dead, along with 35,000 horses. The following year, the Battle of Leipzig would be even bloodier.

> It was now ten o'clock. Murat, whom twelve hours' fighting had not exhausted, again came to ask him for the cavalry of his guard. 'The enemy's army,' said he, 'is passing the Moskwa in haste and disorder; I wish to surprise and extinguish it.' The Emperor repelled this sally of immoderate ardour.
> Philippe Paul de Ségur, *History of the Expedition to Russia*

When Napoléon returned to France in December, Murat was left in command, but he abandoned his post to save his own hold on Naples. Throughout 1813 he wavered between loyalty to the Emperor and negotiation with the Austrians. Napoléon refused to believe his best and most trusted cavalry commander would turn on him, blaming instead his own sister Caroline. In fact, Murat had enjoyed the unwavering support of his young wife, who acted as Regent of Naples while Joachim was campaigning and even supported his decision to betray her own brother in order to retain their crown, making a separate peace with the Allies in 1813.

During the Hundred Days of 1815, Murat rallied to Napoléon and Caroline was again left in charge of Naples. Unsurprisingly, Napoléon refused to give him a military command during the Waterloo campaign, but Murat marched north on his own, claiming that he could unite Italy and expel the Austrians, staking his hopes on an appeal to Italian nationalism. He did win the Battle of the Panaro River, but suffered defeat at Tolentino against General Friedrich Bianchi's Austrians (May 1815).

In October, with just twenty-six men, he made a last, suicidal attempt to recover Naples. Captured by King Ferdinando I's soldiers, he was immediately sentenced to death. Murat faced his destiny with his customary courage. Refusing a confessor or a bandage, he gave the orders to the firing squad himself:

> Soldiers! Do your duty! Straight to the heart but spare my face. Fire!

Following her husband's death, Caroline first went into exile in Austria, before returning to Italy, where she died in 1839. Their eldest son Achille Murat moved to the United States, where he married George Washington's great-grandniece.

> He knew how to conquer, he knew how to reign, he knew how to die.
> Jean-Michel Agar, Comte de Mosbourg, on Murat

Achievements

Murat, the innkeeper's son who became a king, is remembered as the gallant and dashing cavalry commander who actively supported and enabled Napoléon's rise to power. He led decisively in two decades of campaigning all over Europe and the Middle East. Murat was frequently the first to attack, he led cavalry charges that often turned the tide of battle and he pursued his enemies relentlessly, albeit not always with good judgment. His beloved wife Caroline and he proved to be dedicated rulers of Naples, Murat being the first to envisage the creation of a united and independent Italy. Betraying Napoléon, then attempting at all costs to regain his favour, Murat's hesitation contributed to his brother-in-law's defeat at the climactic Battle at Waterloo and spelled his own final doom.

José Gil de Castro, Simón Bolívar, c. 1828, Museo de Arte, Lima. (*Wikimedia Commons*)

Chapter 42

SIMON BOLIVAR
The 'Liberator' of Latin America

Napoléon was great and unique, and also extremely ambitious. Here there is none of that. I am not Napoléon nor do I want to be; I do not want to imitate Caesar, even less Iturbide [short-lived Emperor of Mexico]. Such examples seem to me unworthy of my glory. The title of Liberator is superior to all that human pride has ever received.

Simón Bolivar, Letter to General José Antonio Páez,
6 March 1826

Simón Bolivar was the most prominent leader of the South American revolutions against the Spanish Empire. Although there had been isolated attempts at independence by different regional commanders, they needed to be united under a single inspirational individual. As a general and statesman, through defeats and victories, Bolívar led forces that won independence between 1811 and 1826 for the territories that became Colombia, Venezuela, Ecuador, Peru, Bolivia and Panama. The 'Liberator of Five Nations' also served as President of Gran Colombia and Dictator of Peru.

Born into one of the wealthiest *criollo* (of Spanish descent born in the colonies) families of Caracas in the Viceroyalty of New Granada, Simón Bolívar (1783–1830) was sent to Spain when he was sixteen to receive the best education available at the time. He later travelled in France, Italy, Britain and the United States. The American and French Revolutions, followed by the Napoleonic Wars, had a profound influence on the struggle for independence of the South American continent, and in particular on the formation of what is now Colombia. The Napoleonic takeover of Spain in 1808 triggered resistance in New Spain, and Bolívar became increasingly involved in these revolutionary movements.

> It is a certainty that, as soon as we enter Venezuela, we will be joined by thousands of valiant patriots, who anxiously await our coming in order to throw off the yoke of their tyrants and unite their efforts with ours in the defence of liberty. Let us, therefore, avail ourselves of a time so propitious, lest the reinforcements, which might at any moment arrive from Spain, completely alter the aspect of affairs, and lest we lose, perhaps forever, the welcome opportunity to insure the destiny of these states. The honour of New Granada imperiously demands that she teach these audacious invaders a lesson, by pursuing them to their last entrenchments. Be not insensible to the cries of your brothers. Fly to avenge the dead, to give life to the dying, to bring freedom to the oppressed and liberty to all.
>
> Simón Bolívar, *Cartagena Manifesto*,
> 15 December 1812

At first a staunch supporter of Franciso de Miranda, who planned to liberate and unify all of Spanish America from Spanish rule, Bolivar went into exile in Haiti after eventually handing over Miranda to the Spanish. On 15 June 1813, during the 'Admirable Campaign', Bolívar issued the infamous Decree of War to the Death, permitting the execution of any Spaniard who would not support the Republican cause. The campaign temporarily ended the royalist grip on Venezuela, but irregular forces of *llaneros*, the 'Hellish Legion' commanded by José Tomás Boves, reconquered Caracas in July 1815 and soon restored Spanish authority throughout Venezuela.

Bolívar fled to Jamaica, while Spanish General Pablo Morillo '*El Pacificador*' (a veteran of the Peninsular War alongside Wellington), and Admiral Don Pascual

Enrile besieged Cartagena de Indias with sixty ships, which landed an army of 10,000 men and a siege train of more than 400 cannons. By 6 December 1815, when Cartagena was eventually captured, one third of the city's population had perished in the 105-day siege. More would fall victim to the harsh reprisals during the so-called 'Regime of Terror'. The patriotic cause seemed all but lost; but still Bolívar would not yield:

> The American provinces are fighting for their freedom, and they will ultimately succeed. More than anyone, I desire to see America fashioned into the greatest nation in the world, greatest not so much by virtue of her area and wealth as by her freedom and glory. Although I seek perfection for the government of my country, I cannot persuade myself that the New World can, at the moment, be organized as a great republic. It is a grandiose idea to think of consolidating the New World into a single nation, united by pacts into a single bond. It is reasoned that, as these parts have a common origin, language, customs, and religion, they ought to have a single government to permit the newly formed states to unite in a confederation. But this is not possible. Actually, America is separated by climatic differences, geographic diversity, conflicting interests, and dissimilar characteristics.
>
> Simón Bolívar, Kingston, Jamaica, 6 September 1815

In May 1816, with the support of Alexandre Pétion from Haiti, Bolívar returned to New Granada and established himself as leader of the republican forces in the Venezuelan *llanos* (plains). The *llaneros* had switched their allegiance to the Republicans after they had been disbanded by the European-trained General Pablo Morillo. From there, Bolívar and Francisco de Paula Santander led an army of 3,400 men over the Andes, through the austral winter. Only 1,900 made it to the other side, but the survivors captured Santa Fé de Bogotá after a 77-day campaign that culminated in the Battle of Boyacá on 7 August 1819. Bolívar's audacious campaign in New Granada is considered one of the most daring in military history, sometimes compared to Napoléon's crossing of the Alps in 1800.

> The rebellious Bolívar has occupied the capital of Bogotá, and the deadly outcome of this battle gives him dominion over the enormous resources of a highly populated, abundantly rich nation, from which he will take whatever he needs to prolong the war. In just one day, Bolívar has undone all we have accomplished in five years of this campaign, and in one single battle he has reconquered all the territory that soldiers of the King have won in the course of so many past conflagrations.
>
> General Pablo Morillo to the Spanish War Ministry,
> August 1819

From 1817 to 1824 the 'British' Legion, composed of 6,000 battle-hardened Irish, British and German veterans of the Napoleonic Wars, became a crucial part of Bolívar's and José de San Martin's armies. The young Irishman William Owens Ferguson (1800–28) commanded the Rifles Company, Bolívar's élite unit, and was killed in September 1828 during the failed assassination attempt on the *Libertador*. James Rook (1771–1819) had enlisted in the British Army in 1791, and as Colonel of the 1st Regiment of Hussars of Venezuela, from February to April 1818, led his men in the Battles of Calabozo, El Rio Semén, Ortiz, and Rincón de los Toros. In 1819 he took part in the Campaign of New Granada, assuring Bolívar that, 'if necessary he would follow with the British Legion even beyond Cape Horn!' Rook was mortally wounded at Pantano de Vargas (25 July 1819). A year earlier, another Irishman, the 17-year-old Daniel Florence O'Leary, had joined the forces of the Republicans with the rank of Cornet in the Venezuelan Red Hussars under Colonel Henry Wilson. He would gradually advance to the position of Brigadier General, also serving as Bolívar's aide-de-camp. Bolívar later praised the Legion troops, calling them the 'Saviours of my Fatherland'.

Bolívar's other major military asset was Antonio José Páez's cavalry from the Colombo-Venezuelan plains, used effectively in guerrilla warfare. Páez 'the Centaur' won all the six major battles that he led himself against the Royalists. At the Battle of Las Queseras del Medio in April 1819, his 153 fearless *llaneros* were able to rout their numerically superior foes by applying his famous tactic, a feigned retreat followed by a sudden volte-face that caught the Royalists off-guard.

> Soldiers! You have just achieved the most extraordinary feat that the military history of nations can celebrate. One hundred and fifty men, or rather one hundred and fifty Heroes, led by the undaunted General Páez, have deliberately attacked Morillo's entire Spanish army head-on. Artillery, infantry, cavalry, nothing has been enough for the enemies to defend themselves against the one hundred and fifty companions of the intrepid Páez.
>
> Simón Bolívar, from the Headquarters in Potreritos
> Marrereños, 3 April 1819

The territories of the Viceroyalty gained de facto independence from Spain between 1819 and 1822 after a series of military and political struggles. In the midst of the fight for independence, Bolívar summoned a congress in the city of Angostura to reassert New Granada's autonomy and to create a political system capable of sustaining a new republic.

> We are not Europeans; we are not Indians; we are but a mixed species of aborigines and Spaniards. Americans by birth and Europeans by law, we

find ourselves engaged in a dual conflict: we are disputing with the natives for titles of ownership, and at the same time we are struggling to maintain ourselves in the country that gave us birth against the opposition of the invaders.

Simón Bolívar, Angostura Address, 19 February 1819

The path was prepared for the union of New Granada and Venezuela in the Republic of Colombia (now known as 'Gran Colombia'). It provided Bolívar with the economic and human resources to complete his victory over the Spanish in Venezuela. In November 1820 Bolívar and Morillo met face-to-face at Santa Ana de Trujillo to negotiate a six-month cessation of hostilities.

Bolivar then helped consolidate the independence of Peru and Ecuador, sending his troops south to fight the remnants of the Spanish Army. Rivalry between Peru and Colombia, however, limited cooperation between Bolivar and Argentine General José de San Martín. In June/July 1821, the Battles of Carabobo and the Lake of Maracaibo secured the independence of Venezuela. Quito's independence came with the Battle of Pichincha on 24 May 1822, and Perú was freed on 6 August 1824 after the Battle of Junín. After the victory of Antonio José de Sucre's Independentists at the Battle of Ayacucho in December 1824, the war was virtually over.

The Battle of Ayacucho is the climax of American glory and the work of General Sucre. His plans for battle were perfect and the execution was divine . . . Just as the Battle of Waterloo decided the fate of European nations, that of Ayacucho decided the fate of the nations of Hispanic America.

Simón Bolívar

In 1825 the new republic was named 'Bolivia' in honour of the inspirational leader, now hailed as '*El Libertador*'. Unfortunately, from the outset, Gran Colombia suffered from instability and internal divisions, since many favoured a federal republic, whereas Bolivar supported a strong centralized state. The inevitable collapse of his pan-Hispanic project convinced Bolivar that only a dictatorship could still save the whole experiment, and he declared himself Dictator in February 1828; however, he faced growing criticism for his authoritarianism and attempted assassinations. Gran Colombia went to war with Peru, and Venezuela proclaimed its independence.

Finally acknowledging that his grand experiment was a failure, in April 1830 Bolivar resigned the presidency of Gran Colombia, leaving for Europe in self-exile and abandoning South America to its fate. In June, Sucre, his former lieutenant, the celebrated 'Grand Marshal of Ayacucho', was assassinated by order of Juan José Flores, who would later serve three terms as President of Ecuador after it broke away from Gran Colombia. Weakened, destitute, and bitterly disillusioned, on 17 December 1830 Bolivar died of tuberculosis in Cartagena at the age of forty-seven. His last thoughts were for the citizens of the new nations he had emancipated:

> Colombians, you have witnessed my efforts to establish freedom where tyranny formerly reigned. I have worked unselfishly, giving up my fortune and my tranquillity. I resigned the command when I was convinced that you did not trust my disinterestedness. My foes availed themselves of your credulity and trampled upon what is most sacred to me – my reputation as a lover of freedom. Colombians, my last wishes are for the happiness of our country. If my death can help to destroy the spirit of partisanship, and strengthen union, I shall tranquilly descend to my grave.
>
> Simón Bolívar, 10 December 1830

Achievements

During his lifetime Bolívar experienced extreme highs and lows, from stunning victories to serious setbacks and repeated exile. His successful campaigns in New Granada eventually secured the independence of northern South America. However, shortly after he retired from the Presidency in 1830, Gran Colombia was dissolved and replaced by the republics of Venezuela, New Granada and Ecuador. What followed was a long period of civil wars and revolutions among the states freed from Spanish rule. With time, however, Bolívar's reputation steadily grew. The Liberator's legacy became appropriated by everyone in Latin America, where he is widely considered the greatest leader who ever lived on the continent. In Venezuela, Bolívar remains the nation's guiding deity.

Faisal's party at the Versailles Conference, January 1919. (L to R) Rustam Haidar, Prince Faisal (front), Captain Rosario Pisani (rear), T. E. Lawrence, Faisal's slave (name unknown), Captain Hassan Khadri. (*Wikimedia Commons*)

Chapter 43

COLONEL T. E. LAWRENCE
Leader of the Great Arab Revolt

I never had anything but praise for his work, which, indeed, was invaluable throughout the campaign. He was the mainspring of the Arab movement. He knew their language, their manners, their mentality; in daring, he led them; in endurance, he equalled, if not surpassed, their strongest. There shone forth a brilliant tactician, with a genius for leadership. Praise or blame were regarded with indifference by Lawrence. He did his duty as he saw it before him.

General Edmund Allenby, *The Listener*, 22 May 1935

Lawrence was a British scholar and archaeologist turned intelligence officer. Hailed as a Great War national hero, the self-styled 'Lawrence of Arabia' encouraged and manipulated Arab nationalism in their revolt against the Turks. Through his coordination with General Allenby's Egyptian Expeditionary Force, he played an important role in the eventual success of British forces in the Sinai-Palestine campaign. Seeking glory and recognition, but appalled by his own wartime misdeeds, the self-tortured army officer became a controversial legend in his lifetime, inspiring revolutionary leaders for decades.

The illegitimate son of an Irish aristocrat, Thomas Edward Lawrence (1888–1935) was born in North Wales. As a teenager, he developed an early interest in medieval military architecture. He made his first trip to Syria and Lebanon during the summer vacation of 1909 as a student of archaeology and medieval history, embarking on a dangerous tour of Crusader castles on foot, visiting the Krak des Chevaliers on 16 August, his twenty-first birthday. His 1910 Oxford University thesis, the fruit of his research, was entitled 'Crusader Castles'. During the 1912–13 campaign Lawrence served as Leonard Woolley's assistant at the Hittite site of Carchemish in the *vilayet* (administrative sub-division) of Aleppo. Here he learned to speak Arabic and how to survey.

Soon after the outbreak of the First World War, Lawrence found employment as a subaltern of the Foreign Office. In December 1914, he was sent to the Arab Bureau headquartered in Cairo. The Bureau was tasked to coordinate imperial intelligence in the Middle East, although its activities would largely be confined to the logistical support of the 1916 Arab Revolt and frustrating French imperial ambitions in the region. Its members included other historians, archaeologists and scholars such as acting Director David Hogarth and Gertrude Bell.

> The previous plan of Sherif Abdullah to secure the independence of Hejaz (as a preliminary to the formation of an Arab State) was to lay sudden hands on the pilgrims at Mecca during the great feast. He calculated that the foreign governments concerned (England, France, Italy, and Holland) would bring pressure on the Porte to secure their release. When the Porte's efforts had failed, these Governments would have had to approach the Sherif direct, and would have found him anxious to do all in his power to meet their wishes, in exchange for a promise of immunity from Turkey in the future. This action had been fixed (provisionally) for 1915, but was quashed by the war.
>
> T. E. Lawrence, report to the Arab Bureau, 13 May 1917

Sharif Husayn of the Hejaz rebelled against the Turks in June 1916, taking control of Mecca and Jeddah. In October 1916 Lawrence was ordered to Jeddah to assess the military situation. Now a Captain, he became liaison officer and adviser to Emir Faisal ibn Husayn, the third of the four sons of the revolt's leader. Lawrence later wrote:

> I felt at first glance that this was the man I had come to Arabia to seek – the leader who would bring the Arab Revolt to full glory.
>
> T.E. Lawrence, *Seven Pillars of Wisdom*

With Faisal and his 6,000 irregulars, Lawrence helped to organize and carry out attacks on Ottoman outposts from Aqaba in the south to Damascus in the north. Faisal's army welcomed Lawrence's advice and assistance. The rather frail young man gave the tribesmen hope and an ambitious goal: to take Damascus. Lawrence's own overriding and somewhat contradictory aims were to help the Arabs achieve self-government, while at the same time promoting the interests of the British Empire.

> The value of the Arab army depended entirely on quality, not on quantity. The members had to keep always cool, for the excitement of a blood-lust would impair their science, and their victory depended on a just use of speed, concealment, accuracy of fire. Guerrilla war is far more intellectual than a bayonet charge.
>
> T. E. Lawrence, 'Guerrilla Warfare' in *Encyclopedia Britannica*

The young Captain, soon promoted to Lieutenant Colonel, proved to be a superb tactician and a highly influential theoretician of desert guerrilla warfare. He was the mastermind of a war of extraordinary fluidity, always advocating indirect approach. Advised by Lawrence, Faisal's small but effective irregular forces attacked Turkish communications, telephone wires and supply routes, tying down thousands of Turkish troops while avoiding direct confrontation. Unguarded sections of the Hejaz railway and bridges were blown up by the Hashemite guerrillas, wrecking tracks and derailing trains. On 26 March 1917 Lawrence led an attack on the Aba el Naam station, inflicting seventy casualties on the garrison and taking thirty prisoners.

> The Turkish army was an accident, not a target. Our true strategic aim was to seek its weakest link, and bear only on that till time made the mass of it fall. The Arab army must impose the longest possible passive defence on the Turks (this being the most materially expensive form of war) by extending its own front to the maximum. Tactically it must develop a highly mobile, highly equipped type of force, of the smallest size, and use it successively at distributed points of the Turkish line.
>
> T. E. Lawrence, 'Guerrilla Warfare' in *Encyclopedia Britannica*

On 6 July 1917 the Arab forces led by Auda ibu Tayi and Lawrence won their first major victory, seizing Aqaba, a strategically important Red Sea port, after a two-month march to the edge of the Nefud desert. The capture of Aqaba enabled the rebel Arab forces to be supplied by the British. The British headquarters were astonished when Lawrence, who had travelled 250km by camel across the Sinai Peninsula in fifty hours, arrived in Cairo to request relief and supplies. Emir Faisal, who moved his headquarters to Aqaba, placed himself and his army under the command of British General Edmund 'the Bull' Allenby's Egyptian Expeditionary Force. By then, Lawrence had grown confident he could control and use the Bedouin effectively to Britain's advantage:

> While very difficult to drive, the Bedu are easy to lead, if you have the patience to bear with them. The less apparent your interference, the more your influence. They are willing to follow your advice and do what you wish, but they do not mean you or anyone else to be aware of that. It is only after the end of all annoyances that you find at bottom their real fund of goodwill.
>
> T. E. Lawrence, 'Twenty-Seven Articles', Arab Bulletin,
> 20 August 1917

Success mounted, as the Sharifian Arab forces gradually made their way north, with Jerusalem as the final objective. At Tafas, on 27 September 1918, Lawrence ordered the killing of a column of retreating refugees, an event that haunted him for the remainder of his life.

> We left Abd el Main there and rode on past the other bodies, now seen clearly in the sunlight to be men, women, and four babies, toward the village whose loneliness we knew meant that it was full of death and horror. The Zaggi burst out into wild peals of laughter, in which some of those who were not sick joined hysterically. It was a sight near madness. I said: 'The best of you brings me the most Turkish dead'; and we turned and rode as fast as we might in the direction of the fading enemy. On our way we shot down those of them fallen out by the roadside who came imploring our pity.
>
> Lowell Thomas, *With Lawrence in Arabia*

The Arab-British offensive culminated in Allenby's quasi-Biblical entry with his armies into Jerusalem (December 1917) and Damascus (October 1918). In the Levant, 'The Bull' successfully pioneered cooperation between infantry, cavalry, artillery, armoured cars and aircraft at the Battle of Megiddo against Liman von Sanders' Yildirim Army Group and Mustafa İsmet (September 1918). On the Western Front, the use of combined arms by the Allies had gradually improved since the First Battle of Cambrai (November-December 1917), and by the end of the Great War, the foundations of combined arms warfare were firmly established. Marching north along the Hejaz Railway, Faisal's Sharifian army captured Aleppo on 25 October. Lawrence was then promoted to Colonel.

> Meantime, in the desert to the east and south, a curious campaign was not only helping to weaken the fighting strength of Turkey but shedding some new light on strategy and, in particular, on the indirect approach. This campaign was the Arab Revolt, with Lawrence as its guiding brain. If it falls into the category of guerrilla warfare, which is by its very nature indirect . . . in September 1918 when it had reduced the Turkish forces on the Hejaz railway to a state of paralytic helplessness the main Turkish forces in Palestine were overthrown by a single decisive stroke. In this stroke of Allenby's, however, the Arab forces played a significant part.
>
> Basil H. Liddell Hart, *The Strategy of Indirect Approach*

The newly-appointed commander of the disintegrating Ottoman 7th Army, Mustafa Kemal, was forced to fall back to a final defensive line, which became the basis for the Armistice of Mudros a few days later (30 October). The Ottoman negotiators ceded to the Allies the right to occupy 'in case of disorder' any Ottoman territory, signalling the effective end of the Empire. The Great Arab Revolt of 1916–18 had served its purpose:

> Its value to the British commander was great, since it diverted considerable Turkish reinforcements and supplies to the Hejaz, and protected the right flank of the British armies in their advance through Palestine. Further, it put an end to German propaganda in southwestern Arabia and removed any danger of the establishment of a German submarine base in the Red Sea. These were important services and worth the subsidies in gold and munitions expended on the Arab forces.
>
> General Archibald Percival Wavell,
> *The Palestine Campaigns*

After the fall of Damascus to the Australian Light Horse, Allenby had to advise Emir Faisal, who became part of a new independent Arab government formed after the capture of the city, 'to moderate his aims'. According to the Sykes-Picot agreement, made public in the 26 November 1917 edition of the *Manchester Guardian*, France was to gain control of Syria and Lebanon. However, the provisions of the agreement, and of the Anglo-French Declaration of November 1918, clashed with promises previously made to the Arabs by British High Commissioner Sir Henry McMahon in 1915–16.

The last modest clause concealed a treaty (kept secret, till too late, from McMahon, and therefore from the Sherif), by which France, England and Russia agreed to annex some of these promised areas, and to establish their respective spheres of influence over all the rest. Rumours of the fraud reached Arab ears from Turkey. The Arabs, having tested my friendliness and sincerity under fire, asked me, as a free agent, to endorse the promises of the British Government. I assured them that England kept her word in letter and spirit. In this comfort they performed their fine things: but, of course, instead of being proud of what we did together, I was continually and bitterly ashamed.

T.E. Lawrence, Seven Pillars of Wisdom

Lawrence, by that time an international celebrity thanks to American journalist Lowell J. Thomas, left for London and then the Paris Peace Conferences to lobby for Arab independence. Although the Arabs found themselves freed from centuries of Ottoman rule, Lawrence was particularly disillusioned by his failure to win them genuine independence. Faisal was made King of Syria, but his reign proved short-lived, as the Middle East came under mandate rule by France and the United Kingdom. Instead, in 1921, Faisal was offered the crown of the British mandate of Iraq which he accepted reluctantly. He ruled until his death in 1933 from a heart attack.

In 1921 Colonial Secretary Winston Churchill appointed Lawrence as an adviser, but he resigned a year later. During the 1920s and early 1930s Lawrence, craving anonymity, served in the ranks in both the RAF and the Royal Tank Corps, under assumed names, being sent to British India in 1926–8. Lawrence left the RAF in March 1935, and he died on 13 May 1935, after losing control of his motorcycle on a country road. A full edition of his *Seven Pillars of Wisdom*, an embellished autobiographical account of the Arab Revolt, was not published until after his death.

And in the distant future, if the distant future deigns to consider my insignificance, I shall be appraised rather as a man of letters than as a man of action.

T. E. Lawrence to his editor Edward Garnett,
23 December 1927

Achievements

Although more than a hundred books have been written about this legendary British officer since the 1920s, T. E. Lawrence remains one of the most enigmatic and fascinating characters of the twentieth century. He took on with passion the role of a guerrilla leader of Arab tribesmen during the First World War, organizing the Bedouin warriors as an effective force against the Turks for the British Empire. His influence was lasting, and his writings inspired prominent revolutionary leaders of the twentieth century, including Mao Zedong and Võ Nguyên Giáp. A daring and exceptionally resourceful leader, Lawrence's over-confidence eventually brought about his fall from grace. He sought the goal of Arab unity, but his idealism failed to take into account the inherent difficulties of unifying the Arab tribes. While achieving great fame, the 'uncrowned King of Arabia' became increasingly disillusioned by the schemes of the Western colonial powers to carve up the Middle East, and guilty about the ambiguous part he had played in misleading the Arabs through his military and diplomatic efforts. The infamous Sykes-Picot Agreement launched a process that created the states of the modern Middle East from the former Arab *eyalets* of the Ottoman Empire.

Imperial General Headquarters, January 1917. (L to R) Hindenburg, Kaiser Wilhelm and Ludendorff. (*Robert Sennecke/ Wikimedia Commons*)

Chapter 44

PAUL VON HINDENBURG
Germany's hero of the Great War

One might compare Hindenburg to one of those big firmly-rooted oaks of the Prussian landscape under whose shade so many find protection and rest. He seemed to rise out of an old legend of our forefathers. He incorporated the soul of our nation and one felt awed at its tragic presence.
Helene Nostitz von Hindenburg, *Hindenburg at Home*

A retired officer recalled to active duty at the start of the Great War, Hindenburg would become celebrated as the victor of the decisive Battle of Tannenberg against the Russian Empire, overshadowing his master Kaiser Wilhelm II. Revered as the epitome of Prussian militarism, duty, discipline, loyalty and strength, Hindenburg became a living myth, the towering popular figure of early twentieth century

Germany. Hindenburg's and Ludendorff's symbiotic partnership during the First World War contributed to innovations in strategy that resonated throughout the rest of the century.

Paul von Hindenburg (1866–1934) was born in Posen, Prussia, the son of *Junkers* (estate owners). After his education at cadet schools in Berlin and Wahlstatt, he was commissioned as a Lieutenant in 1866. During the Seven Weeks' War of 1866, his helmet was struck by an Austrian bullet, which he kept with him for the rest of his life as a lucky talisman. A huge man, standing almost 1.98m tall, with a muscular frame and striking blue eyes, Hindenburg could not fail to impress everyone who met him.

During the Franco-Prussian War Hindenburg fought in the bloody Battle of St Privat and witnessed, but did not participate in, the Siege of Paris in 1870–1. In 1878 he was appointed to the General Staff, then taught for five years at the *Kriegsakademie*. He reached the rank of General in 1905. Like many Prussian officers, Hindenburg believed that wars could be won by a few decisive battles. He was an admirer of Scipio Africanus, who sought to win battles of annihilation. Hindenburg retired from the army for the first time in 1911.

> My military career had carried me much farther than I had ever dared to hope. There was no prospect of war, and as I recognised that it was my duty to make way for younger men, I applied in the year 1911 to be allowed to retire.
>
> Hindenburg, *Out of my Life*

The retirement did not last long. Shortly after the outbreak of the Great War, Hindenburg, now aged sixty-six, was recalled to active duty by *Generaloberst* Helmuth von Moltke, the Chief of the German General Staff. In the middle of August 1914, on the Eastern Front, von Moltke replaced 8th Army commander General Maximilian von Prittwitz and his Chief of Staff, Alfred von Waldersee, by Colonel General Paul von Hindenburg and Major General Erich Ludendorff, whom Basil Liddell Hart called the 'Robot Napoléon'. Hindenburg and his junior partner would form a 'happy marriage', until the relationship broke down in October 1918.

> The perfect harmony of their collaboration is not less striking than their apparent contrast – Hindenburg, the most loyal, honourable and unselfish of all Germany's great soldiers, was a veteran of noble birth, called out of retirement to rescue his native province, a shrewd fighting man with no pretence of intellectual distinction. Ludendorff, of middle-class origin,

nearly twenty years his junior, harsh and overbearing in temper, considered nothing outside the province of his restless mind. His power of work and mastery over detail can rarely have been equalled in history.

C.R.M.F. Cruttwell, *A History of the Great War 1914–1918*

Hindenburg and his Chief of Staff arrived at Marienburg on the afternoon of 23 August to take command of the 8th Army. Two Russian armies were threatening East Prussia: the 1st, commanded by General of the Cavalry Paul von Rennenkampf (a Baltic German who had served in the Russian Imperial Army since his youth), in the north-west; and the 2nd, under General of the Cavalry Aleksandr Samsonov, in southern East Prussia. The stakes could not have been higher:

> In first place we opposed a thin centre to Samsonov's solid mass. I say thin, not weak. For it was composed of men with hearts and wills of steel . . . We had not merely to win a victory over Samsonov. We had to annihilate him. Only thus could we get a free hand to deal with the second enemy, Rennenkampf, who was even then plundering and burning East Prussia. Only thus could we really and completely free our old Prussian land and be in a position to do something else which was expected of us, intervene in the mighty battle for a decision which was raging between Russia and our Austro-Hungarian Ally in Galicia and Poland.
>
> Hindenburg, *Out of my Life*

The Germans were helped by being able to intercept Russian wireless communications and use air reconnaissance, therefore staying one step ahead of their enemies. Their operational approach was based on the plan already developed by Lieutenant Colonel Hoffmann. While Rennenkampf planned to capture Königsberg with his 1st Army, General Samsonov was leading the 2nd Army, consisting of five corps, across the border into East Prussia. Hindenburg decided to charge through the gap between the two Russian armies. According to the German operational military doctrine of the time, risk was accepted as a common element of operational planning and its execution in order to exploit opportunities. Pre-war Chief of the Imperial General Staff Alfred von Schlieffen had promoted the theory of *bewegungskriegen*: short wars of rapid movement, aimed at annihilating the enemy's field forces through flank attacks and risky battles of manoeuvre and envelopment.

> To win, we must endeavour to be the stronger of the two at the point of impact. Our only hope of this lies in making our own choice of operations, not in waiting passively for whatever the enemy chooses for us.
>
> Alfred von Schlieffen

The German 8th Army lured Samsonov's central III Corps into a trap by staging a tactical withdrawal. Then Samsonsov's II Corps on the flanks was thrown back on the left by General Hermann von François' I Corps, and on the right by General August von Makensen's XVII Corps. The two attacking German corps then turned inward and sealed the trap behind Samsonov's III Corps in the centre near Allenstein (Olsztyn, in present-day Poland).

> Ludendorff concentrated some six divisions against Samsonov's left wing. This force, inferior in strength to the Russians, could not have been decisive; but Ludendorff, finding that Rennenkampf was still near Gumbinnen, took the calculated risk of withdrawing the rest of the German troops, except the cavalry screen, from that front and rushing them back against Samsonov's right wing. This daring move was aided by the absence of communication between the two Russian commanders and the ease with which the Germans deciphered the Russian wireless orders. Under converging blows, Samsonov's flanks were crushed, his centre surrounded, and his army practically destroyed. If the opportunity was presented rather than created, this brief Tannenberg campaign forms an almost perfect example of the 'interior lines' form of the indirect approach.
>
> Basil H. Liddell Hart, *The Strategy of Indirect Approach*

By 31 August the battle was over. The surrounded Russians were unable to break out, and all their relief efforts failed. Cut off, three of the five corps of Samsonov's 2nd Army had been annihilated. About 78,000 Russians were dead (including General Samsonov, who committed suicide with his revolver), and another 92,000 taken prisoner. Only 10,000 managed to escape.

> The manoeuvre will live as a classic example of how a small force, by using its mobility to strike at a vital point, can paralyze a vastly larger army.
>
> Basil H. Liddell Hart, *Reputations*

Tannenberg, actually credited by Liddell Hart mostly to Ludendorff's genius, is considered a prime example of a successful encirclement, a tactical masterpiece comparable to the Battle of Leipzig in 1813 or the Prussian campaign at Metz and Sedan in 1870; but luck also played a part. With the subsequent Battle of the Masurian Lakes in September 1914, Hindenburg's 8th Army ejected the Russians from East Prussia, Von Rennenkampf's 1st Army suffering another 100,000 casualties.

> Ludendorff claims this was his victory. But if the encircling movement had gone wrong and success had lain on the other side, it is I who would

have been blamed for losing the battle. After all, I know something about the business. I was the instructor in tactics at the Staff College for six years!

Hindenburg to Papen, in Franz von Papen, Memoirs, 1952

In eastern Prussia, Hindenburg had assumed significant risks to achieve his strategic objective. His operational approach employed few forces against a whole enemy army. The two triumphs in a row, at Tannenberg and the Masurian Lakes, achieved in a matter of days, were the major turning point of his life and the beginning of his meteoric rise to fame. The victories in East Prussia established the personality cult surrounding Hindenburg, who came to be compared to the legendary Germanic hero Siegfried. German war propaganda presented them as vengeance for the First Battle of Tannenberg of 1410, when the Slavs had defeated Ulrich von Jungingen's Teutonic knights.

Hindenburg was duly promoted to Field Marshal, and at the end of July 1916 he was made Supreme Army Commander, replacing Erich von Falkenhayn, who had failed at Verdun and had not been able to deal effectively with the Brusilov offensive.

The Kaiser, with the approval of the Emperor Francis Joseph, entrusted to Field-Marshal von Hindenburg the command of the Eastern Front from the right wing of the Austrian 2nd Army in the neighbourhood of Salotsche, east of Lemberg, to the Baltic coast, to date from the 30th July. In the first half of August six more divisions were given to Field-Marshal von Hindenburg, for disposal on the front under his command.

Erich von Falkenhayn, The German General Staff and its
Decisions, 1914–1916, August 1919

Hindenburg now rose even further in German public esteem. He and his deputy Erich Ludendorff then led Germany in a military dictatorship in all but name throughout the remainder of the war, marginalizing German Emperor Wilhelm II. Hindenburg was essentially the figurehead, and his Chief of Staff, First Quartermaster General Ludendorff, was effectively in control of the State and the Army. On 2 October 1917 came the high point of the Hindenburg cult, when his seventieth birthday was celebrated lavishly as a public holiday all over Germany.

Until the end, the German public believed that Hindenburg's masterful command would also bring ultimate victory on the Western Front. For more than four long years, the Hindenburg-Ludendorff duumvirate, still aiming at nothing less than total victory at all costs, was unable to admit defeat or even consider making peace.

Rhetoric, self-adulation and lies plunged Germany into the deepest abyss, when they stifled the sense of reality in our once strong and good people . . . we were now engaged in a struggle in which the very existence of our nation, and not only military glory, or the conquest of territory, was at stake.

Erich von Falkenhayn, *The German General Staff and its Decisions, 1914–1916*, August 1919

Although revolutionary new weapons with a potential for deep penetration and exploitation such as the tank emerged during the Great War, the only tank built in Germany and used in combat was the heavy A7V, and only twenty of them were manufactured in 1918. The British Mark I had been the first mass-produced tank used at the front (in the Battle of Flers-Courcelette, September 1916), but they were exceedingly slow and frequently broke down. The French developed their own tanks in secret. The light, manoeuvrable Renault FT, which entered service in 1917 and was later mass-produced, was the first with that distinctive feature of modern tanks, a rotating circular turret. The Germans never developed a substantial armoured force. Instead, German High Command favoured the development of anti-tank weaponry and tactics, although dozens of knocked-out British Mark IVs were repaired and ended up in German service.

> [June 1918] There was a cluster of shell-shot tanks quite close to the embankment, and I often went to look at them. They were all in a pitiable plight. The little cabin of armoured plate, now shot to pieces, with its maze of pipes, rods and wires, must have been an extremely uncomfortable crib during the attack, when the monsters, hoping to baffle the aim of our guns, took a tortuous course like gigantic helpless cockchafers. I thought more than once of the men in these fiery furnaces.
>
> Lieutenant Ernst Jünger, *The Storm of Steel*

Ludendorff thought tanks were 'very effective' but 'only in masses'; he did not regard them as 'particularly dangerous', and Germany could not afford to 'put masses of tanks in action'. After the last German offensive on the Western Front failed in the spring of 1918, Hindenburg and Ludendorff finally admitted that the war was lost, and they pressed Kaiser Wilhelm II to agree to an armistice. Hindenburg and Ludendorff's partnership eventually broke down in October.

> I reached Kolberg, where Field-Marshal von Hindenburg had set up his last headquarters. His majestic figure looked the same as when I had last seen him in France, but his strong face was marked with care. I retained an ineffaceable impression of the strength of his character and of his modest, unassuming greatness in the hour of Germany's defeat. Here, I felt, was one

personality to whom the nation could turn in time of stress . . . His great military authority and the aura of his personality compensated in a large measure for the disappearance of a dying monarchy, and thus prevented the Army from becoming a political tool.

Franz von Papen, Memoirs, 1952

After the Treaty of Versailles (1919), Hindenburg retired once again. In November of that year he read a statement to the Weimar National Assembly in which he declared that the German Army had remained undefeated and the Fatherland had been 'stabbed in the back'. He was again called from retirement in 1925 and, with the help of his immense prestige, was elected President of the new Republic by universal adult suffrage for a term of seven years. The ageing *Generalfeldmarschall* served a full term and was re-elected in 1932 at the age of eighty-five, nominated by the pro-republican parties who thought only he could prevent the election of Adolf Hitler.

Hindenburg died in office in August 1934, a little over two years after his re-election, having appointed Hitler as Chancellor in 1933. He was buried at the Tannenberg Memorial in East Prussia (now Poland), which was destroyed at the end of the Second World War, its remains then totally dismantled by the Polish authorities during the Cold War. Hindenburg had served three successive states in Germany: the Empire of the Hohenzollerns, the Republic and the dawn of the Third Reich.

Achievements

At the start of the Great War, East Prussia was saved by Hindenburg's leadership and strategic brilliance. He was hailed as saviour of the homeland, an epic hero who became a lasting cult figure in Germany. Throughout the war, the staunch, steadfast Hindenburg and his associate Ludendorff remained the indispensable central figures of the German war effort. Following the bitter Treaty of Versailles, Hindenburg emerged with his reputation intact and was twice elected President of the Weimar Republic. Hindenburg and his former Chief of Staff became largely responsible for promoting the notion that Germany had not been defeated in the field, but had been betrayed from within on the home front. The Army's frustrations with Wilhelm II's ineptitude led it to search for a *Feldherr* (military leader), thinking it had found one in Hindenburg, and later for a *Führer*. The two infamous Hindenburg-class giant airships, the largest aircraft ever built, were named in his honour.

Mustafa Kemal as Commander of the Yıldırım Army Group, 1918. (*Wikimedia Commons*)

Chapter 45

MUSTAFA KEMAL 'ATATÜRK'
Saviour and founder of modern Turkey

We are not defending a line but an area, the area that encompasses the whole of the fatherland. Not an inch of it is to be surrendered until it is drenched with the blood of our citizens . . . even if you see other units falling next to you.

> Mustafa Kemal's orders to the Turkish Nationalist Army at
> the Battle of Sakarya, 26 August 1921

Mustafa Kemal, the hero of Gallipoli, defeated the Greek invasion of his homeland, saving Anatolia from partition during the Turkish War of Liberation (1919–23) in one of the key aftershocks of the Great War. A paternalistic leader and statesman, Kemal dragged his nation into the twentieth century, his modern and independent

Anatolian Turkey rising from the ashes of the Ottoman Empire. The celebrated Ghazi Pasha became the founder and first president of an ethnically united Turkey in 1923, receiving the honorific name Atatürk ('Father of the Turks') in 1934 from the Turkish parliament.

The son of customs official Ali Rıza, Mustafa (1881–1938) was born in Selânik (Salonika), Macedonia. Although his parents wanted him to study business, he sat the military entrance exam and graduated from the Military Academy in Istanbul in 1902. He became an Army Staff Captain in 1905 and was assigned to the Fifth Army, based in Damascus. At this time he joined the 'Motherland and Liberty' revolutionary secret society opposed to Sultan Abdul Hamid II.

Kemal entered service in the Ministry of War in 1911. That same year, he was posted to Tripoli during the war with Italy and took part in the defence of Derne and Tobruk. As a field commander, he first drew attention during the Balkan Wars (1912–13), playing a crucial role in the recapture of Edirne (Adrianople) in July 1913. After the war, he was appointed military attaché in Sofia.

Promoted to Lieutenant Colonel before the onset of the First World War, Mustafa Kemal was already familiar with the Gallipoli peninsula from his operations against Bulgaria in the Balkan Wars. In early 1915 the Ottoman Empire faced Allied offensives on three fronts: the Dardanelles, the Caucasus and the newly opened Mesopotamian Front. In February, Kemal was given the task of organizing and commanding the 19th Division attached to the Fifth Army at Gallipoli, under the command of Marshal Otto Liman von Sanders. He reacted immediately to the Allied landings at Anzac Cove in April 1915, launching successful counter-attacks against the Australians and New Zealanders.

[Chunuk Bair, 25 April] While the Australian troops were digging in on the second ridge, Mustafa Kemal Bey, the Commander of the 19th Division, forthwith placed himself at the head of the 57th Infantry, and rushed for the dominating terrain feature of Chunuk Bair, without regard to the fact that his general reserve had been placed at the disposal of the Commander-in-Chief [von Sanders]. The two opponents clashed at Shain Tepe (Battleship Hill). The Turks succeeded in regaining Dus Tepe (Baby 700), which was a vital point.

Hans Kannengiesser, *The Campaign in Gallipoli*

In a matter of days Mustafa Kemal became a celebrated and outstanding front-line commander. He had realized how capable and resilient was the Turkish soldier when led by his officers from the front. His defining order remains one of the most memorable leadership moments in military history:

Men, I don't order you to fight, I order you to die. In the time it takes us to die, other troops and commanders can come and maintain our positions!

Mustafa Kemal to the 57th Infantry Regiment, 25 April 1915

In the face of determined Turkish resistance, the British and ANZAC Corps remained restricted to just five beachheads. Promoted to Colonel on 1 June, Kemal was assigned to the Headquarters of the Anafartalar Group, in charge of some of the most hotly contested sectors of the Gallipoli peninsula such as Chunuk Bair, Scimitar Hill and Sari Bair (April–August 1915). On 10 August, at Conkbahyri, Kemal led his men downhill in a swift counter-attack which regained lost ground. By September, the Allied High Command, warned by war correspondent Ashmead-Bartlett, had taken the measure of the deadlock.

Our last great effort to achieve some definite success against the Turks was the most ghastly and costly fiasco in our history since the Battle of Bannockburn . . . A few Gourkas obtained a lodgment on Chunuk Bair but were immediately driven off by the Turkish counter-attacks, and the main objective Koja Chemen Tepe was never approached. The 9th Corps miserably mishandled having failed to take the Anafarta Hills . . . We do not hold a single commanding position on the Peninsula and at all three points, Helles, Anzac and Suvla Bay, we are everywhere commanded by the enemy's guns.

Ellis Ashmead-Bartlett, letter to British Prime Minister Asquith, 8 September 1915

Before the end of the year, Major General Fevzi Çakmak took over Group Anafartalar, by which time, in early December, the Allies had successfully completed their withdrawal from the Dardanelles. His task accomplished with honour at Gallipoli, and awarded the Iron Cross by Imperial Germany, in March 1916 Kemal was promoted to General. He was then assigned to the command of the XVI Corps of the Second Army and sent to the Diyarbakir Headquarters to hold the Caucasus front. Fighting a losing war around Lake Van against the Russians and the Armenian insurgency throughout 1916, Kemal nevertheless managed to capture the towns of Bitlis and Muş. In February 1917 the Russian advance came to a standstill following the outbreak of the Revolution at home.

After disagreements with Erich Von Falkenhayn, who had taken command of the Ottoman Yıldırım Army Group, in December 1917 Kemal accompanied Prince Vahîdeddin (the Sultan's brother) on a state visit to Germany. In Berlin they were warmly received by Kaiser Wilhelm II, Hindenburg and Ludendorff, before visiting some of Krupp's armament factories and trenches on the Western Front. Suffering from various ailments, Kemal remained convalescing in Austria during spring and summer 1918, before heading back to Istanbul. In the meantime, Vahîdeddin had succeeded his brother to the Sultanate under the name of Mehmed VI.

Taking command of the Seventh Army in Syria on 18 September 1918, in an attempt to salvage the disastrous situation against Allenby and the Sharifian Army, Kemal realized that the campaign, and the war, were irremediably lost. With the Armistice of Mudros on 30 October 1918, it was indeed all over. Two weeks later, French and British troops landed at Istanbul, inaugurating an Allied occupation of the Imperial capital that would last five years.

> Our horse rode on that evening [30 September] into Damascus, where the burning ammunition dumps turned night into day. Away back at Kiswe the glare was painful, and the roar and reverberation of the explosions kept us all awake. In Damascus, Shukri el-Ayubi and the town council had proclaimed the King of the Arabs and hoisted the Arab flag as soon as Mustafa Kemal and Jemal had gone. The Turk and German morale was so low that they had marched out beneath the Arab flag without protest.
>
> T.E. Lawrence, *Arab Bulletin* No. 106, 22 October 1918

After the war, Kemal steadily gained ascendancy over his political rivals and led the Turkish people in a revolt against the European powers and Greece. Under the Treaty of Sèvres, the Ottoman Empire was to be broken up and large regions transferred to the control of Greece, Britain, France and Italy. Faced with this impending disaster, Mustafa Kemal and other nationalists were determined not to allow Turkey to be dismantled. They organized a campaign of national resistance, setting up a government in Ankara to rival the authorities in Constantinople, gradually building up support through the entire country.

> Mr Kemal of Anafartalar [is] adored by his men and the Islamic crowds. He was to personify the new consciousness which agitated the Turks, the national consciousness. The whole history of the resistance would eventually revolve around him.
>
> Berthe Georges-Gaulis, *Le Nationalisme Turc*

Kemal reformed the Turkish Army and became its Commander-in-Chief. He assembled a group of Turkey's most talented young officers, who developed effective war plans, and taught them to think of defence in terms of area, not lines. On 15 May 1919 the Greek Army landed in İzmir (Smyrna) with the agreement of Britain and France. Simultaneously, the Greeks occupied all of Thrace. The new Turkish National Army was fighting on three fronts: against the French and their *Légion d'Orient* composed of Armenians in Cilicia, the Greeks in Thrace and

Anatolia, and Armenian armed forces in the east. To face the Greek invasion of Anatolia, Kemal stretched his troops thin, conducting a masterly strategic retreat. Irregular forces were invited to join the new Army, and many Circassians instead changed sides. To unite his people, Kemal knew he had to create a new national consciousness. Only a nation state with a solid internal structure could implement a strong foreign policy and establish external security.

> The parts of our territory within national borders constitute a whole; they are inseparable. In the event that foreigners enter our territory and interfere in our affairs and the Ottoman government is demolished, the nation will defend by itself and resist the enemy.
>
> Erzurum Congress Manifesto, 1919

Between January and April 1921 Major General Mustafa İsmet, Kemal's Chief of the General Staff, halted two Greek offensives near İnönü. In May the Allies declared themselves neutral in this conflict, thus leaving the Greeks to wage war on their own, and the French and Italians soon withdrew from Anatolia. The War of Turkish Independence was turning into a stalemate. The Battle of Sakarya River, in August–September, stopped the Greek advance just 80km from Ankara, capital of the Grand National Assembly.

> The Greek Army of Asia Minor, which now stood ready and eager to advance, was the most formidable force the nation had ever put into the field. Its morale was high. Judged by Balkan standards, its staff was capable, its discipline and organization good.
>
> Colonel Edward Spencer Hoare Nairne, British military
> attaché in Athens

At this point, Kemal, Fevzi Çakmak and İsmet decided to retake the strategic initiative and drew up a fully developed operational plan. Concentrating their forces at Dumlupinar to achieve local superiority against the Greek Army of the East, on 26 August 1922, after an opening artillery barrage, they launched a massive counter-attack known as the 'Great Offensive' (*Büyük Taarruz*). Kemal issued his famous order: 'Armies, your first goal is the Mediterranean. Forward!' Breaking through the enemy, catching them in a pincer movement and cutting their supply lines, in a matter of days the Turkish Nationalist Army threw the invaders back to the Aegean Sea. Smyrna (İzmir) fell on 9 September. The Greek soldiers and civilians in their desperate retreat suffered more than 100,000 casualties, and their senior commander, Major General Trikoupis, was captured along with all his staff. Lieutenant General Hatzianestis, who managed to escape, would later be put on trial by a junta for high treason and executed by firing squad.

The Greeks abandoned the field, cast away their rifles, and fled wildly towards the west, towards the sea. There ships waited to rescue them. A breathless six days' chase ensued. Anatolia was a sea of fire. The fugitives burnt everything in their road . . . The fugitive army left in its trail a desolate and terrible scene of ruin and frightfulness . . . The Greek civil population, the Levantines and other foreigners, crazed with fear, fled back to the sea with the troops. On the sixth day the Anatolian cavalry, which had ridden ahead of the main army, drew within sight of the Mediterranean. The order had been carried out. Below them lay the fair city of Smyrna.

Hanns Froembgen, *Kemal Ataturk*

The Battle of Dumlupınar was probably Kemal's finest military hour. By 18 September 1922 the occupying armies had all been expelled from Anatolia. The Armistice of Mudanya brought the War of Independence to an end, but a large Greek army in Thrace still threatened Istanbul. The final settlement was established by the Treaty of Lausanne, which recognized the new Ankara government as legitimate, restored the nation's sovereignty and finalized its new Anatolian borders. By October 1923 the last French, British and Italian contingents had all departed from Istanbul.

Afterward, Mustafa Kemal completed what the Committee of Union and Progress (the 'Young Turks') had started in 1915, the elimination of the Armenian population from Anatolia. With the expulsion of the Greeks, the Turkification of Asia Minor was nearly complete. The bitter Greco-Turkish War, full of horrendous massacres committed by both sides, continues to fuel Turkish and Greek nationalism to this day. From the Albanian Revolt of 1910 to 1925, millions of Christians and Muslims living in the Balkans and the Middle East were the victims of pillage, mass executions and large-scale exchange of populations. A new republican Turkey had to be built from the ground up.

History is a bridge. We must delve into our roots and reconstruct what history has divided.

Mustafa Kemal, 29 October 1933

The next step was the declaration of a Republic and the removal of Sultan Mehmed VI, bringing to an end the 600-year-old Ottoman dynasty. Kemal had long held the view that the Sultanate could not be maintained if Turkey was to take its place as a European nation. In March 1924 the Sharia legal system was abolished. Kemal set himself up as a dictator, with some superficial nods to a multi-party system. He was convinced that only he knew what was best for his country. Promoting a secular Turkish identity, Turkey was the first Muslim country to become a modern democratic nation state.

By the time of his death in 1938, Mustafa Kemal had become a mythical, almost sacred figure. He was given a magnificent state commemoration on 10 November 1953, upon the completion of his mausoleum in Ankara. Kemalism lived on, based on the principle of the unity of an indivisible Turkish state.

Achievements

An outstanding Prussian-trained officer whose exploits during the First World War, including leading the defence against the Allied invasion of Gallipoli, made him a legend, Mustafa Kemal regained control of the Anatolian territories occupied by foreign powers at the end of the Great War. He was also able to unite a variety of forces in the effort to prevent an Armenian state from being constructed in eastern Anatolia. With courage and intelligence, Kemal learned from each stage of his career and applied those lessons to his next campaigns. A passionate nationalist and a consummate politician, Kemal had the vision to lead his nation on the path to a viable future. He ended the Caliphate and created modern Turkey out of the ruins of the Ottoman Empire. Regarded as the founder of secular, modern Turkey, this central, towering figure of twentieth century Turkish history is venerated in his nation to this day, the tutelary figure of one of the world's longest-running personality cults.

Lettow-Vorbeck in 1919. (*Photo studio Hermann Noack, Berlin. Deutsches Historisches Museum, Berlin*)

Chapter 46

PAUL VON LETTOW-VORBECK
The 'Lion of Africa'

Our small band had occupied a greatly superior enemy force for the whole war; 137 Generals had been in the field, and in all about 300,000 men had been employed against us. Yet in spite of the enormously superior numbers at the disposal of the enemy, our small force, the ride strength of which was only about 1,400 at the time of the Armistice, had remained in the field always ready for action and possessed of the highest determination.

Paul von Lettow-Vorbeck, *My Reminiscences*, 1920

During the Great War, *Generalmajor* Paul Emil von Lettow-Vorbeck, Commander-in-Chief of the German *Schutztruppe* in East Africa, conducted one of the most successful guerrilla campaigns in history. Ten Allied commanders, including Generals Jan Christiaan Smuts and Jaap van Deventer, chased von

Lettow-Vorbeck fruitlessly all over East Africa. Facing a combined Allied force of some 250,000 men, Lettow-Vorbeck at the head of few thousand men (mostly native Askaris) remained undefeated throughout the war, only surrendering after the Armistice in November 1918.

Born into a minor noble family in Prussia, Paul von Lettow-Vorbeck (1870-1964) joined a cadet corps in Potsdam. Prior to the Great War, he served in China during the Boxer Rebellion (1900) and in the campaign of repression against the Herero and Nama tribes in German South-West Africa (1904–6). Von Lettow-Vorbeck's experience of colonial campaigning and tackling indigenous insurgencies would prove particularly useful, since he would adapt his tactics to those of native bands, using the terrain brilliantly to his advantage.

> The *Boma* [stockade] had been built as a residence for the local district officials, and as the headquarters of the *Schutztruppe* – the native levies, officered by Europeans and used to keep order among the more turbulent tribes. The 'Wagogos', who live in the plain below, used to be very difficult to manage, and as late as '95 there was a widespread revolt against German rule, which was only suppressed after much trouble, and by the usual Teutonic methods of 'blood and iron'.
>
> Ernest Charles Holtom, *Two Years' Captivity in German East Africa*

In April 1914, as a Lieutenant Colonel, von Lettow-Vorbeck was appointed Commander of the German colonial forces, known as the *Schutztruppe* in German East Africa (present-day Tanzania). At the outbreak of the war, with only 2,472 Askaris and 260 German officers, medical officers, NCOs and settlers, von Lettow-Vorbeck's protection force seemed hopelessly outnumbered. Therefore he opted for a bold strategy: instead of waiting for the enemy to strike at the German colony, he would take the initiative, tying down as many Allied troops as possible with his elusive bush army, a strategy he explained in his memoirs:

> On my first journey of reconnaissance and inspection, commenced in January, 1914, I went by sea from Dar-es-Salaam to Tanga, thence to Usambara, and then on into the country round Kilimanjaro and Meru Mountain. At Usambara I met an old friend whom I had known well since our military college days, Captain von Prince. He was an enthusiastic supporter of the idea that, in case of a war with England, we East Africans should not remain idle spectators, but should take a hand if there should be even a trace of a prospect of relieving the pressure in Europe.
>
> Paul von Lettow-Vorbeck, *My Reminiscences*

Early on, the Germans took the offensive. On 15 August Captain Tom von Prince occupied Taveta, the only British territory to be held by the Germans during the Great War. At the Battle of Tanga, in November 1914, von Lettow-Vorbeck and Captain von Prince repelled a British-Indian force under Major General Arthur Edward Aitken which was nine times their size. Von Lettow-Vorbeck held the invaders with his weak left, while sending in his reserves to outflank the British on the right. General Aitken's troops retreated in confusion, having suffered 1,300 casualties and leaving behind most of their equipment. The news of the disaster was kept secret in Britain for months:

> The news of the failure at Tanga and the withdrawal from Longido was cabled to London on the 5th and 6th November respectively by Major-General Aitken and Sir Henry Belfield. The general situation at the time was gloomy and critical. In Flanders the desperate First Battle of Ypres was still undecided; in the Near East, Turkey had newly come into the war; at sea Admiral Craddock's squadron had just been destroyed by the cruisers of Admiral von Spee. It was felt by the Government that publication of the news of a further reverse would be inadvisable, and accordingly no mention of the events at Tanga was permitted. It was not until several months later that any details of the fighting were given to the public in Great Britain.
>
> Charles Hordern, *History of the Great War: Military Operations East Africa*

The strategic Uganda Railway became a priority target for German guerrilla attacks. In July 1915 the *Schutztruppe* were reinforced by the 180 survivors of the light cruiser SMS *Königsberg*, scuttled after the Battle of the Rufiji Delta. At its peak in early 1916, the number of Askaris in the *Schutztruppe* reached 13,000; these were supported by 45,000 porters, indispensable in regions where railways and roads were virtually non-existent.

After Belgo-Congolese troops had managed to take Tabora from *Generalmajor* Kurt Wahle in September 1916, the Allies established firm control of the African Great Lakes region. The British had also launched simultaneous attacks from British East Africa and Rhodesia. A large part of German East Africa was now in the hands of the Allies, but von Lettow-Vorbeck's *Schutztruppe* had not suffered any defeats and escaped to the south-east region. His men had become experts in jungle guerrilla warfare, frequently setting booby traps for their adversaries:

> As we walked, a man who had fought at Tanga, in the first disastrous assault from the sea, told me how the outlying bush through which our men had passed had been full of these hives, and how the Germans had snared the pathways of the wood with cords which set them in motion, so that when

our attack began the hives were roused, and the wild bees swarmed in their millions, doing more damage to one Indian regiment than the German maxims.

Francis Brett Young, *Marching on Tanga*

In early November 1917, the Zeppelin LZ 104 (L 59) attempted to re-supply von Lettow-Vorbeck's force, flying all the way from Yambol in Bulgaria. *Kapitänleutnant* Ludwig Bockholt's aircraft travelled 6,800km in 95 hours before turning back upon receiving false reports of a German surrender. More than a century later, the LZ 104 ('*das Afrika-Schiff*') mission still holds the record for the longest non-stop flight by a military airship. After this failed attempt, and despite having no other means of re-supply, von Lettow-Vorbeck defeated the British at Mahiwa (incurring serious losses), invaded Portuguese East Africa and routed a Portuguese force sent to stop him at Ngomano.

Living off the land, using captured British and Portuguese weapons and ammunition, his remaining 2,000 men marched as far as Northern Rhodesia. Throughout the 'safari war', von Lettow-Vorbeck often divided his forces to outflank his enemies; his small, mobile, self-sufficient force carried out hundreds of successful deep raids and commando operations against bridges, railways and outposts, successfully fighting off a vastly superior foe. Re-supply remained a dominant concern, and morale was badly affected by shortages of food, medical goods and ammunition. Lettow-Vorbeck often divided his forces to outflank his enemies and continuously preyed on their supplies lines.

Huns kept on sniping at us giving us bursts of M.G. In the afternoon the whole battalion moved out & wheeled round the *boma* intending to attack Von Lettow, No.4 Coy forming screen, No.3 on left flank, and the others completing the diamond. We didn't go far tho' for some reason & returned to the *boma* for tea. Manned the trenches again at night. Von Lettow's camp fires visible about 2 miles away. Quiet night. Moult with patrol today got alongside Hun porters on march. They had been passing across our front.

John Bruce Cairnie, *The Great War Diaries*, 27 August 1918

Moving with incredible stealth through the dense forest and rough terrain of the African wilderness in ever more harrowing conditions, the *Schutztruppe* evaded the might of the British, South African, Portuguese, Belgian and Rhodesian forces sent after them, until 23 November 1918. A day after the Armistice had been signed in Europe, von Lettow-Vorbeck captured Kasama in Northern Rhodesia (present-day Zambia), which the British had evacuated in haste.

Finally, the survivors of the defiant German East African bush army surrendered to General William Frederick Edwards at Abercom, twelve days after the

Armistice. At that time the force consisted of only 155 Europeans, with fewer than 2,000 Askaris and 3,000 bearers. A monument in Mbala, Zambia, commemorates this event. On their surrender, many of the German veterans of East Africa fell ill, having been exposed to the infamous 'Spanish' influenza; 10 per cent of the men who had survived years of gruelling *buschkrieg* died in the epidemic.

> Von Lettow surrendered with 155 whites, 1,186 African ranks, 37 M.G.s, 200,000 S.A.A. He & some of his party passed thro' by train yesterday and spent an hour on the platform where they were met by practically the whole of the German population – women & girls mainly. They looked very fit indeed, their clothes a bit worn certainly but no signs of crumpling up with fever. I couldn't help admiring them. They are a tough lot.
>
> John Bruce Cairnie, *The Great War Diaries*, 8 December 1918

Despite von Lettow-Vorbeck's best efforts and the untold sacrifices of his loyal troops, at the end of the Great War in Europe, Germany's African colonies (Togoland, Kamerun, South-West Africa and East Africa) were all occupied by France and Britain. When the Treaty of Versailles dismantled the German colonial empire, the *Schutztruppe* were officially disbanded. Opposing them, the native Africans, the British, the Belgians and the Portuguese had lost hundreds of thousands of lives, many to illness and malnutrition. The huge number of porters who had been forced into service suffered a particularly high rate of attrition.

> That the enemy had to contend with sickness and with sameness if not with scarcity of food is certain, but in a minor degree, since his white men were more acclimatised to German East Africa and his native soldiers indigenous to the country. He had the advantage of falling back upon interior lines and of his power of living on the country as he retired. This last was accentuated by the fact that whereas we are accustomed to take and pay for only what the villagers can spare, the Germans have no scruples about taking all. And after using men, women, and children as porters, so far as they require, they send them back in a starving condition, thus increasing the difficulties of our advancing troops.
>
> Major General Reginald Hoskins' dispatch, 1917, in Herbert
> Charles O'Neill, *The War in Africa and in the Far East*

Von Lettow-Vorbeck was shipped back by the British with 114 German veterans. They reached Germany in February 1919. The undefeated von Lettow-Vorbeck and *Kapitän zur See* Max Looff, commander of the SMS *Königsberg*, were treated as heroes of the fatherland and cheered by the people as they paraded through the streets of Berlin. *Generalfeldmarschall* Hindenburg hailed the Lion of Africa as 'the truest German soldier'. In the immediate post-war years, a flood of histories and reminiscences of the East Africa campaign was produced, and von Lettow-Vorbeck was acclaimed as the greatest of the *Kolonialhelden* (colonial heroes). Although it took him many years, Lettow-Vorbeck ultimately persuaded the Weimar government to pay the veteran Askaris what they were owed for their wartime service, acknowledging that the German presence in East Africa could not have been maintained without their contribution.

> If we East Africans received so kindly a reception in the homeland, it was because everyone seemed to think that we had preserved some part of Germany's soldierly traditions, had come back home unsullied, and that the Teutonic sense of loyalty peculiar to us Germans had kept its head high even under the conditions of war in the tropics.
>
> Paul von Lettow-Vorbeck, *My Reminiscences*

After the war, the Weimar authorities gave von Lettow-Vorbeck command of a brigade, but following his involvement in the abortive Kapp-Lüttwitz Putsch of October 1920, he was dismissed from the *Reichswehr*. It is interesting to note that he enjoyed lifelong friendships with some of his former adversaries, including the South African leader Jan Christiaan Smuts. At the 1929 reunion of the British East African Expeditionary Force in London, he was even made the guest of honour. Von Lettow-Vorbeck would survive the Second World War, dying in Hamburg in 1964, having outlived almost all of his generation. He was given a state funeral by the government of West Germany in the presence of elderly Askaris flown from Tanganyika for the event.

Achievements

Von Lettow-Vorbeck's improvised tactics and extreme mobility earned him the reputation of being an exceptionally talented guerrilla commander. A master of the art of survival, his highly unconventional campaign of bush warfare and his evasive skills compelled the British to commit significant resources to the East African theatre throughout the war, in an attempt to neutralize his ghost army. Von Lettow-Vorbeck's *Schutztruppe*, despite suffering constant supply shortages, frequently won battles against great odds and became enduring symbols of German military prowess. They had the distinction of being the only Germans of the Great War to occupy British and Portuguese territories and to be the last to lay down their arms. Von Lettow-Vorbeck's spectacular exploits captured the imagination of his countrymen and earned him the nickname of 'Lion of Africa'.

Erich von Manstein and Hermann Breith planning Operation Zitadelle, (Kursk), 1943.

Chapter 47

ERICH VON MANSTEIN
Hitler's ablest battlefield commander

The general verdict among the German generals I interrogated in 1945 was that Field Marshal von Manstein had proved the ablest commander in their Army, and the man they had most desired to become its Commander-in-Chief. It is very clear that he had a superb sense of operational possibilities and an equal mastery in the conduct of operations, together with a greater grasp of the potentialities of mechanised forces than any of the other commanders who had not been trained in the tank arm. In sum, he had military genius.

Basil Henry Liddell Hart,
preface to *Lost Victories*, 1958 edition

Among the chief military commanders of the Second World War, Manstein had arguably one of the most impressive records. The principal architect of the invasion plans of Poland and France, he later captured Sevastopol and the Crimea in spite of facing tremendous odds. He skilfully extricated German forces from entrapment in the wake of the Stalingrad disaster, then led a brilliant counter-offensive at Kharkov. After the Battle of Kursk, Manstein was to lead one of the most masterful fighting retreats in history, until his dismissal after repeated arguments with Hitler. A general who led from the front, Manstein was the Wehrmacht's best tactician. Marshal Malinowsky judged him to be the Soviet Union's 'most dangerous opponent'.

Erich von Lewinski (1887–1973) came from an aristocratic Prussian family. Adopted as a young child by General Georg von Manstein, he was destined for a military career, like his uncle Paul von Hindenburg and his father and adoptive father, both Prussian generals. He spent six years in the Prussian cadet corps before entering the War College in Berlin. He would then fight throughout the Great War, on both the Western and Eastern Fronts. After the war he remained in the *Reichswehr* and had risen to the rank of *Generalleutnant* by April 1939.

> I have decided upon a solution by force. The attack against Poland is to be carried out according to preparations for Operation *Weiss* with the modifications resulting from the Army's having been almost completely deployed in the meantime.
>
> Hitler's War Directive N. 1, 31 August 1939

As Chief of Staff of Gerd von Rundstedt's Army Group South, Manstein developed the *Fall Weiss* operational plans for the September 1939 invasion of Poland in collaboration with Colonel Günther Blumentritt. Despite their bravery, the Poles, attacked by the Red Army from the east and forced to fight on two fronts, surrendered on 6 October.

In the wake of the occupation of Poland, Manstein, now Chief of Staff of Army Group A, participated with Heinz Guderian in the creation of *Fall Gelb* No. 3, the risky plan to tackle France and the BEF using the invasion of Belgium as a decoy, then switching to a main thrust through the Ardennes, before crossing the Meuse and reaching the Channel coast.

The strategic objective was to defeat France quickly in a *Blitzkrieg* campaign, in order to avoid the stalemate of the Great War's Western Front. Rapid movement was indeed the essence of armoured warfare: victory would only be achieved through surprise and shock resulting from maximum exploitation of the tanks' speed. *Blitzkrieg* breakthrough-focused campaigns would combine deep-penetrating armour units, with close support from motorized infantry, artillery and air power with a viable communications architecture. In February 1940, Hitler was convinced by Manstein of *Fall Gelb*'s feasibility.

> The Army High Command, spurred on by Hitler to mount an offensive, was intending to use, once again, the so-called 'Schlieffen Plan' of 1914. It is true that this had the advantage of simplicity, though hardly the charm of novelty. Thoughts therefore soon turned to alternative solutions. One day in November, Manstein asked me to come to see him and outlined his ideas on the subject to me; these involved a strong tank thrust through southern Belgium and Luxembourg towards Sedan, a breakthrough of the prolongation of the Maginot Line in that area and a consequent splitting in two of the whole French front. He asked me to examine this plan of his from the point of view of a tank man. After a lengthy study of maps and making use of my own memories of the terrain from the First World War, I was able to assure Manstein that the operation he had planned could in fact be carried out.
>
> Heinz Guderian, *Panzer Leader*

The gamble would indeed prove stunningly successful. The Germans, humiliated by their defeat in 1918 and having developed the strategy and tactics of tank warfare, achieved spectacular early victories. On 10 May 1940 Germany invaded Belgium, the Netherlands and France. Army Group A, commanded by *Generaloberst* Gerd von Rundstedt, outflanked the best Allied troops with massed Panzer forces (mostly light Panzer I and II variants armed with machine guns or 20mm cannons), taking France out of the war by 25 June. Manstein's corps, part of Günther von Kluge's 4th Army, had achieved the first breakthrough east of Amiens and had been the first to cross the Seine. Disorganized French units and the retreating BEF had to be evacuated from Dunkirk in dire conditions.

> Very cheering developments in 4th Army sector. Under very good leadership, it has established itself firmly in the part of Rouen north of the Seine, has seized Les Andelys with forces under Manstein's command, and is covering its left wing with 1st Cav. Div. Its right wing, pressing on in direction of Dieppe is attacking from the rear the British group which is still holding out on the coast. The bulk of its armed forces is pushing on to Le Havre.
>
> Franz Halder, *War Journal*

A year later, at the outset of Operation Barbarossa (June 1941), Manstein was appointed commander of the LVI Panzer Corps, a subdivision of Army Group North led by Field Marshal Wilhelm von Leeb, which was tasked to advance from East Prussia toward Leningrad. The Eastern Front would soon turn into the greatest and most brutal land conflict in history. Manstein's corps moved swiftly:

by the end of June, 4th Panzer Group had reached the Dvina River, covering 315km in just 100 hours!

> Manstein had aged since he had visited our division in Poland in 1940, but his reputation had grown with the years, and his exploits in the initial advance into Russia, and subsequently in the conquest of the Crimea, had raised his fame higher than that of any commander on the Eastern Front. As an expert on siege warfare he had been sent to the Leningrad sector to plan the capture of the old Russian capital, whence he had been hastily summoned to restore the situation on the Don and open a way to Stalingrad.
>
> Friedrich von Mellenthin, *Panzer Battles*

On the Southern Front, on 12 September 1941, when the LIV Army Corps reached the Isthmus of Perekop, Colonel General von Schobert was killed after landing his liaison aircraft in a minefield. Manstein, now General of Infantry, was sent to replace him at the head of the 11th Army. After encountering fierce resistance, the 11th Army entered Crimea via the narrow Isthmus of Perekop. Manstein pursued the retreating Soviet troops, and by 16 November his army had captured the whole region, including its capital Simferopol, leaving only Sevastopol in enemy hands.

> A true battle of annihilation had been fought to a victorious finish! Eleventh Army still faced the hardest task of all: the conquest of Sevastopol.
>
> Erich von Manstein, *Lost Victories*

Soviet naval infantry and the 'Maxim Gorky I' coastal heavy batteries held off the initial attack on Sevastopol. The Germans, however, had brought their Karl-Gerät self-propelled howitzers 'Odin' and 'Thor'. Built by Rheinmetall AG, at 126 tons these were two of the seven largest self-propelled howitzers ever built and used in combat. In June and July they fired 197 2.2-ton shells at Sevastopol, causing massive devastation to the concrete bunkers. Krupp's 800mm 'Big Dora' supergun, initially designed to operate against the Maginot Line, was also brought by railway to bombard Sevastopol from a distance of almost 50km.

> In making its artillery preparations for the attack, 11th Army dispensed with the intensive barrage so popular with our opponents. 11th Army had naturally called in every gun within reach for the attack, and O.K.H. [Army High Command] had made available the heaviest pieces. The heavy siege artillery included batteries of cannon up to a calibre of 19cm, as well as independent howitzer and heavy-howitzer batteries with calibres of 30.5, 35 and 42 cm. Furthermore, there were two special 60cm guns

and the celebrated 80cm Big Dora. At no other time on the German side in World War II can artillery ever have been more formidably massed – particularly as regards the high calibres used – than for the attack on Sevastopol.

Erich von Manstein, Lost Victories

The siege would last 250 days. With his masterful combination of air, land and super-heavy artillery firepower, by July 1942 Manstein's outnumbered 11th Army had been able to overwhelm Sevastopol and clear Soviet bridgeheads in the Kerch Peninsula. A few weeks later, Manstein's 21-year old son Gero was killed on the Eastern Front.

Promoted to Field Marshal for his successes in Crimea, Manstein would almost succeed in relieving Paulus' 6th Army encircled at Stalingrad (Operation *Wintergewitter*, 12 December 1942). The 6th Army was ultimately unable to escape encirclement, since they had neither fuel nor horses and very limited supplies. *Generaloberst* Hermann Hoth did achieve impressive gains in the first 24 hours, some units even covering 60km of ground, but Hoth Group's progress was halted on 19 December at the Mischkova tributary river by the 2nd Guards and 5th Shock Army while still 48km short of its objective.

We fought for six days to prevent Hoth's panzer army from reaching the Myshkova River. The Verkhne-Kumskiy farmstead changed hands several times. We fought with no sleep and rest, and, it may be said, with no food either . . . On the morning of 19 December the troops of Malinovsky's powerful 2nd Guards Army and the 2nd Mechanized Corps arrived in our deployment area. Having taken up the defence, Malinovsky's army immediately went into action. Now, together with them, we repulsed all the attacks of von Manstein's forces.

Vasiliy Krysov, Panzer Destroyer

Unsurprisingly, controversy has always surrounded Manstein's precise role in the Stalingrad debacle. In the aftermath of the Soviet victory at Stalingrad, the Red Army's push liberated Kharkov and Kursk with Operations *Zvezda* (Star) and *Skachok* (Gallop). Knowing that the *Stavka* (Headquarters of the Supreme Commander-in-Chief) was politically obliged to commit to continuous offensives wherever there was a perceived weakness, Manstein reasoned that the best way to defeat the Red Army was to lure it into a trap by executing a tactical retreat, drawing the Soviet forces into pre-prepared pockets where they could be cut off and annihilated in battles of encirclement. This strategy resulted in the Third Battle of Kharkov (February–March 1943), in which Manstein supervised the most successful German counter-offensive of the entire war.

Manstein was perfectly calm; indeed, he watched the Russian manoeuvre with satisfaction. On 17 February Hitler visited him again to demand the immediate recapture of Kharkov, but Manstein explained that the farther the Russian masses advanced to the west and south-west, the more effective would be his counter-stroke.

Friedrich von Mellenthin, Panzer Battles

As the stubborn defence of Army Group South wore down the over-extended Soviet spearheads, which were losing their cohesion, Manstein redeployed the Fourth and First Panzer Armies, before unleashing his unexpected 'backhand punch' at the critical moment. Despite his forces being outnumbered 5-1 (350,000 v. 70,000), Manstein's 350 tanks in ten divisions outnumbered the Soviets at the focal point, giving the Germans tactical numerical superiority. Wolfram von Richthofen's *Luftflotte* 4 also quadrupled their average daily sorties to 1,000, providing vital air support. The Soviet forces were broken, and the Soviet 6th Army was encircled and destroyed. Outflanked from the west, Kharkov was recaptured. The Red Army, lured into a trap, had lost 52 divisions. Von Manstein's forces drove north-east and occupied Belgorod on 18 March.

On March 29th I flew to the headquarters of Army Group South, at Zaporozhe, to see Field-Marshal von Manstein. Here a considerable victory had recently been won; by using armoured formations in the correct operational way Kharkov had been recaptured. I once again realized what a pity it was that Hitler could not tolerate the presence of so capable and soldierly a person as Manstein in his environment. Their characters were too opposed: on the one hand Hitler, with his great will-power and his fertile imagination: on the other, Manstein, a man of most distinguished military talents, a product of the German General Staff Corps, with a sensible, cool understanding, who was our finest operational brain.

Heinz Guderian, Panzer Leader

Manstein then strongly recommended following up with an immediate pincer movement while the Soviets were still recovering from their rout. Most of OKH supported Manstein's proposal, but Hitler hesitated. An immediate offensive against the Kursk salient could have resulted in a major German victory. To hold 900km of front, Manstein had four armies at his disposal. Awaiting reinforcements, Operation *Zitadelle*, which called for a double envelopment of six Soviet Armies, was delayed until 5 July, by which time the Red Army had had weeks to prepare its defence in depth. The German southern flank, composed of Hoth's 4th Panzer Army and Detachment Kempf, did fulfil its objectives by effecting a breakthrough of the first Soviet lines. The elite II SS Panzer Corps *Sonderverbände*, despite being heavily outnumbered, decimated the Soviet reaction forces on 12 July at Prokhorovka, in one of the largest tank engagements in world history (losing just ten AFVs, including four Panzer IVs, while knocking out 192 enemy tanks and assault guns). Overall, 1,000 AFVs fought at Prokhorovka. However, the northern flank of the pincer stalled after nine days when confronted with the well-prepared Soviet defence in depth.

> When I was entrusted with the duties of Chief of the Army General Staff, I frequently proposed to Hitler that Manstein be appointed Chief of the OKW in place of Keitel, but always in vain. It is true that Keitel made life easy for Hitler; he sought to anticipate and fulfil Hitler's every wish before it had even been uttered. Manstein was not so comfortable a man to deal with; he formed his own opinions and spoke them aloud.
>
> Heinz Guderian, *Panzer Leader*

Manstein implored Hitler to allow him to throw in the reserves to finish off the Soviets, who had been severely mauled (in all, more than 6,000 tanks and assault guns were written off on the Red Army's side!), but Hitler refused, insisting on disengaging, since German troops needed to be redeployed urgently to Italy. After the losses and ultimate failure at Kursk, the German High Command became almost completely defensively minded. In the early stages of the Second World War, German Blitzkrieg warfare had seemed unbeatable, but by 1943 the Red Army had learned how to defend in depth before launching decisive counter-attacks.

By late 1943 the Wehrmacht, having lost the strategic initiative, was fighting a series of delaying battles back to the pre-invasion lines. In March 1944 Manstein was attempting to hold the Dnieper line with the remnants of his spent Panzer forces. Breaking out of an encirclement manoeuvre in direct violation of Hitler's 19 March directive that 'every defensive position be held to the last man', Manstein successfully saved the XI and XXXXII Corps from annihilation. He was then, to the delight of the Soviet High Command, relieved of his command for challenging the Führer's direct orders:

> We considered the hated Manstein our most dangerous opponent. His technical mastery of every, and I mean every situation was unequalled. Things would perhaps have gone much worse for us if every general in the German Wehrmacht had possessed his stature.
>
> Marshal Rodion Malinovsky

Though awarded the Swords to the Oak Leaves of the Knight's Cross in recognition of his outstanding services, Manstein was not given another command. A product of his age and of his Prussian military upbringing, Manstein ultimately declined to join any clandestine plot against Hitler, believing the Führer's downfall would cause even more chaos to his homeland. Even though he constantly opposed Hitler on operational details, he considered obedience to the Führer was not only legitimate, but also a question of honour. Sentenced to eighteen years' imprisonment by a British war tribunal at Hamburg in 1949, Manstein was released as a result of Cold War *realpolitik* in 1953 after serving less than one-fifth of his sentence.

> Von Manstein has got no more than he deserved, there is no need . . . for anyone on this side of the Channel to wax sentimental because retribution has at last caught up with a man who plied his grim trade of death and destruction with such ruthlessness.
>
> Editorial in the *Hull Daily Mail*, 20 December 1949

Manstein went on to advise the West German government on the creation of its new army within NATO. In his *Verlorene Siege* (Lost Victories), first published in Germany in 1955, Manstein largely claimed credit for the German victories, while blaming Hitler and his fellow generals for most of the defeats suffered by the Wehrmacht. Manstein, the last but one surviving German Field Marshal, died on 9 June 1973 at the age of eighty-five. He was laid to rest with full military honours at Dorfmark, Lower Saxony.

Achievements

In a military career spanning four decades, the aristocratic Prussian Erich Von Manstein served the Imperial German Army, the Weimar Republic, the Third Reich and the *Bundeswehr* (as adviser). A master of manoeuvre, Manstein combined strategic brilliance with impressive powers of leadership as commander of a corps, army and army group. An 'extraordinary military leader' according to Kenneth J. Campbell (2016), Manstein's fellow generals bowed to his superiority. No one in the Wehrmacht was credited with greater conceptual vision and tactical prowess. His skill and sound decision-making were based on his 'iron nerve' (von Mellenthin), his experience and his knowledge of the true capabilities of his own forces and of his adversary. Manstein's 'backhand punch' against the Soviet spearhead during the Third Battle of Kharkov became a classic manoeuvre. Considering the massive Soviet superiority in men and materiel, his strategy and the execution of this operational masterpiece were nothing short of outstanding. This victory certainly prolonged the war in Europe by several months. The Eastern Front, on which Manstein's abilities were so brilliantly displayed, was arguably the war's decisive theatre, determining the course of world history up to the end of the Cold War.

Georgy Zhukov (second left) with Montgomery and Rokossovsky at the Brandenburg Gate, Berlin, 12 July 1945. (*Imperial War Museum/ Wikimedia Commons*)

Chapter 48

GEORGY ZHUKOV
Stalin's champion against the Third Reich

The Germans stumbled upon the mass heroism of our troops, their vigorous resistance, their persistence, the unparalleled patriotism displayed by the Army and the people. It is hard to draw a demarcation line between the role of weaponry, military materiel and the significance of the troops' morale. It is a fact that under equal conditions, large-scale battles and whole wars are won by troops which have a strong will for victory, clear goals before them, high moral standards, and devotion to the banner under which they go into battle.

Georgy Zhukov, *The Memoirs of Marshal Zukhov*

German power was broken on the Eastern Front. Zhukov, the most important Soviet military commander of the Second World War, is considered by many to be the hero of the Red Army which eventually defeated Hitler and took Berlin. Zhukov could be authoritarian, but he got the job thoroughly done. His reputation was that of a patriot and an independent-minded general who remained a key figure in Stalin's high command throughout the 'Great Patriotic War'. Zhukov lives on in public consciousness in Russia and is arguably the twentieth century's most famous general.

Georgy Konstantinovitch Zhukov (1896–1974) was born at Strelkovka in the Kaluga Governate, south-west of Moscow, to a poor family. His father was a shoemaker, his mother a farmer. At the age of eleven young Georgy's prospects improved when he was sent to Moscow to become an apprentice furrier and fur-trader under his maternal uncle. Four years later (in 1912), Zhukov was taken into partnership; the young man was on his way to becoming a successful petty bourgeois businessman. He worked as a craftsman until the beginning of the First World War, when he was drafted; in August 1915 he was assigned to the 10th Cavalry Division and was sent to the front in August 1916. He was awarded two Crosses of St George, but was wounded and spent the rest of the war in hospital at Kharkov and in the rear.

Following the October Revolution of 1917 Zhukov deserted. In August 1918 he joined the Red Army and became a member of the Bolshevik Party. Fighting in the Russian Civil War, Zhukov continued in the cavalry, serving with Semyon Budyonny's and Kliment Voroshilov's famous 1st Cavalry Army. In 1920–1 Zhukov commanded a cavalry squadron that put down the Tambov Rebellion; using scorched-earth tactics against the Union of Working Peasants, Zhukov was awarded the Order of the Red Banner. From 1923 to 1930 he commanded the 39th Cavalry Regiment. In 1924 and 1925 he attended the Leningrad Higher Cavalry School, where he met Rokossovsky, Timoshenko and Yeryomenko. In 1929, he was sent to the Frunze Academy, where he became familiar with operational art theories defined by Aleksandr Svechin and Nikolai Varfolomeev, along with the concepts of deep battle and mechanized warfare. A constant feature of Zhukov's tactical doctrine would be operational encirclement and annihilation, in itself a Prussian concept. We plunged into our studies with a will, especially Zhukov, who gave himself up completely to mastering the subtleties of military science. Whenever we dropped into his room he would be crawling about over a map spread on the floor. Even then there was nothing higher for him than duty.

Konstantin K. Rokossovsky, *A Soldier's Duty*.

In February 1931 Zhukov was appointed assistant to General Budyonny, and there is no doubt that this connection helped his career. In the following years, he commanded the 4th Cavalry Division and was awarded the Order of Lenin, and in 1938, surviving Stalin's purges, he was promoted to Deputy Commander of the Belorussian military district. Like most people at the time, Zhukov was in awe of Stalin and would remain so until the day the Soviet dictator passed away.

In early June 1939 Zhukov was sent to the Russian Far East, on the Mongolian-Manchurian border, to fend off the Japanese 6th Army's incursion into this disputed territory. His operational plan was approved by Stalin, but it required weeks of logistical preparation, and reconnaissance carried out in total secrecy. In August, at the Battle of Khalkhin-Gol (or Nomonhan), Zhukov suddenly counter-attacked with 500 BT-5 and BT-7 fast light tanks, supported by 550 aircraft and a large quantity of field artillery. The Mongolians also provided cavalry. Pinned down by Soviet fighter-bomber attacks and an intense artillery barrage, elements of Michitarō Komatsubara's 23rd Division were simultaneously attacked from the rear by Soviet armour. Surrounded, they lost 25,000 men, more than 50 per cent to artillery fire.

We had heard of the frightful Soviet artillery fire, but the intense, around-the-clock pounding we received from the Soviet artillery far surpassed our imagination. Although their lines of communication were four or five times longer than ours, the Russians seem to have stockpiled a stupendous amount of ammunition at Nomonhan by using over 10,000 trucks.
> Diary of field artillery Captain Kusaba Sakae (3rd Battalion,
> 7th Battery) in Georgy Zhukov, *Reminiscences and*
> *Reflections* (appendix)

Indeed, throughout the Second World War, the Soviet forces' strongest weapon would be the artillery. Khalkhin-Gol was the Red Army's first effective combined-arms attack. Historian Alexei Isaev once remarked, 'Khalkhin-Gol for Zhukov was like Toulon for Napoléon Bonaparte' – in essence, a turning point. Former Red Army officer Ruslanov, who served under Zhukov in the Belorussian Military District, highlighted the impact of this success in the Far East on Zhukov's rise to fame and subsequent promotions:

Zhukov's appointment could not have been made without Stalin's knowledge, and it was not accidental. The significance of the Khalkhin Gol River battles must not be underestimated. The whole world followed their outcome; the matter involved the international prestige of the USSR, and, primarily, it was a rare opportunity to test new material and tactics under actual combat conditions. Zhukov himself knew that this appointment was a test of his competence and one which he had to pass.
> P. Ruslanov, *The Russian Review*, April 1956

Khalkhin-Gol also had immediate sinister consequences for Poland. A ceasefire was agreed between the Japanese Kwantung Army and the Soviet Union on 16 September, and thus relieved of the threat of fighting a two-front war, the very next day the Red Army invaded the 'Land of the Fields' from the east, in accordance with the Molotov–Ribbentrop Pact that included a plan for the partition of Poland by the Third Reich and the Soviet Union. The brutal invasion culminated with the mass execution of 22,000 captive Polish officers by the NKVD at Katyn in March 1940.

Zhukov now received the first of his four Hero of the Soviet Union awards, and in the summer of 1940 he was put in command of the Southern Front when the Red Army occupied Bessarabia and Northern Bukovina. He was promoted to General and Chief of the General Staff of the Red Army in the early days of 1941 after his brilliant performance in January's military exercises. Then Operation Barbarossa was unleashed. On 30 July Zhukov was sacked after recommending that Kiev be abandoned. Stalin refused to agree, and as a result, Field Marshal Gerd von Rundstedt captured the city and inflicted 700,000 casualties on the Soviets. Zhukov was then sent to Leningrad to organize its defence. Upon arrival there on 14 September, he made it clear that everyone was to hold the line:

> All commanders, political officers and rank and file who leave the line of defence without prior written instruction of the Front or Military Council are to be shot on sight.
>
> Zhukov's Order No. 0064 for the Leningrad Front,
> 17 September 1941

Stalin had ordered the scuttling of the Red Banner Baltic Fleet, but Zhukov cancelled it, planning instead to use the heavy guns of the two battleships (*Oktyabrskaya Revolyutsiya* and *Marat*) and two *Kirov*-class heavy cruisers for fire support. In any case, by the fall of 1941 the Soviet Union's utter defeat seemed a foregone conclusion.

Then, when Moscow was directly threatened by Operation Typhoon, Stalin recalled Zhukov and gave him command of the battered forces defending the capital. Soviet regiments stationed in the Far East were hastily transferred across the vast expanses of the USSR. With his fresh 'Siberian' troops, Zhukov succeeded in defending the city. On 5 December 1941, while the temperature fell to a glacial -40° Celsius, these reinforcements and new units assembled by *Stavka* attacked the German lines around Moscow, supported by new T-34 tanks and Katyusha rocket-launchers. These divisions were better prepared for winter warfare than their foes, and they included several ski battalions. By 7 January 1942 the exhausted and freezing Germans had been pushed back 100–250km from Moscow.

Our attack on Moscow had broken down. We had suffered a grievous defeat which was to be seriously aggravated during the next few weeks thanks to the rigidity of our Supreme Command: despite all our reports those men, far away in East Prussia, could form no true concept of the real conditions of the winter war in which their soldiers were now engaged. The troops were no longer strong enough to capture Moscow . . . The Russians are pursuing us closely, and we must expect misfortunes to occur. Our casualties, particularly from sickness and frostbite, have been bad.

Heinz Guderian, *Panzer Leader*

In August 1942 Zhukov was named deputy Commissar of Defence and first deputy Commander-in-Chief of the Soviet armed forces. Feared as well as respected, proud and irascible, his leadership style was authoritarian and coercive, and he demanded nothing less than perfection and absolute obedience from his subordinates. He took charge of the defence of Stalingrad and became the chief member of Stalin's personal Supreme Headquarters. From that point on, Zhukov figured prominently in the planning or execution of almost every major engagement of the Eastern Front. Engaged in strategic or operational planning, he was often away from the front.

We are here, on the steep banks of the Volga. Our spirit is stronger than ever, our will is as strong as steel, our hands are not tired of crushing the enemy. We have decided to stand to the last man at the walls of Stalingrad!

Oath taken by Red Army troops at Stalingrad, 6 November 1942

Operation Mars, aiming at tying down German forces in the Rzhev sector and preventing them from reinforcing Stalingrad at the end of 1942, was an epic military disaster and Zhukov's worst defeat, with 100,000 Red Army soldiers killed and another 200,000 wounded in the Rzhev meat grinder. Historical records of this botched offensive were actually suppressed to preserve Zhukov's reputation. But then Operation Uranus, which Zhukov also planned, effectively enveloped and surrounded the Wehrmacht's 6th Army in Stalingrad. Launched on 19 November 1942, the massive operation ended with the capture of 265,000 German personnel after *Generalfeldmarschall* Paulus' surrender on 2 February 1943. Stalingrad was saved!

The first period of the war, which ended with the Battle of Stalingrad, was a great school of armed struggle with a powerful enemy. The Soviet Supreme Command, the General Staff, the commands and staffs of the troops in the field acquired invaluable experience in organizing and executing active defensive battles and counter-offensive operations.

Georgy Zhukov, *Reminiscences and Reflections*

Zhukov then oversaw Operation Spark, which opened a route into the besieged city of Leningrad in January 1943, and for his achievements he was promoted to Marshal of the Soviet Union on 18 January. Leningrad would still be subjected to a partial siege and bombardment until January 1944. Zhukov was heavily involved in the Battle of Kursk opposite Manstein (July–August 1943). He persuaded Stalin to wait for the German offensive, in order to wear the enemy out, before launching a decisive counter-attack:

In the first phase the enemy, collecting their best forces – including 13–15 tank divisions and with the support of a large number of aircraft – will strike Kursk with their Kromskom-Orel grouping from the north-east and their Belgorod-Kharkov grouping from the south-east . . . It would be better to make the enemy exhaust himself against our defences, and knock out his tanks and then, bringing up fresh reserves, to go over to the general offensive which would finally finish off his main force.

Zhukov to Stalin, 8 April 1943

In the initial stage of Operation *Zitadelle*, the Wehrmacht, despite bringing in new Tiger and Panther tanks and Ferdinand *jagdpanzers* (tank destroyers), was unable to break through the nine Soviet successive defensive belts, being caught off guard by the Red Army's large operational reserves and strategic depth (extending to no less than 250 km!). Manstein and Hoth believed a breakthrough into open ground by the 4th Panzer Army could be achieved, had the XXIV Panzer Corps held in reserve been committed to exploit the gains, but Hitler then called a halt to the offensive because of the Allied landing in Sicily.

At 2.20 a.m. the order was issued to begin the counter-preparations. A terrible rumbling was heard and a very great battle began in the Kursk Bulge area. The sounds of the heavy artillery, the explosions of bombs and the M-31 rocket projectiles, the outbursts of the Katyushas and the constant hum of the aircraft engines merged into what was like the strains of a 'symphony' from hell.

Georgy Zhukov, *Reminiscences and Reflections*

The Germans failed to take Prokhorovka, but nor did the Soviets manage to destroy the II SS Panzer Corps and they suffered monumental losses in tanks and personnel in the process. Nevertheless, it was the first time that the Red Army had managed to halt a Wehrmacht summer offensive. The Battle of Kursk, which involved more than 3 million soldiers, 10,000 AFVs and 8,000 aircraft, was the final strategic offensive the Germans were able to launch on the Eastern Front, a reality which Hitler refused to acknowledge.

> The outstanding victory of our forces near Kursk was an indication of the growing might of the Soviet state and its armed forces. The victory was forged at the front and in the rear by the efforts of all Soviet people under the leadership of the Communist Party . . . The defeat of the Nazi troops was of vital international significance and raised the authority of the Soviet Union even higher.
>
> Georgy Zhukov, *Reminiscences and Reflections*

In early 1944 Zhukov directed the Soviet sweep across Ukraine. He commanded the Soviet Operation Bagration through Belorussia (summer-autumn 1944), which resulted in the collapse of Army Group Centre and of the German occupation of Poland and Czechoslovakia. By the time of the D-Day landings in Normandy in June 1944, the Wehrmacht was but a shadow of its former self.

On 12 November 1944 Stalin appointed Zhukov to command the 1st Belorussian Front, replacing Rokossovsky. After the capture of Poland and East Prussia, spearheading the Soviet thrust into Germany, Zhukov's men defeated the Germans at Oder Neisse and Seelow Heights, before encircling Berlin. Hitler committed suicide on 30 April under the Reich Chancellery; two days later, completing the Soviets' total victory, elements of the 3rd Shock Army gained control of the Reichstag. Nazi Germany had fallen and the war in Europe was finally over.

On the night of 8 May 1945 Zhukov was selected by Stalin to personally accept the German Instrument of Surrender in Berlin. For all his achievements during the 'Great Patriotic War' Zhukov was later allowed to ride the great white horse 'Kumir' (Idol) at the Victory Parade in Red Square. At the end of the magnificent ceremony, 200 soldiers carrying German banners threw them down at the foot of the Lenin Mausoleum with a 'contemptuous gesture', as instructed.

> Moscow, June 24, 1945. Here it is, a long-awaited and unforgettable day! The Soviet people firmly believed that it would come. Heroic warriors, inspired by the party of Lenin, under the command of their famous commanders have passed a difficult four-year battle path and ended it with a brilliant victory in Berlin.
>
> Georgy Zhukov, *Reminiscences and Reflections*

Once the war was over, Zhukov was made Supreme Military Commander of the Soviet occupation zone in Germany. However, his extraordinary popularity caused him to be regarded as a potential threat by Stalin, who then assigned him to serve in subordinate commands in post-war Europe. After the death of the dictator in 1953, Zhukov returned to favour, personally arresting Lavrentiy Beria and serving as Defence Minister.

> Stalin was very much interested in assessments of comrade Zhukov as a military leader. He asked me often for my opinion of Zhukov. I told him then, 'I have known Zhukov for a long time. He is a good general and a good military leader.' After the war Stalin began to tell all kinds of nonsense about Zhukov. Among it [was] the following: 'You praised Zhukov, but he does not deserve it. They say that before each operation at the front Zhukov used to behave as follows: he used to take a handful of earth, smell it and say, "We can begin the attack", or its opposite, "The planned operation cannot be carried out." I stated at the time, 'Comrade Stalin, I do not know who invented this, but it is not true.' It is possible that Stalin himself invented these things for the purpose of minimizing the role and military talents of Marshal Zhukov.
>
> Nikita Khrushchev, Special Report of the 20th Congress of
> the Communist Party, 24–25 February 1956

Though temporarily on the same side, on 26 October 1957 Zhukov was formally dismissed as Minister of Defence by Khrushchev, and a week later, still considered a serious political rival for supreme power, he was removed from his party posts. He was finally allowed to bring out his autobiography, *Marshal of Victory*, in 1969, although some chapters were only published by *Pravda* in 1989. In his memoirs he tended to take credit for practically all the decisive victories the Red Army had won. Greatly admired worldwide, Zhukov received long and resounding standing ovations at every public occasion he attended. He died in Moscow from a stroke on 18 June 1974, and his state funeral was the biggest such occasion since Stalin's death. His ashes were buried at the Kremlin Wall Necropolis.

Achievements

A man of humble origin who began his military service as a private in the Imperial Russian forces and rose to the head of the mighty Red Army, Zhukov deserves more acknowledgment than he has received from the West for an impressive career that spanned most of the Soviet period and for his strategic grasp during the 'Great Patriotic War'. Zhukov had mastered the concept of combined-arms warfare before Operation Barbarossa. He carefully orchestrated infantry, armour, artillery and air power to complement and support each other in order to overwhelm the enemy. He also became a master of the grand envelopment. Zhukov played a critical role in salvaging the perilous situation in the winter of 1941, leading the Red Army to an amazing reversal of fortune in 1942–3 and eventual victory just two years later. He stopped the Wehrmacht at the very gates of Moscow, rescued Leningrad, was instrumental in the hard-fought victory of Stalingrad and won the Battle of Kursk, the true turning point of the war in Europe. His men were the first Allies to enter Berlin. This was all made possible by the patriotism and heroism of the ordinary Russian people. It is estimated that 80 per cent of all Germany's miltary deaths occurred on the Eastern Front. For its part, the Soviet Union lost 25 million people, including 6 million soldiers. The 'Great Patriotic War' or the 'Great Fatherland War' of 1941–5 is today more than ever a centrepiece of the nation's consciousness in Russia. Tough and resolute, Zhukov also knew how to navigate the dangerous waters of Soviet politics. He never questioned Stalin's brutal methods, but for the period he was something of a free thinker, and it was this quality that Stalin valued and made Zhukov so successful. Indeed, one of his crucial talents was knowing how to deal with Stalin and survive! With time, he became just too important and popular to be eliminated. It was Zhukov who was selected by Stalin to formally accept Germany's unconditional surrender on 8 May 1945, although after the war, fearing his immense popularity, Stalin eventually demoted him and took personal credit for having saved the nation. For Russians to this day, despite his flaws and mistakes, Zhukov has achieved near-mythical status, becoming their enduring symbol of victory.

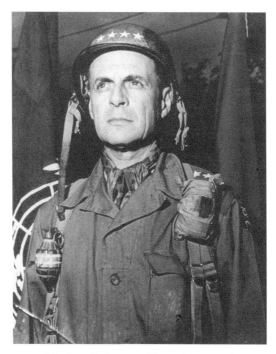

Matthew Ridgway in Korea. (*U.S. Army*)

Chapter 49

MATTHEW RIDGWAY
The Airborne General who saved Korea

D-Day saved a continent, and so, a world. And Ridgway helped save D-Day. Heroes come when they're needed; great men step forward when courage seems in short supply. World War II was such a time. And there was Ridgway.

US President Ronald Reagan, 12 May 1986

Matthew Ridgway was one of the foremost combat leaders in US history. In charge of the elite 82nd Airborne Division, he led this newly activated unit in all its major operations from the campaign of Sicily to the invasion of Germany. In Korea, leading from the front, the veteran paratrooper rescued the beaten Eighth Army from the brink of defeat against North Korean and Chinese forces. Succeeding

General Douglas MacArthur as Supreme Allied Commander in the Far East, Ridgway ended his eventful career as NATO Commander in Europe and US Army Chief of Staff.

A Virginian, son of an artillery colonel, Matthew Bunker Ridgway (1895–1993) graduated from West Point in 1917. Having missed deployment on the Western Front, Ridgway received a series of inter-war assignments, serving under George C. Marshall in the 15th Infantry in Tientsin, China, and also in Nicaragua and the Philippines. He attended the Army War College, graduating in 1937. His commanding officer and mentor was impressed by his industry:

> I know you have enough brains to perform your military duties in a superior fashion but I doubt very much whether you have enough sense to take care of the human machine – very few men have, and unfortunately when you burn out a fuse you cannot substitute another twenty minutes later. Seriously, you must cultivate the art of playing and loafing; there is no need for you to demonstrate any further you are an energetic, able workman.
>
> Brigadier General George C. Marshall to Major Matthew Ridgway, 24 August 1936

He was still Marshall's assistant Chief of Staff in Washington at the time of the attack on Pearl Harbor, and served in the War Plans Division until January 1942, when he was promoted to Brigadier General. In April he was promoted to the rank of Major General, and in August he was placed in command of the 'All American' 82nd Infantry Division previously organized by Omar Bradley. As the advent of the Second World War ushered in a need for highly mobile units capable of being airdropped into battle zones by parachuting, the 82nd Infantry Division was selected to be converted and re-designated as the 82nd Airborne Division, becoming the first US Army Airborne division. Training started at Camp Claiborne and Fort Benning.

Although the first US airborne operation was by the 509th Parachute Infantry Battalion in November 1942 (Operation Torch against French North Africa), the Soviet forces had led the way a decade earlier, developing airborne tactics through a series of trials. Germany (1935), France (1936), Italy (1938), the United Kingdom and Japan (1940) followed suit. The first wartime jumps came during the German invasions of Norway and Denmark (Operation *Weserübung*). The elite *Fallschirmtruppe* pioneered vertical envelopment, conducting successful airborne operations in Norway, Denmark, Belgium, Holland and France. During the Campaign of Crete, in the spring of 1941 (Operation *Merkur*), Kurt Student's *Fallschirmjäger* parachute and glider troops captured the island but suffered 3,800 dead and 2,600 wounded; this should have alerted the US theoreticians of airborne warfare to the high risks of lightly-equipped infantry acting independently.

> We had learned, from the very beginning in Sicily, that it is better to land near an objective and take heavy landing losses rather than to have to fight on the ground to get it.
>
> James Gavin, *On to Berlin*

The 82nd took part in Operation Husky, the Allied invasion of Sicily, and the Division's baptism of fire came during the combat jumps of 11 July (when the 504th was decimated by friendly fire), and at Salerno on 13 September 1943. Other airborne operations, such as the attempted reinforcement of the Gela beachhead in Sicily and the night drop of the 509th Parachute Battalion at Avellino in Italy, ended in disaster. In Sicily the 82nd Airborne lost 148 men killed, 501 wounded and 348 missing, also suffering 290 non-battle casualties. Ridgway himself, considered too old to jump, reached Sicily by sea. The Airborne Division's equipment was deemed too light, especially when facing German Panzer divisions, a serious issue that Ridgway was not able to correct before the subsequent Normandy invasion.

> Part of the fault lay with Troop Carrier itself where too intricate an operation had been planned for the inadequately trained C-47 crews. They had been directed to fly a tricky overwater course at night with few markers to guide their inexperienced navigators. So difficult was the mission that even today Lieutenant General Matthew B. Ridgway, wartime commander of the 82nd, contends we never developed during the war proficiency enough to have executed that drop as it was planned. A share of the failure he ascribed to insufficient training of troop-carrier crews with the airborne troops. This problem of interservice training had harassed those airborne units since the organization of their first division. It was to haunt them throughout the remainder of the war.
>
> Omar Bradley, *A Soldier's Story*

During Operation Overlord, the 82nd landed inland to capture Sainte Mère l'Eglise, which was on the main road to Cherbourg, and two bridges over the Merderet River. The Division's third major combat drop prevented units of the German 91st Infantry Division and 243rd Division from interfering with the landings on Utah Beach. General Bradley used the 82nd in ground campaigning far longer than expected. This time, Ridgway had jumped with his men. By the time the Division was relieved in early July, the 82nd had seen more than a month of severe combat; 5,245 troopers were killed, wounded, or missing, a total casualty rate of 46 per cent.

The 82nd fought for 33 days of action without relief, without replacements. Every mission accomplished. No ground gained ever relinquished.

Major General Ridgway's report, 26 July 1944

Following the Normandy campaign, the 82nd returned to Britain for a much-needed refit before future operations. Ridgway was given command of the newly organized XVIII Airborne Corps, which consisted of the 17th, 82nd and 101st Airborne Divisions. The command of the 82nd went to James Gavin. During the Battle of the Bulge, Eisenhower committed both the 82nd and the 101st as reinforcements in an attempt to halt the German offensive. Transported by trucks to the front in a matter of hours, the 82nd was tasked with facing *Kampfgruppe Peiper*, while the 101st participated in the defence of Bastogne.

In the third week of March 1945, XVIII Airborne Corps planned and executed Operation Varsity (a component of Operation Plunder). This was the largest airborne operation in history, involving 16,000 paratroopers, and it helped secure a foothold across the Rhine in German territory, in preparation for the final push toward Berlin, already threatened by Marshal Zhukov's 1st Belorussian Front.

He was a great combat commander. Hard as flint and full of intensity; so much so, I thought, 'The man's going to have a heart attack before it's over.' Sometimes it seemed as though it was a personal thing: Ridgway versus the Wehrmacht . . . He was brave under fire to the point of being exhibitionistic.

James Gavin, *On to Berlin*

Following VE Day, Ridgway was promoted to Lieutenant General. He was sent to the Pacific, but the war came to an end after President Harry Truman's fateful decision to vaporize Hiroshima and Nagasaki with radioactive bombs in August 1945. These dramatic events instantly and radically changed the face of warfare, and they also altered the balance of power in the early phase of the Cold War, since the Americans were then the sole possessors of the ultimate weapon of mass destruction and the means to deliver it in the form of their Superfortresses.

On 26 December 1950, while a new war was raging in Korea, Ridgway arrived at General of the Army Douglas MacArthur's headquarters in Tokyo. The Airborne General was to take over the Eighth Army after General Walton Walker's death in a jeep accident. When Ridgway asked if he was allowed to attack, given the right conditions, a pessimistic MacArthur replied, 'The Eighth Army is yours, Matt. Do what you think is best.' This was in the midst of the 'Chinese New Year Offensive' by the PVA (People's Volunteer Army) and KPA (Korean People's Army). The situation on the ground was so compromised that, a day before Ridgway's landing in Tokyo, MacArthur had submitted a list of thirty-four 'retardation targets' identified for attack in China, Manchuria and Korea using Mark-4 plutonium bombs. Ridgway arrived at Taegu with a grenade hanging from a shoulder strap; this was the origin of his famous nickname 'Ole Iron Tits'.

> Some people thought I wore the grenades as a gesture of showmanship. This was not correct. They were purely utilitarian. Many a time, in Europe and in Korea, men in tight spots blasted their way out with grenades.
>
> Matthew Ridgway, *Soldier*

The PVA and KPA captured Seoul for the second time on 4 January 1951, and Incheon had to be abandoned the following day. The Communist offensive now threatened to push the UN forces into the sea. Less than two weeks later, Ridgway managed to halt the longest retreat of any US military unit in history, some 80km south of Seoul. The front was stabilized, the broken Eighth Army rebuilt and re-motivated with a new fighting spirit. Ridgway provided training and equipment, revitalized morale and placed the emphasis on leadership from the front.

> The job of the commander was to be up where the crisis of action was taking place. In time of battle, I wanted division commanders to be up with their forward battalion, and I wanted corps commanders up with the regiment that was in the hottest action. If they had paperwork to do, they could do it at night. By day their place was up there where the shooting was going on. I held to the old-fashioned idea that it helped the spirits of the men to see the Old Man up there, in the snow and sleet and the mud, sharing the same cold, miserable existence they had to endure.
>
> Matthew Ridgway, *Soldier*

Providing close infantry support, the M24 Chaffees and M4A3 tanks were outclassed by the Soviet-built T-34/85s, but the M26 Pershings and the introduction of a growing number of M46A1 Pattons throughout 1950–1 definitely tipped the balance in the UN's favour. Regaining the initiative with Operation Thunderbolt, the Eighth Army advanced for the second time toward the 38th parallel. Incheon was recaptured on 10 February, and Communist resistance south of the Han River collapsed.

> There was a common G.I. joke: 'There's a right way, a wrong way and a Ridgway.'
>
> Eddie Deerfield, Second World War and
> Korean War veteran

Contrary to MacArthur's advice, the Truman administration opted for a limited war, called a 'police action', with conventional weapons and forces, in order to prevent further escalation of hostilities with the Chinese, or with the Soviets, who had given a demonstration of their own nuclear capability in August 1949. The use of atomic weapons was indeed considered in Washington but was discarded, since analysts estimated that it would not produce a decisive victory, but might rather trigger World War III. President Truman was not prepared to risk the fate of the world over Korea.

Ridgway was thus bound to launch counter-offensives with the massive use of artillery, strategic bombing (by B-26s and B-29s), napalm and close air support, to grind down the Communist forces, devastating literally every city, village and piece of infrastructure in North Korea. The UNC's air superiority did not go uncontested, however. At the end of November 1950 agile Soviet and Chinese MiG-15s appeared in the skies over Korea, effectively challenging the American F-80 straight-wing jets and intercepting the lumbering Second World War-era bombers. Avoiding total war, and using limited means, Operations Killer and Ripper (February–March 1951), aiming at annihilating enemy forces, were nevertheless highly successful. UN forces retook Seoul in mid-March, before reaching the 38th parallel.

> He [Ridgway] stopped his jeep and came over and asked us what our biggest problem was, and in those days the problems were no food and no writing materials. He said he'd have the things we needed by tomorrow, and, by God, the next day the airplanes came and dropped materials and we had hot food. To me he was a wonderful general.
>
> Ernest Sarianides, Korean War veteran

In the next two years the conflict became a war of attrition, reaching a protracted stalemate over the defensive lines near the 38th parallel, the pre-war border, while ceasefire negotiations dragged on. On 11 April 1951 Ridgway replaced the sacked MacArthur as Commander-in-Chief UN Command in Tokyo. In May, while being promoted to four-star General, Ridgway requested the forward deployment of thirty-eight atomic weapons into the theatre of operations. As with his predecessor, the request was denied.

Concurrently, Ridgway oversaw the end of the US military occupation of Japan a year later. In May 1952 Ridgway left Korea to replace General Eisenhower (who was running for President) as NATO Commander in Europe, and he later became US Army Chief of Staff (1953–5), succeeding General J. Lawton Collins.

Ridgway retired in June 1955, and in 1956 he published his memoirs entitled *Soldier*. His second book, *The Korean War: How We Met the Challenge*, was published in 1967. In recognition of his outstanding military career, Ridgway was awarded the US Presidential Medal of Freedom in 1986 by Ronald Reagan and the US Congressional Gold Medal by President Bush in 1991, two years prior to his death at the age of ninety-eight. He was buried at the Arlington National Cemetery.

Achievements

Together with Omar Bradley, the charismatic staff officer Matthew Ridgway oversaw the conversion of the 82nd Infantry Division to the 82nd Airborne Division. He then led the 82nd in the campaigns of Sicily, Italy and Normandy. Later, as part of the XVIII Airborne Corps, he was given command and led his paratroopers at the Battle of the Bulge and in the invasion of Germany. Learning from the near-failure of the mission in Sicily, the progressive application of the elements of operational art in the following operations until the end of the war indicates that Ridgway's leadership was developing and maturing over time. In Korea, the famed Airborne commander restored the demoralized Eighth Army to combat effectiveness in a matter of weeks, rallying the defeated United Nations forces and turning the tide of the war. These achievements were, according to General Omar Bradley, 'the greatest feat of personal leadership in the history of the Army'. In this brutal conflict, Ridgway's intervention eventually ensured the survival of the Republic of Korea. In Europe and Korea, Ridgway's leadership style was popular with his troops, ensuring their confidence and loyalty. An adviser to four US Presidents, Matthew Ridgway stands out as one of the greatest figures in United States military history.

Vo-Nguyen-Giap in 1967. (*HO -Vietnam News Agency - AFP*)

Chapter 50

VÕ NGUYÊN GIÁP
Master of revolutionary warfare

The French and the Americans underestimated our strength. They had better weapons and enormous military and economic potential. They never doubted that victory would be theirs. And yet, just when the French believed themselves to be on the verge of victory, everything collapsed around them. The same happened to the Americans in the spring of '65. Just when Washington was about to proclaim victory in the South, the Americans saw their expectations crumble. Why? Because it wasn't just an army they were up against but an entire people.

General Giáp interview, in 'Guerilla Wars', PBS, 1999

Over thirty-five years, from 1944 to 1979, Giáp relentlessly fought off the Japanese, France, the United States, the Republic of South Vietnam, the Khmer Rouge and China, with virtually no pauses between conflicts. He served as the military leader of the Viet Minh resistance against the Japanese occupation of Vietnam during the Second World War, and in the following decades was one of the principal commanders in the Indochina War (1946–54) and the Vietnam War (1960–75). Giáp earned a reputation as one of Asia's outstanding military tacticians and one of the finest strategists of the twentieth century.

Võ Nguyên Giáp (1911–2013) was born in the village of An-Xa in Quang-Binh Province. His father was a poor scholar in pre-colonial Vietnam. At twelve, young Giáp was sent to the Lycée National at Hué, where he first came to the attention of the French police. He then became involved in leftwing revolutionary groups and spent two years in a French prison in Lao Báo. After his release in 1932 Giáp joined the Indochinese Communist Party (ICP). In the mid-1930s he studied politics at the University of Hanoi, before taking a job as a history professor.

During the Second World War Giáp joined other insurgents to fight the Japanese invaders in northern Vietnam. In May 1940 he travelled to China, met Hồ Chí Minh and became a member of the Viet Minh. Giáp was placed in charge of a Viet Minh unit responsible for recruitment, training and discipline. He became an avid student of revolutionary warfare, taking inspiration from Sun Tzu, Napoléon Bonaparte's campaigns, T. E. Lawrence's guerrilla tactics, and of course Vladimir Lenin.

Giáp's reputation as a skilled tactician and strategist earned him a ministerial post in Hồ Chí Minh's government at the end of 1945. When the First Indochina War broke out against French colonial rule in 1946, Giáp returned to a military role, leading an army of more than a quarter of a million men. It was Giáp who defined the role of the People's Army of Vietnam (PAVN) as being 'the instrument of the Party and the revolutionary state for the accomplishment, in armed form, of the tasks of the revolution'. He was the main instigator of the struggle against the nationalist parties, competing with the Viêt Minh. During the 10-year long Indochina War, Giáp's guerrilla forces were transformed into a competent and disciplined regular army.

With the development of our forces, guerrilla warfare changed into a mobile warfare. In this process of development of guerrilla warfare and of accentuation of the mobile warfare, our people's army constantly grew and passed from the stage of combats involving a section or company, to fairly large-scale campaigns bringing into action several divisions.

General Giáp, *People's War, People's Army*

Throughout the Indochina War, in the Battles of Lạng Sơn (1950), Hòa Bình (1951–2) and Điện Biên Phủ (March–May 1954), Giáp fought against veteran French generals of the Second World War such as De Lattre de Tassigny, Raoul Salan and Henri Navarre. Employing the guerrilla tactics used by Mao Zedong, Giáp's army slowly gained control of large areas of northern and central Vietnam. Though they suffered high rates of attrition, his planning and intrepid tactics led eventually to the decisive French defeat at Điện Biên Phủ, which stunned the world.

> Our victory at Điện Biên Phủ will make it possible for our forces to intensify their actions on various fronts, thus creating conditions for the annihilation of important enemy forces and foiling his plans for pacification.
>
> Giáp, quoted in 'Contributions to the History of Điện Biên Phủ', *Vietnamese Studies* No.3, 1965

At Điện Biên Phủ, to deliver one kilo of rice to the soldiers involved in the siege, four had to be consumed during transport. Giáp used 260,000 porters, over 20,000 bicycles, 11,800 rafts, 400 trucks and 500 horses. Operation Vulture, the air intervention planned by the Eisenhower administration to save the French garrison, was vehemently opposed by US Army Chief of Staff Matthew Ridgway, who wished to avoid direct American military involvement in Indochina. Ridgway expressed concern that the United States had already forgotten the lessons of the Korean War:

> The experience of Korea, where we had complete domination of the air and a far more powerful air force, afforded no basis for thinking that some additional air power was going to bring decisive results on the ground.
>
> Matthew B. Ridgway to Admiral Arthur Radford, 22 March 1954, Matthew B. Ridgway Papers, USAHEC

The PAVN's victory at Điện Biên Phủ led directly to the end of seventy years of French colonial rule in South-East Asia. By June 1954 the US began to consider the possibility that rather than supporting the French war effort, it would be preferable to replace them altogether and support the new Indochinese states of South Vietnam, Laos and Cambodia. In other words, to substitute their own control for that of the former European colonial power .

Once the French withdrawal was complete in January 1957, the US, fearing South Vietnam might fall to communism, started to send 'advisers' to support the fight of Ngô Đình Diệm's regime against the armed communist 'insurgency'. In November 1961 General Maxwell Taylor recommended to President John F. Kennedy the introduction of US ground combat troops. These forces eventually reached a total of more than half a million men alongside the Army of the Republic of Vietnam (ARVN), but they proved unable to respond adequately to the unconventional warfare waged by the Viet Cong (founded in December 1960), facing sabotage, hit-and-run attacks, infiltration and assassination campaigns against alleged 'traitors'. Since Stanley Karnow reported it in 1983, Giáp's alleged statement has often been quoted:

> Every minute, hundreds of thousand of people die on this Earth. The life or death of a hundred, a thousand, tens of thousands of human beings, even our compatriots, means little.

While US military policies dehumanized their opponents, measuring success by body counts, the Viet Cong, following Hanoi's Central Office for South Vietnam (COSVN) guidelines, progressively won the battle of 'hearts and minds', successfully using intimidation and propaganda in many rural areas of South Vietnam. Counter-insurgency, a notoriously brutal form of combat, did not even have the excuse of securing US victory in Vietnam. It was just a matter of time before the Communist cause would prevail.

> We fought and won against the Mongols in the thirteenth century. Now it is the Americans. We are conscious of our historic role. We have shaken the largest country in the world. In a war like this, one bends or gets stronger.
>
> General Giáp to Marc Riboud, *Look* magazine,
> 21 January 1969

As North Vietnamese Defence Minister and Commander-in-Chief of the PAVN, Giáp continued to advocate a total war using guerrilla strategy against the US and their local ARVN allies. He was involved only reluctantly in the Tết Offensive (January 1968), decided on by the Politburo and based on an operational plan prepared by General Nguyễn Chí Thanh, Lê Duẩn and the Military Operations Command. During the Lunar New Year holiday, North Vietnamese and Viet Cong forces launched a coordinated attack against more than a hundred targets in South Vietnam. Both the Viet Cong and the PAVN suffered heavy casualties, and the popular uprising of the southern population did not happen as expected, but the military defeat still proved to be a turning point in the conflict, a propaganda and political success for the communist forces. Contrary to the official narrative, US military victory was clearly nowhere in sight.

> Of course, he was a formidable adversary. Let me also say that Giáp was trained in small-unit, guerrilla tactics, but he persisted in waging a big-unit war with terrible losses to his own men. By his own admission, by early 1969,

I think, he had lost, what, a half million soldiers? He reported this. Now such a disregard for human life may make a formidable adversary, but it does not make a military genius. An American commander losing men like that would hardly have lasted more than a few weeks.

William Westmoreland, on Giáp, interview for *George* magazine, November 1998

A new policy of 'vietnamization' was now implemented, and US troop strength was gradually reduced from 543,000 to 49,000 between 1968 and 1972. Deserted by most of their American allies, the ARVN was first routed at the Battle of Lam Son in January 1971; then, taking advantage of their perceived weakness, the 'Easter Offensive', planned by Giáp and Lê Duẩn, was launched on 30 March 1972. Three North Vietnamese divisions crossed the demilitarized zone (DMZ) and invaded the Republic of Vietnam's northernmost provinces. The operation was aimed at defeating elements of the ARVN, with the stated objective of demonstrating that vietnamization of the conflict was not working for the South. Though the offensive was eventually defeated, PAVN forces succeeded in occupying about 10 per cent of South Vietnamese territory. To counter the Easter Offensive, the Nixon Administration endorsed the military option of an escalation through increased strategic bombing of North Vietnam.

For years, the military had been complaining about being held on a leash by the civilian leadership. But when Nixon pressed them for new strategies, all they could think of was resuming the bombing of the North.

Henry Kissinger, on the NSC meeting of 25 January 1969, in *The White House Years*

With the Soviets' technical assistance, Giáp had supervised the building of an air defence system against escalating US bombing, which was mostly characterized by deep strikes against the North, and Hanoi in particular. North Vietnamese headquarters received advance warnings from Soviet intelligence, as well as SA-2 surface-to-air missiles, AZP S-60s, 61-Ks and ZU-23s anti-aircraft autocannons, ammunition and a great deal of other military equipment.

On 4 April 1972 Richard Nixon declared to members of his staff, 'The bastards have never been bombed like they're going to be bombed this time!' The Presidential promise was duly fulfilled: during Operations Freedom Train and Linebacker I and II, North Vietnam was crushed by 165,000 tons of bombs, more than twice the tonnage that fell on the British Isles during the whole of the Second World War! Collateral damage was extensive, including 1,600 civilian deaths, but by mid-December Hanoi had fully repaired its railway connection with China and adjusted its supply routes to compensate for the US naval blockade. Owing to the efficient North Vietnamese defence system, from 10 May to 29 December 1972 the US lost 132 aircraft in combat (including fifteen B-52s), with another thirty destroyed as a direct consequence of the missions.

> We all feared the B-52 at first because the US said it was invincible, but after the first night, we knew the B-52 could be destroyed just like any other aircraft. The US said they wanted to bomb Vietnam back to the Stone Age. This was a mistake. You cannot use power to destroy the will of the people.
> Lieutenant General Nguyễn Văn Phiệt, *Air & Space Magazine*, December 2014

The last phase of the strategic bombing campaign, Operation Linebacker II, did play a decisive role in a return to the negotiating table, with the signing of the Paris Accord on 27 January 1973. 'Peace with honour' had been achieved at last! Two months later, the last US military unit left Vietnam, and the final Hồ Chí Minh campaign led by Văn Tiến Dũng saw the rapid collapse of the 1 million-strong ARVN and the climactic fall of Saigon on 30 April 1975. The two nations, unified by conquest, would adopt the name 'The Socialist Republic of Việt Nam'. The victors ignored the provisions of the Paris peace agreements, but suffered no consequences.

> When I was young, I had a dream that one day I'd see my country free and united. That day, my dream came true. When the political bureau reunited Hanoi with Laos, there were first reports of evacuation. Then the Saigon government capitulated. It was like turning the page on a chapter of history.
> General Giáp, PBS interview, 1999

Giáp's forces demonstrated great tactical flexibility. His own patient approach to planning, and to preparing and equipping his forces in each phase of the war, was remarkable. In the field of logistics, his most astonishing achievement was the clever use of terrain, with the development of the Truong Son Strategic Supply Route, better known as the 'Hồ Chi Minh trail', an immense and elaborate maze of tracks hidden in the jungle, running from North Vietnam to the South through Laos and north-eastern Cambodia. From October to November 1965 the Hồ Chí Minh trail disgorged 4,500 Vietnamese troops per month and 300 tons of supplies per day!

Traffic on the trail was little affected by massive bombing campaigns, even when the US resorted to defoliants, napalm and the dropping of hundreds of thousands of mines and anti-personnel devices. Two million tons of explosives were dropped on the Laos portion of the trail alone! Relative to its size and population, Laos became the nation which had suffered the most extensive bombardment in history. The possibility of employing tactical nuclear weapons against the trail was even discussed by the Pentagon. The tracks were kept open by 300,000 full-time workers (half of them women) and almost as many part-time farmers. By the early 1970s the trail had evolved into a well-defined series of jungle roads and underground support facilities.

In the end, US tactical victories were irrelevant, as the 8 million tons of bombs dropped on South-East Asia from 1964 to 1973. Giáp's ideologically indoctrinated 'peasant armies' had imposed a strategic defeat on a superpower in the midst of the Cold War. The PAVN and Viet Cong had inflicted sufficient casualties to undermine US morale and weaken support for the war at home. The US military had 47,434 servicemen killed in action in Vietnam, plus another 11,000 non-combat deaths. Leaving aside the Vietnamese losses (those fighting on behalf of foreign powers), these casualties are comparable to the 47,674 French colonial (mostly Africans and *Légionnaires*) and metropolitan troops killed in Indochina between 1945 and 1954, men who had only a fraction of the manpower, equipment and firepower available to the US military a decade later.

> The entire population took part in the fighting; every commune had its fortified village, every district had its regional troops fighting under the command of the local branches of the Party and the people's administration, in liaison with the regular forces in order to wear down and annihilate the enemy forces.
>
> General Giáp, *People's War, People's Army*

For their part, according to North Vietnamese sources, the military forces arrayed against the US and its allies suffered 1,100,000 casualties, and probably more than 3 million casualties overall (including civilians), taking into account both wars. In a conflict waged for political and diplomatic reasons, Giáp was fighting not only a civil war but also a war against one of the world's superpowers, whose stated mission was to kill as many of the enemy as possible. However, these heavy losses did not accomplish what the US sought to achieve.

Apart from his military role and leadership, Giáp also served as a member of the Politburo of the Việt Nam Workers' Party, which in 1976 became the Communist Party of Việt Nam. He served as Defence Minister of the Socialist Republic of Việt Nam until 1980, overseeing his country's swift victory against the Cambodian Khmer Rouge in January 1979. The PAVN armies also pushed back the Chinese 'comrades and brothers' who briefly moved into border areas of Việt Nam a month later, ostensibly to punish the Vietnamese for invading their ally Cambodia. This Chinese aggression in turn caused a serious diplomatic crisis between Beijing and Moscow.

After his retirement in 1980, during those rare foreign visits on which he was sent by the Politburo, Giáp often wore his white uniform. He died a highly respected figure in October 2013 at age of a hundred and two, was given a state funeral and was buried within the Hồ Chí Minh Mausoleum at Hanoi.

Achievements

A legendary figure of the Communist revolution and the Indochina War, Giáp embodied the triumph of Điện Biên Phủ. Alongside Hồ Chí Minh, he was the most prominent commander of the subsequent Vietnam War against the US. Through his personal authority, logistical genius and sound strategic and tactical approach, Giáp was responsible for most of the major operations until the final victory and the reunification of Vietnam in 1975. During three decades of warfare he managed to maintain the morale and elan of his troops. Giáp once more demonstrated that the mobilization of an entire nation could, in the long run, triumph over a much stronger foe unwilling, because of civilian control of the military, to conduct a total war by all available means. A legacy of the Cold War era, this lesson remains valid today. Toward the end of his life, a cult of personality began to centre on Giáp. As the epitome of Vietnamese righteousness and heroism, his simple conduct and lifestyle became a role model for many of his compatriots. In 2012 the Vietnamese Association of Historical Science decided to dedicate a museum to Hồ Chí Minh's faithful lieutenant.

FINAL CONSIDERATIONS

Our journey through space and time has taken us from the deserts of Syria to the jungles of South-East Asia, over a span of some 2,600 years. It has involved countless feats of personal bravery, numerous cases of limited warfare, the effective use of guerrilla tactics and the complex logistical organization behind continental campaigns; all of this is testimony to the prodigious versatility of human genius and its instinct for survival in any given environment. Effective leadership, ingenious tactics and good discipline were always the foundations on which military success has been built. Strength of will, boldness and decisiveness have always been the essential character traits of any battlefield commander.

Military leadership is contingent upon an array of abilities. In recent studies, classification of leadership strengths and virtues has been attempted by Peterson and Seligman (2004), Niemiec (2013) and Boe and Bang (2017). Assessment of the particular sample of gifted commanders introduced in this book has revealed that the most successful military leaders exhibit an impressive set of capabilities which truly sets them apart. These traits can be summed up in character, which is an innate pattern of qualities that can be developed, and competence, which is something acquired and enhanced. As pointed out by Zaccaro, Kemp and Bader (2003), the influence of these traits derives from their joint application. Unsurprisingly, character is foremost, but other determinant traits appear in action, in particular when facing tough challenges. Below is a list of leadership attributes that could be highlighted:

Character	**Competence**
personal courage	leads through example
endurance	delegates authority
self-discipline and control	excels in logistics
humility and self-confidence	masters military intelligence
knowing one's limits	wins trust and loyalty
authority and charisma	diplomatic skills
integrity	superior communicator
resilience	technical expert
quick-thinking	cares for his men
initiative and decisiveness	remains focused
determination and flexibility	accepts feedback
intuition and foresight	long-term planner
creativity	team worker

learns from his mistakes

effective influence

accepts responsibility

inspires confidence and respect

strong willed

sound judgment/common sense

remains consistent

ability to cope with stress

open-mindedness

conflict manager

physical fitness

Finally, we cannot disregard 'luck' or 'destiny', depending on whether we interpret events as random, partially random, or the consequence of supernatural intervention. These phenomena, and the ability to be at the right place at the right time, cannot be conjured naturally and remain independent of one's will and efforts.

Contrary to the adage, fortune does not always favour the brave. However, a leader with a record of past successes gains confidence from subordinates and superiors alike. It was the habit of Napoléon I, when listening to an officer being praised for his military competence, to comment, 'Very well, but is he lucky?' None of these successful commanders, whatever their eventual fate, could have fared that well without a consistent amount of 'luck'. As Matthew Ridgway put it in his memoirs, 'No field commander ever attains much success without a full measure of good fortune.'

In conclusion, although ranking is always a delicate and very subjective affair, based on the information that has come down to us through history, among these fifty outstanding leaders there are a few who can be said to have particularly distinguished themselves. They constitute the elite of the 'underrated', ticking most of the criteria and attributes listed above.

At sea, no admiral in history accumulated such an impeccable battle record as Yi-Sun-sin, who paid the ultimate price to save his nation – like Ruyter or Nelson after him, although Yi-Sun-sin is probably in a league above the Dutch and British admirals. On land, when it comes to the sheer size of territory conquered or liberated, the masterful use of command and control over large expanses, the clever use of tactics and deception, Cyrus, Khālid ibn al-Walīd, Subotai and Zhukov are unrivalled in their lasting legacy to world history.

Although not as universally recognized, without doubt these men deserve their position among the very best, the supreme 'Gods of War', the equals of Alexander or Napoléon I. Every military college and, indeed, anyone fascinated by military history, could gain from the study of the personal, organizational, strategic and tactical skills of these five men, and indeed of the entire selection of fifty of the most outstanding leaders who ever lived.

Fools say that they learn by experience. I prefer to profit by others' experience.
Otto von Bismarck

SELECT BIBLIOGRAPHY

1. Cyrus II The Great
Xenophon, *Cyropaedia,* fourth century BC, translation Walter Miller, 1914.
Herodotus of Halicarnassos, *The Histories*, Book I.
William H. Shea, 'The Nabonidus Chronicle: New Readings and the Identity of Darius the Mede', *Journal of the Adventist Theological Society*, 1996.
Pierre Briant, *From Cyrus to Alexander: A History of the Persian Empire*, 2002.
Amélie Kuhrt, *The Persian Empire: A Corpus of Sources from the Achaemenid Period*, 2007.
Maria Brosius, *A History of Ancient Persia: The Achaemenid Empire*, 2020.

2. Themistokles
Herodotus, *Histories*, Book VIII (Urania), fourth century BC
Thucydides, *The Peloponnesian War,* fourth century BC
Plutarch, *Parallel Lives*, Book IV, second century AD
Peter Green, *The Year of Salamis*, 1970.
Russell Meiggs, *The Athenian Empire*, 1972.
Barry Strauss, *The Battle of Salamis: The Naval Encounter that Saved Greece and Western Civilization*, 2005.
John R. Hale, *Lords of the Sea: The Epic Story of the Athenian Navy and the Birth of Democracy*, 2009.

3. Epaminondas
Xenophon, *Hellenica*, Book VII, fourth century BC
Diodoros Siculus, *Bibliotheca Historica*, Book XV, first century BC
Cornelius Nepos, *Life of Epaminondas,* first century BC
Plutarch, *Parallel Lives*, Books VII (missing) XIV and XXI, second century AD
Aelian, *Varia Historia*, second century AD
John Buckler, *The Theban hegemony, 371–362 BC*, 1980.
Victor Davis Hanson, 'The General as Hoplite'. *Hoplites: the Classical Greek Battle Experience*, 1993.
Paul Cartledge, *Thebes: The Forgotten City of Ancient Greece*, 2020.

4. Demetrios Poliorketes
Diodoros Siculus, *Historical Library,* first century BC
Asclepiodotos, *Tactics*, first century BC
Pliny the Elder, *Natural History,* first century AD
Plutarch, *Parallel Lives, Life of Demetrius*, second century AD
Polyaenus: *Stratagems*, second century AD
Bob Bennett and Mike Roberts, *The Wars of Alexander's Successors 323–281 BC*, 2008, 2 vols.
Edward Anson, *Alexander's Heirs: The Age of the Successors*, 2014.
Pat Wheatley and Charlotte Dunn: *Demetrius the Besieger,* 2020.

5. Bai Qi Of Qin
Sun Tzu, *The Art of War*, fifth century BC
Sima Qian, *Records of Grand Historian (Shiji)*, *Biographies of Bai Qi and Wang Jian,* first century BC, partial English translation by Burton Watson, 1961. French translation by Jacques Pimpaneau, Max Kaltenmark and Yves Hervouet, 2015, 9 vols.

Sima Guang, *Comprehensive Mirror in Aid of Governance (Zizhi Tongjian)*, 1084 AD, Volume 1 to 8 (403–207 BC) translated by Joseph P. Yap, 2016.
Anonymous, *Annals of the Warring States*, edited by James I. Crump Jr. as *Chan-kuo ts'e*, 1970.
Michael Loewe and Edward L. Shaughnessy (Dir.), *The Cambridge History of Ancient China, From the Origins of Civilization to 221 BC*, 1999.
Yuri Pines, *Envisioning Eternal Empire: Chinese Political Thought of the Warring States Era*, 2009.
Xiaolong Wu, *Material Culture, Power, and Identity in Ancient China*, 2017.

6. Marcus Agrippa
Plutarch, *Parallel Lives*, *Life of Mark Antony*, first century AD
Suetonius, *The Twelve Caesars*, Book II, Augustus, second century AD
Appian of Alexandria, *The Civil Wars*, second century AD
Cassius Dio, *Roman History*, third century AD
Meyer Reinhold, *Marcus Agrippa, a biography*, 1933.
Jean-Michel Roddaz, *Marcus Agrippa*, 1984.
Lindsay Powell, *Marcus Agrippa: Right-Hand Man of Caesar Augustus*, 2014.

7. Germanicus
Tacitus, *Annals*, Book I and II and *Germania*, Book VIII.
Strabo, *Geography*, Book VII.
Suetonius, *The Twelve Caesars*.
Stephen Dando-Collins, *Blood of the Caesars: How the Murder of Germanicus Led to the Fall of Rome*, 2008.
Lindsay Powell, *Germanicus: The Magnificent Life and Mysterious Death of Rome's Most Popular General*, 2013.
Lindsay Powell, *Roman Soldier vs Germanic Warrior, 1st Century AD*, 2014.

8. Attila
Vegetius, *De re militari*, fourth century AD
Jordanes, *The Origin and Deeds of the Getae [Getica]*, and *Romana*, sixth century AD
Simon Kézai, *The Deeds of the Hungarians* [*Gesta Hungarorum*], c. 1280.
William Herbert, *Attila, King of the Huns*, 1838.
Colin D. Gordon and Arthur E. R. Boak, *The Age of Attila: Fifth- century Byzantium and the Barbarians*, 1960.
Patrick Howarth, *Attila, King of the Huns*, 1995.
John Man, Attila: *The Barbarian King Who Challenged Rome*, 2005.
Peter Hether, *The Fall of the Roman Empire: A New History*, 2006.
Christopher Kelly, *Attila the Hun: Barbarian Terror and the Fall of the Roman Empire*, 2008.
Priscus of Panium, *The Fragmentary History of Priscus: Attila, the Huns and the Roman Empire, AD 430–476*, translated by John P. Given, 2015.
Hyun Jin Kim, *The Huns*, 2015.
Evan Michael Schultheis, *The Battle of the Catalaunian Fields AD 451: Flavius Aetius, Attila the Hun and the Transformation of Gaul*, 2019.

9. Flavius Belisarius
Procopius of Caesarea: *History of the Wars* and *Secret History*, sixth century AD
John Malalas, *Chronographia*, sixth century AD, translated by Elizabeth Jeffreys under the title *The Chronicle of John Malalas*, 1986.
Philip Henry Stanhope, *The Life of Belisarius: The Last Great General of Rome*, 1829.
Robert Graves, *Count Belisarius*, 1938.
George T. Dennis, *Three Byzantine Military Treatises*, 1985.

Warren T. Treadgold, *Byzantium and its Army, 284–1081*, 1995.
James Alla Stewart Evans, *The Age of Justinian*, 1996.
Ian Hughes, *Belisarius: The Last Roman General*, 2014.
Peter Heather, *Rome Resurgent: War and Empire in the Age of Justinian*, 2018.

10. Khalid Ibn Al-Walid
Al-Balâdhurî, *Book of the Conquests of Lands*, ninth century. English translation by Phillip Hitti, 1916 (vol. 1) and Francis Clark Murgotten, 1924 (vol. 2).
Al-Tabari, *History of the Prophets and Kings*, tenth century, 16 volumes (in particular vols. 10–14).
Ibn Kathīr, *Al-Bidāya wa-n-Nihāya (The Beginning and the End)*, fourteenth century, 10 volumes.
'Abd al-Raḥmān ibn Abī Bakr al-Suyūṭī, *History of the Caliphs*, fifteenth century, English translation by Henry Sullivan Jarret, 1881.
Agha Ali Ibrahim Akram, *Sword of Allah: Khalid Bin Al-Waleed, His Life and Campaigns*, 1969.
Fred McGraw Donner, *The Early Islamic Conquests*, 1981.
Hugh Kennedy, *The Armies of the Caliphs: Military and Society in the Early Islamic State*, 2001.
Hugh Kennedy, *The Great Arab Conquests: How the Spread of Islam Changed the World we Live in*, 2007.

11. Charles Martel
Fredegarii Chronicorum Liber Quanus cum Continuationibus, seventh/eighth century, edited and translated by J. M. Wallace-Hadrill, 1960.
Liber Historiae Francorum, eighth century Neustrian Chronicle.
Chronicles of Saint-Denis, twelfth century.
Bernard Bachrach, 'Charles Martel, Mounted Shock Combat, the Stirrup, and Feudalism', *Studies in Medieval and Renaissance History*, Vol. VII (1970).
Pierre Riché, *Les Carolingiens: Une famille qui fit l'Europe*, 1983.
Paul J. Fouracre, *The Age of Charles Martel*, 2000.
Ed West, *The Path of the Martyrs: Charles Martel, The Battle of Tours and the Birth of Europe*, 2019.

12. Robert Guiscard
William of Apulia, *Gesta Roberti Wiscardi*, c.1098.
Goffredo Malaterra, *The Deeds of Count Roger of Calabria and Sicily and of Duke Robert Guiscard, his brother*, c.1099. Translated by Graham A. Loud (unpublished), 2005.
Anna Komnene, *The Alexiad*, c.1150. Translations by Elizabeth A. Dawes, 1928, and by Edgar Robert Ashton Sewter, 1969.
John Julius Norwich, *The Normans in the South 1016–1130*, 1967.
Huguette Taviani Carozzi, *La Terreur du Monde, Robert Guiscard et la conquête normande en Italie*, 1996.
Graham Loud, *The Age of Robert Guiscard: Southern Italy and the Northern Conquest*, 2000.
Gordon S. Brown, *The Norman Conquest of Sicily and Southern Italy*, 2002.
Richard Brown, *Robert Guiscard: Portrait of a Warlord*, 2016.

13. Subotai
The Chronicle of Novgorod (1076–1471), translated by Robert Mitchell and Nevill Forbes, 1914.
The Secret History of the Mongols. The life and times of Chinggis Khan. Translated by Urgunge Onon, 2001.
The Secret History of the Mongols: A Mongolian Epic Chronicle of the Thirteenth Century. Translated by Igor de Rachewiltz, 2004.
Friar Giovanni di Plano Carpini, *The story of the Mongols whom we call the Tartars*, 1240s. Translated by Erik Hildinger, 1996.

'Ala-ad-Din 'Ata-Malik Juvayni, *History of the World-Conqueror*, 1260s. Translated by John Andrew Boyle, 1997.

René Grousset, *The Empire of the Steppes*, 1939.

Christopher Dawson, *The Mongol Mission: Narratives and Letters of the Franciscan Missionaries in Mongolia and China in the Thirteenth and Fourteenth Centuries*, 1955.

Richard A. Gabriel, *Genghis Khan's Greatest General: Subotai the Valiant*, 2004.

Timothy May, *The Mongol Art of War: Chinggis Khan and the Mongol Military System*, 2007.

Franck McLynn, *Genghis Khan: His Conquests, His Empire, His Legacy*, 2016.

Yuan Shi (History of Yuan, fourteenth century), translated in Pow, Stephen and Jingjing Liao, 'Subutai: Sorting Fact from Fiction Surrounding the Mongol Empire's Greatest General', *Journal of Chinese Military History* 7, 2018.

14. Aleksandr Nevsky

'The tale of the Life and Courage of the Pious and Great Alexander Nevsky' in *Second Pskovian Chronicle*, thirteenth century.

The Chronicle of Novgorod (1076–1471), translated by Robert Mitchell and Nevill Forbes, 1914.

Hypatian Codex, Galician-Volynian Chronicle, thirteenth century, translated by George A. Perfecky, 1973.

'Ala-ad-Din 'Ata-Malik Juvayni, *History of the World-Conqueror*, 1260s. Translated by John Andrew Boyle, 1997.

René Grousset, *The Empire of the Steppes*, 1939.

George Vernadsky, *The Mongols and Russia*, 1953.

Christopher Dawson, *The Mongol Mission*, 1955.

Nicholas Valentine Riasanovsky, *A History of Russia*, 1963.

Sergey Zenkovsky, *Medieval Russia's Epics, Chronicles, and Tales*, 1974.

Charles J. Halperin, *Russia and the Golden Horde: The Mongol Impact on Medieval Russian History*, 1987.

Janet Martin, *Medieval Russia*, 1995.

Mari Isoaho, *The Image of Aleksandr Nevskiy in Medieval Russia*, 2006.

Lindsey Stephen Pow, *Deep ditches and well-built walls: a reappraisal of the Mongol withdrawal from Europe in 1242*, 2012 (Thesis).

15. Bertrand Du Guesclin

Jehan Cuvelier, *La Chanson de Bertrand Du Guesclin*, c.1385.

Jehan Froissart, *Chroniques*, Book I, c. 1400. Translated as *Chronicles of Froissart* by John Bourchier and Lord Berners, 1908.

Christine de Pisan, *Livre des fais et bonnes meurs du sage Roy Charles V*, 1404.

F.W.D. Brie, *The Brut of England* or *The Chronicles of England*, 1906.

Philippe Contamine, *War in the Middle Ages*. Translation by Michael Jones, 1984.

Georges Minois, *Du Guesclin*, 1993.

Richard Vernier, *The Flower of Chivalry: Bertrand du Guesclin and the Hundred Years War*, 2007.

Bernard Guenée, *Du Guesclin et Froissart: La fabrication de la renommée*, 2008.

Thierry Lassabatère, *Du Guesclin*, 2015.

16. John Hawkwood

Chronicle of Geoffrey le Baker of Swinbrook, fourteenth century, translated and edited by David Preest, 2012.

'Cronica volgare di anonimo fiorentino: dall'anno 1385 al 1409; già attribuita a Piero di Giovanni Minerbetti', edited by Elina Bellondi in *Rerum Italicarum Scriptores II*, vol. 27, part 2, 1915–1918.

Jean Froissart, *Chroniques*, Book II, c. 1400. Translated as *Chronicles of Froissart* by John Bourchier and Lord Berners, 1908.

John Temple-Leader and Giuseppe Marcotti, *Sir John Hawkwood, Story of a Condottiere*, 1889.

Alfred H. Burne, *The Crécy War: A Military History of the Hundred Years War from 1337 to the Peace of Bretigny in 1360*, 1955.

Mario Tabanelli, *Giovanni Acuto capitano di ventura*, 1975.

Terry Jones, *Chaucer's Knight: The Portrait of a Medieval Mercenary*, 1980.

Duccio Balestracci, *Le armi, i cavalli, l'oro. Giovanni Acuto e i condottieri nell'Italia del Trecento*, Rome, 2003.

Frances Stonor Sanders, *Hawkwood: Diabolical Englishman*, 2005.

Frances Stonor Sanders, *The Devil's Broker: Seeking Gold, God, and Glory in Fourteenth-Century Italy*, 2005.

William Caferro, *John Hawkwood: An English Mercenary in Fourteenth-Century Italy*, 2006.

Carlo Ciucciovino, *La cronaca del Trecento italiano, giorno por giorno*, 2007.

G. M. Varanini and F. Bianchi, *La 'Cronaca carrarese' di Bartolomeo e Andrea Gatari per la storia della battaglia del Castagnaro. La guerra scaligero-carrarese e la battaglia del Castagnaro (1387)*, 2015.

Kelly DeVries, *Castagnaro 1387: Hawkwood's Great Victory*, 2019.

17. Jan Žižka

Vavřinec of Březová, *Husitská kronika; Píseň o vítězství u Domažlic*, translated by František Heřmanský and Jan Blahoslav Čapek, 1979.

Friedrich von Bezold, *König Sigismund und die Reichskriege gegen die Husiten*, 1872–1877, three vols.

Otakar Frankenberger, *Naše velká armáda*, 1921, three vols.

Frederick G. Heymann, *John Žižka and the Hussite Revolution*, 1955.

Howard Kaminsky, *A History of the Hussite Revolution*, 1967.

Thomas A. Fudge, *The Crusade against Heretics in Bohemia, 1418–1437: Sources and Documents for the Hussite Crusades*, 2002.

František Šmahel, *Die Hussitische Revolution*, 2002, three vols.

Victor Verney, *Warrior of God: Jan Zizka and the Hussite Revolution*, 2009.

Alexander Querengässer, *Hussite Warfare: The Armies, Equipment, Tactics and Campaigns 1419–1437*, 2019.

Thomas A. Fudge, *Origins of the Hussite uprising: the chronicle of Laurence of Březová (1414–1421)*, 2020.

18. Mehmet II

Niccolò Barbaro, *Diary of the siege of Constantinople 1453*. Translation by John Melville-Jones, 1969.

Michael Kritovoulos of Imbros, *History of Mehmet II*, 1467. Translated by Charles T. Riggs, 1954.

George Sphrantzes, *The Fall of the Byzantine Empire: A Chronicle, 1401–1477*. Translated by Marios Philippides, 1980.

Nestor Iskander, *The Tale of Constantinople (of its Origin and Capture by the Turks in the Year 1453)*, early sixteenth century. Edition by Walter K. Hanak, 1998.

Franz Babinger, *Mehmed the Conqueror and his Time*, 1953.

Halil İnalcık, *The Ottoman Empire: The Classical Age 1300–1600*, 1973.

André Clot, *Mehmed II, le conquérant de Byzance (1432–1481)*, 1990.

Marios Philippides, *Mehmed II the Conqueror and the fall of the Franco-Byzantine Levant to the Ottoman Turks*, 2007.

John Freely, *The Grand Turk: Sultan Mehmet II, Conqueror of Constantinople and Master of an Empire*, 2009.

Roger Crowley, *Constantinople, the last Great Siege, 1453*, 2013.

Marios Philippides, *The Siege and the Fall of Constantinople in 1453: Historiography, Topography, and Military Studies*, 2017.

Aristotle Kakaliagos and Nikolaos Ninis, *Damage and failure of Orban's gun during the bombardment of Constantinople walls in 1453*, 2019.

19. Matthias Corvinus

Antonio Bonfini, *Rerum Ungaricarum decades*, 1486.

Jan Długosz, *Annales seu cronicae incliti Regni Poloniae*, fifteenth century. Translated by Maurice Michael under the title *The Annals of Jan Długosz: A History of Eastern Europe from AD 965 to AD 1480*, 1997.

Gertrud Buttlar, Gyula Rázsó, and Leopold Auer, *The campaigns of King Matthias Corvinus in Lower Austria, 1477–1490*, 1973.

Marianna D. Birnbaum, *The Orb and the Pen: Janus Pannonius, Matthias Corvinus and the Buda Court*, 1996.

Jörg K. Hoensch, *Matthias Corvinus: Diplomat, Feldherr und Mäzen*, 1998.

Kubinyi, András, *Matthias Corvinus: Die Regierung eines Königreichs in Ostmit-teleuropa 1458–1490*, 1999.

Pál Engel, *The Realm of St Stephen: A History of Medieval Hungary, 895–1526*, 2001.

András Kubinyi, *Matthias Rex*, 2008.

Attila Bárány, and Attila Györkös (eds), *Matthias and his Legacy: Cultural and Political Encounters between East and West*, 2008.

Marcus Tanner, *The Raven King – Matthias Corvinus and the Fate of His Lost Library*, 2008.

Antonín Kalous, *Matyáš Korvín (1443–1490): Uherský a český král*, 2009.

Győző Somogyi, *The Army of King Matthias 1458–1526*, 2014.

20. Dom Francisco De Almeida

Gaspar Correia, *Lendas da Índia*, 1556, published by M. Lopes de Almeida, 1975.

Joaquim Pedro d'Oliveira Martins, *História de Portugal*, 1879, vol. I.

Richard Stephen Whiteway, *The Rise of Portuguese Power in India, 1497–1550*, 1899.

José Moreira Campos, *Francisco de Almeida, 1° vice-rei da Índia*, 1947.

Mathew Kuzhippalli-Skaria, *Portuguese and the Sultanate of Gujarat 1500–1573*, 1986.

Saturnino Monteiro, *Batalhas e Combates da Marinha Portuguesa*, 1989, eight volumes.

Theresa M. Schedel de Castello Branco, *Na Rota da Pimenta*, 2006.

Jorge Nascimento Rodrigues and Tessaleno C. Devezas, *1509, a batalha que mudou o domínio do comércio global*, 2008.

Roger Crowley, *Conquerors: How Portugal Forged the First Global Empire*, 2015.

21. Gonzalo Fernandez De Cordoba

Niccolò Machiavelli, *The Art of War*, 1521.

Jerónimo Zurita y Castro, *Historia del rey Don Fernando el Católico. De las empresas, y ligas de Italia*, 1580.

Francisco de Herrera, *Historia de las proezas y hazañas del Gran Capitán Don Gonzalo Fernández de Córdoba*, 1669.

Luis María de Lojendio, *Gonzalo de Córdoba (El Gran Capitán)*, 1942.

René Quatrefages, *Los tercios españoles (1567–1577)*, 1979.

René Quatrefages, *La revolución militar moderna: el crisol español*, 2002.

José Enrique Ruiz-Domènec, *El Gran Capitán: retrato de una época*, 2002.

Michael Mallett and Christine Shaw, *The Italian Wars 1494–1559: War, State and Society in Early Modern Europe*, 2012.

Julio Albi de la Cuesta, *De Pavía a Rocroi: Los tercios españoles*, 2017.

22. Hernán Cortés

Hernán Cortés, *Cartas y relaciones de Hernan Cortés al emperador Carlos V*. Edited by Pascual de Gayangos, 1866.

Bartolomé de Las Casas, *Historia de Indias*, 1527–1547, Book III.

Francisco López de Gómara, *Historia general de las Indias y todo lo acaescido en ellas dende que se ganaron hasta agora y La conquista de Mexico, y de la Nueva España*, 1553.

Bernal Díaz del Castillo, *Historia verdadera de la conquista de la Nueva España*, 1568.

Hugh Thomas, *Conquest: Cortes, Montezuma, and the Fall of Old Mexico*, 1995.

Jared Diamond, *Guns, Germs, and Steel*, 1997.

Buddy Levy, *Conquistador: Hernan Cortes, King Montezuma, and the Last Stand of the Aztecs*, 2008.

23. Khayr Al-Din Barbarossa

Jehan de la Vega, *Le Voyage du Baron de Saint Blancard en Turquie*, 1538.

Francisco López de Gómara, *Crónica de los Barbarrojas*, 1545.

Giacomo Bosio, *Dell'istoria della sacra Religione, dell' illustrissima milizia di Santo Giovanni Gierosolimitano*, 1594, 3rd volume.

Ernle Bradford, *The Sultan's Admiral: the Life of Barbarossa*, 1968.

John Francis Guilmartin Jr., *Gunpowder and Galleys. Changing technology and Mediterranean Warfare at Sea in the Sixteenth Century*, 1974.

Jean-Louis Belachemi, *Nous, les frères Barberousse, corsaires et rois d'Alger*, 1984.

Salvatore Bono, *Corsari nel Mediterraneo: cristiani e musulmani fra guerra, schiavitù e commercio*, 1993.

Gábor Ágoston, *Guns for the Sultan: Military Power and the Weapons Industry in the Ottoman Empire*, 2005.

Emrah Safa Gürkan, *Ottoman corsairs in the Mediterranean 1505– 1535, and their place in the Ottoman-Habsburg rivalry*, 2006.

Roger Crowley, *Empires of the Sea: The Final Battle for the Mediterranean 1521–1580*, 2008.

Ernle Bradford and Selby Disgate, *The Sultan's Admiral: Barbarossa, pirate and empire-builder*, 2009.

Daniel Nordman, *Tempête sur Alger. L'expédition de Charles Quint en 1541*, 2011.

24. Francis Drake

Nicholas Breton, *A discourse in commendation of the valiant as vertuous minded gentleman, Maister Frauncis Drake*, 1581.

Richard Hakluyt, *The Principal Navigations, Voyages, Traffics and Discoveries of the English Nation*, 1589.

Francis Drake (his nephew), *The World Encompassed by Sir Francis Drake*, 1628.

Francis Drake, *Sir Francis Drake Revived*. Edited by Philip Nichols, 1653.

Sir Julian S. Corbett, *Sir Francis Drake*, 1890.

James Alexander Williamson, *The Age of Drake*, 1938.

George Malcolm Thomson, *Sir Francis Drake*, 1972.

Neville Williams, *The Sea Dogs: Privateers, plunder and piracy in the Elizabethan Age*, 1975.

John Sugden, *Sir Francis Drake*, 1990.

Robert Samuel Bawlf, *The Secret Voyage of Sir Francis Drake, 1577– 1580*, 2001.

Luis Gorrochategui Santos, *The English Armada: The Greatest Naval Disaster in English History*, 2018.

Brian Best, *Elizabeth's Sea Dogs and their War Against Spain*, 2021.

Laurence Bergreen, *In Search of a Kingdom: Francis Drake, Elizabeth I, and the Perilous Birth of the British Empire*, 2021.

25. Yi Sun-Sin
Yu Sŏngnyong, *The Book of Corrections (Chingbirok)*, 1604. Translated by Choi Byonghyon, 2002.
Yu Deuk-gong, *Collected works of Admiral Yi Sun-sin*, 1795, eight volumes.
Annals of the Joseon Dynasty, Volume 42, 221.
Toyotomi Hideyoshi, *101 Letters of Hideyoshi: The Private Correspondence of Toyotomi Hideyoshi*. Edited and translated by Adriana Boscaro, 1975.
Yi Sun-si, *Nanjung ilgi* or *War Diary of Admiral Yi Sun-sin*, seven volumes, translated by Tae-Hung Ha, 1977.
Yi Sun-si, *Admiral Yi Sun-Sin's Memorials to Court*, translated by Tae- Hung Ha, 1981.
Samuel Hawley, *The Imjin War: Japan's Sixteenth-Century Invasion of Korea and Attempt to Conquer China*, 2005.
Kim Jae-Woong, *Admiral Yi Sun-sin: A brief overview of his life and achievements*, 2005.
Kenneth M. Swope, *A Dragon's Head and a Serpent's Tail: Ming China and the First Great East Asian War, 1592–1598*, 2009.

26. Akbar the Great
Antonio Montserrate, *Relaçam do Equebar, Rei dos Mogores*, 1582. Translated by J. S. Hoyland as *The Commentary of Father Monserrate, S.J., on his Journey to the Court of Akbar*, 1922.
George Bruce Malleson, *Akbar and the Rise of the Mughal Empire*, 1903.
Vincent Arthur Smith, *Akbar the Great Mogul, 1542–1605*, 1917.
Henry Beveridge, *The Akbar Nama of Abu-l-Fazl*, 1902–1939, three vols.
Douglas E. Streusand, *The Formation of the Mughal Empire*, 1989.
John F. Richards, *The Mughal Empire*, 1993.
Iqtidar Alam Khan, *Gunpowder and Firearms: Warfare in Medieval India*, 2004.
Douglas E. Streusand, *Islamic Gunpowder Empires*, 2010.
Jorge Flores, *Nas margens do Hindustão: O Estado da Índia e a expansão mogol, ca. 1570–1640*, 2015.
Andrew de la Garza, *The Mughal Empire at War: Babur, Akbar and the Indian Military Revolution, 1500–1605*, 2017.
Ira Mukhoty, *Akbar: The Great Mughal*, 2020.

27. Tokugawa Ieyasu
Hayashi Gahō, *Nihon Ōdai Ichiran*, 1652.
Arthur Lindsay Sadler, *Maker of Modern Japan: The Life of Tokugawa Ieyasu*, 1937.
Ryotarô Shiba, *Haō no ie*, 1973.
Noel Perrin, *Giving up the Gun: Japan's Reversion to the Sword, 1543–1879*, 1979.
Conrad Totman, *Early Modern Japan*, 1993.
Olof, G. Liden, *Tanegashima, the arrival of Europe in Japan*, 2002.
Stephen Turnbull, *War in Japan, 1467–1615*, 2014.
Tonio Andrade and Xing Hang, *Sea Rovers, Silver, and Samurai: Maritime East Asia in Global History, 1550–1700*, 2016.
Danny Chaplin, *Sengoku Jidai. Nobunaga, Hideyoshi, and Ieyasu: Three Unifiers of Japan*, 2018.
Shigeo Sugawa, *The Japanese Matchlock: A Story of the Tanegashima*, 1990.

28. Michiel De Ruyter
Gerard Brandt, *Het Leven en bedryf van den Heere Michiel de Ruiter*, 1687.
Samuel Pepys, *The Diary of Samuel Pepys from 1659 to 1669*. Edited by Richard Griffin 3rd Baron Braybrooke, 1825, two volumes.

Petrus Johannes Blok, *Michiel Adriaanszoon de Ruyter*, 1928.
Johan Carel Marinus Warnsinck, *Luitenant-admiraal Willem Joseph baron van Ghent*, 1934.
Charles Ralph Boxer, *The Anglo-Dutch Wars of the 17th Century*, 1974.
Jaap Ruurd Bruijn, *The Dutch navy of the seventeenth and eighteenth centuries*, 1993.
Jaap Ruurd Bruijn and Femme Simon Gaastra, *Ships, sailors and spices: East India companies and their shipping in the 16th, 17th and 18th centuries*, 1993.
James R. Jones, *The Anglo-Dutch Wars of the Seventeenth Century*, 1996.
Jaap Ruurd Bruijn, *De 7 Provinciën: een nieuw schip voor Michiel de Ruyter*, 1997.
Roger Hainsworth and Christine Churches, *The Anglo-Dutch Naval Wars 1652–1674*, 1998.
Femme Simon Gaastra, *The Dutch East India Company: Expansion and decline*, 2003.
Gijs Rommelse, *The Second Anglo-Dutch War (1665–1667)*, 2006.
Jaap Ruurd Bruijn, Ronald Prud'homme van Reine, and Rolof van Hövell tot Westerflier, *De Ruyter: Dutch Admiral*, 2011.
David Ormrod and Gijs Rommelse, *War, Trade and the State: Anglo- Dutch Conflict, 1652–89*, 2020.

29. Shivaji
Abbé Carré, *Travels in India and in the Near East*, 1672–74. Translated by Lady Fawcett, 1947.
Krishnaji Anant Sabhasad, *Sabhasad Bakhar*, 1697, (in Marathi).
John Fryer, *A new account of East-India and Persia, in eight letters being nine years travels begun 1672 and finished 1681*, 1698.
Robert Orme, *Historical Fragments of the Mogul Empire, the Morattoes and English Concerns in Indostan from the year 1659*, 1782.
Jadunath Sarkar, *Shivaji and his Times*, 1919.
Nilkanth Sadashiv Takakhav, *The Life of Shivaji Maharaj: Founder of the Maratha Empire*, 1921.
Shiva-Charitra Karyalaya (ed), *English records on Shivaji, 1659–1682*, 1931.
Dennis Kincaid, *Shivaji: The Grand Rebel*, 1937.
Govind Sakharam Sardesai, *New History of the Marathas*, 1946.
Stewart Gordon, *The New Cambridge History of India, The Marathas 1600–1818*, 1993.
Ranjit Desai, *Shivaji: The Great Maratha*, 2017.

30. Grand Condé
James II, *Memoirs of James II, His Campaigns as Duke of York, 1652– 1660*.
Pierre du Prat, *Portrait du Maréchal de Gassion*, 1664.
Edward Hyde, *The History of the Rebellion and Civil Wars in England*, 1708, three vols.
Voltaire, *The Age of Louis XIV*, 1751.
Joseph Louis Ripault, *Histoire de Louis de Bourbon*, 1766–68, four vols.
Pierre Lenet, *Mémoires de Pierre Lenet contenant l'histoire des guerres civiles des années 1649 et suivantes*, 1826.
Henri d'Orléans, *Histoire des Princes de Condé*, 1869–1895, seven vols.
David M. A. Maland, *Europe in the Seventeenth Century*, 1966.
Michael Duffy, *The Military Revolution and the State 1500–1800*, 1980
John A. Lynn, *The Wars of Louis XIV, 1667–1714*, 1999.
Katia Béguin, *Les princes de Condé. Rebelles, courtisans et mécènes dans la France du Grand Siècle*, 1999.
Dominique Paladilhe, *Le Grand Condé: Héros des armées de Louis XIV*, 2008.
David P. Miller, *Ballistics of 17th Century Muskets*, 2010 (Thesis).
Mathieu Deldicque, *Le Grand Condé: Le rival du Roi-Soleil?*, 2016.

31. Francesco Morosini
Alessandro Locatelli, *Racconto Historico Della Guerra in Levante*, 1691.
Camillo Contarini, *Istoria della Guerra di Leopold Primo Imperatore*, 1710.

Giuseppe Bruzzo, *Francesco Morosini nella guerra di Candia e nella Conquista della Morea*, Forli, 1890.

Cesare Augusto Levi, *Navi da guerra costruite nell'Arsenale di Venezia dal 1664 al 1896*, 1896.

Mario Nani Mocenigo, *Storia della Marina veneziana: da Lepanto alla caduta della repubblica*, 1935.

Roger Charles Anderson, *Naval Wars in the Levant, 1559–1853*, 1952.

Ekkehard Eickhoff, *Venedig, Wien und die Osmanen: Umbruch in Südosteuropa 1645–1700*, 1970.

Kenneth Meyer Setton, *Venice, Austria, and the Turks in the Seventeenth Century*, 1991.

Özkan Bardakçı and François Pugnière, *La dernière croisade, Les Français et la Guerre de Candie, 1669*, 2008.

Robert Dankoff and Sooyong Kim, *An Ottoman Traveller: Selections from the Book of Travels of Evliya Çelebi*, 2010.

Eric Pinzelli, *Venise et l'Empire Ottoman, les Guerres de Morée (1684–1718)*, 2020.

32. Jan III Sobieski

François-Paulin Dalerac Chevalier de Beaujeu, *The Secret History of the Reign of John Sobieski the Third*, 1699. English translation 1700.

Johann Peter von Valckeren, *Vienne assiégée par les Turcs et délivrée par les Chrestiens, ou Journal du siège de Vienne*, Bruxelles, 1684.

Abbé Gabriel-François Coyer, *Histoire de Jean Sobieski*, Paris, 1761, three vols.

Lettres du roi de Pologne Jean Sobieski à la *reine Marie Casimire, pendant la campagne de Vienne*, published by Narcisse-Achille de Salvandy, 1826.

Karl August Schimmer, *Wiens Belagerungen durch die Türken und ihre Einfälle in Ungarn und Österreich*, 1845.

Janusz Woliński, *Pamiętniki z czasów Jana Sobieskiego. Diariusz i relacje z l. 1691–1696*, 1958.

Thomas M. Barker, *Double Eagle and Crescent, Vienna's second Turkish siege*, 1967.

Ekkehard Eickhoff, *Venedig, Wien und die Osmanen: Umbruch in Südosteuropa 1645–1700*, 1970.

Kenneth Meyer Setton, *Venice, Austria, and the Turks in the Seventeenth Century*, 1991.

Romuald Romański, *Cudnów 1660*, 1996.

Marek Wagner, *Wojna polsko-turecka w latach 1672–1676*, 2009, vol I.

Radosław Sikora, *Husaria w walce*, 2015.

Grzegorz Jasiński and Wojciech Włodarkiewicz (editors), *Polish Battles and Campaigns in 13th–19th Centuries*, 2016.

Eric Pinzelli, *Venise et l'Empire Ottoman, les guerres de Morée (1684– 1718)*, 2020.

33. Marquis De Vauban

Sébastien Le Prestre, Marquis de Vauban, *Traité de l'attaque et de la défense des places*, 1704. Edited by Pierre de Hondt, 1737.

Sébastien Le Prestre, Marquis de Vauban, *Mémoire pour server d'instruction dans la conduite des sièges et dans la défense des places*, 1740 (though written in 1672).

Sébastien Le Prestre, Marquis de Vauban, *A Manual of Siegecraft and Fortification*. English translation by George A. Rothrock, 1968.

Jacques-Antoine-Hippolyte de Guibert, *Essai général de tactique*, 1770.

Jacques-Antoine-Hippolyte de Guibert, *Défense du système de guerre moderne*, 1779.

Louis de Rouvroy, Duc de Saint-Simon, *Mémoires*, 1829.

Christopher Duffy, *Fire and Stone. The Science of Fortress Warfare, 1660–1860*, 1975.

Christopher Duffy, *The Fortress in the Age of Vauban and Frederick the Great, 1660–1789*, 1985.

F. J. Hebbert and George A. Rothrock, *Soldier of France: Sebastien Le Prestre de Vauban, 1633–1707*, 1989.

John Lynn, *Giant of the Grand Siècle: The French Army 1610–1715*, 1997.

John Lynn, *The Wars of Louis XIV, 1667–1714*, 1999.

John Childs, *Warfare in the Seventeenth Century*, 2001.

Michèle Virol, *Vauban: De la gloire du roi au service de l'État*, 2003.

Jamel Ostwald, *Vauban under Siege: Engineering Efficiency and Martial Vigor in the War of the Spanish Succession*, 2006.

Sébastien Le Prestre, Marquis de Vauban, *Les Oisivetés de Monsieur de Vauban*, 2007 (first edition).

Thierry Martin and Michèle Virol, *Vauban, architecte de la modernité?* 2008.

Jean Denis Lepage, *Vauban and the French Military under Louis XIV: An Illustrated History of Fortifications and Sieges*, 2009.

34. Karl XII

Captain James Jefferyes, *Letters to the Secretary of State, Whitehall, from the Swedish army, 1707–1709*. Edited by Ragnhild Hatton, 1954.

Captain John Perry, *The State of Russia under the present Czar*, 1716.

Daniel Defoe, *The History Of The Wars Of His Late Majesty Charles XII, King Of Sweden: From His First Landing In Denmark, To His Return From Turkey To Pomerania*, 1720.

Anonymous, *The History of the Wars, of his late Majesty Charles XII. King of Sweden, from his first landing in Denmark, to his return from Turkey to Pomerania, with a continuation to the time of his death*, 1720.

Voltaire (François-Marie Arouet), *Histoire de Charles XII, Roi de Suède*, 1731.

Jöran Andersson Norberg, *Konung Carl den XII: S Historia*, 1740.

Robert Nisbet Bain, *Charles XII and the collapse of the Swedish Empire 1682–1719*, 1895.

Ragnhild Marie Hatton, *Charles XII of Sweden*, 1968.

Göte Göransson and Alf Åberg, *Karoliner*, 1976.

Robert Kinloch Massie, *Peter The Great*, 1980.

Peter Englund, *The Battle That Shook Europe: Poltava and the Birth of the Russian Empire*, 2003.

Oskar Sjöström, *Fraustadt 1706: ett fält färgat rött*, 2008.

Pavel Konovalchuk and Einar Lyth, *Vägen till Poltava, Slaget vid Lesnaja 1708*, 2009.

Boris Megorsky, *Peter the Great's Revenge: The Russian Siege of Narva in 1704*, 2018.

Michael Glaeser, *By Defeating My Enemies: Charles XII of Sweden and the Great Northern War, 1682–1721*, 2020.

35. Duke of Marlborough

Anonymous, *The New Exercise of Firelocks & Bayonets; Appointed by his Grace the Duke of Marlborough to be used by all the British Forces*, 1708.

John Wilson, *The Journal of John Wilson an 'Old Flanderkin Serjeant' of the 15th Regiment and later of the 2nd Troop of Life Guards, who served 1694–1727*. Edited by David Chandler, in *Military Miscellany II, Manuscripts from Marlborough's Wars*, 2005.

Robert Parker, *Memoirs of the most remarkable military transactions from the year 1683 to 1718*, 1747.

Jacques-François de Chastenet de Puységur, *Art de la Guerre par principes et par règles*, 1748.

Archibald Alison, *The Life of John, Duke of Marlborough with some account of his contemporaries and of the War of Succession*, 1852.

Winston S. Churchill, *Marlborough: His Life and Times*, 1933.

Hilaire Belloc, *The Tactics and Strategy of the Great Duke of Marlborough*, 1933.

Ivor F. Burton, *The Captain-General: The career of John Churchill, Duke of Marlborough from 1702–1711*, 1968.

David Chandler, *Marlborough as Military Commander*, 1973.

Henry L. Snyder, *The Marlborough-Godolphin Correspondence*, 1974–1975, three vols.

David Chandler, *The art of warfare in the age of Marlborough*, 1976.

John A. Lynn, *The Wars of Louis XIV 1667–1714*, 1999.

Eric Goldstein, *The socket bayonet in the British army, 1687–1783*, 2000.

Richard Holmes, *The British Soldier in the Age of Horse and Musket*, 2001.

Jamel Ostwald, *Vauban under Siege: Engineering Efficiency and Martial Vigor in the War of the Spanish Succession*, 2006.

Richard Holmes, *Marlborough: England's Fragile Genius*, 2008.

James Falkner, *Marlborough's War Machine, 1702–1711*, 2014.

David John Blackmore, *Destructive and Formidable: British Infantry Firepower 1642–1765*, 2014.

Mark A. Shearwood, *The Perfection of Military Discipline, The Plug Bayonet and the English Army 1660–1705*, 2020.

36. Prince Eugene of Savoy

Thomas Amaulry, *Campagnes de M. le Prince Eugene en Hongrie et des généraux Vénitiens dans la Morée*, 1718.

Luigi Ferdinando Marsigli, *Stato militare dell' Imperio Ottomano*, 1732.

Dimitrie Cantemir, *The History of the Growth and Decay of the Ottoman Empire*, 1734.

Claude Alexandre de Bonneval, *Mémoires du Comte de Bonneval*, 1737.

Eléazard de Mauvillon, *Histoire du prince François Eugène de Savoie, généralissime des armées de l'Empereur et de l'empire*, 1741.

Maurice de Saxe, *Reveries or Memoirs concerning the Art of War*. Translation by Sir William Fawcett, 1759.

Charles Joseph Prince de Ligne, *The life of Prince Eugene of Savoy, from his own original manuscript*, 1812.

Joseph von Hammer-Purgstall, *Geschichte des osmanischen Reiches*, 1827–1835, ten vols.

Archibald Alison, *The Life of John, Duke of Marlborough with some account of his contemporaries and of the War of Succession*, 1852.

Alfred Ritter von Arneth, *Prinz Eugen von Savoyen*, 1858, 3 vols.

George Bruce Malleson, *Prince Eugene of Savoy: the Life of a Great Military Commander of the 17th & 18th Centuries*, 1888.

Paul Frischauer, *Prince Eugene 1663–1736: A Man and a Hundred Years of History*, 1934.

Nicholas Henderson, *Prince Eugen of Savoy, a Biography*, 1964.

Max Braubach, *Prinz Eugen Von Savoyen: Aufstieg*, 1963–1965.

Derek McKay, *Prince Eugene of Savoy*, 1977.

John P. Spielman, *Leopold I of Austria*, 1977.

Michael Hochedlinger, *Austria's Wars of Emergence 1683–1797*, 2003.

Henri Pigaillem, *Le Prince Eugène*, 2005.

James Falkner, *Prince Eugene of Savoy, A Genius for War Against Louis XIV and the Ottoman Empire*, 2022.

37. Blas De Lezo

Anonymous, *Vernon's glory. Containing Fifteen New Songs, occasion'd by the Taking of Porto-Bello and Fort Chagre*, 1740.

Edward Vernon, *A second genuine speech, deliver'd by Admiral Vernon, on board the Carolina, to the officers of the Navy, immediately after the salley from Fort St. Lazara*, 1741.

Tobias Smollet, 'An Account of the Expedition against Cartagena' in *A Compendium of Authentic and Entertaining voyages*, 1756.

Herbert Richmond, *The Navy in the War of 1739–48*, 1920.

Charles E. Nowell, 'The defence of Cartagena', *The Hispanic American Historical Review*, Vol. 42, No. 4, 1962.

Enrique Marco Dorta, *Cartagena de Indias puerto y plaza fuerte*, 1988.

Kristian Matthew Marks, *Like Thunder and Lightning: British Force Projection in the West Indies* (Thesis), 1999.

John Robert McNeil, *Mosquito Empires, Ecology and War in the Greater Caribeean, 1620–1914*, 2010.

Francisco Hernando Muñoz Atuesta, *Diarios de Ofensa y Defensa. Ataque inglés sobre Cartagena de Indias*, 2015–2018, four vols.

Gonzalo M. Quintero Saravia, *Don Blas de Lezo: Biografía de un marino español*, 2016.

José Antonio Crespo-Francés y Valero, *Blas de Lezo y la defensa heroica de Cartagena de Indias*, 2016.

Carolina Aguado Serrano and Mariela Beltrán García-Echániz, *La última batalla de Blas de Lezo*, 2018.

Robert Gaudi, *The War of Jenkins' Ear: The Forgotten Struggle for North and South America 1739–1742*, 2021.

Craig S. Chapman, *The Tragic British-American Expedition to the West Indies during the War of Jenkins' Ear*, 2021.

38. Robert Clive

Joseph François Marquis Dupleix, *Mémoire Pour Le Sieur Dupleix Contre La Compagnie Des Indes*, 1759.

William Bolts, *Considerations on India Affairs*, 1772.

Harry Verelst, *A View of the Rise, Progress, and Present State of the English Government in Bengal*, 1772.

Robert Orme, *A History of the Military Transactions of the British Nation in Indostan from the year 1745*, 1778, two vols.

Ğulām Husayn Khan, *The Siyar-ul-Mutakherin: a history of the Mahomedan power in India during the last century*. Translation by Haji Mustefa, and collated with the Persian original by John Briggs, 1832.

Thomas Babington Macaulay, *Lord Clive*, 1840.

George Bruce Malleson, *History of the French in India*, 1893.

William Hunt, *The Political History of England*, 1905, volume X.

Mark Bence-Jones, *Clive of India*, 1974.

Huw V. Bowen, *Revenue and Reform: The Indian Problem in British Politics, 1757–1773*, 1991.

Robert Harvey, *Clive: The Life and Death of a British Emperor*, 2000.

Nicholas Dirks, *The Scandal of Empire, India and the Creation of Imperial Britain*, 2006.

Brad C. Faught, *Clive: Founder of British India*, 2013.

William Dalrymple, *The Anarchy: The East India Company, Corporate Violence, and the Pillage of an Empire*, 2019.

39. Nathanael Green

Nathanael Green, *The Papers of General Nathanael Green*. Edited by Richard K. Showman and Dennis Conrad, 1976–2015, thirteen vols.

George Washington Greene, *The Life of Nathanael Greene: Major- General in the Army of the Revolution*, 1867, three vols.

Francis Vinton Greene, *Life of Nathaniel Greene, Major General in the Army of the Revolution*, 1893.

Theodore Thayer, *Nathanael Greene: Strategist of the American Revolution*, 1960.

Piers Mackesy, *The War for America, 1775–1783*, 1993.

Terry Golway, *Washington's General: Nathanael Green and the Triumph of the American Revolution*, 2005.

John J. Tierney, *Chasing Ghosts: Unconventional Warfare in American History*, 2006.

Steven E. Siry, *Greene: Revolutionary General*, 2006.

Gerald M. Carbone, *Nathanael Greene: A Biography of the American Revolution*, 2008.

David Lee Russell, *The American Revolution in the Southern Colonies*, 2009.
Rick Atkinson, *The British Are Coming: The War for America, Lexington to Princeton, 1775–1777*, 2019.
John Ferling, *Winning Independence: The Decisive Years of the Revolutionary War, 1778–1781*, 2021.

40. Marquis De La Fayette

John Quincy Adams, *Oration of the Life and Character of Gilbert Motier de Lafayette. Delivered at the request of both houses of the Congress of the United States, before them, in the House of Representatives, at Washington, on the 31st December, 1834*, 1835.
Gilbert Du Motier La Fayette, *Mémoires, correspondance et manuscrits du général Lafayette*, three vols, 1837.
Gilbert Du Motier La Fayette, *Lafayette in the Age of the American Revolution, Selected Letters and Papers, 1776–1790*, Edited by Stanley J. Idzerda, 1977–1981, four vols.
Charlemagne Tower Jr., *The Marquis de La Fayette in the American Revolution*, 1895.
Etienne Charavay, *Le général Lafayette, 1757–1834*, 1898.
Sabra Holbrook, *Lafayette, Man in the Middle*, 1977.
Stanley J. Idzerda, *Lafayette, Hero of Two Worlds: The Art and Pageantry of His Farewell Tour of America, 1824–1825*, 1989.
Harlow Giles Unger, *Lafayette*, 2003.
Jason Lane, *General and Madam De Lafayette: Partners in Liberty's Cause in the American and French Revolution*, 2003.
James R. Gaines, *Liberty and Glory: Washington, Lafayette, and their Revolutions*, 2007.
Philippe Bourdin, *La Fayette, entre deux mondes*, 2009.
Laura Auricchio, *The Marquis: Lafayette Reconsidered*, 2014.
Larrie D. Ferreiro, *Brothers at Arms: American Independence and the Men of France and Spain who Saved it*, 2016.

41. Joachim Murat

Philippe-Paul de Ségur, *History of the Expedition to Russia Undertaken by Emperor Napoléon in the year 1812*, 1825.
Elzéar Blaze, *La Vie Militaire sous le Premier Empire, ou Moeurs de garnison, du bivouac ou de la caserne*, 1837.
Aymar de Bonneville, *Recollections of Colonel de Bonneville*, 1875.
Philippe Paul de Ségur, *Un aide de camp de Napoléon. Mémoire du général Comte de Ségur*, 1894–1895.
Joachim Joseph Murat, *Murat, Lieutenant de l'Empereur en Espagne, 1808, d'après sa correspondance inédite et des documents originaux*, 1897.
Albert Dufourcq, *Murat et la question de l'unité Italienne en 1815*, 1898.
Paul Jules Joseph Le Brethon, *Lettres et documents pour servir à l'histoire de Joachim Murat, 1767–1815: publiés par S. A. le prince Murat*, 1908.
Andrew Hilliard Atteridge, *Joachim Murat: Napoleon's Great Commander of Cavalry*, 1911.
Ronald Frederick Delderfield, *The March of the Twenty-Six: The Story of Napoleon's Marshals*, 1962.
David Johnson, *Napoleon's Cavalry and its Leaders*, 1978.
Jean Tullard, *Murat ou l'Eveil des Nations*, 1983.
John Robert Elting, *Swords around a Throne: Napoleon's Grande Armée*, 1988.
Hugh S. Bonar Jr., *Joachim Murat: Lieutenant of the Emperor*, 1989.
Michel Lacour-Gayet, *Joachim et Caroline Murat*, 1996.
Frédéric Hulot, *Murat: la chevauchée fantastique*, 1998.
James R. Arnold and Ralph R. Reinertsen, *Crisis in the Snows: Russia Confronts Napoléon – The Eylau Campaign 1806–1807*, 2007.

42. Simon Bolivar

José Manuel Restrepo, *Historia de la Revolución de la República de Colombia en la América Meridional*, 1858.

Simón Bolivar, *Correspondencia general del Libertador Simón Bolívar*. Edited by Felipe Larrazábal, 1865.

José Felix Blanco, *Documentos Para La Historia de la Vida Publica del Libertador de Colombia, Peru Y Bolivia*, 1875.

Daniel Florence O'Leary, *Cartas del Libertador, Memorias del General O'Leary*, 1879–1888, 32 vols.

Alfred Hasbrouck, *Foreign Legionnaires in the Liberation of Spanish South America*, 1928.

Simón Bolivar, *Selected Writings of Bolivar*. Edited by Lewis Bertrand, 1951.

Francisco Antonio Encina, *Bolívar y la independencia de la América española: Independencia de Nueva Granada y Venezuela*, 1961.

Augusto Mijares, *El Libertador*, 1964.

Manuel Pérez Vila, *Bolívar el libro del sesquicentenario 1830–1980*, 1980.

Hector Bencomo Barrios, *Bolívar Jefe Militar*, 1983.

Ramón José Velásquez, *Los pasos de los héroes*, 1988.

Manuel Pérez Vila, *El legado de Bolivar*, 1989.

Gilette Saura, *Simon Bolivar, le Libertador*, 1990.

Richard W. Slatta, and Jane Lucas De Grummond, *Simon Bolivar's Quest for Glory*, 2003.

Frederick H. Fornoff and David Bushnell, *El Libertador: Writings of Simón Bolívar*, 2003.

Moisés Enrique Rodriguez, *Freedom's Mercenaries: British Volunteers in the Wars of Independence of Latin America*, 2006, two vols.

John Lynch, *Simon Bolivar: A Life*, 2008.

Marie Arana, *Bolívar: American Liberator*, 2013.

43. T. E. Lawrence

Lowell Jackson Thomas, *With Lawrence in Arabia*, 1924.

T. E. Lawrence, *Seven Pillars of Wisdom*, 1926.

Archibald Percival Wavell, *The Palestine Campaigns*, 1928.

T. E. Lawrence, 'Guerrilla Warfare' in *Encyclopedia Britannica*, 1929.

Basil Henry Liddell Hart, *T.E. Lawrence in Arabia and After*, 1934.

T. E. Lawrence, *Crusader Castles*, 1936.

Basil H. Liddell Hart, *The Strategy of Indirect Approach*, 1941.

Elie Kedourie, *England and the Middle East*, 1956.

Peter Brent, *T.E. Lawrence*, 1976.

John Mack, *A Prince of Our Disorder: The Life of T.E. Lawrence*, 1976.

Bruce Westrate, *The Arab Bureau: British Policy in the Middle East, 1916–1920*, 1984.

Jeremy Wilson, *The Authorized Biography of T.E. Lawrence*, 1989.

Lawrence James, *The Golden Warrior: The Life and Legend of Lawrence of Arabia*, 1990.

James Barr, *Setting the Desert on Fire: T.E. Lawrence and Britain's Secret War in Arabia*, 2009.

Scott Anderson, *Lawrence in Arabia: War, Deceit, Imperial Folly And The Making Of The Modern Middle East*, 2013.

Neil Faulkner, *Lawrence of Arabia's War: The Arabs, the British and the Remaking of the Middle East in WWI*, 2016.

Robert Johnson, *Lawrence of Arabia on War: The Campaign in the Desert 1916–18*, 2020.

44. Paul Von Hindenburg

Alfred von Schlieffen, *Cannae*, 1913.

Paul von Hindenburg, *Aus meinem Leben*. Translated as *Out of my Life* by F. A. Holt, 1920.

Erich von Falkenhayn, *The German General Staff and its Decisions 1914–1916*, 1920.
Ernst Jünger, *The Storm of Steel,* 1920.
Erich von Ludendorff, *Meine Kriegserinnernungen 1914–1918*, 1921.
Major General Sir Edmund Ironside, *Tannenberg: The First Thirty Days in East Prussia*, 1925.
Max Hoffmann, *Tannenberg wie es wirklich war*, 1926.
Basil Henry Liddell Hart, *Reputations*, 1928.
Helene Nostitz von Hindenburg, *Hindenburg at Home: An intimate biography*, 1931.
Charles Robert Mowbray Fraser Cruttwell, *A History of the Great War 1914–1918*, 1934.
Gert Von Hindenburg. *Hindenburg 1847–1934, Soldier and Statesman*, 1935.
Basil Henry Liddell Hart, *The Strategy of Indirect Approach*, 1941.
Franz von Papen, *Memoirs.* Translated by Brian Connell, 1952.
Martin Kitchen, *The Silent Dictatorship: The politics of the German High Command under Hindenburg and Ludendorff, 1916–1918*, 1976.
Werner Maser, *Hindenburg: Eine politische Biographie*, 1990.
Dennis E. Showalter, *Tannenberg: Clash of Empires, 1914*, 1991.
John Sweetman, *Tannenberg 1914*, 2002.
Perry Pierk, *Tannenberg: Erich Ludendorff and the Defence of Eastern German Border in 1914*, 2004
Dennis E. Showalter and William J. Astore, *Hindenburg: Icon of German Militarism*, 2005.
David J. A. Stone, *The Kaiser's Army: the German Army in World War One*, 2015.
Prit Buttar, *Collision of Empires: The War on the Eastern Front in 1914*, 2016.

45. Mustafa Kemal Atatürk

Berthe Georges-Gaulis, *Le Nationalisme Turc*, 1921.
Berthe Georges-Gaulis, *Agora-Constantinople-Londres, Moustafa Kémal et la politique anglaise en Orient*, 1922.
Berthe Georges-Gaulis, *La Nouvelle Turquie*, 1924.
Hans Kannengiesser, *The Campaign in Gallipoli*, 1927. English translation, 1940.
Harold Courtenay Armstrong, *Gray Wolf: The Life of Kemal Ataturk*, 1933.
Hanns Froembgen, *Kemal Ataturk*, 1935.
Bernard Lewis, *The Emergence of Modern Turkey*, 1961.
Patrick Balfour Kinross, *Atatürk: The Rebirth of a Nation*, 1964.
Michael Llewellyn Smith, *Ionian Vision: Greece in Asia Minor, 1919– 1922*, 1973.
İsmet Görgülü, *Büyük Taarruz: 70 nci Yıl Armağanı*, 1992.
Nur Bilge Criss, *Constantinople under Allied Occupation 1918–1923*, 1993.
Edward J. Erickson, *Ordered to Die. A History of the Ottoman Army in the First World War*, 2001.
Andrew Mango, *Ataturk: The Biography of the Founder of Modern Turkey*, 2002.
Taner Akcam, *A Shameful Act: The Armenian Genocide and the Question of Turkish Responsibility*, 2006.
Edward J. Erickson, *Gallipoli & the Middle East 1914–1918*, 2012.
George W. Gawrych, *The Young Atatürk: From Ottoman Soldier to Statesman of Turkey*, 2015.
Sean McMeekin, *The Ottoman Endgame: War, Revolution, and the Making of the Modern Middle East, 1908–1923*, 2015.
Ryan Gingeras, *Fall of the Sultanate: The Great War and the End of the Ottoman Empire, 1908–1922*, 2016.
Konstantinos Travlos (ed), *Salvation and Catastrophe: The Greek- Turkish War, 1919–1922*, 2020.
Edward J. Erickson, *The Turkish War of Independence: A Military History, 1919–1923*, 2021.

46. Paul Von Lettow-Vorbeck

John Bruce Cairnie, *The Great War Diaries*, 1915–1919.
Francis Brett Young, *Marching on Tanga: With General Smuts in East Africa*, 1917.

Ludwig Deppe, *Mit Lettow-Vorbeck durch Afrika*, 1919.

Ernest Charles Holtom, *Two years' captivity in German East Africa*, 1919.

Herbert Charles O'Neill, *The War in Africa and in the Far East, 1914– 1917*, 1919.

Paul von Lettow-Vorbeck, *My Reminiscences of East Africa*, 1920.

Richard Wenig, *Kriegs-Safari*, 1920.

Paul von Lettow-Vorbeck and Walter von Ruckteschell, *Heia Safari! – Deutschlands Kampf in Ostafrika*, 1920.

Paul von Lettow-Vorbeck, *Was mir die Englander über Ostafrika erzählten: zwanglose Unterhaltungen mit ehemaligen Gegnern*, 1932.

Hans von Chamier-Glisczinski, *Leben und sterben in Afrika*, 1938.

Ascan Roderich Lutteroth, *Tunakwenda: auf Kriegssafari in Deutsch- Ostafrika*, 1938.

Charles Hordern, *History of the Great War: Military Operations East Africa, August 1914– September 1916*, 1941.

Ludwig Boell, *Die Operationen in Ost-Afrika: Weltkrieg 1914–1918*, 1951.

Brian Gardner, *German East: The story of the First World War in East Africa*, 1963.

William Roger Louis, *Great Britain and Germany's Lost Colonies, 1914–1919*, 1967.

J. R. Sibley, *Tanganyikan guerilla: East African campaign 1914–18*, 1971.

Edwin Palmer Hoyt, *Guerilla! Colonel von Lettow-Vorbeck and Germany's East African Empire*, 1981.

Eckard Michels, *'Der Held von Deutsch-Ostafrika'. Paul von Lettow- Vorbeck. Ein preußischer Kolonialoffizier*, 2008.

F. Jon Nesselhuf, *General Paul von Lettow-Vorbeck's East Africa Campaign: Maneuver Warfare on the Serengeti* (Thesis), 2012.

Thomas A. Crowson, *When Elephants Clash – A Critical Analysis of Major General Paul Emil Von Lettow-Vorbeck*, 2014.

Robert Gaudi, *African Kaiser: General Paul von Lettow-Vorbeck and the Great War in Africa, 1914–1918*, 2017.

47. Erich Von Manstein

Franz Halder, *War Journal of Franz Halder*, 1947, nine vols.

Basil Henry Liddell Hart, *The Other Side of the Hill. Germany's Generals: Their Rise and Fall, with their own Account of Military Events, 1939–1945*, 1951.

Reginald Thomas Padget, *Manstein: His Campaigns and His Trial*, 1951.

Heinz Guderian, *Panzer Leader*, 1952.

Erich von Manstein, *Lost Victories*, 1955.

Friedrich von Mellenthin, *Panzer Battles*, 1956.

Alan Clarck, *Barbarossa: The Russian-German Conflict, 1941–45*, 1965.

James Lucas, *War on the Eastern Front, 1941–1945*, 1979.

Otto Carius, *Tigers in the Mud: The Combat Career of German Panzer Commander Otto Carius*, 1985.

David M. Glantz, *From the Don to the Dnepr: Soviet Offensive Operations, December 1942–August 1943*, 1991.

David M. Glantz and Jonathan M. House, *The Battle of Kursk*, 1999.

Marcel Stein, *Generalfeldmarschall Erich Von Manstein. Kritische Betrachtung des Soldaten und Menschen*, 2002.

Marcel Stein: *Der Januskopf. Feldmarschall von Manstein – eine Neubewertung*, 2004.

Oliver von Wrochem: *Erich von Manstein. Vernichtungskrieg und Geschichtspolitik*, 2006.

Chris Bellamy, *Absolute War: Soviet Russia in the Second World War*, 2007.

Mungo Melvin, *Manstein: Hitler's Greatest General*, 2010.

Vasiliy Krysov, *Panzer Destroyer: Memoirs of a Red Army Tank Commander.* Edited by Stuart Britton, 2010.

Robert Forcyzk, *Where the Iron Crosses Grow. The Crimea 1941–44*, 2014.
Russel H. S. Stolfi, *Hitler's Panzers East: World War II Reinterpreted*, 2014.
Aleksei Isaev, *The End of the Gallop: The Battle for Kharkov February–March 1943*, 2018.

48. Georgy Zhukov
Aleksandr A. Svechin, *Strategy*, 1927, edited by Kent D. Lee, 1992.
John Frederick Charles Fuller, *The Second World War, 1939–1945: A Strategical and Tactical History*, 1948.
Friedrich von Mellenthin, *Panzer Battles*, 1956.
Vasili I. Chuikov, *The Beginning of the Road: The Story of the Battle for Stalingrad*, 1963.
Alexander Werth, *Russia at War, 1941–1945*, 1964.
Vasili I. Chuikov, *The Fall of Berlin*, 1967.
Earl Frederick Ziemke, *From Stalingrad to Berlin: The German defeat in the East*, 1968.
Konstantin K. Rokossovsky, *A Soldier's Duty*, 1968.
Georgy K. Zhukov, *The Memoirs of Marshal Zukhov*, 1969.
Otto Preston Chaney, *Zhukov*, 1971.
Albert Seaton, *The Russo-German War, 1941–45*, 1971.
Georgy K. Zhukov, *Marshal Zhukov's Greatest Battles*, edited by Harrison Salibury, 1971.
Georgy K. Zhukov, *Reminiscences and Reflections*, 1985.
Alvin D. Coox, *Nomohan: Japan against Russia, 1939*, 1990.
William J. Spahr, *Zhukov: The Rise and Fall of a Great Captain*, 1993.
Edwin Palmer Hoyt, *199 Days: The Battle of Stalingrad*, 1993.
Antony Beevor, *Stalingrad: The Fateful Siege: 1942–1943*, 1998.
Richard Overy, *Russia's War: A History of the Soviet Effort, 1941– 1945*, 1998.
David M. Glantz, *Zhukov's Greatest Defeat: The Red Army's Epic Disaster in Operation Mars, 1942*, 1999.
Geoffrey Roberts, *Stalin's General: The Life of Georgy Zhukov*, 2012.
Stuart Douglas Goldman, *Nomonhan, 1939; The Red Army's Victory That Shaped World War II*, 2012.
Jean Lopez and Lasha Otkhmezuri, *Jukov: L'homme qui a vaincu Hitler*, 2013.
Georgy K. Zhukov, *Marshal of Victory: The Autobiography of General Georgy Zhukov*, edited by Geoffrey Roberts, 2015.
Roman Toeppel, *Kursk 1943: The Greatest Battle of the Second World War*, 2018.

49. Matthew Ridgway
Department of the Army Historical Division, *Utah Beach to Cherbourg*, (American forces in action series), 1947.
Omar Nelson Bradley, *A Soldier's Story*, 1951.
Matthew Bunker Ridgway, *Soldier: The Memoirs of Matthew B. Ridgway*, 1956.
John Miller jr., Owen J. Curroll, and Margaret E. Tackley, *Korea, 1951–1953*, 1956.
Allen S. Whiting, *China Crosses the Yalu: The Decision to Enter the Korean War*, 1960.
Matthew Bunker Ridgway, *The Korean War: How We Met the Challenge*, 1967.
Edwin Palmer Hoyt, *On to the Yalu*, 1984.
James M. Gavin, *On to Berlin*, 1985.
Clay Blair, *Ridgeway's Paratroopers: The American Airborne in World War II*, 1985.
Clay Blair, *The Forgotten War: America in Korea, 1950–1953*, 1987.
Paul M. Edwards, *General Matthew B. Ridgway: An Annotated Bibliography*, 1993.
T. Moffatt Burriss, *Strike and Hold: A Memoir of the 82nd Airborne in World War II*, 2000.
George C. Mitchell, *Matthew B. Ridgway: Soldier, Statesman, Scholar, Citizen*, 2002.
Tim Saunders, *Nijmegen: U.S. 82nd Airborne Division, 1944*, 2008.

Mark Alexander and John Sparry. *Jump Commander: In Combat with the 82nd Airborne in World War II*, 2010.

Joseph R. Kurz, *General Matthew B. Ridgway: A Commander's Maturation of Operational Art*, 2012.

Mitchell A. Yockelson, *The Paratrooper Generals: Matthew Ridgway, Maxwell Taylor, and the American Airborne from D-Day through Normandy*, 2020.

50. Võ Nguyên Giáp

Alphonse Juin, *Le Viêt Minh, mon adversaire*, 1956.

Võ Nguyên Giáp, *People's War, People's Army*, 1961.

Võ Nguyên Giáp, *Big Victory, Great Task; North Viet-Nam's Minister of Defence Assesses the Course of the War*, 1968.

Võ Nguyên Giáp, *Military Art of People's War: Selected Writings of General Võ Nguyên Giáp*, 1970.

John T. McAllister Jr. and Paul Mus, *The Vietnamese and Their Revolution*, 1970.

Telford Taylor, *Nuremberg and Vietnam: An American Tragedy*, 1970.

Douglas Pike, *The Viet Cong Strategy of Terror*, 1971.

Võ Nguyên Giáp, *How We Won the War*, 1975.

Georges Boudarel, *Võ Nguyên Giáp*, 1977.

Henry Alfred Kissinger, *The White House Years*, 1979.

Harry G. Summers Jr., *On Strategy: A Critical Analysis of the Vietnam War*, 1982.

Stanley Karnow, *Vietnam: A History,* 1983.

Douglas Pike, *PAVN: People's Army of Vietnam*, 1986.

Mark Clodfelter, *The Limits of Air Power: The American Bombing of North Vietnam*, 1989.

Peter MacDonald, *Giap: The Victor in Vietnam*, 1993.

Jeffery Record, *The Wrong War: Why We Lost in Vietnam*, 1998.

Jacques Dalloz, *Dictionnaire de la Guerre d'Indochine*, 2006.

Huy Đức, *The Winning Side*, 2012, two vols.

James A. Warren, *Giap: The General who Defeated America in Vietnam*, 2013.

Virginia Morris and Clive A. Hills, *Ho Chi Minh's Blueprint for Revolution: In the Words of Vietnamese Strategists and Operatives*, 2018.

Max Hastings, *Vietnam: An Epic Tragedy, 1945–1975*, 2018.